The Emergence
of the Welfare States

M. & J. Walzer
December 1988
Princeton

The Emergence
of the Welfare States

DOUGLAS E. ASHFORD

BASIL BLACKWELL

First published 1986
First published in USA 1987
First published in paperback 1988

Basil Blackwell Ltd
108 Cowley Road, Oxford OX4 1JF, UK

Basil Blackwell Inc.
432 Park Avenue South, Suite 1503
New York, NY 10016, USA

British Library Cataloguing in Publication Data
Ashford, Douglas E.
    The emergence of the welfare states.
    1. Welfare states——-History
    I. Title
    361.6'5'09   HN16

    ISBN   0–631–15211–3
    ISBN   0–631–16023–X Pbk

Library of Congress Cataloging in Publication Data
Ashford, Douglas Elliott.
    The emergence of the welfare states.
    Includes index.
    1. Welfare state. 2. Social policy. 3. Democracy.
I. Title.
HN28.A84   1986   361.6'5   86–12925
ISBN   0–631–15211–3
ISBN   0–631–16023–X (pbk.)

Typeset by Photo-Graphics
Printed in Great Britain by Billing & Sons Ltd, Worcester.

Contents

Preface

The welfare state has been frequently assessed in terms of its performance and equity, but less often in terms of its historical importance in the transformation of modern democratic institutions. The aim of this book is to contribute to such an evaluation. In doing so, my assumption has been that how the early liberal democracies adapted to social policies was not only a function of social need and social justice, but also a function of how their political and administrative structures might best accommodate what were, and often still remain, entirely new demands on the institutional structure of democratic governance. On such criteria the conventional rankings of welfare states by amounts of benefits and effective redistribution of incomes takes on less importance and emphasis is placed on how institutional and political adaptation took place.

When this study began my expectation was that an adequate institutional evaluation might be made covering the past century. The more I read about the late nineteenth-century debates over social reform, the internal party struggles, and the institutional uncertainties generated by new social policies, the more convinced I became that an institutional assessment of the years since 1950 could not be made without more detailed analysis of many fundamental structural changes made before 1950. This has involved extracting quite mercilessly from numerous historical studies, biographies and administrative histories. I am acutely aware that in doing so I frequently compress major historical controversies. To settle all these disputes in a single volume touching on five countries would be impossible, but I try to acknowledge different historical interpretations. The effort has left me with a renewed respect for how difficult it is to arrive at what we label 'truth' and a renewed suspicion that much contemporary social science treats many fundamental questions all too simply.

From the beginning of work on the study there was an important question of whether to include some materials on Germany, Sweden and the United States. In these cases I rely largely on secondary studies so my interpretations are more easily disputed, yet the risk seemed acceptable in order to extend the range of comparison. In the case of Germany, it is important to see that providing more social benefits and social security does not necessarily reinforce democratic government. In the case of Sweden, it is also important to see that the more ambitious approaches to welfare state policies were often possible only because of unique historical and political circumstances. And lastly, it is important to see why the United States remains the least developed of welfare states despite the enormous advances made in recent years. Without making such broad comparisons, the unique contribution of each democracy to the advance of the welfare state notion does not acquire relief. More important perhaps, without fully exploring the intricate historical and institutional changes that new social policies entailed, we are likely to fall into the trap of thinking that welfare states experienced the same political and institutional problems.

The main burden of the book is Britain and France. In the case of France such concentration may seem more justified. Although there are several excellent histories in French, there is almost nothing in English elaborating how the French reacted to welfare state questions. Taking institutional and political circumstances into account, my conclusion is that the French did not do all that badly despite their unfavourable ranking by many of the conventional quantifiable measures. The attention to Britain may seem less justifiable, but, as will appear, the evidence of basic institutional change in this venerable political system leads to very different conclusions that are often found if one deals with Britain in isolation. The superb social and administrative histories of Britain make comparison an easier task, but one that those immersed in British history are less likely to undertake. If the conclusions reached here are less complimentary to British policy-making capabilities than has often been assumed, my hope is that these conclusions will not be interpreted in any way as an effort to diminish the historical importance of Britain's pioneering effort as a welfare state.

Such an ambitious study could obviously not have been undertaken without much support and encouragement. Having completed a similar comparison of territorial policymaking in Britain and France in 1981, the Center for International Studies at Cornell University very generously provided me with an incentive grant to begin a discussion of comparative social policy. The Center later contributed to the costs of an international conference, partly supported as well by the Council on European Studies, so that a collection of scholars and policymakers from several countries might meet. The results of this effort have been published separately in *Nationalizing Social Security* (JAI Press, 1986).

On the basis of these early investigations and discussions, I became persuaded that an institutional assessment was needed and possible. Without the generous support of the John Simon Guggenheim Fellowship over 1983–84 the book would probably never have been completed. Over that year I also enjoyed a sabbatical support from the University of Pittsburgh and was substantially helped by research funds attached to the Andrew W. Mellon Professorship. Over both 1983 and 1984 my work was further assisted by visiting appointments at the Institut d'Etudes Politiques at the University of Bordeaux and at the Faculty of Law and Administration, University of Paris I. For all this support I am permanently grateful though none of these parties bears any responsibility for the contents of the study.

A great many libraries and librarians have been dependably helpful as the study was assembled. Several months were spent in the new British Public Records Office whose convenience and comfort must surely be one of the most important encouragements to modern British historical research. In addition, the libraries of both the London School of Economics and Political Science and the Royal Institute of Public Administration were unfailingly cooperative. A number of French libraries also provided invaluable assistance. Perhaps the most important at early stages of inquiry was the charming Musée Social in Paris. Additional Third Republic documents and records were found by the efficient staff of the Bibliothèque Administrative of the Parisian Hotel de Ville. Work was also done in the Bibliothèque Municipale of Bordeaux, and the libraries of the Bordeaux and Paris Institut d'Etudes Politiques.

For a middle-aged scholar, noting individual assistance is likely to be a whimsical task because many persons have had the patience and interest to contribute to my efforts. Two persons deserve special mention for they acted as my historical watchdogs and read the entire manuscript: Jose Harris and Vincent Wright, both at Oxford University. In addition, I received useful comments and criticisms from Gösta Esping-Anderson, Norman Furniss, Peter Hall, Hugh Heclo, Arnold Heidenheimer, Richard Kuisel, Rodney Lowe, Robert Paxton, Guy Peters, Gaston Rimlinger, Timothy Tilton and John Weiss. As usual in academic endeavour, advice freely given was freely used, but none of these persons bear responsibility for the use I have made of their knowledge. Final mention should be made of the priceless assistance of the Comité d'Histoire de la Securité Sociale under Pierre Laroque's direction. He and his assistant in this formidable effort, Mme. Sursuz, made a number of key documents available to me.

Final words are for my family Karen and Matthew, who so often were alone while I was in France or Britain. Nonetheless, when we could travel together there were unforgettable surprises and pleasures for which I am eternally grateful.

Douglas E. Ashford
University of Pittsburgh
January 1986

1

The Welfare State as an Institutional Challenge

The transformation of the nineteenth-century liberal state, and its diverse manifestations throughout Europe and North America, into the contemporary welfare state is perhaps the most remarkable accomplishment of democratic governance. No sooner had the fundamental concepts of modern democratic governance been established than did the fledgling democracies begin to debate how to share the social costs of caring for the less fortunate. Even before mass democracy took its present form in the late nineteenth century, policymakers in most of the democracies began to ruminate over how to expand the array of social benefits and social services to be offered to newly enfranchised citizens. In fact, it is probably historically inaccurate to measure the politics of the welfare state against an abstract model of the classical liberal state. The democracies had very different origins and very different traditions. Over the twentieth century, each formulated different ways to fit the goals of social equality and social justice into their institutional and political frameworks, the frameworks themselves the issue of the peculiar circumstances influencing the rise of democratic government in their country. While the liberal model of governance was a very powerful one in terms of political rights and political organization, it was also very fragile once the complexities of modern social policymaking were added to modern states.

Tempting as it may be to read the development of the welfare state in terms of the adequacy and breadth of social benefits, the political saga is much more complicated and a tribute to the

ingenuity of democratic governance. Defining social goals and
social objectives was a more difficult problem for political theorists
than for political actors. While many nineteenth-century leaders
were convinced of the sanctity of property and the virtue of work,
they were also acutely aware of the social problems of their countries and often anticipated the social stress and strain of mass
democracy much better than did the philosophers of government,
the liberal economists and the rising tide of socialist thinkers. One
of the great difficulties of arriving at a satisfactory definition of
the welfare state arises precisely because of this problem. There
never was one view of how social justice was to be achieved any
more than there was one route by which to achieve effective
democratic governance. Historically sensitive policy analysis enters
into the picture because the many forms of the contemporary
welfare state are the manifestation of the complex and diverse
compromises forged by political leaders and administrative officials
over many years.

Some of the historical anomalies bear mentioning because they
are intrinsic to understanding the diverse routes of the long march
toward mass democracy to which the struggle for social justice
and social equality was a sequel. For one thing, much of the
progress toward building the welfare state can be attributed to the
conservative elements of the early democratic governments. More
ideological versions of this transformation often attribute social
reform to fears of class struggle and apprehensions over working
class movements. While conservative values were certainly threatened by the turmoil of creating industrial societies, the actual
reactions of policy makers were more often pragmatic solutions
to immediate problems which were accepted by most important
political actors as crucial problems of the day. By viewing the
history of social policy apart from the political conflicts and political pressures that such leaders actually encountered, and ig-
noring the concern that they often felt over meeting visible rather
than imagined social needs, one injects a form of historicism into
our account of the metamorphosis of democratic governance from
the late nineteenth century to the present day.

These comments may serve to alert the reader that in this study,
the term 'welfare state' is not being used in its conventional sense.
The book is not intended to be a study of why we have expanded
social assistance and social protection, but how governments went

about doing so. Indeed, the common term to designate the development of social policies under the aegis of the state contains an important ambiguity which, as will be argued in more detail in Chapter 2, can only be unraveled by recognizing that states existed well before welfare, at least in the sense of state intervention to assist certain classes of citizens, to relieve them of the risks of advanced forms of industrialization and to assure that those without incomes had some minimal protection. In general, the claim is made that while states certainly were not completely autonomous in deciding how to provide relief and protection, political, institutional and even constitutional issues affected the transition from liberal to welfare state as much as economic and social realities. In short, there were some reasonably specific independent political factors involved in each country's transformation. The result, as Higgins has suggested,[1] is different 'states of welfare' rather than an ideal state particularly suited to providing welfare.

Approaching the development of the welfare state through the political process means that the social and economic definitions that have figured so heavily in many accounts of how welfare states developed take on less significance. The idea of a welfare state is a distinct contribution of modern democratic governance to the contemporary political lexicon.[2] The political context of the welfare state varied considerably in each democracy. It varied not only in terms of whom governments felt were in most need of assistance and in terms of how much income redistribution might be justified, but in terms of the instrumentalities at the disposal of government, the internal struggle among ministries to share the rewards of an expanding governmental structure, and the incentive offered politicians and officials. Few of these concerns were determined by social policies alone, but by the historical, political and organizational structure of the state.

In such a context, the institutional setting of the various governments takes on special meaning. In one sense, developing welfare

[1] Joan Higgins, *States of Welfare: Comparative Analysis in Social Policy*, Oxford; Martin Robertson, 1981.
[2] According to Henry Pelling, *The Labour Governments*, London; Macmillan, 1984, pp. 88–90, the term 'welfare state' was first used by Alfred Zimmern in *Quo Vadimus*, 1934, and again by Sir George Schuster in a 1937 lecture, later published as *United Empire*, 1937. By the time of Archbishop Temple's campaigns in the late 1930s, the term was common currency in Britain.

states was not about welfare at all, but simply about how governments might extend existing capabilities and practices to unfam-
iliar problems. There was never an historical turning point where
leaders sat around the table and said to each other that we must
now devise a 'welfare state'. On the contrary, it was a gradual
and often uninformed process propelled as much by ambitious
politicians and rather visionary civil servants as by an abstract
notion of a crumbling social order or of fears of major social unrest.
Important as the various external threats to government may be
in social history, leaders were not overwhelmed by a sense of social
obligation nor by a sense that society was crumbling. To be sure,
the late Victorians, for example, investigated the various social
and economic ills they saw around themselves for several decades,
but their many investigations into the cause of labour unrest, poor
housing, the inefficiency of local government as a social provider,
etc., were never a coherent view of how the state was changing.

If at the level of government the process was diffuse and uncertain, the question of how to get some conceptual grasp of the
metamorphosis of government remains. Perhaps the first observation to be made is that our standard political explanations of
how states change are not particularly helpful. On the one hand,
the pluralist notion of the state, if indeed we can say the pluralists
even acknowledge some sort of organized body holding authority
over a society, is, as Carnoy notes, an 'empty state'.[3] From the
pluralist perspective, government seems no more than an undirec-
ted and somewhat opportunistic search for improvised solutions
to dimly perceived problems. At least from a policy making perspective, leaders and officials are exempt from exercising any
particular wisdom and foresight. Sensing the immediate demands
of the electorate and pressing for change in policies only to the
point of acceptable opportunity costs is sufficient. As will be
apparent in many parts of this analysis, in building new social
policies, and very probably in other policy areas as well, political
life at the top has never been that simple. In more historical
language, the constituted authority of a state does develop its
own rules, habits and, above all, institutional regularities to solve
problems. If nothing else emerges from a political and institutional
analysis of the transformation of states over the past century, it is

[3] Martin Carnoy, *The State and Political Theory*, Princeton; Princeton University
Press, 1984, p. 51.

that however halting and uncertain the introduction of social policies was, the major actors in the process of change accepted new activities. Regardless of partisan, party or electoral concerns, governments knew that they were accepting major new obligations and commitments.

On the other hand, the alternative view of the state as a helpless creature of social and economic necessity does not serve our purposes very well either. At the extreme there are the early Marxist views of the bourgeois state as an epiphenomenon of the system of production. As we shall see in more detail in Chapters 2 and 5, the controversies about the state within the Marxist eschatology sowed confusion among the nascent socialist parties at the turn of the century. While it is not the purpose of this study to reconstruct the evolution of Marxist theory, it is important to see that because of such differences, the left missed many golden opportunities to move toward its utopian goals. One of the major lessons to be learned about the institutional foundations of the modern state in fact lies in the interwar experience of the left. The socialists were slow to adapt their social and economic ideas to institutional limitations which, in turn, fundamentally affected the institutionalization of new social policies in the immediate postwar period. In any event, the overdetermined concept of the state that influenced socialists well into the twentieth century does not square with much of the behaviour of actual governments. However unsatisfactory the results may be in terms of aligning the state with class interests, the concepts of social class, social need and social equality were not workable ideas as new social policies were developed. Governments were not unaware of these considerations, but neither could policies be formulated in ways that permitted governments to redirect the capabilities of the state toward utopian goals.

If the more extreme theories of how states behave are unsatisfactory, then what shall be used as a framework for understanding how political and policy choices entered into the development of welfare states? The definition of the state that seems appropriate for such an institutional analysis sees the institutional foundations of the state in constant interaction with the formation and implementation of new social policies. In other words, what is needed is a concept of the state that neither reduces it to the infinitely flexible apparatus of the pluralist state nor to the mindless robot of the Marxist state. Institutions are not confined to the legal foundations of the state, though these are often of more importance than the more abstract theories of the state recognize, but represent the nature of constituted authority within each state. One of the most difficult problems is of course to state clearly what is meant by 'constituted authority'. Institutions are the manifested expressions of how a people limit the use of collective authority. The problem of both the pluralist and Marxist definitions of the state is that government is made indiscriminate, in the first instance because theoretically speaking it is able to do anything and in the second instance because it can do nothing. The institutional definition is meant to specify that we can state with some precision what resources, methods and capabilities are attached to the exercise of authority in each political system.[4]

Making an institutional definition of the state operation is not as difficult as it may seem. The ground rules for exercising authority within each political system are not all that vague. They are found in the basic practices attached to the work of political executives, the organization and powers of the bureaucracy and the accepted methods of formulating, implementing and evaluating policies. As may be apparent, this is a very different view of the welfare state than that derived from some external measure of welfare. More specifically, a political and policy-based notion of the state is based on institutional capacities for change. Expanding welfare is of course only one of many kinds of modern democratic experience. The proliferation of social policies to relieve social distress and to provide a measure of social security created very different institutional problems for each state. Put into the somewhat misleading language of variance in the case of welfare and any other policy issue, institutions are the intervening variable between some ideal solution and the capabilities of government itself.

Fixing the meaning of the welfare state on a comparison of institutional capabilities is a two-step process of explanation. There is first the question of what are the dominant values of each government, that is, the limitations placed on the use of institutionalized or collective authority.[5] How institutions may behave

---

[4] In a somewhat different theoretical context, Harry Eckstein argued some years ago that an adequate theory of collective authority was not likely to answer many economic and social questions about politics. See his article, 'Authority Patterns: A Structural Basis for Inquiry,' *American Political Science Review*, **67**, December 1973, pp. 1142–61.

is historically defined. For present purposes, for example, the basic institutional features of British democracy were visible from the late seventeenth century,[6] while the institutional fabric of France was still in question as late as the Dreyfus affair at the turn of the century. Put differently, the process of developing welfare states cannot be divorced from fundamental institutional questions about each democracy. It is probably fruitless to ask when the advance of social policies governed institutional choice, as is implied in a class or Marxist concept of the state, or when institutions in their wisdom simply gave way to new organized pressures, as is implied in the pluralist concept of the state. Historically, the causal relationship was always an intricate and changing process. Sometimes the institutional precedents prevailed, and sometimes social needs prevailed. From an institutional perspective, the problem is more one of trying to see which condition was more important, not which should be more important.

The institutional dynamics of such an interaction are visible in how policies were defined, implemented and evaluated. This is essentially why policy analysis is so critical to a proper understanding of how institutions change. Policy analysis has been defined as the study of how demands are made[7] or of how results are achieved.[8] Within an institutional context policy making is more nearly an intricate and reversible relationship between policy

[5] The common social science term for this limitation is 'legitimacy.' However, there are important differences between the social and historical meanings of legitimacy. Over time, the meaning of legitimacy is recast not only by changing preferences and changing social conditions, but by the effectiveness and authenticity attributed to institutions.

[6] See J. H. Plumb, *The Growth of Political Stability in England 1675–1725*, London; Penguin Books, 1969; and Christopher Hill, *The Intellectual Origins of the English Revolution*, Oxford; Clarendon Press, 1965.

[7] Robert H. Salisbury, 'The Analysis of Public Policy: A Search for Theories and Roles,' in Austin Ranney, ed., *Political Science and Public Policy*, Chicago; Markham, 1978, pp. 151–78.

[8] This is a common feature of policy analysis which assumes that the most desirable policies improve class relationships. See, for example, Walter Korpi, *The Democratic Class Struggle*, London; Routledge and Kegan Paul, 1983. On the British perspective of class and the welfare state, see Michael Barratt Brown, 'The Welfare State in Britain,' *The Socialist Register*, London; Merlin Press, pp. 185–223; and Dorothy Wedderburn, 'Facts and Theories of the Welfare State,' *Socialist Register*, London; Merlin Press, 1965, pp. 127–46.

making and institutional values.[9] In this respect, the welfare state is of political interest not so much because it changed society or because society changed institutions, but because it provides a wealth of situations where policymakers saw opportunities, exploited controversies within government, and redirected institutional capabilities within the institutional limitations of each state. With the possible exception of Germany, the institutional challenge took place after a prolonged period of rule under the minimalist notion of the liberal democratic state. The next chapter outlines the major forces affecting the transition from the liberal to the various forms of the welfare state. For the moment, it is important to specify several implications of approaching the welfare state as a dynamic process of institutional transformation.

THE VALUE PREMISES OF THE WELFARE STATE

Viewing the transformation of the welfare state as the interaction of democratic institutions with the tasks of a vastly enlarged area of governmental activity meant changing the ground rules of democratic governance. The acquisition of major social and economic responsibilities is perhaps the most momentous change in the development of democratic institutions. The more empirical approaches to the welfare state, to be outlined below, evaluate democratic governance in terms of its ability to manage new social demands or in terms of the adequancy of its results. Under these paradigms the most important political consideration is submerged. How were liberal democratic states, lacking the machinery, the resources and clear proposals, to justify becoming important social actors, and to redefine old institutional procedures and practices? Perhaps the main reason a politically oriented study of the transformation of liberal into welfare states is needed is that

---

[9] On policies as normative constructs, see Charles W. Anderson, 'The Place of Principles in Policy Analysis,' *American Political Science Review*, **73**, September 1979, pp. 711–23, Also his essay, 'The Logic of Public Problems: Evaluation in Comparative Policy Research,' in D. Ashford, ed., *Comparing Public Policies*, Beverly Hills, CA; Sage Publications, 1978, pp. 19–42. The ethical implications of this approach are outlined by Lawrence H. Tribe, 'Policy Science: Analysis or Ideology?,' *Philosophy and Public Affairs*, **2**, 1972, pp. 66–110.

this delicate and uncertain task is simply excluded from many contemporary analyses of welfare policies. In effect, the most creative accomplishment of democratic governance is never recognized. While it is true that we could barely imagine the welfare state today without democratic institutions, this relationship was by no means clear a century ago, not so much because governments were unwilling to provide social benefits and social protection, but because democratic values were removed from such questions.

Specifying the values to be preserved depended very much on how well existing institutions seemed to express a viable form of democracy. After many centuries of philosophical debate over the limits and nature of human reason the French Revolution inalterably changed the course of modern politics. Although there are important historical controversies over why the revolution took place,[10] essentially the appeal to traditional and religious authority was demolished and people were left to construct their own form of governance. For nearly half a century Europe lived in fear of the French Revolution. To be historically accurate a political account of the development of the welfare state should probably begin with 1848 when those grasping the remains of aristocratic power realised that major institutional adjustments were needed. Indeed, many of the continuing dilemmas in building a French welfare state can be dated from the divergent, and eventually unsuccessful, experiments of the Second Republic such as the ill-fated *ateliers*.[11]

The revision of democratic values needed as welfare states emerged required a very different logic of political change. The 'successful' welfare states were those which were sufficiently ingenious and imaginative to keep the fundamental democratic values alive while making massive institutional changes. There is no absolute or external measure of 'successful' other than the persistence of basic democratic practices, which should help explain

[10] A useful guide to these controversies is Lynn Hunt, *Politics, Culture and Class in the French Revolution*, Berkeley, CA; University of California Press, 1984, especially pp. 1–51.
[11] The Parisian *ateliers* or worker cooperatives of Louis Blanc established the right-to-work principle in French labour history. For a summary, see Georges Lefranc, *Histoire du travail et des travailleurs*, Paris; Flammarion, 1957, especially pp. 85–98; and B. Schnapper, 'Les sociétés de production pendant le Seconde République: l'exemple girondin,' *Revue d'Histoire Economique et Sociale*, 1965, pp. 162–91.

why the delicate process of reconstructing democratic governance tends to elude the more highly determined views of the state stemming from Marxism and also the highly permissive state in the pluralist mould. Neither concept of the state allows us to pose the most difficult political question of how institutional values were adjusted to include the values of social need and social equality.

Despite the intensive feelings aroused by the rise of socialism, the adaptation of the liberal state to welfare state needs was never a question of building a utopian society or of leading government to the whim of changing demands. The problem was how to reconcile the basic tenets of liberalism with an elaborate and growing set of social policies. This puts Germany's development in a very different perspective from that of most social and economic assessments of the welfare state. Quite simply, the question did not arise because Germany did not have democratic institutions when welfare state policies were introduced. German social accomplishments are easily included in social and economic theories of the welfare state, but are an anomaly in a democratic theory of the welfare state. In fact, Germany is the exception that proves the rule in that social reform was used by Bismarck to delay democratic development and to manipulate democratic forces within German society. In the logic of democratic institutional change, Germany was a failure even though by economic and social measures it was an immense success.

WELFARE AND POLITICAL IMAGINATION

Shifting to the institutional level puts political ideas in the forefront of the explanation of welfare states. As will be elaborated in more detail in Chapter 2, the abstract notions of social equality and social need had to be translated into institutional and political possibilities. The highly determined and the less determined views of the state leave very little room for ideas, symbols and political ingenuity, not to mention skill in political subterfuge and internecine political warfare among those competing for power within democratic institutions. Many have suggested that ideology was invented by the French Revolution, that is, for the first time in the history of human governance there was a clear institutional need, as well as a more general popular need, to discriminate among competing assertions about the reconstruction of societies and polities. It is not simply a pedagogical accident that for many years in the nineteenth century rhetoric was a required subject in the Ecole Normale Supérieure and that the teaching of foreign languages was viewed with suspicion until the turn of the century. Although there are good practical reasons why France needed to standardize its language in the early nineteenth century, politicizing the language was a natural consequence of the French Revolution.

Nor should it escape us that in the early transition to the welfare state, British government was still dominated by leaders for whom the Oxbridge study of classical languages and civilizations prevailed. As we shall see in more detail in Chapter 2, the British ruling class was sheltered not only by there being no secular revolution,[12] but by there being a common moral and philosophical foundation of the British state that predated modern ideology. In fact the principles of British governance were so well established by the nineteenth century that the term 'state' was seldom used.[13] One does not need to subscribe to a determinist view of how ideas develop to compare the agonized and tortured concerns of nineteenth-century German political philosophy[14] with British confidence in their democratic framework. If doubt occurs at high levels of British government, it is after the quest for social reform begins in the Edwardian period. Restoring political ideas to prominence makes the political transition from liberal to welfare state a less dramatic change than may be implied by social and economic accounts of its growth. Moral certainty in political life was destroyed with absolute monarchy. It was only a matter of time until social and economic questions acquired significance in ideological competition that democracy unleashed.

Within the mundane world of practical politics, the clearest effect of developing social policies as part of the burden of democratic governance was to doom the classical liberal view of governance. As T. H. Marshall[15] and others have pointed out, there was

[12] See Samuel H. Beer, *British Politics in the Collectivist Age*, New York; Knopf, 1965, for the classic statement of British governmental capabilities.

[13] See Michael Walzer, *The Revolution of the Saints: A Study in the Origins of Radical Politics*, Cambridge; Harvard University Press, 1965.

[14] Though a controversial work, Guenther Roth, *The Social Democrats in Imperial Germany: A Study in Working Class Isolation and National Integration*, Totowa, NJ; Bedminster Press, 1963, is probably the major study on the roots of ideological conflict in the Germany labour movement.

[15] T. H. Marshall, *Class, Citizenship and Social Development*, London; Heinemann, 1963.

no way to confine the democratic state to protecting only juridical and political rights. The inadequacy of the social and economic view of the development of the welfare state is to assume that the inadequacy of liberal ideas as a viable source of political solutions was self-evident. Many of the basic political questions provoked by awareness of official responsibility for social needs were being thrashed out well before social policies proliferated. Put differently, the principles governing institutional behaviour had to be revised if welfare states were to thrive. Sometimes these issues arose in ways that were far removed from the actual cares and needs of citizens. The Irish Land Act of 1881, for example, was hotly debated because it recognized that contracts among persons of highly unequal resources were not binding. Likewise, throughout the nineteenth century in France the laws of association were a constant preoccupation and seen by many moderate republicans in the 1880s as a crucial aspect of the social reconstruction of France.[16] However important we may consider popular pressures and social disarray in producing welfare states there were nonetheless fundamental questions about the design of democratic institutions that had to be considered, too.

Without indulging unduly in historical hindsight, it is important to note the decline of liberal parties throughout Europe in modern political history. Their ability to survive into the age of the welfare state is directly associated with the stability of political institutions. The British Liberal Party was the natural heir of Whig radicalism and until the 1920s still thought to be the main threat to Tory rule. As we shall see in Chapter 4, the Liberals produced some highly persuasive and original ideas about social and economic policy over the 1920s even though by then the Party was fatally divided.[17] In the doctrinaire sense of classical liberal thought, there probably never was a prototypical French liberal party. As we shall see, the Radicals and Radical Socialists, the closest thing to liberal parties in France, forged their compromise over social reform in the midst of a democratic crisis, often with the support of the more badly divided socialists.[18] In Germany, the old Liberal

[16] Pierre Sorlin, *Waldeck-Rousseau*, Paris; Colin, 1966, especially on his efforts as Minister of the Interior, pp. 236–98.
[17] On the decline of the Liberal Party, see George Dangerfield, *The Strange Death of Liberal England, 1910–1914*, New York; Putnam (Capricorn Books), 1965.
[18] On the whole, French leaders and scholars were agreed that British utilitarian ideas had no appliction to France. The classical study is Elie Halévy, *The Growth of Philosophic Radicalism*, London; Faber and Faber, 1928.

Party was perhaps the most unwitting victim of Bismarck's manipulation of political power and steadily declined under Weimar, only to be virtually excluded when competitive party politics revived after World War II.[19] Similarly in Sweden the Liberal Party never developed a social base or a political appeal that might have made it a viable alternative to the Social Democrats.[20]

The plight of the Liberals was not so much that they did not see the need for social and economic policies, but that they had great difficulty making institutional choices. Indeed, they often had clearer ideas about new policies than did socialist or conservative parties. Conservatives could either totally reject the new policies as happened in Germany, with disastrous political consequences for the development of the German democracy, or could assume the benevolent posture of the British Conservative Party by gradually yielding to social needs and thereby survive as a credible alternative. As will be elaborated more in Chapter 2, the left was consistently confused by the development of social policies, sometimes because of their suppression as in Germany and sometimes because of their internal ideological differences as in France. Thus, one of the major misperceptions about the political development of welfare states cultivated by a short historical perspective is that the rise of social policy to prominence was a socialist accomplishment.[21] Where party politics was not brutally manipulated as in Germany, the early transition from liberal to welfare state was much more the product of a murky, dimly understood contest between conventional liberal and old conservative forces neither of which fully understood the institutional consequences of their acts.

---

[19] Except for brief moments of recovery after 1868, the German Liberals never again regained their parliamentary strength. See Gordon Smith, *Democracy in Western Germany: Parties and Politics in the Federal Republic*, New York; Holmes and Meier, 1979, p. 12.

[20] Douglas Verney, 'The Foundations of Modern Sweden: The Swift Rise and Fall of Swedish Liberalism,' *Political Studies*, **20**, March 1972, pp. 42–59.

[21] Only the British Labour Party was in a position to potentially affect social legislation early in the century. Though historically controversial, it seems clear that their social aims were confused. See Kenneth O. Brown, *The Labour Party and Unemployment, 1900–1914*, Totowa, NJ; Rowman and Littlefield, 1971; Pat Thane, 'The Labour Party and State "Welfare"', in K. D. Brown, ed., *The First Labour Party, 1906–1914*, London; Croom Helm, 1985, pp. 183–216; and John Brown, '"Social Control" and the Modernisation of Social Policy,' in P. Thane, ed., *The Origins of British Social Policy*, London; Croom Helm, 1978, pp. 126–46.

Stressing ideas in relation to institutional adaptation suggests an open-ended definition of the welfare state and makes performance and need less prominent in explaining the rise of welfare states. If institutions are the main arena of political interaction where decisions are made by balancing old and new values, historical continuities loom larger and the significance of external conditions common to empirical explanations of the welfare states diminish. The assurances of positivist explanation are sacrificed because we cannot build simple measures of institutional behaviour across countries.[22] While there are certainly some reliable measures of rising expectations and of economic growth, these are not true measures of institutional capabilities. This is not to say that the quantitative measures of the welfare state are irrelevant to an institutional analysis, but only that their full meaning can only be extracted by placing their results in the context of institutionalized power in each democratic state. Put differently, the acceptable and workable manifestation of democratic values in each democratic polity varied enormously.

In this respect, the book is not really about social policies as such but how social policies were blended with pre-existing institutional norms and practices to permit the state to engage in entirely new endeavours. Demand and performance, or the 'inputs' and 'outputs' of government, are of less concern to an institutional analysis though obviously how institutions shaped the expression of demands and provision of new social goods is important. Perhaps the most extreme version of the behavioural model of the state was that advocated by Easton who simply banished the term 'state' from his wholly empirical theory of how political systems work.[23] Only a long methodological diversion would establish why such unpredictable elements as intention, political imagination and political ambition are part of the process of institutional adaptation.[24] What may suffice is to note only that each democracy formed its particular form of democratic compromise to respond

[22] In general, the public choice theorists argue that complex organizations, possibly even institutions, might be reconstructed with behavioural methods. For a selection of these ideas, see Judith A. Gillespie and Dina Zinnes, eds., *Missing Elements in Political Inquiry: Logic and Levels of Analysis*, Beverly Hills, CA; Sage Publications, 1982.
[23] David Easton, *The Political System: An Inquiry into the State of Political Science*, New York; Knopf, 1953, pp. 111–15.
[24] Douglas E. Ashford, 'Structural Analysis and Institutional Change,' *Polity*, March 1986.

to the uncertainties and risks of basing the state on human reason. As an institutional problem, the welfare state is no more than an extension of the initial democratic assumption. To assume that the historical and philosophical context within which democratic states were organized simply disappears because we are now more involved with calculating the social and economic effects of the state would seem to sacrifice the most challenging question about democratic governance. One might even argue that the welfare state may not have progressed as rapidly as its advocates wished because they failed to treat institutional values seriously while, at the other political extreme, those who dogmatically resisted the extension of institutional values to new social questions eventually fail because they underestimate democratic governance.

INSTITUTIONAL DYNAMICS OF DECISIONMAKING

If there is an inescapable relational quality imbedded in democratic governance, the positivist explanations can only be a partial explanation of how states change. But we must also have some method of inquiry that seems appropriate to understanding how institutions respond to changing social needs and social demands. This brings us to the third, and possibly the most crucial step, in an institutional analysis of the emergency of welfare states. At the level of institutions, the working out of the compromises or the new capabilities of the state took place in the process of initiating, designing and implementing new policies. To be sure, the rigid rules of secrecy such as exist in Britain make these decisions hard to follow in the recent past. An important reason for delving into the early transition of the welfare state is of course that the ample supply of memoirs, biographies and released official documents make the reconstruction of what actually did happen much easier. Moreover, it stands to reason that as important social and economic burdens were first imposed on government we are likely to obtain a sharper account of the institutional dilemmas and institutional conflicts than is possible in an age of extraordinarily complex decisionmaking. There are also very good descriptive histories of social policy for most European countries though they often do not provide much detail on how and why political decisions were made.

The study of decisionmaking is not easily standardized to fit the assumptions used in absolute comparisons of how states behaved as they embarked on building welfare states. Fixing the limits of the policy process in ways that satisfy the requirements of more rigorous, empirical explanation is no easier than is the direct measurement of institutional differences. But this may also be a misleading formulation of the question because how politicians, officials and larger bureaucracies affecting policymaking takes place within the setting of institutional norms and practices, and the key actors are sensitive to such restraints. Any governmental decision balances rhetoric and reality, calculates political risks against political rewards, and weighs numerous national problems against social and economic proposals. One attraction of the policy-based approach to institutional change is that the major actors are indeed speaking the language of their own institutional setting. The methodological price of greater validity is that we cannot claim the reliability of more positivist explanations. Having shown how institutions relate to a particular decision at one point in time provides no guarantee, statistical or otherwise, that the politicians or officials will behave the same way were the question to arise at a later time.

Policy analysis is shooting at a moving target. For purposes of evaluation we can make policies 'stand still' for a brief moment in quantitative models, but no one, least of all the governmental consumers of policy research of this kind, are fooled by such methodological assumptions. Institutional policy analysis is very different because it focuses on how risks, uncertainties and anticipations relate to an institutional setting rather than to an external measure of policy. But if we cannot specify the elusive, imperative quality of decisionmaking, we can map institutional continuities in decisions through time. Put differently, decisionmaking is a way of seeing how institutionalized values impinge on politics. As we shall see throughout this study, whether such decisions coherently relate to an economic, social or, for that matter, political model of how best to make policies for some given reason has only a marginal bearing on outcomes. The approach used may be best described as interactive,[25] that is, searching for regularities in the

[25] For an elaboration of this view, see Douglas E. Ashford, 'The Structural Analysis of Policy or Institutions Really Do Matter,' in D. E. Ashford, ed., *Comparing Public Policies: New Concepts and Methods*, Beverly Hills, CA; Sage Publications, 1978, pp. 81–98.

institutional constraints on policies and, in turn, how policies gradually change institutional constraints. As will be elaborated in the conclusion, the critical interaction between institutional settings and the aspirations, schemes and visions of policymakers is at the core of democratic political theory.

Although the intricacy of both institutions and the policy processes means that direct comparisons are impossible, how new policies affected the emergence of welfare states can be specified with some precision. As is now relatively clear in various versions of the social democratic state, perhaps most advanced in Sweden, once states began to provide more social benefits and social protection they unavoidably affected wages and redistributed incomes. Indeed, the major reason that the classical liberal view of government was soon bankrupt, at least in so far as it adhered to classical economics as an assumption of any democratic state, was disagreement over wage policy rather than social policy. Liberals were quite prepared to extend education, to build public housing and to provide pensions for the elderly. What they had difficulty imagining was how to reconcile the growing impact of social benefits and social protection on wages and incomes. To be sure, in each country their options were hemmed in by the nature of the labour movement and by the aims of the socialist parties, but these were hardly major political obstacles until social democratic parties began to assume political importance in the 1930s.

In some countries, such as Germany, liberals never had a chance to establish the ground-rules of democratic governance as they did in most of Europe so the issue becomes moot. In Britain, the Liberal Party was permanently identified with social reform after the 1911 National Insurance Act, but was distracted first by Lloyd George's betrayal of Asquith in 1915 and later by his schemes to resurrect a coalition government with the Tories after World War I. As we shall see, their doom was sealed not by social caution, but by their clash with Tory ideas about land values and taxation. In France, Leroy-Beaulieu was a leader among the outspoken exponents of a totally untouched labour market, but he hardly represented French political thinking over the 1920s. France continued to make steady, if not spectacular, progress toward building new social policies. The political argument was really over the nature of labour associations and labour organization in the context of French democracy. Although the Swedish Liberals had made progress toward providing some basic social benefits prior to the rise of the Social Democrats,[26] they were easily eclipsed by the political coalition of industrial and agrarian interests assembled by the Social Democratic Party. Only the diffuse structure of American politics enabled liberal ideas to persist. Having lost his fight with the Supreme Court over a national economic policy, Roosevelt never suggested that social security might link to reconstructing a wage and incomes policy.

Whether the ambitious idea of integrating labour and social policies associated with Sweden is desirable is not our primary concern, but from the earliest forms of social assistance wages and incomes were being distorted. At the policymaking level, concern about the private labour market was seldom a major obstacle to new social policies. The effect was that, with the exception of Sweden, social policies led the way toward reconsidering wage policies. One of the remarkable characteristics of the British welfare state is how readily government intervened in all kinds of social policies, but how reticent it was to suggest that wage and income policies were politically and economically linked to social policy. By this criteria, one of the highest performers in terms of social policy was also one of the least successful performers in articulating the interdependence of the social and real wages. For various reasons, the sharp differentiation of social and wage policy was never as firmly implanted in the politics of the other European democracies. From the debates of the 1890s onwards France considered how workers might be involved in implementing social policies, and later accepted family and child protection under the guise of a *salaire normale*. For political reasons more than economic and social necessity, Sweden inverted the normal sequence of building social policies by first considering how wage policies provide a foundation for social policy. In Germany, the rapid advance of social policy under anti-democratic forces had the perverse effect of 'stealing the thunder' of the powerful Social Democratic Party and forcing it toward a corporatist organization of both social and labour policies.

The development of what might be considered the fully fledged welfare state was of course only dimly perceived at the turn of the century, and the specific circumstances will be discussed more in Chapter 5. But the early choices about social policies affected the

---

[26] Hugh Heclo, *Modern Social Politics in Britain and Sweden*, New Haven; Yale University Press, 1974, pp. 180–91.

policy response to wage policy fifty and a hundred years later. Moreover, the constraints observed in setting the welfare state in motion were not as much economic dogmas about private enterprise or frantic efforts to quell labour unrest, but politically contested and politically designed actions within the institutional framework of each democracy. For this reason the functional comparison of policies is not particularly suitable for an institutional analysis of policy change and its relation to the welfare state.

Although the direct comparability of major public policies probably increases as the complexities of the welfare state proliferate in more recent years, in the early stages of welfare states, embarking on social reforms and intervening in the economy generated different political controversies in each country. Education, for example, had extremely different political implications for France and Britain. One might almost write the history of the Third Republic in terms of the educational reforms of the moderate republicans in the 1880s and the extreme secularization of education under the Bloc des Gauches.[27] In Britain, education was certainly controversial for religious reasons, but first in 1871 and again in 1902 (as well as in 1944) the Tories managed to skirt the political pitfalls of expanding public education.

In an historical perspective, when major social issues impinged on government makes a great difference. British government was still largely in the hands of aristocrats when the disastrous epidemics of the mid-nineteenth century struck.[28] The Victorian history of local government can be written around the problems of 'standpipes and sewers' and Parliament was greatly perplexed by the organization of the public health. Sir John Simon was a major actor in mid-Victorian policymaking, and his contribution to British public health policy sets in motion governmental changes that anticipate the National Health Service.[29] In other words, the political salience of social and economic policies is not wholly

[27] See, for example, Katherine Auspitz, *The Radical Bourgeoisie: The Ligue de l'Enseignement and the Origins of the Third Republic, 1866–1885*, Cambridge; Cambridge University Press, 1982.
[28] See Sydney Checkland, *British Public Policy, 1776–1939: An Economic, Social and Political Perspective*, Cambridge; Cambridge University Press, 1983; and W. M. Frazer, *A History of English Public Health, 1834–1939*, London; Baillere, Tundall and Cox, 1950.
[29] Royston Lambert, *Sir John Simon, 1816–1904 and English Social Administration*, London; MacGibbon and Kee, 1963.

determined by need or demand. From an institutional perspective, the unexplained variance is most important because it reflects the political circumstances of the day. The early decisions became the precedents for solving later problems. Governmental capabilities, administrative organization and vested political interests were taking shape long before anyone imagined a welfare state. Policymakers only partially anticipated the consequences of their actions, not only in terms of the specific form and precedence that social problem-solving would take in each democracy, but in how their decisions would ultimately impinge on long-standing institutional and political values.

WELFARE: OBJECT OR SUBJECT OF THE STATE?

In varying degrees the recent analyses of the welfare state have assumed that the welfare objectives of the modern democracies can be translated into objective language with relative ease. By underscoring the priority of democratic governance, the role of ideas in shaping welfare policies and the uncertainties surrounding policymaking of any kind, this study tries to revive awareness of the subjective dimension in the growth of welfare states. In general, the more an approach relies on direct measures of need and demand as an explanation of the change, the less important become the institutional and political constraints with all their subjective complications. Without hoping to provide a thorough assessment of the alternative schemes, it is perhaps useful to review briefly how the central problem of this study fares when treated in other ways.

Macro-studies of the welfare state are not easily categorized, but may perhaps be summarized in four groupings. There are, first, the political sociological analyses which might be characterized as seeing the welfare state as demand-driven. There are of course various formulations of how and why demand for more social protection arose, many of them stemming from the seminal work of Bendix on industrialization.[30] As populations became concentrated in cities, more highly differentiated occupationally and

[30] Reinhard Bendix, *Nation-Building and Citizenship*, New York; Wiley, 1964.

more readily mobilized for political purposes, governments provided more social assistance. The most complete account of the development of welfare states as a consequence of industrialization has been written by Rimlinger.[31] Another variation, stressing the importance of mobilization and applied more to developing countries, is Huntingdon's analysis of the potential imbalance of mobilization and institutionalization.[32] Perhaps the most ambitious effort is the extensive effort of Flora and Alber to link the growth of the electorate to the timing and nature of major social reforms.[33]

The fundamental problem of the demand-based theories of state and society is that they attempt to combine an aggregated concept of societal change with a structural notion of politics. They convey a picture of states either disintegrating as the excesses of societal mobilization destroy legitimacy or states having an apparently bottomless reservoir of resources and ingenuity to reconstruct their legitimacy. The critical importance of enfranchisement, voter pressures and social protests is not in question, but we are left with little guidance to differentiate between total success and total failure. The latter possibility makes mobilization theories especially attractive to Marxist critics of the liberal state,[34] and the theory naturally draws fire from more conservative analysts such as Huntingdon.[35] Neither assessment of how states respond to increasing demands deal with a number of crucial questions.

For one thing, the aggregated measure of growing demand conceals very different structures. The repressive capabilities of the Junker three-class voting system is not equivalent to the uncertain

[31] Gustav V. Rimlinger, *Welfare Policy and Industrialization in Europe, America and Russia*, New York; Wiley, 1971.

[32] Samuel P. Huntingdon, *Political Order in Changing Societies*, New Haven; Yale University Press, 1968.

[33] Peter Flora and Jens Alber, 'Modernization, Democratization, and the Development of Welfare States in Western Europe,' in P. Flora and A. Heidenheimer, eds, *The Development of Welfare States in Europe and America*, London and New Brunswick; Transaction Books, 1981, pp. 37–80.

[34] For example, Alan Wolfe, *The Limits of Legitimacy: Political Contradictions of Contemporary Capitalism*, New York and London; Free Press and Macmillan, 1977.

[35] Huntingdon, *Political Order and Political Decay* . . . was criticized for suggesting that mobilization was more likely to undermine legitimacy than heavy-handed institutions. If the legitimacy problem is differentiated from effectiveness, then the two problems (popular support and governmental effectiveness) can be differentiated. A good critique of these limitations in economic terms is Ole P. Kristenen, 'On the Futility of the "Demand Approach" to Public Sector Growth,' *European Journal of Political Research*, **12**, September 1984, pp. 309–24.

bumbling of Napoleon III. Secondly, one can easily find social factors that operated independently of overall trends in industrialization and mobilization to affect how demands were indeed made. The prolonged controversy between the more bourgeois socialists of Saxony under Bebel's influence and the more militant Berlin socialists under Liebknecht is one example, as are the almost endless schisms inhibiting the power of the French socialists in the 1890s. Third, the demand theories suggest that governments react to social pressure in similar ways. Asquith's 1908 Pension Act, for example, may correlate with growing labour unrest and more working class voting, but the Act itself was hastily prepared and many thought an extravagant electoral gesture. By 1908 pension plans had been debated for nearly thirty years and were soon to be completely re-examined by the Royal Commission on the Poor Laws. Fourth, there is a growing literature linking welfare to precapitalist values.[36] Thus, the historical timing and institutional links between increased demand and increased social protection vary widely among countries. The demand theories have an unassailable persuasiveness, but they do not help us isolate how states differed internally in meeting welfare demands.

A second grouping might be made of supply-based theories of the welfare state that are associated with political economy writings. Essentially, the political economists argue that the imperfections of the private marketplace are multiplied in the provision of public goods and services. As stated more modestly by Mancur Olson, for example, sharing of social costs leads to sub-optimal levels of production.[37] The economic logic is impeccable, but the question

[36] A summary of the pre-capitalist argument is John Hall, 'The Conscious Relegitimation of Liberal Capitalism: Problems of Transition,' in A. Ellis and K. Kumar, eds, *Dilemmas of Liberal Democracies: Studies in Fred Hirsch's Social Limits to Growth*, London; Tavistock Publications, 1983, pp. 65–79. See also A. Hirschman, *The Passions and the Interests*, Princeton; Princeton University Press, 1977, and Arnold J. Heidenheimer, 'Secularization Patterns and the Westward Spread of the Welfare State, 1893–1973,' in R. F. Tomasson, ed., *The Welfare State, 1883–1983*, vol. 6, Comparative Social Research Annual, Greenwich CN; JAI Press, 1983, pp. 3–37. For more historical analysis, see for example, A. Macfarlane, *The Origins of English Individualism*, Oxford, Basil Blackwell, 1978; Martin J. Wiener, *English Culture and the Decline of the Industrial Spirit, 1850–1980*, Cambridge; Cambridge University Press, 1981; and Clive Treblicock, *The Industrialization of Continental Powers*, New York; Longman, 1982.

[37] Mancur Olson, *The Logic of Collective Action: Public Goods and the Theory of Groups*, Cambridge; Harvard University Press, 1965, and *The Rise and Decline of Nations: Economic Growth, Stagflation, and Social Rigidities*, New Haven; Yale University Press, 1982.

remains whether these economic calculations are immune to political and traditional values.[38] Again, one finds the curious way in which supply-side views of state and society can be used with equal skill by both conservatives and radicals. For conservative political economists marketplace conditions need only be restored in the public sector, most often by various devices to allow individuals to maximize their values in selecting among public goods.[39] For more radical theorists, the public sector, and social policies in particular, should be used to demolish the marketplace.[40] Instead of using social policies to remedy inadequate care and loss of employment, the radicals would prefer a system where wages and social benefits become indistinguishable. The logic remains close to that of the conservatives in so far as under these circumstances individuals will presumably be aware that everyone is being treated equally and therefore accept the specified distribution of production. The main difference between them is that conservatives would like the optimal distribution to take place by individual decisionmaking and the radicals see no alternative other than optimal distribution being enforced by the state.

While the 'push' theory of the welfare state must rely on aggregate measures of demand, the 'pull' theory of the welfare state relies on aggregate measures of supply. This raises the first difficulty because the internal structure of the various economies of course varies immensely. In a society such as Sweden with highly concentrated capital and highly organized labour, the possibility of eliminating market forces may exist.[41] More to the point, the

---

[38] The issue is perhaps most clearly drawn by Fred Hirsch, *Social Limits to Growth*, Cambridge; Harvard University Press and London; Routledge and Kegan Paul, 1977. See the penetrating critiques in Adrian Ellis and Krishan Kumar, eds, *Dilemmas of Liberal Democracies: Studies in Fred Hirsch's 'Social Limits to Growth'*, London; Tavistock Press, 1983.

[39] The narrow interpretation of political economy is often associated with the American public choice theorists, in particular James M. Buchanan, *Theory of Public Choice: Political Applications of Economics*, Ann Arbor; University of Michigan Press, 1972.

[40] A typical example being Gösta Esping-Andersen and Walter Korpi, 'Social Policy as Class Politics in Post-War Capitalism: Scandinavia, Austria, and Germany,' in J. Goldthorpe, ed., *Order and Conflict in Contemporary Capitalism: Studies in the Political Economy of Western European Nations*, Oxford; Clarendon Press, 1984, pp. 179–208.

[41] Although the corporatist writing has not been directly applied to the welfare state, the Swedish case is probably the best example of how close cooperation among business, government and unions may result in an advanced form of the

ease of objectifying need may be questionable, both for the individual and the state. For example, it is striking that much of British social policy in the early twentieth century was often based on the nearby and peculiar problems of the London labour market although the basic industrial problems were in the north.[42] It now seems that the British may have exaggerated the problem of poverty,[43] which caused endless distortions in designing the British welfare state, and may also have produced serious misperceptions of the severity of unemployment in the 1930s.[44] Put differently, the 'correct' supply of social services is no more obvious than the 'correct' response to ever-rising expectations. From a political and policy perspective on the welfare state, government may be only an intricate system of approximating the best relationship of supply and demand, not an infallible tool of reason.

A third group of studies are the statistical and quantitative evaluations of welfare states of which the work of Pryor,[45] Wilensky[46] and Peacock and Wiseman[47] are among the most noteworthy. To these might be added the many quantitative stud-

welfare state. The problems of the theory centre on how easily it accomodates the differences among economic structures. See Philippe C. Schmitter and Gerhard Lehmbruch, eds, *Trends Toward Corporatist Intermediation*, Beverly Hills, CA; Sage Publications, 1979.

[42] The Fabians and most London labour organizations were preoccupied with 'casual labour', in particular the plight of the dockworkers. See John Lovell, *Stevedores and Dockers: A Study of Trade Unionism in the Port of London, 1870–1914*, New York; A. M. Kelley, 1969. There has been a remarkable amount of historical research into the early conditions of the British labour movement, much of which will be noted in Chapter 5. An excellent introduction is C. J. Wrigley, ed., *The History of British Labor Relations, 1875–1914*, Amherst; University of Massachusetts Press, 1982.

[43] On the concentration of public assistance needs in a few Poor Law areas, see Eveline M. Burns, *The British Unemployment Program, 1920–1938*, Washington, D.C.; Social Science Research Council, 1941, p. 37.

[44] The testimony of one high official dealing with the 1930s legislation suggests that the severity of unemployment was exaggerated. Ronald C. Davison, *British Unemployment Policy: The Modern Phase Since 1930*, London; Longman's Green, 1938, p. 49.

[45] Frederic L. Pryor, *Public Expenditures in Communist and Capitalist Nations*, New Haven; Yale University Press (The Economic Growth Center), 1968.

[46] Harold L. Wilensky, *The Welfare State and Equality: Structural and Ideological Roots of Public Expenditures*, Berkeley; University of California Press, 1975.

[47] Alan T. Peacock and Jack Wiseman, *The Growth of Government Expenditure in the United Kingdom*, London and New York; Allen & Unwin, 1967, rev. ed.

ies of income redistribution in the welfare state,[48] but these studies have less relevance to the early stages of welfare state development. As Pryor acknowledges,[49] the quantitative studies permit broad, macro-comparisons of welfare states in terms of their performance, but do not bear very directly on the norms that have governed varying degrees of redistribution nor on the relative merits of different ways that governments have assessed the costs and benefits of specific programmes. As he writes, it is 'extremely difficult to derive many convincing hypotheses linking institutions to actual expenditures' so that institutional and political factors can only be treated in an 'interpretative' way.[50] Although Wilensky shifts his ground in more recent writing,[51] in his early statistical comparison he, too, agreed that public expenditure 'comes close to capturing the idea of the welfare state,[52] an assumption that many historical sociologists would dispute.

As should be apparent, the quantitative studies exclude the role of ideas and institutions. The motives linked to new social policies, the grounds for advancing reforms, and the political intricacies of obtaining agreement are methodologically irrelevant because they cannot be measured in standard terms across countries. Not surprisingly, the idea that spending accurately reflects political ideas and political realities has been hotly disputed.[53] On the whole, economists are more restrained in making such interpretations of

---

[48] There have been dozens of quantitative studies and comparisons of social security systems of which one of the earliest and most useful is Henry Aaron, 'Social Security: International Comparisons,' in Otto Eckstein, ed., *Studies in the Economics of Income Maintenance*, Washington, D.C.; the Brookings Institution, 1967.

[49] Pryor, *Public Expenditures* . . ., p. 312.

[50] Pryor, *Public Expenditures* . . ., p. 48 and p. 34.

[51] Harold L. Wilensky, 'Leftism, Catholicism, and Democratic Corporatism: The Role of Political Parties in Recent Welfare State Development,' in P. Flora and A. J. Heidenheimer, eds, *The Development of Welfare States in Europe*, New Brunswick and London, Transaction Books, 1981, pp. 345–82.

[52] Wilensky, *The Welfare State and Equality* . . ., pp. 2–3.

[53] Among the many articles on this issue, see J. M. Fesmire and G. C. Beauvais, 'Budget Size in Democracy Revisited: The Public Supply of Private, Public and Semi-Public Goods,' *Southern Economic Journal*, **45**, 1979, pp. 277–93; Ole P. Kristenen, 'The Logic of Political-Bureaucratic Decisionmaking as a Cause for Government Growth,' *European Journal of Political Research*, **8**, pp. 249–64; F. G. Castles and R. D. McKinlay, 'Public Welfare Provision, Scandinavia, and the Sheer Futility of the Sociological Approach to Politics,' *British Journal of Political Science*, **9**, 1979, pp. 157–71; and David Collier and Richard Messick, 'Prerequisites versus Diffusion: Testing Alternative Explanations of Social Security Adoption,' *American Political Science Review*, **69**, 1975, pp. 1296–315.

their work, but this may also mean that implied causes are misleading. In the Peacock and Wiseman study, for example, the pattern of expenditure growth is clearly associated with wartime surges in public spending. As a Treasury document of 1931 shows,[54] the imputed cause may not explain welfare increments. Between 1891 and 1921 government spending on five major social programmes multiplied five times, but the increment could be entirely traced to laws passed before World War I. Unless we assume that the late Victorian and Edwardian policymakers were anticipating the war as a way to establish their programmes (if anything they feared the war would curtail their programmes), the 'displacement' theory is extremely misleading. As we shall see in more detail in Chapter 3, in fact, the war derailed nearly all the ambitious ideas for expanding the British welfare state, which is not to say that British government could ignore the growth of social spending.

The fourth and last grouping might be labelled historical sociological studies which stress how social change impinges on the structure of the state, and less clearly perhaps on the development of institutions. Again, we find distinctly Marxist interpretations such as Anderson's work on the Third World[55] and Mayer's assessment of the influence of the aristocracy,[56] as well as more standard social histories such as the well-known studies of the social change in peasant societies by Moore and Skocpol.[57] The main theoretical problem differentiating these works appears to be the extent to which the various authors wish to treat the historical

---

[54] 'Public Social Spending,' *Financial Acts of the United Kingdom, 1930–1931*, London; Parliamentary Papers, 1932.

[55] Perry Anderson, *Lineages of the Absolutist State*, London; New Left Books, 1974.

[56] Arno Mayer, *The Persistence of the Old Regime*, New York; Pantheon, 1981, might also be seen as a study of how pre-democratic values penetrate democratic governance. A class analysis of state transformations may exclude important evidence on how the aristocracy actually maintained their influence; and make the logical error of attributing to one class a characteristic that is widespread in the society. Compare Mayer, for example, with F. M. L. Thompson, *English Landed Society in the Nineteenth Century*, London; Routledge and Kegan Paul, 1963; A. P. Thornton, *The Habit of Authority: Paternalism in British History*, London and Boston; Allen & Unwin, 1966; and James Camplin, *The Rise of the Rich*, New York; St Martin's, 1979.

[57] Barrington Moore, Jr, *The Social Origins of Dictatorship and Democracy: Lord and Peasant in the Making of the Modern World*, Boston; Beacon Press, 1966; and Theda Skocpol, *States and Social Revolutions*, Cambridge; Cambridge University Press, 1979.

transformation of social classes as economically determined. To the degree that they do so, institutional and political influences necessarily receive less weight. Thus, the major controversy surrounding these studies becomes the state as an autonomous actor and ultimately whether we may distinguish strong and weak states. Strong states are presumably able to redirect and channel social forces and social conflict to national purposes, while weak states topple or resort to totalitarian controls in the face of social unrest.

There are a number of questions to be resolved before the historical studies can become a reliable foundation to compare institutional changes over time. First, the borderline between society and state is often vague and of course there is no reason to assume that even if agreement could be reached that such borderlines are historically constant. In this respect, the historical social analyses explain failure better than success. There would be little disagreement, for example, that Britain is a strong state, but is it because of its success in incorporating new social classes into the state or because those who might have toppled the state rarely considered revolutionary change? Whatever the weaknesses of British governance, as Beer argues,[58] British leaders were remarkably adept at anticipating and defusing social conflict. Second, there is the problem of strong states which took very different courses. Surely it is not meant that Britain and Germany are in some sense equivalent even though both dealt harshly with their peasant populations. Third, there is the as yet unravelled issue of why some strong states seem to experience policymaking failures and others less so. To take the British welfare state as an example, there is ample evidence that, at least over the past century, few British policies dealing with basic social issues worked very well. Thus a state may be strong in relation to its social setting, but not very effective in solving policy problems.

As will be stressed throughout this study, there is increasing historical and political evidence that the emergence of the welfare state was by no means the product of market forces that were somehow super-imposed on nineteenth-century liberal democracies. Perhaps the welfare state was neither pushed nor pulled into existence by inexorable economic and social forces as much as it was the product of institutionalized searching, experimentation, and accumulation within the democratic framework

[58] Samuel H. Beer, *British Politics in the Collectivist Age*, New York; Knopf, 1965.

of each country. Historical ebbs and flows are easily·forgotten. Kumar points out, for example, the existence, in early Victorian Britain, of the remarkable consensus of Tory and radical opinion that Marx observed and which led him to think that Britain would become the first truly communist state.[59] Asa Briggs bases his entire case to explain the welfare state on the early agreement that market intervention was essential.[60] There is an intense historical controversy over the collectivist impact of Bentham on Britain,[61] but it is perhaps clear that in no continental country were the vagaries of the marketplace acceptable in the pursuit of national goals. One of the most influential of the nineteenth-century German economists in the *Sozialpolitik* school that helped devise Germany's brand of state socialism was persuaded that no Smithian could ever hold an academic chair in Germany.[62]

The main reason for more explicitly dealing with the subjectivity of institutions and politics is primarily to restore balance in our understanding of the modern democratic state. Many who once argued that the complex transition from liberal to welfare state might be evaluated in primarily objective terms are changing their views. In a re-assessment of his work, Wilensky finds that Catholicism is an important explanatory factor in the distribution of German social benefits.[63] Goldthorpe, one of the major advocates of the radical political economy view of the welfare state, writes that the liberal impulse behind industrial society 'could be fairly described as a political, far more than an economic liberalism'.[64] However discouraging these suggestions may be for those viewing the state as the product of uncontrollable forces, it is

[59] Krishan Kumar, 'Pre-Capitalist and Non-Capitalist Factors in the Development of Capitalism: Fred Hirsch and Joseph Schumpeter,' in A. Ellis and K.Kumar, eds, *The Dilemmas of Liberal Democracies* . . ., p. 162.
[60] Asa Briggs, 'The Welfare State in Historical Perspective,' *Archives Europeene Sociologie*, **2**, 1961, pp. 221–58, especially p. 228.
[61] L. J. Hume, 'Jeremy Bentham and the Nineteenth-Century Revolution in government,' *Historical Journal*. **4**, no. 4, 1967, pp. 361–75; and Valerie Cromwell, 'Interpretations of Nineteenth-Century Administration: An Analysis,' *Victorian Studies*, **9**, The Welfare State. . ., March 1966, pp. 245–55.
[62] Briggs, p. 242.
[63] Wilensky, 'Leftism, Catholicism and Democratic Corporatism . . .' in P. Flora and A. Heidenheimer, *The Development of Welfare States* . . ., pp. 345–82.
[64] John H. Goldthorpe, 'The End of Convergence: Corporatist and Dualist Tendencies in Modern Western Societies,' in J. Goldthorpe, ed., *Order and Conflict in Contemporary Capitalism* . . . . p. 321.

possible that the democratic state was in fact never that closely associated with unfettered capitalism. The desire for a more humane and equitable society may never achieve the absolute standards imposed by objective measures, but perhaps democracies never subscribed to these material measures of accomplishment as completely as many analyses of the welfare state suggest.

Does this mean that the empirical study of the emergence of the welfare state is then adrift in an existential sea? If one takes seriously the intense debates and enormous effort made to initiate social policies over the past century this would hardly seem the case. The rules governing access to government, the organization of government and the powers of government were steadily tested, not only by the proliferation of social policies but by the introduction of new principles of governance. The early democratic compromises underwent revision and redefinition. Institutions were radically altered, budgets grew at what was thought a dizzying pace, and government officials multiplied to be a common element in political life. In grasping the complexity of this transformation, possibly the best starting point is to survey what appear to be the major political components of this historic change in modern democracies.

2

Images of Welfare

Perhaps the most brutal distortion imposed on our interpretation of welfare states by the socio-economic analyses is that the formulation and transmission of concepts and ideas necessarily becomes a residual problem. In order to achieve clarity in comparing states, the intricacies of the struggle of ideas are excluded. To the historians of ideas, the rigid rules imposed on the data are a form of rhetoric that enables such writers to ignore the fact that our knowledge of the past is necessarily incomplete.[1] At the root of this controversy is a difficult philosophical debate over the meaning of intentions and the correct way to deal with antecedent conditions here.[2] Possibly the most concise formulation of the issue is Pocock's discussion of 'authoritative language' (rhetoric) and prescriptive language which seeks to uncover the diverse meanings of ideas.[3] In its most general sense the continuing argument is over the nature of explanation in social sciences and, as expounded by Kuhn, the use of paradigmatic knowledge in advancing understanding.[4]

While the accumulation of ideas and the raging intellectual controversies that accompanied the development of the idea of welfare states cannot be satisfactorily presented in a few pages,

[1] John Dunn, 'The Identity of the History of Ideas,' *Philosophy*, **43**, no. 164, April 1968, pp. 85–104; Quentin Skinner, 'Meaning and Understanding in the History of Ideas,' *History and Theory*, **8**, 1969, pp. 3–53.
[2] P. F. Stawson, 'Social and Morality and Individual Ideal,' *Philosophy*, **36**, no. 136, January 1961, pp. 1–17.
[3] J. G. A. Pocock, *Politics, Language and Time: Essays on Political Thought and History*, New York; Atheneum, 1971, p. 18.
[4] Thomas Kuhn, *The Structure of Scientific Revolutions*, Chicago; University of Chicago Press, 1962.

the aim of this chapter is to suggest that the assumptions and
rules associated with the early democratic state, labelled the liberal
state, were in question long before welfare states were constructed.
In each instance the debates evolved from particular historical
and political circumstances. For this reason, many of the crucial
steps toward defining welfare states occurred decades before positivist meanings could be attached to the state. At the same time,
many of the early philosophical and political advocates of increased
social protection and social assistance were themselves positivists
of many kinds. Thus, from the perspective of an historian of ideas,
the recent positivist explanations of the welfare state are a rigid,
rhetorical amount of subjective meanings.

By equating social justice and social progress with material
indicators the positivists divorce the history of ideas from the
changing concept of the state. The main problem of the nineteenth-
century liberal thinkers was not that they lacked an image of
welfare, but that they had too many of them. In linking policies
to politics there were endless controversies over the correct way to
add social obligations to democratic liberal states. Well before the
issues of social insurance present clearer choices involving immense
sums of money and major institutional changes, the battles were
being fought over the extension of the franchise, most notably in
the prolonged mid-Victorian debate over the Reform Bill of 1867,
and over the expansion of education. In France, the violent clash
of ideas in the Revolution provided sharper differences which may
account for the continuity of social concern in French political
debate, while in Germany a paternal state forestalled the free
discussion of the meanings and instruments of their version of the
welfare state. The ascendancy of social democratic ideas in Sweden
was more rapid than elsewhere, but even in Sweden the liberal
cause was powerfully represented by Bertil Ohlin and the Stock-
holm School of Economics, and the Social Democratic Party was
under severe political uncertainties in the 1930s. Only in the
United States were social purposes relatively insulated from the
clash of political ideas.

In the search for the institutional roots of welfare states, the
positivist approach extracts empirical objectivity at enormous cost
to the history of ideas, and, most importantly, to the ingenuity
and imagination that in fact were exercised a century or more
before welfare states were firmly institutionalized. Mobilizing the
intellectual energies of the liberal democracies was highly contested

at every stage, not only because of fears of the working class and the obvious costs of early industrialization, but also because the questions were intrinsically difficult. Their resolution is still contested, but their political meanings persist in charting the course of welfare states. First, in the early welfare state debates political and social issues were intermingled. Unlike the somewhat dichotomized accounts that emerge from positivist accounts of recent periods, political calculations blended with social issues, as, for example, in the early concerns of Labour Members of Parliament (MPs) that they be paid. Paying representatives was not a major social issue, but it was vital to assuring continued and widespread representation of the working class. Similarly, the divisive controversies among French socialists over 'ministerialism' or the acceptance of responsibility in liberal governments in 1898 helped define the welfare state in the context of French politics. The great risk of the recent studies of welfare states is, of course, that their simplified accounts of how welfare states are built neglects more fundamental questions about redefining political values and adapting political institutions to immediate needs.

Second, translating the development of welfare states into performance, its adequacy and equity, submerges the more fundamental political question of how the left influenced the growth of welfare states and, more basically, how the left itself is affected by the growth of social protection. The ambiguities of contemporary socialist ideas is not the issue. What can be seen historically is the great difficulty that socialists had in reconciling liberal democracy with social reform at the turn of the century. There is perhaps no sharper contrast than the British and French cases. In both countries the early socialist movement was an amalgam of Marxist interpretations of society and politics. With the lure of parliamentary power the British socialists came under the influence of the Independent Labour Party (ILP) underscored by the secret electoral pact of MacDonald in 1906. In contrast, the French socialists retained a revolutionary posture while participating in the early social reform debates. The greatest ambivalence appears in Germany where the socialists were suppressed by Bismarck, attempted a reconciliation with the Kaiser, and were later the valiant, if ineffective, defenders of the Weimar Republic. The result was that the clash of socialist and liberal thinking impregnated the development of welfare policies in France and Germany, while in Britain the ideological debate was subdued.

Both France and Germany produced major social theorists, Weber and Durkheim, in part due to the intensity of the debate over how states might fulfill their newly-conceived social functions.

Third, the emergence of welfare states not only took place in specific political situations, but was influenced by the appeal of early positivists themselves. Imagining welfare states posed very different problems for each country. In a curious way, from a relatively early date British social issues were captured by social investigators such as Mayhew, Booth and Rowntree who presumed that empirical evidence of poverty and suffering could, and often in their terms, should, be immediately translated into public policies. From the earliest studies of British social problems there was what Letwin has called the 'pursuit of certainty'.[5] As we shall see, the mixture of ideas that moved British policymakers in this direction was complex, running from the arrogant claims of Sir Edwin Chadwick in the Royal Commission on Poor Laws of 1834 through Sir Robert Morant's pleas for 'central guidance' of educational policies,[6] and on into the Labour government of 1945. The presumption was not only that there were rational solutions to social issues, but that ministers and Parliament were quite capable of finding them. Annan summarizes this view admirably in his essay on the strength of positivist thinking in British social theory[7] which, as we shall explore below, helps explain the failure of new liberal idealism to make an impact on British government at the turn of the century. As most vividly displayed in the political roles of Weber and Durkheim, the transformation of continental states required a more elaborate rationalization. Put differently, many intellectuals in France, Germany and Sweden were aware of the redefinition of the state and for historical reasons met the issue head-on.

RECOGNITION OF LIBERAL VULNERABILITIES

As Heclo concludes in his comparison of British and Swedish social policies, problem recognition is an essential aspect of how

[5] Shirley Letwin, *The Pursuit of Certainty*, Cambridge; Cambridge University Press, 1965.
[6] Bernard M. Allen, *Sir Robert Morant: A Great Public Servant*, London; Macmillan, 1934.
[7] Noel Annan, *The Curious Strength of Positivism in English Political Thought*, London; Oxford University Press, 1959.

governments change.[8] Less clear are the reasons why some governments see these problems differently from others, and why some
remain bound to ineffective or contradictory policies. Beneath the
actual response of governments to social questions lies the murky
question of how social and political philosophers, not to mention
numerous social investigators, provide the setting for a re-examination of the role of government and enter into the actual transformation of democratic practices. The intensity of the social
debate at the turn of the century is easily forgotten. The nineteenth-
century liberals were fully conscious of the vulnerability of their
principles. In many respects, the true 'crisis' of the welfare state
ran from roughly 1850 to 1900 when liberal leaders in all countries
were searching for new answers. Their belief in individual rationality meant that they could not reject social issues, most importantly educational reform, but at the same time such measures
threatened an entire framework of democratic practice as then
understood. The decline of doctrinaire liberal parties in all the
European countries is perhaps the best demonstration that their
best efforts failed. Oddly enough, the practical results were the
least durable in Britain where the philosophical issue consumed
liberal leaders and thinkers for half a century.

Although the philosophical debates over the nature of the welfare
state can be traced back to Cobden, Bright[9] and John Stuart
Mill,[10] their modifications of mechanical utilitarian thought only
set the stage for what became an intense controversy over the
relationship of collectivism and individualism in late Victorian
Britain. By the 1880s a new generation of political philosophers,
T. H. Green,[11] Leslie Stephens,[12] Leonard Hobhouse[13] and the
elder Arnold Toynbee generated a new intellectual atmosphere

[8] Hugh Heclo, *Modern Social Politics in Britain and Sweden*, New Haven; Yale
University Press, 1974.
[9] On the early Victorian social debate, see Gertrude Himmelfarb, *The Idea of
Poverty: England in the Early Industrial Age*, New York; Random House, 1983.
[10] On Mill's links to early Victorian liberalism, see Gertrude Himmelfarb, *On
Liberals and Liberalism: The Case of John Stuart Mill*, New York; Knopf, 1974.
[11] Melvin Richter, *The Politics of the Consensus: T. H. Green and His Age*, London;
Weidenfeld and Nicolson, 1964.
[12] Noel Annan, *Leslie Stephens: His Thought and Character Relation to His Time*,
London; McGibbon and Key, 1951.
[13] Stephan Collini, *Liberalism and Socialism: L. T. Hobhouse and Political Argument
in England, 1880–1914*, Cambridge; Cambridge University Press, 1979.

that was to have profound effects on the coming generation of high civil servants and political advisors who tried to fashion new social legislation. Alongside the idealists, ranged the Social Darwinist, Herbert Spencer, and the more conventional liberal W. S. McKechnie.[14] Even the more orthodox liberal economist, Henry Sidgwick, roughly the British equivalent to the French liberal economist Leroy-Beaulieu, admitted that 'Individualism of the extreme kind has clearly had its day'.[15] For comparative purposes, the important consequence was how little effect the prolonged Victorian debates actually had on British politics and policy-making, and ultimately on redefining the British state. Green and his contemporaries set the tone of 'new liberalism' which became the hallmark of Edwardian thinking about society and politics, and inspired much of the Edwardian social legislation. But British concepts of state and society were relatively untouched during the initial phase of social legislation, and, as we shall see in Chapter 4, by 1920 these debates were forgotten. The output of studies on the new relationship between the individual and the state was prodigious, but the effects on British politics were meagre.

There are many plausible explanations of their failure to have an impact on British politics. For one thing, the new thinkers never followed German idealism to its logical conclusion so that it became a pallid representation of the deep philosophical debate raging in Germany. As Richter comments, Green was 'Hegel with a Puritan accent'.[16] In contrast, the introduction of German idealism into French political thinking, most importantly by Lucien Herr and his circle of young socialists at the Ecole Normale, was passionately joined to divisions within the Socialist movement and to critical events in French politics.[17] Reconciling individualism and collectivism in France was never the languid discourse found in Oxford Common Rooms. Second, the philosophical discussion of liberalism in Britain never lost its moralizing tone.

---

[14] See Herbert Spencer, *Man vs. State*, London; Williams and Norgate, 1884; and W. S. McKechnie, *The State and the Individual: An Introduction to Political Science with Special Reference to Socialistic and Individual Theories*, Glasgow; J. MacLehose, 1896; and Henry Sidgwick, *The Elements of Politics*, London and New York; Macmillan, 1891. On the influence of the Social Darwinists, see Greta Jones, *Social Darwinism and English Thought*, Atlas Highlands, NJ; Humanities Press, 1980.
[15] Collini, *Liberalism and Socialism* . . ., p. 14.
[16] Richter, *The Politics of Consensus* . . ., p. 82.
[17] See Daniel Herr and Pierre-Andre Meyer, *Lucien Herr: Le Socialisme et son destin*, Paris; Calmann-Levy, 1977.

Morality became the 'Trojan horse' of British liberalism so that Sidney Ball, the Oxford Fabian, worried whether social reform might lead to the 'moral destruction of the next generation' and Godsen feared that doing too much for the poor would 'sap forever the self-reliance of a class.' Green's best student was Bishop Gore, the founder of the Christian Social Union, and his best known disciple, Bernard Bosanquet, became a staunch defender of the Charity Organisation Society and the Poor Law mentality. As Collini so neatly sums up, the new liberal thinker 'wants to have his cake of socialism and to eat it in accordance with Liberal principles.'[18]

From a policymaking perspective, however, there are additional reasons to consider in explaining why the British welfare state never became a radical departure from British political traditions. The elitist character of British policymaking was surely one factor. In an atmosphere created by the famous Master of Balliol, Jowett, the High Church exclusiveness of Oxford was gradually turned into a 'Broad Church.' To achieve his ends Jowett set out to infiltrate Whitehall with idealistic young Oxonians, a case of permeation that was infinitely more successful than the similar tactic of the Fabians twenty years later. The result was a new generation of Edwardian policymakers that were in close contact with the new social philosophers, an association that never developed in Germany except for the conservative Catholic group, the *Kathedersozialisten*, and which reached intense heights in the French republican debates of the 1890s over *solidarité sociale*. A Prussian political elite could brush aside new ideas while the radical republicans and socialists were in desperate need of new ideas. In Britain, the process of infiltration was more clearly displacing outworn civil servants in a stable parliamentary system. In addition, there were direct lines through the elitist university system itself. Asquith was Green's student and his impetuous, if ill-considered, reforms no doubt link to Balliol in the 1880s. Lord Haldane, perhaps the most adroit political leader with an admiration of German accomplishments, was a direct contact, but skipped through a quarter of a century in Parliament without leaving clear traces.

New ideas about collective obligation and the state never took root because it was too easy to change policies. Even though there

[18] Collini, *Liberalism and Socialism* . . ., p. 134.

was a widespread feeling of despair among British leaders after
the 1890s, and in particular after the bungled Boer War, Britain
did not confront the fateful political choices of France or Germany.
Jowett sent his socially conscious acolytes off to settlement houses
in East London with the clear intention that they became social
policy pioneers, but certainly not with the intention of shaking the
foundations of British government. They were to arouse political
concern *within* Whitehall and Westminster, not to question the
British political traditions. To be sure, their task was easier because
British socialism never accepted the revolutionary and syndicalist
socialism that captivated turn of the century Marxists on the
continent, but it is doubtful that even such fiery ideology would
have substantially changed the course of British policymaking.
The new leaders were skilful civil servants, like Smith, Morant
and Beveridge, or benevolent politicians, like Asquith. Their intellectual fervour was tempered by evangelical efforts such as the
Christian Social Union, by enlightened support for workers such
as adult education, and by exclusive political clubs such as the
Rainbow Circle. Unlike many French and German leaders around
1900, most British leaders had never been excluded from power
and the moral fervour inspired by brief forays into the world of
the poor never needed to be translated into radical political action.
The reformers that the new liberal philosophers sent out into the
real world belonged to the same clubs, summered in the same
country houses, and moved about in the same fashionable London
circles.

As we shall see, the individualistic assumptions prevailing in
the British debate over new liberalism were later manifested in
the organization of new social legislation, the design and extension
of social benefits, and, most dramatically, in the persistence of the
Poor Laws. Unlike Britain, France never whole-heartedly
embraced laissez-faire liberal assumptions, and except for only
brief moments in history, most notably the July Monarchy, never
adopted a consistently liberal view of the state. However slow the
actual progress of the welfare state in France, reconciling the needs
of state and society was a constant preoccupation of nineteenth-
century French political philosophers. A number of circumstances
account for the direct link between political ideas and social action
in France. First, republican ideas were nurtured by the Revolution
and by the structure of Napoleonic education, most importantly
by the continued reflection and political awareness cultivated in

the Ecole Normale Supérieure.[19] Alongside the Ecole Normale, there were other prestigious intellectual institutions which were actively cultivated and consulted by political leaders, such as the Académie des Sciences Morales et Politiques and the Collège de France. The fiercely competitive exams for the *aggrégation* produced a chain of philosophers concerned with the social meaning of the French state.[20] They were duly elevated to chairs at the Sorbonne or lodged within the Ecole Normale where their influence was not confined to a few socially conscious and privileged sons of the upper class as in Britain, but spread throughout the entire educational establishment.

Secondly, the political turbulence itself stimulated philosophical awareness of the conflicts between individual liberty and a strong state. Many of the philosophers who helped construct a social philosophy for the French state refused to sign the oath of loyalty to Napoleon III. They detested both Bonapartist and clerical domination of France, and in particular the restraints placed on free education. Many of the critics of unrestrained liberalism were in fact professors of pedagogy, including Durkheim himself once he was called to the Sorbonne. Charles Renouvier, who played a role similar to T. H. Green in introducing neo-Kantian ethics in France, wrote the *Manuel Républicain* for primary schools under the Second Republic.[21] Unlike Britain, the force of new liberal thinking was not dissipated in party politics, but was concentrated at the pinnacle of the educational system.

Constructing an intellectual framework for the French welfare state was much less of a problem than in Britain, and as it was constructed it became the rationale for state intervention. To the chain of philosophers devoted to perfecting the republican ideal 'naked utilitarianism' was an anathema and could only lead to the breakdown of social solidarity. Starting from Renouvier, they agreed that limits had to be placed on inequality, including such

---

[19] For a careful history of the Ecole, see Robert J. Smith, *The Ecole Normale Supérieure and the Third Republic*, Albany; State University of New York Press, 1982. Also Jean-Francoise Sirinelli, 'The Ecole Normale Supérieure and Elite Formation and Selection during the Third Republic,' in J. Howorth and P. G. Cerny, eds, *Elites in France*, New York; St Martin's, 1981, pp. 66–77.

[20] See the superb account of their lives and ideas by William Logue, *From Philosophy to Sociology: The Evolution of French Liberalism, 1871–1914*, Dekalb, Ill.; Northern Illinois University Press, 1983.

[21] Logue, p. 53.

measures as a progressive income tax, providing workers with some security similar to that property provided for the middle class, and some voluntary means to achieve social reform. In effect, they became 'lay preachers for a democratic republic'.[22] To French new liberals such as André Fouillée, for example, only a *liberalism réformiste*, based on a *sociologie réformiste*, could enhance individual capabilities while preserving social solidarity. The contractual basis of society was dismissed and governmental growth was seen as the natural result of progress. Durkheim, of course, was the heir to these ideas and his work might be seen as the climax of a long intellectual struggle to demonstrate the interdependence of social solidarity.[23]

In a fragmented and conservative Germany, the ideas propelling German social insurance were dispersed and cautious. Nonetheless, there was a vigorous social policy debate well before Bismarck's benevolent legislation of the 1880s. Perhaps the most active group was a collection of social science professors of conservative, Catholic background, the *Kathedersozialisten*, which included such notable early sociologists as Werner Sombart and Ferdinand Tonnies. But little could be accomplished in a disunited Germany. Under Bismarck's *Kulturkampf* Catholic organizations were to suffer the same fate as German trade unions. As in most countries, the earliest legislation was on workmen's disability but Bismarck was unhappy with the early Liberal efforts such as the 1871 Liability Act.[24] If there was a single formulation acceptable

---

[22] Logue, p. 93.

[23] A good summary of this debate is found in Judith Stone, *The Search for Social Peace: Reform Legislation in France, 1890–1914*, Albany; State University of New York Press, 1985, pp. 25–54. On the consolidation of French new liberalism, see the excellent account by J. E. S. Hayward, 'Solidarist Syndicalism: Durkheim and Duguit,' *Sociological Review*, Part I, **8**, July 1960, pp. 17–36; and Part II, **8**, December 1960, pp. 185–202. On Durkheim's influence and ideas, Steven Lukes, *Emile Durkheim: His Life and Times: A History and Critical Study*, London; Allen Lane, 1973; and Steve Fenton, *Durkheim and Modern Sociology*, Cambridge; Cambridge University Press, 1984.

[24] See H. P. Ullman,, 'German Industry and Bismarck's Social Security System,' in W. J. Mommsen, ed., *The Emergency of the Welfare State in Britain and Germany*, London; Croom Helm, 1981, pp. 133–49; and Detlev Zollner, 'The Federal Republic of Germany,' in P. Kohler and H. Zacher, eds, *A Century of Social Security, 1881–1981: The Evolution in Germany, France, Great Britain, Austria and Switzerland*, Munich; Max Planck Institute, 1982, pp. 15–37.

to Bismarck it was Adolf Wagner's view of state socialism.[25] Wagner's concept of benevolent social reform put reform at the service of a powerful state and supported strong industry and so was compatible with Bismarck's views, though it is by no means clear that Bismarck in fact followed Wagner's ideas closely. As we shall see in more detail, social legislation under the Second Reich had the important political purpose of crippling whatever democratic impulse might arise in the form of social democracy or enlightened Catholicism. As Dyson has shown at length,[26] there were competing concepts of the German state none of which helped forge a direct link between social reform and democratic development. The paradox, to which we shall return, was that by 1890 Germany built the most complete system of social insurance in the world, but democratic forces were effectively excluded and unable to use social reform as a way of building a stable democratic tradition.

Unlike the philosophical foundations of the welfare state in Britain, France and Germany, where new ideas were more clearly linked to political change, in both the United States and Sweden the intellectual advocacy of expanded social services and social insurance was relatively pragmatic. The important difference between the United States and Sweden is of course that in Sweden the central core of Social Democratic thinkers made their party into the vehicle for social reform, while in a pluralist America no consolidation of political power was possible. In both countries, liberal inspired social legislation preceded the major efforts of the 1930s,[27] and in both countries new proposals were not grounded as much in new values as in political realities. After its defeat in the 1928 elections, the Swedish Social Democratic Party (SAP) agreed that it must fashion a new relationship between the labour movement and private business, and it dropped its association with the Communist Party. Although the 'Swedish miracle' is most often seen in terms of class politics,[28] the social democratic strategy

[25] See Richard Musgrave and Alan Peacock, eds, *Classics in the Theory of Public Finance*, New York; Macmillan, 1958, pp. 1–16.
[26] Kenneth H. F. Dyson, *The State Tradition in Western Europe*, New York; Oxford University Press, 1980.
[27] On pre-Social Democratic Sweden, see Steven Koblik, ed., *Sweden's Development from Poverty to Affluence, 1750–1970*, Minneapolis; University of Minnesota Press, 1975, especially Chapters 5 and 6.
[28] For example, Walter Korpi, *The Democratic Class Struggle*, London; Routledge and Kegan Paul, 1983.

was a carefully crafted set of principles that were politically attractive to a rapidly industrializing country where the power of both labour and business were remarkably concentrated. Aware of the enormous risks as well as the virtually unique opportunity this provided for a genuine social democratic experiment, a small group of socialist thinkers, most importantly Ernst Wigforss, designed a political strategy that reversed the normal sequence of building new labour policies after social reforms.

The result was that prolonged soul-searching of the French and German socialists never took place nor was there the capitulation to parliamentary realities found in Britain. A very small circle of politicians led the Social Democratic Party toward a new vision of social harmony. Working from established ideas Wigforss saw 'socialism as the logical extension of liberalism rather than its antithesis.'[29] More important, both social and economic conditions made the social democratic alternative feasible. Both industry and agriculture were in severe depression over the 1920s. The possibility of uniting workers and farmers behind the SAP made a Social Democratic coalition possible, whereas in most of Europe farmers had independently established their political base, and had begun to extract their own economic and social concessions from government. Thus, the Swedish welfare state was much more a revolution based on social and economic planning than widespread, political clash of ideas. As Heclo notes,[30] the foundation was a fiscal policy that provided suitable assurance to both labour and business. Devising such policy preceded concern for specific social benefits and new social insurance. As the contemporary writing on 'decomodification'[31] implies, social reform was not to be the product of government as much as the vehicle to achieve wage stability and income redistribution. In no other major European state was it politically possible to reverse the usual sequence of social and economic policymaking.

[29] Timothy A. Tilton, 'A Swedish Road to Socialism: Ernest Wigforss and the Ideological Foundations of Swedish Social Democracy,' *American Political Science Review*, **73**, July 1977, pp. 505–20.
[30] Hugh Heclo, *Modern Social Politics in Britain and Sweden*, New Haven; Yale University Press, 1974, p. 102. Wigforss sets forth his own strategy in 'The Financial Policy during Depression and Doom', *Annals of the American Academy*, **197**, 1938, pp. 25–39.
[31] Gösta Esping-Anderson, 'Politics against Markets: Decomodification in Social Policy', paper presented to Arne Ryde Symposium on the Economics of Social Policy, Lund, Sweden, 1981.

The cultural and political heterogeneity of the United States make any summary account of the ideas woven into the American welfare state incomplete.[32] But the ferment of new social thinking in turn of the century United States was no less vigorous than that in Europe. If there was a common theme that set the United States apart from Britain and France, it was the emphasis on social engineering, itelf a function of the unwieldy and complex governmental process that early reformers encountered. The American settlement house movement, for example, was no less developed than its European counterparts. The famous settlement house leaders such as Graham Taylor in Chicago, Robert A. Woods in Boston and Arthur C. Holden in New York were well-known figures at British and French charitable association meetings. Like their Victorian colleagues, the American settlement movement sought to bring the virtues of middle-class existence to the poor, and its workers were themselves overwhelmingly the offspring of pious, Protestant ministers.[33] In addition, there were important studies of poverty modelled on Booth's studies of London, notably the Pittsburgh Survey, by the pioneering social researchers gathered around the Russell Sage Foundation. By 1914 the United States was as aware of poverty and social inequality as most European countries but lacked the institutional capacity to weave the diverse strands of social concern, including fears over the assimilation of immigrants,[34] into legislation.

Perhaps it is not surprising that in a nation so resistant to ideology that social engineering became the dominant theme. If there was a single organization that focused these interests around social insurance, it was the American Association for Labor Legislation (AALL). As might be expected, it was dominated by labour historians and labour experts, the foremost being John R. Commons[35] and his student John B. Andrews. In a federalist America,

[32] See Walter, I. Trattner, *From Poor Law to Welfare State*, New York; Free Press, 1959, 2nd edn.; and James Leiby, *A History of Social Welfare and Social Work in the United States*, New York; Columbia University Press, 1978.

[33] Allan Davis, *Spearheads for Reform: The Social Settlements and the Progressive Movement, 1890–1914*, New York; Oxford University Press, 1967.

[34] The cultural heterogeneity of the United States is a major difference from European countries and of course played into politics in strange ways. See, among other works, John Higham, *Strangers in the Land: Patterns of American Nativism, 1860–1925*, New Brunswick; Rutgers University Press, 1955; and John F. McClymer, *War and Welfare: Social Engineering in America, 1890–1925*, Westport CN; Greenwood Press, 1980.

[35] John R. Commons, *Principles of Labor Legislation*, New York; McGraw Hill,

the different approaches developed in the more progressive states, Wisconsin, New York, Massachusetts and Pennsylvania. The leaders fought bitterly which accounts for the later exclusion of all of them from the consideration of New Deal legislation. Abraham Epstein, active in Pennsylvania's voluntary pension organizations, formed a separate group, the American Association for Old Age Security to fight AALL, and was in bitter disagreement with Isaac Max Rubinow, who in later life worked in Ohio and favoured compulsory insurance.[36] As it turned out, Andrew's organization in Wisconsin provided most of the experts for the Social Security Act of 1935, but as we shall see, Roosevelt carefully eschewed any clear political philosophy for American social reform.

The modern welfare state is, in part, the product of how political ideas passed through the screen of political opportunity and political possibility in the various democracies. Often neglected in more socio-economic explanations of the welfare state, the translation of ideas into policy had great influence on the contemporary welfare state. Indeed, for those interested in the dynamics of democratic principles and practice, the welfare state and its development is a neglected subject. For those primarily concerned with advancing social equality, it is barely relevant. For partisans of a classic liberal state, it is an unwelcome embarrassment. Around 1900 policy changes and new ideas joined in peculiar ways and devised the welfare state, often under the influence of remarkably few persons of foresight and imagination. In this sense, the transformation of the liberal into welfare state is relatively simple because we can easily identify the key figures. But in a larger sense the intricacy of the policy changes made the translation of ideas into action very complex. In each case the principles of social progress and social change had to pass the hurdle of the policy process. Linked to the transformation, and perhaps the key explanatory element, is the advance of knowledge about social problems in the late nineteenth century, something that can often

1927; and *Industrial Goodwill*, New York; McGraw Hill, 1919. On his impact, see George C. Somers, ed., *Labor, Management and Social Policy: Essays in the J. R. Commons Tradition*, Madison; University of Wisconsin Press, 1963.
[36] Material for this paragraph comes from the account of Roy Lubove, *The Struggle for Social Security, 1900–1935*, Cambridge; Harvard University Press, 1968. On the internal dispute, see I. M. Rubinow, *The Quest for Social Security*, New York; Holt, 1934; and Abraham Epstein, *Insecurity: A Challenge to America: A Study of Social Insurance in the United States and Abroad*, New York; H. S. Smith and R. Haas, 1933.

be taken for granted in the late twentieth century. For this reason, the role of translators and how they fitted into the politics of the day is crucial in understanding how welfare states developed.

EDUCATION: THE LIBERAL ACHILLES HEEL

The concept of the modern welfare state is, roughly speaking, the product of two major intellectual revolutions. The first, dating from the sixteenth century, was the notion that individual reason could better allocate authority than divine authority. It is impossible to do justice to the long development of the basic justification of the secular state, but it is easily forgotten that it was an essential first step toward building modern states. Social need and social protection were then appended to the initial political assumptions of liberal democracy. The historical parameters of most studies of the welfare state exclude this early struggle of ideas, though the setting and progress of this debate left indelible imprints on each democracy. More often, contemporary analyses begin with the early nineteenth century, which may help explain why the later convergence of economic and political liberalism in the classical liberal state is often used as a base line for measuring change. The result is an implicit, and sometimes explicit, economic determinism that excludes the complexity of adding social policy to the normal political process of the liberal state.[37]

For obvious reasons, it is the second stage of the transformation that most occupies this study. The early development of political ideas is not excluded for it became the institutional and constitutional framework which social reformers encountered in the liberal state. This is not to say that what Crouch calls the 'refined view' of laissez-faire economics,[38] namely, the growing awareness of the economic externalities, is irrelevant to the development of the welfare state, but only that such phraseology and conceptualization

---

[37] There is an intense historical controversy over whether Britain was indeed a laissez-faire nation in the nineteenth-century. See J. B. Brebner, 'Laissez-Faire and State Intervention . . .,' and David Roberts, *Victorian Origins of the Welfare State*, New Haven; Yale University Press, 1960.

[38] R. L. Crouch, 'Laissez-Faire in Nineteenth Century Britain: Myth or Reality?,' *The Manchester School*, **35**, 1967, pp. 199–215. Crouch directs the reader to the earlier assessments of Jacob Viner and Lord Robbins.

make the social goals of the state a secondary problem. For the economist, social problems confound economic rationality, as most recently expounded with skill by Mancur Olson.[39] From the perspective of this study, conceptualizing social problems in this way makes politics less significant. The irrationality of social choices divides political science from economics, but the two approaches are not necessarily contradictory. The state is a way of making irrational situations manageable, but maximizing economic rationality does not embrace all political choices.

These problems are not likely to be easily resolved, but for present purposes it may suffice to begin with the flood of ideas that arose over the nineteenth century concerning the social goals of democratic governance. In Britain, France, Germany, Sweden and the United States there were vast differences in how these ideas were presented,politically justified, and organized into policy proposals. Most important, to understand the impact of new ideas on the liberal state one needs to see the direct policymaking role that many intellectuals acquired. Bentham had immense influence through his disciples in many parts of British government; Le Play was an adviser to Napoleon III; and Adolf Wagner was consulted, if not observed, by Bismarck. In addition, the slower pace of government in the nineteenth century made it possible for many important officials to engage in scholarship, to participate actively in the deluge of societies and organizations to study social problems, and to conduct their own investigations where evidence was sparse. In a way that is no longer possible, the discovery of social problems was often being translated into policy by the same persons.

What differentiates the lively intellectual exchanges of the nineteenth-century liberal democracies is the ease with which new social ideas and needs could be integrated with existing democratic traditions and institutions. The extent to which there was a fundamental re-examination of the state as the vehicle of collective authority seems to vary inversely with the readiness of liberal political forces to accept social problems as a legitimate function

[39] Mancur Olson, *The Rise and Decline of Nations: Economic Growth, Stafflation, and Social Rigidities*, New Haven; Yale University Press, 1982. There is, of course, a similarity between the economists' desire to maximize rational behaviour by defining social costs and the Marxist view that social costs are totally unmanageable and will eventually destroy modern democratic governance. See James O'Connor, *The Fiscal Crisis of the State*, New York; St Martin's Press, 1973.

of government. Britain is, of course, the interesting test case for it was there that stable institutions and strong parties made it possible for both Conservative and Liberal leaders to consider social reform as a distinct issue.

While it is correct that the Anglo-Saxon legal tradition had much to do with the ease with which constitutional concerns could be put aside, this is an overly legalistic explanation that seems to appeal to those who see the social role of the state developing independently of other political changes. The crisis over the 1909 budget and increasing income and land taxes could hardly be called an insignificant event in the development of British democracy.[40] Limiting the House of Lords legislative veto signifies the final exclusion of aristocratic power over social policy, and is surprising more for its delay than for its necessity. More interesting in terms of the transformation of ideas, the political leaders most responsible for these changes, Asquith, Churchill, and Lloyd George, implemented few reforms in the way they were envisaged and designed by the social thinkers of their time.

While the British constitutional arrangements certainly made it easier to avoid fundamental questions about the state, this view does not explain why so many British politicians, unlike their European counterparts, were so willing to do so. Though MacDonald will never be considered an original socialist thinker, it is symptomatic of this difference that he marvelled at the richness of debate over the social role of the state that was immediately visible in European bookstalls.[41] One must understand the dilemmas of redefining the state for the left in order to understand the evasiveness of the British social policy debate for the nascent Labour Party. Practical politics decided their strategy, for they did not want to be crushed between the militant Social Democratic Federation and the new liberal reformers. As Marquand notes, the social ideas of the Edwardian Labour leaders were 'reminiscent of a Calvinist hymn'. In a survey done of the most popular reading

[40] P. Ford, *Social Theory and Social Practice*, Shannon, Ireland; Irish University Press, 1968, p. 189, points out that the crisis was over a very small part of the budget, the increase in the land tax, and could have easily been avoided if Lloyd George wished to do so. By 1914 the major new tax had produced only three-quarters of a million pounds. On the central political significance of arguments over taxation, see Bruce K. Murray, *The People's Budget 1909–10: Lloyd George and Liberal Politics*, Oxford; Clarendon Press, 1980.
[41] Marquand, *MacDonald*, p. 88 and p. 96.

among new Labour MPs in 1906, the most cited works were the Bible, Carlyle, Dickens and Ruskin. There is more historical convenience than accuracy in the later attacks of Miliband and other Marxists on the feeble socialism of the Labour Party. The British left had no political incentive to espouse more militant socialism, nor were the leaders exposed to the intense socialist debate that was commonplace in France and Germany throughout the late nineteenth century.[42]

For those who see social justice or social equality as the sole justification of collective authority, it is as easy to simplify the past as the future. In contrast to Britain, the French could never forget the unfulfilled Revolutionary claims of La Rochefoucault-Liancourt, 'If there exists the right to say to society: help me live; then society has equally the right to respond: give me work.' The Declaration of the Rights of Man of 1793 stipulated 'Public assistance is a sacred debt. Societies owe subsistence to unfortunate citizens either by finding them work or by assuring them the means to exist without work.' Again, before the Committee on Public Safety, the committee on the poor (*mendacité*) of de Barrière reports, it was not enough to redistribute income and resist foreign economic penetration, but it remained 'necessary to make the subjection of basic (*prémiers*) needs disappear from the soil of Republic, (to end) the slavery of misery and the hideous inequality among men which makes some intemperate of wealth and others intemperate of the agonies of need.'[43] Thus, the social task of the French state, if slow to appear in policies, was indelibly inscribed on the foundations of republican France. Despite the bitter political fights that accompany the development of French democracy over the nineteenth century, the continuous reference to the revolutionary rhetoric of equality marks the emergence of the French

---

[42] There is immense political irony in that the dominant Marxist versions of a socialist state came from England. Engel's 1844 work on the British working class was not translated into English until 1887, and then in the United States. Marx's *Communist Manifesto* was not widely circulated until the 1870s, and by then both Marx and Engels were heavily occupied with their conflicts with continental socialists. See P. Ford, *Social Theory and Social Practice*, pp. 35–9.

[43] Quotes taken from Hatzfeld, *Du paupérisme à la securité sociale*, pp. 278–9. On the eighteenth-century origins, see Camille Bloch, *L'assistance et l'Etat en France à la veille de la Révolution*, Paris; 1908; on actual conditions early in the nineteenth century, see Louis Chevalier, *Les classes laborieuses et classes dangereuses à Paris pendant le première moitié du XIXe siècle*, Paris; Plon, 1958.

welfare state, and could not be ignored by either its advocates or its antagonists.

As in Germany and Sweden, leaders wanted the welfare state to have intellectual coherence, and in various ways this led them into revising their concept of the state. Action and thought were not as easily divorced as in stable Britain or a pluralist United States. While it might be comforting to partisans of utopian socialism to think that the blend of ideas and decisions that emerged around 1900 is a function of class politics, on the whole liberals gave way for more prosaic, internal political reasons, rooted in their own awareness that the liberal concept of the state needed revision. This is not to say that the ideological debates and class protest in Britain and France were irrelevant, but that political logic was more closely attached to political realities. Just as the early twentieth-century Liberal reformers in Britain were not particularly alarmed over the appearance of the Labour Party, so also French leaders of the Third Republic may be excused if they found the doctrinal battles of the nascent socialist party obscure and confusing. The intellectual justification, and eventually the work of the key translators of social thinking into policy, were more accurately the product of a long period of accumulated learning about social problems. Of course, having a clearer idea of what one meant by the social role of the state did not necessarily mean that democracy thrived, as the case of Germany demonstrates, but it did mean that social policies became parts of a more general rationalization of collective authority. On the whole, this task was avoided in Britain.

In surveying how ideas changed in France, it is important to keep Soltau's warning in mind. 'Neither in practice nor in theory did any criticism emerge of current conceptions of government as embodied in the *ancien régime*; the relations of the individual to the state, the scope and functions of the state, the nature of sovereignty, the sphere and aims of law – these were all taken for granted.'[44] Essentially, there is more continuity of the concept of the state in France than in most democracies. Conservative republicans could use the same principles to delay the development of social policy,

---

[44] Roger Soltau, *French Political Thought in the Nineteenth Century*, New Haven; Yale University Press, 1931, p. xxi. Similar conclusions arise from Theodore Zeldin's critique of solidarism, *France 1848–1945*, Oxford; Clarendon Press, 1973, v.1, pp. 654–82.

but for political reasons French thinkers and politicians were compelled to use the state as their frame of reference. As in Germany a century later, the political struggle for unification and democracy was so intense that a purely individualistic rationale for the state was inadequate, the unvarnished liberalism of Britain and the United States was inapplicable. This helps explain why the classical liberal ideas, though visible in all democracies, seldom took root on the continent and, in turn, why simple socio-economic arguments about the political roots of capitalism and the economy are particularly misleading when applied to France, Germany, and, much later, Sweden.

As the debates of the radical republicans and socialists at the turn of the century show, inventing the welfare state meant re-examining the postulates of republican France. Liberalism only endured under the harsh regimes of the Restoration and the July Monarchy. Guizot comes the closest to a classical liberal leader that France could produce, while conventional liberalism still thrived in late Victorian Britain. But social policy did not advance at this time. Even Tocqueville, though ready to sacrifice order to increase participation, had few well-developed ideas about social policy. In the fragment that exists of his commentary on the British Poor Laws, his views are not terribly different from aristocratic opinion of the day. Like Le Play, who also feared that indiscriminate charity would breed more social ills than benefits, Tocqueville wrote that a permanent administrative structure to fill the needs of the poor would stifle political democracy.[45] This is not to say that important ideas about social reform were not developing in France in the early nineteenth century, especially concerning the nature of mental illness and child care,[46] but that as in Britain and the rest of Europe social problems were not yet politically salient.

Nonetheless, it is clear that the early ravages of British industrialization, which help account for the early development of social

---

[45] Alexis de Tocqueville, 'Memoir on Pauperism,' *Public Interest*, v., 19, p. 110 and pp. 118–19. His ideas were in fact extremely Malthusian and his view on charity etirely consistent with the position of other conservative republicans later in the century. The full account is translated by Seymour Drescher, *Tocqueville and Beaumont on Social Reform*, New York; Harper, 1968.

[46] In the mid-nineteenth century French progress in medicine and mental health was well known in the United States. See Eduard Laboulaye, *Paris en Amerique*, Paris; Chapentier, 1863.

reform, strongly impressed continental observers, especially in France. Indeed, were not Marx and Engels so preoccupied with the German socialists, early French socialism might have advanced more rapidly than it did. Sismondi, for example, was appalled by the deterioration of civic life in British cities.[47] Even so, like a good eighteenth-century Revolutionary, he argued that the state cannot deprive the common man (meaning the peasant) of his property. Le Play was a keen observer of Britain, whose system of property inheritance he greatly admired as a way of preserving family strength and unity.[48] But at the same time, he saw how the expanding industrial and commercial preoccupations of the British middle class were a threat to family life. Saint Simon was influenced by Jeremy Bentham, Robert Owen, and J. S. Mill, but his quest for a more rational society gravitated toward state control of industrial development, something that British lawmakers assiduously avoided. His secretary, Comte, was in direct contact with Mill, but even Comte's vision of rational society made concessions to the deeply religious roots of the French middle class. The late nineteenth-century analysts of republican France, Taine and Renan, were impressed by British institutional stability, but not because they had any firsthand knowledge of Victorian social reform. As Soltau concludes, political thinking in nineteenth-century France was a 'medley of contradictions'[49] which, in turn, made it easier for political leaders to pick and choose among political ideas. When major social reforms began, notably with education in the 1880s, and with social issues in the 1890s, neither conservative nor radical republicans could find much to copy from British social policy. As in the case of decentralization, French political thinkers and leaders wanted the stability of British politics, but their firsthand knowledge of the price paid for institutional stability was slight.[50]

[47] Patrick de Laubier, *L'Age de la politique sociale*, Editions Techniques et Economiques, Paris; 1978, p. 63.

[48] M. F. Le Play, *La Réforme sociale en France*, Paris; Plon, 1864, v. 1, p. 35.

[49] Soltau, *French Political Thought . . .*, p. 253. The views of the additional political thinkers on Britain are also from Soltau. To understand the diversity it is important to see the multiplicity of academic and educational channels for new social thinking. See, for example, Terry Nichols Clark, *Prophets and Patrons: The French University and the Emergence of the Social Sciences*, Cambridge, MA; Harvard University Press, 1973.

[50] French self-deception in emulating Britain carries on into the Fourth and Fifth Republics. Michel Debré, de Gaulle's constitutional expert in 1945 and first

Two factors seem crucial in explaining why the pragmatic brand of British liberalism could not take root in France. First, the Revolution had created a nation of small landed proprietors. Their republican virtues were rooted in the small-scale, agrarian nature of French society. Fiercely independent, they could not accept social reform for the practical reasons advanced in late Victorian Britain, but had to await the clear challenge to republican governance of the 1930s and 1940s to rise to the challenge. As we shall see, there were the remnants of patriarchal power advocating charity and self-reliance, much like the British aristocracy, but in France they were aligned with the anti-republican forces of the Catholic Church and so politically unpersuasive. Second, in Britain liberalism served as a bridge between the continuing influence of the aristocracy and the rising middle class. The early nineteenth-century French liberals had a similar strategy in mind, but brought democratic participation into tune with new political demands. The political manipulation of the Second Republic demonstrated how easily liberalism could be twisted to political advantage, most notably in Napoleon III's wishful thinking about building a true middle class on solid economic foundations.[51]

Political and economic self-interest could be joined in Britain, and mass democracy could be adjusted to the growth of government, but the Revolution made this compromise impossible for France. In 1789, French citizens had acquired political rights and, as the rhetoric of the period shows, they were considered virtually indistinguishable from social and economic rights. In short, a middle-class revolution had accomplished at one blow what Britain took the entire nineteenth century to accomplish.[52] Social reforms as an apology for shortcomings of the state were not acceptable to Frenchmen. There were of course exponents of liberal economics in France such as Leroy Beaulieu and Edmund Villey, and their

Prime Minister in 1958, had high hopes of transplanting the discpline of British politics on French soil. See, for example, Michel Debré, *La République et son pouvoir*, Paris; Nagel, 1950.

[51] See James M. Thompson, *Louis Napoleon and the Second Empire*, New York; Columbia University Press, 1983, pp. 232–54.

[52] In fact, the economic dimensions of classical liberalism were not easily accepted in Britain. A good argument can be made that mass democracy became the instrument of liberalism in Britain. See J. B. Brebner, 'Laissez faire and State Intervention in Nineteenth-Century Britain,' *Journal of Economic History*, **8**, 1948, pp. 59–73.

conservative views on social reform only carried weight between the wars. Their persuasiveness was not derived from a politically convenient alliance of class interests as in Britain, but from French economic nationalism and protectionism following World War I. However lamentable, French leaders were not particularly attracted to liberalism in its pure form nor did French intellectuals find Jeremy Bentham or Adam Smith attractive models for French society.

But the diverse relationships between politics and the economy, which are all too easily generalized into a theory of the welfare state, should not blind us to the essential bankruptcy of liberal ideas in most democracies once social reform became a political issue. What is similar across political systems is that liberal parties and liberal leaders soon ran out of steam. Only one social reform was naturally incorporated with their individualism: education. Although there are important national differences among the democracies in the way that primary and secondary education was generalized to the entire population, liberal principles could incorporate the notion that a better educated public would naturally be better able to judge its individual self-interest. The intricate political process by which Britain accomplished a measure of universal education is worth reviewing because of the contrast with the politics of education expansion in France. But even in Britain, the growth of educational opportunity was by no means the uncontroversial affair associated with the later development of the British welfare state.

The mid-century Victorian debate over educational reform was a rehearsal for the turn of the century debate over social reform. Education provided a springboard for idealists who were central to the social policy debate, and in fact became the prototype for an elitist approach to social problems. The controversies also displayed the impotence of the early socialists and how easily their demands for strong, secular intervention could be deflected in British politics. The first issue was primary education where the system was divided between 'voluntary schools', where middle-class students paid fees for superior education in schools usually run by the Church of England, and the 'board' or local schools, supported by local taxes (rates) and government grants. The issue acquired political urgency in the 1860s when the young Joseph Chamberlain, Sir Charles Dilke, Charles Bradlough and Annie Besant (later a fervent Fabian), saw the radical potential of free, universal education. Their National Secular Society was perhaps as close as Britain ever came to having a radical republican reform similar to the one which dominated French political debate from the 1880s into the twentieth century. The issue was well chosen because the nascent worker movement was strongly committed to adult education, Sunday Schools and free education to advance their social status.[53] Thus, education held the threat of a divided Britain, and many aristocrats saw the possibility of using educational reform to build links to the workers, where 'unrestrained social intercourse' with their betters would teach the proper values. The Workingmen's Clubs would become the lower class equivalent of the posh London clubs. Half the dukes in Britain subscribed to the adult education movement.[54]

Getting something done was of course quite another matter. The Forster Education Act of 1870, generally taken as the dawn of free primary education in Britain, was preceded by the Endowed Schools Act of 1869 that entrenched the potentially threatened secondary system of fee-paying grammar schools and the formation of the Headmasters' Conference of 1868 to protect the elite secondary or 'public' schools. Collusion would be too strong a description, but clearly the privileged saw both the opportunity to defuse a controversy and were wise enough to insulate their privileged institutions from reform efforts. In fact, continued controversy meant that primary education was not compulsory until 1880 and it was not free until 1891. Even so, until 1893 about half the primary school children were still 'half-timers' in order to provide labour for textile mills. Nonetheless, by the 1890s the voluntary schools were under financial pressure. Many of these designs emerged from the Education Committee of the Privy Council (there was no ministry until 1945) where Sir John Gorst, the President of the Council, worked to obtain grants of over £600,000 for voluntary schools, moved regulation of arts and science education to counties (where supervision would be more conservative), and finally in 1899 merged several educational committees into the Board of Education, a body to oversee reform which in fact never met.

[53] See Brian Simon, *Education and the Labour Movement, 1870–1920*, London; Lawrence and Wishart, 1965; and Olive Banks, *Parity and Prestige in English Secondary Education*, London; Routledge and Kegan Paul, 1965.
[54] See the account of Henry Solly and hopes that worker education would forge new bonds between upper and lower classes, Simon, pp. 72–7.

In such ways a politically charged issue was converted into a parliamentary problem, and within Parliament exclusive control was established at the top. This process was essentially repeated in social legislation, but never as successfully exploited as in education, especially under the skilful manipulation of Sir Robert Morant who became the Secretary of the Board of Education and was 'bitterly contemptuous of the parliamentary machine.'[55] From the perspective of reformulation of ideas, the curious aspect of these changes was how easily the idealists were seduced. Gorst, for example, was a friend of Canon Barnett and agreed with him that 'wide counsel' and 'social salvation' could be achieved by judicious, but controlled, concessions. Schools might become social cement for threatened institutions, but not at the cost of compromising the elite educational system of grammar and public schools, which Haldane, a Germanophile among the reformers, considered the sole place where 'leaders could be adequately trained.'[56] Despite the impressive array of royal commissions on education in late Victorian Britain,[57] the stratified educational system, which corresponded so closely to the presumed needs of British institutions, was not dislodged.

That nearly all this legislation, including the 1945 reforms, were Tory bills suggests how institutional aims and policymaking powers converge. The Education Act of 1902, also a Tory law, was the centerpiece of fifty years of struggle. Most agreed that the independent school boards were an anachronism, but Conservatives feared that they would become the focal points of radical educational demands, so that placing them under local authorities in 1902 was a clever way of playing towns against the countryside. The voluntary schools were given access to local tax revenues, but under an intricate system of local supervision that meant Conservative localities would have no difficulty using public monies for Church schools. The entire issue of modern secondary

---

[55] Simon, p. 171.

[56] Simon, pp. 186–96.

[57] As in the case of much later social legislation, the 1870 Act seemed to have resolved few basic educational questions. Amidst the array of late Victorian inquiries were the Royal Commission on Scientific Instruction (Devonshire Commission), 1870–75; the Royal Commission on Technical Education, 1881; the Royal Commission on Elementary Education (Cross Commission), 1886–88; and the Royal Commission on Secondary Education (Bryce Commission), 1894. Simon describes how each of these studies were done to repel new threats to the elite educational system.

education was postponed until 1945, at which time the Conservatives again produced an improvised solution to protect the grammar and public schools. As we shall see in the next section, similar institutional manipulation allowed the elite universities to keep their grip on higher education.

The episode displays many characteristics of British social reform to the present. First, if politicians and civil servants could devise a system which performed well then the underlying moral and social dilemmas might be avoided. In fact, under the determined skill of Morant, lower education thrived after 1902. By 1906, the number of secondary schools had nearly doubled (from 341 to 681) as had enrolment (from 28,000 to 68,000).[58] Second, largely under the aegis of Morant, government became accustomed to powerful civil servants who might press their ideas regardless of political obstacles. He insisted that Britain must have 'a really expert Central Authority for the whole of our National Education, a localized "guidance of brains", which shall watch, consider and advise upon *all* our national educational arrangements of all grades, of every type, *as a whole*.'[59] Third, reform was possible because of an unholy alliance of interests, in this case between Chamberlain, by 1902 a Unionist Tory, who insisted that voluntary schools should not receive aid and the Duke of Devonshire, then Lord President of the Privy Council, who wanted local taxes minimized. Political deals are of course not new, but the compromise effectively submerged any deeper consideration of the future of British education.

Lastly, and perhaps most interesting in the development of new ideas about welfare, the issue reveals the impotence of the Liberals. Education was the central issue of the 1906 election, especially for Lloyd George whose fame began with non-conformist rejection of state aid to church schools. As part of their pact with the nascent Labour Party, the Liberals promised to revise the 1902 Act, but never did. The bill to do so was amended to death by the local

[58] Read, *Edwardian England*, p. 160. To be fair to Balfour, it should be added that in the debate he acknowledged that school managers would have the final word on whether religious instruction would be permitted in the schools, which raised an outcry from Conservative Church of England backers. The administrative sequel to these concessions will be further developed in Chapter 3 because from this time education became largely an administered policy.

[59] Bernard M. Allen, *Sir Robert Morant: A Great Public Servant*, London, Macmillan, 1934, p. 126. Morant's italics.

government lobby, then heavily Tory, and eventually dropped. Education, not social policy, was the burning issue in Edwardian Britain. The 1902 Act had been debated for nearly two months in Parliament, and eventually passed by liberal application of the rules to limit debate. As Allen points out, the key political question, whether Britain should have a universal and free secondary educational system (Scotland worked out a compromise in 1872), was simply ignored.[60] After the 1910 election the Liberals were dependent on Catholic support from the Irish nationalists so it never became politically feasible to raise the issue again. By default, the Tories obtained the solution best suited to their interests, and many would argue that the issue was never raised again until the controversy over comprehensive schools in the 1960s.

Perhaps more than any other democracy, France saw education as a central policy concern of the state, more accurately, that education was such an important attribute of the state that it was conceptually inseparable. It is interesting that Henri Monod, in presenting his case for more liberal public assistance in 1900, cited the rise of educational spending throughout the nineteenth century as evidence of France's dedication to public service. From the end of the Second Empire to 1887, the national education budget multiplied ten times,[61] in part the product of the fierce dedication of republican moderates to education. From the Restoration there was to be one boys' primary school in each commune, and from 1850 one for girls in every commune over 800 persons. In 1881, primary education was free, and the following year primary education was made obligatory from age 6 to 13 years. This was of course the result of republican dominance after 1877, and specifically the policy of Jules Ferry, who remained Minister of Public Instruction for four and a half years.

Education was never separable from national pride in France, but the republicans pushed the notion of state further and education became inseparable from the integrity of the state. In a way that anticipates the later debates about pensions, the aged and unemployment, social policy was part of French political development, in part because the Catholic right so persistently worked against republican politics. Ferry forbade all but five religious

[60] Allen, *Sir Robert Morant*, p. 200.
[61] Henri Monod, *L'Assistance publique en France en 1889 et en 1900*, Paris; Imprimérie Nationale, 1900, p. 10.

orders to teach in public schools, placed limits on the 'unau-
thorized' orders (mainly Jesuits), ejected religious orders from
sitting on university examination juries, and excluded the religious
orders from the Conseil Supérieur de l'Instruction Publique.[62]
An ardent Protestant republican, and later a strong supporter of
increasing social assistance in the school system, Ferdinand
Buisson became Director of Primary Education and remained in
the post for 20 years. The comparison with Britain is not simply
that practical politics demanded a stronger reaction to conservative
religious influence in the educational system. This was no less
strongly felt by non-conformists in Britain. But in France education
involved the integrity of the state, and opened the way for social
reforms of other kinds. More comprehensive change followed
because of the necessity to establish a republican image of the
state.

All that is not to say that having a strong concept of the state
may not have negative effects on policy and become political
opportunism. In some respects, the Liberal crisis over the House
of Lords is the historical counterpart to the Dreyfus scandal,
which infused republican passions. Both were directed against
reactionary, aristocratic control of policymaking. The second wave
of educational reform in France was associated with the Dreyfus
scandal and conducted by an uninspiring President of the Council,
Combes, whom Soltau describes as being moderate on everything
except religion.[63] With the support of the socialist deputies surrounding Jean Jaurès, Combes forbade all public instruction by
members of religious orders, closed 10,000 Catholic primary
schools (6,000 re-opened as secular schools), and tried to seize all
the assets of Catholic institutions and orders. In the words of his
education minister, Clemenceau, who acquired new popularity as
a result of these policies, the republicans of the 1880s had

[62] Adrien Dansette, *Histoire religieuse de la France contemporaine*, Paris; Flammarion,
1951, pp. 74–91. Ferry also started a separate Ecole Normale Supérieure for
women at Sèvres. Sanford Elwitt, *The Making of the Third Republic: Class and
Politics in France 1868–1884*, Baton Rouge, LA; Louisiana State University Press,
1975, pp. 170–229.
[63] Soltau, *French Political Thought . . .*, p. 360. On the role of educational reform
in establishing republican control after 1877, see Katherine Auspitz, *The Radical
bourgeoisie: The Ligue de l'Enseignement and the Origins of the Third Republic 1866–1885*,
Cambridge; Cambridge University Press, 1982, pp. 123–60.

dethroned the Pope and now the state must expunge God.[64] The effects were more apparent in primary than in secondary education. By 1914 the number of primary school pupils in the '*école libres*' or Church primary schools dropped by over half a million (from 1.6 to 1.0 million) and secondary school enrolment by less than 7,000 (from 91,000 to 84,000). The attack on the *écoles libres* remained dormant for eighty years, that is, until the ambitious Socialist government of 1981 decided in vain to complete the secularization of French schools.

All the European educational systems came under fire as the liberal democracies accepted wider social responsibilities. Because political and cultural factors could not be excluded from school reforms, they are perhaps the best illustration of how liberal states tried to reconcile their individualist assumptions with collective needs. One possible explanation of the decline of the liberals in Germany and Sweden might be that this controversy was excluded from political debate, in the first instance by an autocratic regime and in the second by a social democratic government that constructed an agenda without raising school (and many other social) controversies. Bismarck's manipulation of middle-class concerns about secondary school reform in the 1887 election was the prelude to suppression of the Social Democrats and the rise of imperial sentiment.[65] In effect, the Liberals conceded power to Bismarck for protection of an elite school system, which may be an important factor in their decline. In a more culturally homogeneous Sweden, Liberals never had a chance to raise the issue. But for older, more established liberal parties, as in Britain and France, the implications of educational reform could not be avoided. In doing so, British and French liberals learned about the associated social issues of poor nutrition, poor health and bad housing and were

---

[64] Dansette, *Histoire religieuse* . . ., p. 312. The description in this paragraph comes from Dansette, pp. 301–38, which provides full details of the purge. An important element in the separation was to expunge religious influence on higher education, especially by strict control of the Ecole Normale Supérieure and altering requirements for the *aggrégation*, the certificate for the exalted positions of lycée professors. See Georges Blondel, 'Les influences de l'enseignement secondaire et l'essor économique du pays,' *Réforme Sociale*, **39**, January–July, pp. 193–208, and August–December, 1900, pp. 439–60.

[65] Arnold Heidenheimer, 'Education and Social Entitlements in Europe and America,' in P. Flora and A. Heidenheimer, eds, *The Development of Welfare States in Europe and America*, New Brunswick and London; Transaction Books, 1981, pp. 269–304, p. 281.

inextricably drawn into wider social reforms. Educational reform was of no less concern in the highly decentralized American political setting, but the United States adopted a strategy of 'substituting education for techniques of social action'.[66] America's cultural pluralism made education a poor springboard for national social reforms.

Much more could be written about the political links between early school reforms and the foundations of welfare states. As we shall see, the ingenious, and sometimes unparliamentary, educational reforms of Morant laid the foundations for free public health and improved child care. But in doing so the relation of state education to democracy never crystallized as it did in France. In both the Liberal and Conservative parties the flicker of radical republican sentiments for free, universal schooling were extinguished.[67] Nonetheless, education was a divisive and fateful issue as liberals tried to reconstruct their doctrine. Where they moved toward more ambitious social reforms, as in Britain, they were split over issues demanding more aggressive state intervention; and where they compromised their values to join with conservatives, their political doom was sealed. To the extent that this fateful choice is excluded from our explanations of the rise of welfare states, as is done in most positivist accounts, a fundamental clash of values is brushed aside as irrelevant to the future structure of welfare states.

BRITISH LIBERALS SEARCH FOR THE STATE

State socialism cut the ground from under German liberals, just as it spread despair among German socialists.[68] But the notion of the state as the protector of society easily predates Bismarck. In 1794 the Landreich acknowledged the right of all citizens to work and the obligation of the state to protect the poor. Neither the

---

[66] Quoted in Heidenheimer, p. 275, from Rush Welter, *Popular Education and Democratic Thought in America*, New York; Columbia University Press, 1962.
[67] The Tory splinter group that flirted with republican ideas was led by Lord Randolph Churchill, the young A. J. Balfour and Gorst in the Primrose League. See Simon, p. 94.
[68] William Harbutt Dawson, *Bismarck and State Socialism*, London; Sonnenschein, 1890.

autocratic government of the German Reich before the war nor
the confusion of the Weimar Republic after the war (compounded
by the confusion of German Social Democrats following the Knapp
putsch and the socialist uprisings) allowed liberals to reform their
ranks and make a claim on the German state tradition. From the
viewpoint of liberal political and economic thinking, state socialism
as propounded by Wagner and others integrated social and economic decisions in ways that left liberals stranded. The effort to
find policy solutions transcending simple economic interpretations
of politics, the search began in 1873 with the *Verein für Sozialpolitik*,
and has more or less continued to the present day in the many
Social Democratic policy centres in the German Federal Republic.
But in comparison to both Britain and France, Germany kept
alive the tradition of institutional economics, begun by Wilhelm
Henrich Riehl and Lorenz von Stein, who, like Le Play in France,
considered unbridled industrialization a threat to family and social
values. Their ideas were later integrated by Otto von Zweidineck-
Sudenhorst and set a standard for social policymaking that helps
account for the originality of German social policy in the 1950s
and 1960s, when most other democracies were developing few
new ideas about the welfare state.[69]

Late developers have particular advantages. In the case of the
development of ideas about the welfare state, the delayed political
development of Sweden has particularly beneficial results. From
1932 until 1976 the Liberal Party never became a viable alternative to the Social Democrats.[70] The Social Democrats could take
advantage of the Keynesian concepts developed early in the century by Wicksell.[71] The party leaders were well-informed and,
since the party's defeat in 1928, had abandoned orthodox Marxist
thinking. Both industry and labour accepted the interdependence
of increased productivity and redistribution so that while economic

---

[69] For the development of the *Sozialpolitik* concept, see Werner J. Cahnman and
Carl M. Schmitt, 'The Concept of Social Policy (Sozialpolitik)', *Journal of Social
Policy*, **8**, 1979, pp. 47–59. Their article is phrased as a critique of Asa Brigg's
essentially liberal view of the welfare state.

[70] The Liberal Party never became a major party after the rise of Bismarck. In
1871 they had 155 Reichstag members, and with one small recovery, by 1912
they had only 45 members. Gordon Smith, *Democracy in Western Germany: Parties
and Politics in the Federal Republic*, New York: Holms and Meiser, 1979, p. 32.

[71] Knut Wicksell is often regarded as the founder of demand-based economics.
His works later translated into English were *Value, Capital and Rent*, New York;
Rinehart, 1954; and *Lectures in Political Economy*, New York; Macmillan, 1935.

growth favoured the Swedes their model of the welfare state worked remarkably well. As Leif Lewin argues, liberalism was bankrupt.[72]

Often considered the bastion of liberal ideas, the United States baffles European observers. It is worth recalling that when the Webbs visited the United States (in the late 1890s when opportunities for 'permeation' in Britain appeared slight), they were struck by there being 'no responsible government.' For a couple who so carefully avoided the discussion of political values, this is curious indeed. More indicative of how they and other British political thinkers of the turn of the century thought, only the tightly organized political communities of Mormon Salt Lake impressed them.[73] Had they taken Tocqueville more seriously, they might have noticed that the politics of policymaking in the United States is severely localized.[74] Given the Webbs' devotion to social engineering, it is strange that they were not more attracted to the peculiar difficulties of reshaping the American liberal state in order to accommodate social reform.

Nineteenth-century official and popular views toward social assistance in the United States were not unlike those in Europe. In some instances, as in the development of settlement houses and the liberal inspired charity movement, the United States was considered a leader. The strong feelings of self-reliance among Sam Gompers' craft unionists were similar to those found in Britain and France. The striking difference was that mobilizing these ideas for political purposes could not be easily elevated to national politics. For constitutional and political reasons, there was little room for a concept of the state, much less the experiments with linking social and wage policies that mark the dawn of the advanced welfare state. In this respect, Lowi's title, *The End of Liberalism*,[75] is a misnomer. Under Kennedy and Johnson the amount of federal social assistance increased significantly, but the principles justifying social assistance changed little. The liberal foundations for social assistance remained relatively unshaken in

[72] Leif Lewin, 'The Debate on Economic Planning,' in Steven Koblik, ed., *Sweden's Political Development from Poverty to Affluence, 1750–1970*, Minneapolis; University of Minnesota Press, 1975, pp. 282–302.

[73] Norman and Jean MacKenzie, *The First Fabians*, pp. 256–68.

[74] Grant McConnel, *Private Power and American Democracy*, New York; Random House, 1966.

[75] Theodore Lowi, *The End of Liberalism*, New York; Norton, 1968.

the 1980s and social assistance remained, for political purposes, a question of individual need.

In a country like the United States, social problems were often regarded as a temporary misfortune. For most European countries there were few such optimistic speculations to rationalize growing social distress. European liberals had been revising and expanding old formulas to assist the poor for some years, but at the turn of the century many of these improvisations were clearly unworkable. Undoubtedly, the situation was the most severe in Britain. The perennial Irish question continued to sow bitterness and to immobilize Parliament; the call for trade protection reversed a century of economic dominance and imperial splendour; the discovery of rotting cities and their human victims shocked informed citizens; and the Boer War revealed that the working man was ravaged by neglect.[76] Unlike a dispersed and distracted America, in the Edwardian period awareness of social decline crystallized in the thinking of the new liberals who began to re-examine the more temporary solutions of Victorian Britain, and, more importantly, to ask fundamental questions about the organization of British politics and society. The 'undecided prophets', a loosely collected group of Liberal Party dissidents, drifted among the complex intellectual currents of the day, but clearly saw that the old order was changing.[77] Typical, and perhaps most influential of the group, was C. F. G. Masterman, a minor minister in most Liberal governments until 1914. In assessing his ideas, Hynes reveals the new Liberals' failure as policymakers. The Liberals were unable to escape from their evangelical and sentimental notions of Victorian Britain. Masterman's popular book, *The Condition of England*, was a call for moral and spiritual regeneration, not a programme for the future. 'When he looked to the conditions of modern civilization, it was with the evangelical rather than the reforming eye; he looked,

[76] The shock of the Boer was both political and social. The aristocratic officer class was revealed as incompetent, and the brutal war carried on against Dutch settlers seemed a far cry from the more orderly wars of the past. Among 10,000 recruits from Manchester, 8,000 were found physically unfit to carry a rifle, and half of those accepted were in weak condition. See Arnold White, *Efficiency and Empire*, 1901, quoted in Eric J. Evans, ed., *Social Policy 1830–1914*, London; Routledge and Kegan Paul, 1978, p. 224. See also the fine account found in Donald Read, *Edwardian England 1901–1915*, pp. 21–86.

[77] The phrase is Samuel Hynes' title for the excellent summary of Masterman's thinking in *The Edwardian Turn of Mind*, Princeton; Princeton University Press, 1968, pp. 54–86. The quotes are from p. 69 and p. 86, his italics.

that is, not *at* the social problems but *behind* them, and there he found spiritual causes of the condition of England.' His thinking is important in understanding the transformation of British politics because it asked so much and proposed so little. Political means and political ends were lacking, leaving the way open for a new breed of more aggressive and more opportunistic politicians like Lloyd George and Churchill. As Hynes concludes, 'The Liberal Party needed vision to meet the great occasion, but the prophets who rose to prophecy were sad and undecided, and the occasion passed.'

The failure to fashion the strenuous efforts at the turn of the century into a form that might change the institutional and political assumptions of British politics would be easier to explain away as the misfortune of an early developer or as a curious political accident were it not that Balfour, Asquith, MacDonald and Lloyd George were all so aware that change was needed. Behind them lay the voluminous writing and research of late Victorian Britain. Part of the answer is that there was no clear political framework, no concept of the state, that helped the leaders and thinkers of the period assemble their ideas and programmes. 'A certain uneasiness about what is taking place in the British social order pervades the writings of all of them, a fear that it was being menaced within and without.'[78] Except for the austerely rational thinking of the Fabians, utilitarian thinking had lost its grip. But in some respects the intellectual continuity reflected in the new proposals was remarkable, not so much because the justification and content of new policies changed, but because the ways of approaching pervasive and obvious problems changed so little. As in the case of local reform and reorganization, Britain somehow managed to do new things, but always in the same way. In a policy perspective, there could be adventurous and commendable reforms, but the process of reform had little effect on politics and policymaking.

Politicians will, of course, always pick and choose among the ideas offered up by intellectuals. Although Adam Smith did much to enshrine the virtues of a free economy, it is important to note that he probably had less effect on social policymaking than did

---

[78] David Owen, *English Philanthropy 1660–1960*, Cambridge, MA; Harvard University Press, 1964, p. 103.

Bentham. Smith was primarily opposed to the restraining influences of mercantilist practices in the late eighteenth century. His main attack was on the destructive influence of a rural economy over the potentionally more productive industrial economy. Though we have learned two centuries later that costly and unfair restraints can also operate in the production and distribution of public goods, his ideas did not directly affect the workings of government. More important was Ricardo, who more mercilessly attacked the unearned income of the landed and defended cheap food. In doing so, he at least laid the groundwork for a growth theory of the welfare state. Real incomes could increase without destroying the wage structure. Unfortunately, the early Victorian political economists did not learn this lesson. As Sir Edwin Chadwick, Bentham's disciple, noted in the debate over the 1834 Poor Laws, 'as labour is the source of wealth, so is poverty of labour.'[79] Accepting misery as the natural condition of labour meant that the way toward a more constructive view between wages and social policy was blocked, and, for a variety of reasons, so it remained in Britain until the present.

There were two main intellectual strands deeply buried in the early nineteenth century. The first was the evangelical movement of such leaders as Wilberforce, Oastler and Sadler who brought religious fervour to reform.[80] There was secondly the Benthamites whose rational fervour was no less intense. The evangelicals wanted (and made substantial progress toward) the protection of mothers and children in factories, the termination of the brutal suppression of Ireland, the aboliton of slavery, and better treatment of agricultural workers. Social issues did not figure prominently in the writing of Bentham, whose rational state was grounded in a system of ethics and law that would make the 'felicific calculus' a reality. With the support of the Whigs, the Benthamites also accomplished a large measure of what they set out to do, most notably in the 1834 Poor Law Amendment Act

[79] Cowherd, *Political Economists and the English Poor Laws*, Athens, OH; Ohio University, p. 245.
[80] For a summary of evangelical thinking, see Derek Frazer, *The Evolution of the Welfare State*, London; Macmillan, 1973, pp. 15–22. See also Fred K. Brown, *Fathers of the Victorians*, Cambridge; Cambridge University Press, 1961; and Harold Perkin, *The Origins of Modern English Society, 1780–1880*, Toronto; University of Toronto Press, 1969; and David Roberts, *Paternalism in Early Victorian England*, New Brunswick; Rutgers University Press, 1979.

and the 1835 Municipal Reform Act, but neither law was enforced in the ways that Benthamites hoped. What links the early Victorian social reformers to the Edwardians is that their assumptions were so different but their conclusions were so similar. The evangelical creed of self-reliance and self-improvement was, by definition, unable to construct a collective view of society as finally demonstrated by the decline of its Victorian stronghold, the Charity Organization Society.

Given the philosophical importance of the utilitarians, and their close association with many of the leading politicians and social reformers of early Victorian Britain, it is important to see why they did not contribute to developing the British concept of the state. Like the orthodox Marxists, they wanted a wholly rational state. They had no patience with either the practical or ethical problems that make the exercise of authority less than rational. It is the pervasiveness of their policy influence that makes their failure remarkable. Many prominent statesmen of the day, such as Nassau Senior, adopted the new political economy. Patrick Colquhoun collected elaborate statistics to demonstrate the ineffectiveness and waste of the penal system. Sir Edwin Chadwick was the tireless administrative expert, accumulating a formidable, and sometimes biased, array of information that propelled the 1834 Poor Law Act through Parliament.[81] Through Francis Place and Joseph Hume, Bentham had his own parliamentary agents, and through the *Westminster Review* his own channel to informed opinion.

The reasons for the Benthamite failure as policymakers concern us because, had they been more effective, they might have formulated a concept of the British state. First and most important they were true believers. Thinking that they had the key to political rationality, they ignored the important political and social changes in early Victorian Britain and, though not opposed to political rights, had little interest in how democracy could be reconciled with their theories and proposals. The momentous political changes of the early nineteenth century were the disestablishment

[81] See the excellent biography of Samuel Finer, *The Life and Times of Sir Edwin Chadwick*, London; Methuen, 1952. Like many Benthamites, Chadwick was arrogant and demanding. His Poor Law Report omitted many of the actual changes that were occuring as Poor Law officials themselves perceived the faults of the system and as local government itself began to modify the harshness of the system.

of the Church in Ireland, the right to vote for Catholics, and the initial, though very limited, reform of parliamentary boroughs and elections.[82] The dynamics of British politics were changing but the utilitarians had little confidence in democratic politics. Second, they lacked the essential political skill of later successful operatives, such as Sir Robert Morant, of unobtrusively working with available resources and influence. Chadwick lived until 1898, but he never recovered his fame of 1834. He quarrelled with the new wave of social reformers within government, most notably Sir John Simon, the architect of public health in mid-Victorian England, because they would not accept his sacred principles, and with political activists outside government.[83] The Fabians had many of the same intellectual weaknesses, and they followed a very familir political strategy to promote their ideas and proposals.

But the Benthamite movement has broader implications for our study because of the ensuing debate over whether Bentham and his disciples laid the foundations of British collectivism. Compared to the rest of Europe, Britain's difficulties in coming to grips with the welfare state are revealed in the energy and care scholars devote to answering a question that would be quite easily and simply answered for any other European country. Putting aside the intrinsic philosophical interest of the question, the extended debate over the nature of utilitarian collectivism may be seen as an apology for there being no workable concept of the state in Britain. Having no framework with which to construct a sense of direction and accomplishment from diverse social initiatives, the use of collective authority for social purposes mystifies rather than clarifies. British intellectuals have engaged in a long debate over whether an analytical construct, collectivism, might be the surrogate for the concept of state as revealed in law, institutions and administration in the rest of Europe.[84] In the logic of this study,

[82] See David Moore, *The Politics of Deference: A Study of the Mid-Nineteenth Century English Political System*, New York; Barnes and Noble, 1976.

[83] On Chadwick's useless quarrels, see W. H. Greenleaf, 'Toulmin Smith and the British Political Tradition,' *Public Administration Review*, **53**, 1975, pp. 25–44.

[84] For a good summary, see Geoffrey K. Fry, 'Bentham and Public Administration,' *Public Administrtion Bulletin*, **24**, August 1977, pp. 32–40. See also L. J. Hume, 'III. Jeremy Bentham and the Nineteenth Century Revolution in Government,' *The Historical Journal*, **10**, no. 4, 1967, pp. 361–75, and Jennifer Hart, 'Nineteenth Century Social Reform: A Tory Interpretation on History,' *Past and Present*, **31**, July 1965, pp. 39–61. Among the books taking various stances on the issue are David Roberts, *Victorian Origins of the Welfare State*, New

it goes far toward explaining why devising social policy and setting social priorities remained so difficult a century after the utilitarians.

Because the 1834 Act becomes the pivotal point in so much debate about social policy in Britain, it is worth examining the law as a policy instrument.[85] First, the law abandoned much of the reasoning behind the Elizabethan Poor Laws. Though enshrined in the royalist ideas of the sixteenth century, the original laws conveyed a much broader notion of the state's responsibility for the disadvantaged and poor. The 1834 Law tried to substitute a single logic, and in doing so became the prototype of British social reform until the present day. The preoccupation with poverty is important for what it omits, that is, the relation of social reform to many other social questions such as the improvement of the labour force, industrial adjustment to social needs and working conditions. Why was Britain, the richest and most forceful nineteenth-century power, so ill-prepared to integrate the labour movement into British politics? Of course, many of the ancillary problems were dealt with in separate legislation, but that is precisely the point. Over the Victorian period, and even into the twentieth century, each piece of social legislation devised its own political justification, and in so doing no coherent image of the British welfare state emerged. The Poor Law Amendment Act was directed toward a specific problem, namely, that the cost of poor relief had tripled from 1776 to 1802.[86] Some of the local expedients, such as the Speenhamland proposal to pay the poor the equivalent of a living wage, had much wider implications for the future of social policy, but then as now alternative proposals were easily pushed aside in British politics.

Secondly, although there is no reason to expect the aristocratic lawmakers of early Victorian Britain to think otherwise, the 1834 Act was in many respects a defensive act not an effort to build a system that might adjust to future social problems. Although the industrial revolution in Britain was half a century old, political

Haven; Yale University Press, 1960; Oliver MacDonagh, *A Pattern of Government Growth 1800–1860*, London; MacGibbon and Kee, 1961; William C. Lubenow, *The Politics of Government Growth: Early Victorian Attitudes Toward State Intervention 1833–1848*, Hamden, CN; Archon Books, 1971.

[85] For a full account of these developments, see the remarkable study of Gertrude Himmelfarb, *The Idea of Poverty*.

[86] Maurice Bruce, *The Coming of the Welfare State*, London; Batsford, p. 91.

power still rested with the landholders. Their interest was to protect themselves against the cost of caring for rural labourers who had migrated to cities or who had been rendered penniless in the countryside. Thus, the undebated premise of the 1834 Law was that the power of the landholders should be preserved. Blaming policymakers for lack of foresight is an easy game, but it is remarkable that with the appearance of the industrial revolution the leading industrial power made such inadequate preparations, or, more accurately, accepted legislation that was so difficult to adjust to new industrial problems over the nineteenth century. Just as the landed aristocracy engendered feelings that industrialization was a rather dirty and mechanical affair to be left to others,[87] so also they preferred a solution to Britain's major social problem of the period that would allow the gentry to manage social distress at minimum expense and with minimal disruption of rural harmony. Central to this reasoning was the concern that local taxation be kept under control.[88] That the administrative arrangements to achieve this end were cumbersome and involved an extraordinary assignment of powers to national government mattered little. Paradoxically, by depriving local agencies of revenues for social needs, the landed contributed to the crisis of 1909–11, and made the income tax a necessity to finance social reform.

Third, in placing such emphasis on the mechanics of social assistance, the 1834 Act devised a rigid notion of social benefits and why democracies undertake social tasks. It is interesting to note that the French political economist, Boutmy, detected the latent conflict between wage and social policy in British Poor Law legislation, and, therefore, the great difficulties the British might have in arriving at fair labour prices.[89] The key provision of the law was the 'workhouse' test or a crude means-test. As Chadwick proudly explained, 'if the claimant does not comply with the terms on which relief is given, he gets nothing; and if he does comply,

---

[87] See Martin J. Weiner, *English Culture and the Decline of the Industrial Spirit 1850–1980*, Cambridge; Cambridge University Press, 1981. On the extent to which much Victorian legislation was designed to protect the landed, see Anwer Offer, *Property and Politics 1870–1914*, Cambridge; Cambridge University Press, 1981.
[88] See Ashford, *British Dogmatism and French Pragmatism*, 1982. The theme runs right to the Thatcher government whose efforts to totally control local spending are, in part, motivated by the fear that local authorities will replace lost social expenditure.
[89] Boutmy, *The English People*, p. 248.

the compliance proves the truth of the claim – namely, his destitution.'[90] Both the nonsense and the cruelty of the test were perceived by many Poor Law officials and the law was in fact unevenly enforced. Parliament itself saw the inapplicability of the law and in 1847 brought the 'Three Wisemen of Somerset House,' the peak administrators of this administrative paradise, under parliamentary control. In Chapter 3 we shall pursue in more detail the extent to which means-testing became the hallmark of the British welfare state, and as such has diverted both political and administrative energies from seeking more constructive solutions to British social problems.

In effect, the British devised an eighteenth-century solution for a nineteenth-century problem. The time lag is not a curious product of socio-economic conditions, but a demonstration of the power of landed aristocracy that continued until the Edwardian period. But by then Britain had accumulated a vast array of social legislation, and the administrative machinery was already beginning to replace parliamentary deliberation. The political dilemma of the new liberals, and in a broader sense, the strange limitations of the British welfare state, were repeated at the turn of the century. The social problem was widely recognized and policy proposals were forthcoming from all sides. In a radical Liberal Birmingham, Joseph Chamberlain tried to revive local enterprise and local social responsibility, but when he explained his public works scheme in 1886 he reassured them that it would be 'very strict with the loafer and the confirmed pauper.' Ritchie, the liberal minister for the Local Government Board under Lord Salisbury, and thus responsible for the Poor Laws, considered the 'only real remedy (to unemployment) was greater thrift, less drunkenness, more industry and fewer marriages.'[91] As late as 1909, a Liberal minister testifying to the Poor Law Commission could accept that a 'decent man', even through no fault of his own, might be forced into the workhouse 'for the general good of the body politic.'[92] Beneath his response lurks the unanswered question of what the body politic, or the nature of the state is.

The British government was pushed ahead, and not all that

[90] Jose Harris, *Unemployment and Politics: A Study in British Social Policy 1886–1914*, Oxford; Clarendon Press, pp. 76–7.
[91] Jose Harris, *Unemployment and Politics . . .*, p. 77.
[92] Bruce, *The Coming of the Welfare State*, p. 98.

rapidly, by the growing cost of poor relief,[93] which, as in the 1830s, monopolized the attention of policymakers. But the Edwardian policymakers understandably boggled at placing a tenth of the population in the poor house. Thus, policymaking was always in the situation of catching up with the past, rather than trying to carve out the future. But in countries where the concept of the state was more developed, the link between state and society was more clearly framed. In addition, what is often forgotten is that much of the legislation we associate with liberal democracy in Britain was not produced by mass politics, but by crusading, evangelical aristocrats such as Brougham, Shaftesbury, Althorp and John Russell. Until the 1867 Reform Act only five percent of the British population voted. Both Queen Victoria and most of the Lords greeted the first steps toward mass democracy in 1884 with skepticism or resignation. Until 1911 the political dynamics of the British welfare state were feeble, and policymaking, partly as a result, was disconnected and reactive.[94]

Despite the strong moral overtone of new liberal writing, it was encapsulated in Victorian thinking. One recollects the Victorian idealist, Sidney Ball, instructing one of the leading new Liberals, J. L. Hammond, that the 'poor man's poverty is his moral opportunity.'[95] But, as Freeden notes, the failure of progressive liberalism to take root in Britain 'cannot be attributed to the intellectual failure of its theorists.'[96] T. H. Green, F. H. Bradley and Bernard Bosanquet brought German idealism to British intellectual life, and to their credit lived by many of its presumptions, but the soil was not prepared.[97] They could tap the moral fervour of the

[93] Harris, p. 145, notes that between 1870 and 1905 the cost of poor relief multiplied by ten.

[94] Though it says little about policymaking, the internal contradictions of British democratic development are the central concern of Elie Halévy, *The Growth of Philosophic Radicalism*, London; Faber and Faber, 1928. Like his French colleague, Boutmy, he is sensitive to the contradictions of the utilitarians; see pp. 249–315. For a superb case study of how Liberals operated in the nineteenth century, see A. B. Cooke and John Vincent, *The Governing Passion; Cabinet Government and Party Politics in Britain 1885–86*, New York; Harper and Row, 1974.

[95] Clarke, *Liberals and Social Democrats*, Cambridge; Cambridge University Press, 1978, p. 74.

[96] Michael Freeden, *The New Liberalism: An Ideology of Social Reform*, Oxford; Clarendon Press, 1978, p. 1.

[97] See W. S. Fowler, 'The Influence of Idealism Upon State Provision of Education,' *Victorian Studies*, **4**, June 1961, pp. 337–44. For other interpretations of the British idealists, see Melvin Richter, 'Intellectual and Class Alienation: Oxford

evangelicals, the labour movement and their friends in government, but they could not sink roots into the political structure. Their failure requires a backward glance at where they came from and how they began to think about the social complexities of late Victorian Britain.

As in the case of reforming the school system, university reform was a way 'to broaden the establishment itself' by broadening the base of the intellectual, and then largely clerical, aristocracy of the universities.[98] Their ideas were a curious mixture of Coleridge's 'clerisy', a kind of intellectual priesthood; Thomas Arnold's passionate faith in the reasonableness of common people; and Comte's Religion of Humanity. Their gigantic historicism was to believe that if we could discover the rules of history, then policy and politics might disappear. Under Thomas Arnold's tutelage much of this intellectual ferment began at Rugby where admiration for the 'all-rounder' and self-made man became a deceptively simple formula for reconciling the social elite to working class aspirations. Well before the Edwardian new liberals, many of them with Rugby backgrounds, set out to redirect liberal aspirations, the young John Morley put forth their principles in his study, appropriately entitled, *On compromise* (1886).[99] As a Comtian enthusiast, Morley extolled the possibilities of reason, the virtues of a unified and broad-based elite. As for many British, his confidence in the rationality of the common man was personified by the early Gladstone. Active in adult education, workingmen's clubs and Ruskin College, the workingman's Oxford college, his ideas were subversive and progressive. As we shall see, there is a common thread leading to Jowett at Balliol and his dedication to sending bright, socially conscious young scholars, such as Beveridge, off to the London slums.

To understand the inability of the new liberals to anchor their

Idealist Diagnoses and Prescriptions,' *Archives Européenes de Sociologie*, **7**, 1966, pp. 1–26; W. L. Weinsten, 'The Concept of Liberty in Mid-Century English Political Thought', *Political Studies*, **13**, 1965, pp. 145–162; and David Nicholls, 'Positive Liberty 1880–1914,' *American Political Science Review*, **56**, 1962, pp. 114–128.

[98] Christopher Kent, *Brains and Numbers: Elitism, Comtism, and Democracy in Mid-Victorian Britain*, Toronto; University of Toronto Press, 1978, p. xii.

[99] Morley dropped out of Oxford because his father refused to support him when Morley abandoned the respectable career of the clergy. Morley went on to fulfill Comte's desire that there be a series of studies linking (and hopefully transforming) the pallid revolution of 1688 into the French revolution. He wrote books on Diderot, Rousseau, and Voltaire. See Kent, pp. 117–35.

ideas in a more solid framework, it is helpful to examine briefly
the dispersion of Edwardian reformist thinking. Herbert Spencer
advanced Social Darwinism as a creed, and its appeal, particularly
after the Boer War disaster, spawned an Efficiency Movement.[100]
For obvious reasons – its emphasis on world domination and
national strength – it appealed to Conservative and Liberal imperi-
alists. Haldane, who had studied in Germany and admired the
country, was among the most attracted, and, in turn, he was able
to interest the laconic Lord Rosebery. Efficiency principles also fit
well with Fabian thinking, and helped form their liaison with
Rosebery.[101] Though the Webbs never tired of promoting their
policies, the high point of their influence came with their link to
Rosebery through Haldane. There was also an array of associated
organizations, such as the Eugenics Society, the Administrative
Reform Association and the Rainbow Circle. As history demonstrated, efficiency suited neither the left nor the right. Whatever
may be the sins of omission of Stanley Baldwin, the distracted and
nostalgic leader of the Conservatives from 1923 to 1937, he was
not sufficiently persuaded to make a simplistic efficiency formula
the rallying cry for his party. Oddly enough, it was the left that
drifted into efficiency notions as the solution to social ills, as seen
in Oswald Moseley's defection to fascism and in the respect for
Soviet communism that Sidney and Beatrice Webb discovered in
their waning years.

Another strand of revisionist thinking that had more direct
policy impact was the charity movement, inspired by nineteenth-
century evangelical thinking. Its efforts were renewed in late Victorian Britain by Bernard Bosanquet, whose *Philosophical Theory of
the State* (1899) was a popular book among students of German
idealism. The charity movement was consolidated in 1869 with
the formation of the Charity Organization Society. With the Queen

[100] See J. D. Y. Peel, *Herbert Spencer: The Evaluation of a Sociologist*, New York;
1971. His influence on British sociology, namely its preoccupation with theory,
is outlined by Philip Abrams, *Origins of British Sociology 1834–1914*, Chicago;
University of Chicago Press, 1968.
[101] See Searle, *The Quest for National Efficiency*, 1971. Their group, the Coefficients,
is described in Robert J. Scaly, *The Origins of Lloyd George Coalition: The Politics
of Social Imperialism, 1900–1918*, Princeton; Princeton University Press, 1975, pp.
73–95. Under Spencer's influence one anti-collectivist organization did spring
up with clear concerns about property and rights. See Edward Bristow, 'The
Liberty and Property Defense League and Inidividualism', *Historical Journal*, **18**,
1975,   761–89.

as their patron and the Archbishop of Canterbury as their president, it is clear what their political sympathies were, though the principles of self-reliance were widely accepted throughout Victorian society. For forty years, the CSO secretary, C. S. Loch, was a major voice in British social reform, serving on the Royal Commissions on the Aged Poor (1883–95), the Feeble-Minded (1904–08) and the Poor Laws (1905–09).[102] Six of the nineteen members of the Poor Law Commission had links to the CSO, and Octavia Hill, one of the most active members of the Commission, was a tireless worker in the charity organization in the Marylebone area of London. The Society opposed every pension proposal presented over the 1880s and 1890s, but concentrated their fire on the Poor Laws. In fact, their view of the Poor Laws was not an unreasonable one: social assistance without the individual care that helps the victims of poverty regain a normal and productive life is likely to fail.

The charity movement's objections to poor relief were not so much that aid should not be given, but that it must be coupled with good housing, family care and personal health. In one sense, they were years before their time, because their interest in community care became central to advanced concepts of welfare in the 1960s and 1970s. But in one crucial respect they were also mired in the past. Their patronizing attitude and their rejection of national support without firm conditions was no longer feasible by 1900. While it may be true that the Poor Laws were 'a permanent obstacle to thrift and self-reliance,'[103] it is also true that their idea of aligning volunteer aid with Poor Law assistance would be little more than using public assistance to force compliance with their social values. In testifying before the Royal Commission on the Aged Poor, Alfred Marshall saw their weakness. 'They belong to the old world, in this way, that their basis consists exclusively of those people who used to be the governing classes but who are not the governing classes now.'[104]

---

[102] Loch was a student of T. H. Green at Balliol like many of the young liberal reformers. See Charles Mowat, the *Charitable Organization Society*, London; Methuen, 1961.

[103] Mowat, p. 68. From Loch writing on the Poor Laws in the 11th edition of the *Encyclopedia Britannica*.

[104] Quoted in Mowat, p. 129.

In brief, their view of how to alleviate poverty meant giving a self-appointed group power over the poor. As the 1911 Act demonstrated, their scheme was not politically attractive because it responded to neither the growing financial burdens of social assistance nor to the need for political incentives.

Had the Webbs any coherent philosophy, they might have formed a third strand in the search for ideas in the British welfare state. The fascinating policy aspect of the Webbs' thinking is that they produced so many proposals, but had so few successes. However much social policy advocates may despair over the logic of politics, the turn of the century politicians were not persuaded by their mindless rationality. But 'pragmatic socialism' fell between political stools. On the one hand, it could not inspire the dedicated following that the early socialist thinkers assembled in France and Germany; and, on the other hand, its notion of 'discreetly regulated freedom'[105] was not likely to appeal to those who lived by the ballot box. It is interesting that the perpetually perceptive and ambitious Churchill objected to their advice because, as he said, one must avoid 'mixing morality with mathematics.'[106] Many of their most able sympathizers, among them Hammond, Beveridge, Graham Wallas and J. A. Hobson, drifted away from the inner circle of planners because they did not like the manipulative dimension of Fabian thinking.

In a curious way, the shadow of evangelical sentiment always hung over the Fabian circle, but they never managed to produce a clear statement of their values. Edward Pease, the Fabian Society secretary for most of his life, was an unhappy Quaker. An original member, Hyndman, was an evangelical turned socialist. Graham Wallas had strong evangelical origins.[107] As the Mackenzies note, the Fabians always saw 'reform of social conditions as a palliative for original sin.'[108] Their political network was constantly shifting, but at times included Asquith, MacDonald, Haldane, Arthur Acland and Sidney Buxton, all influential politicians. Important administrators, such as Beveridge, Morant and Llewellyn Smith

---

[105] Read, p. 97.
[106] Clarke, p. 123.
[107] See Martin Wiener, *Between Two Worlds: The Political Thought of Graham Wallas*, Oxford; Oxford University Press, 1971.
[108] Norman and Jean MacKenzie, *The First Fabians*, p. 59. See also A. M. McBriar, *Fabian Socialism and English Politics, 1884–1918*, Cambridge; Cambridge University Press, 1962, especially pp. 146–62.

were in close touch at times, but as they were sensitized to the political limitations of policymaking, they too drifted away. The Fabians were actually more successful in reforming London government than British government, and London became the proving ground for their schemes. But as often happens with intellectuals closely associated with power, the Webbs soon became ornaments. By the early 1900s it was quite clear that national policy would not follow their recommendations. In defence of Beatrice Webb's minority report to the Poor Law Commission, 'utopia in a bluebook' according to the MacKenzies,[109] they organized a national campaign which certainly did not endear them to leading politicians.

Because the British policy process so often failed to rethink the British welfare state, or, perhaps more accurately, to state why Britain made such a heavy commitment to the welfare state, it is worth reflecting on why this group of industrious policy designers never had an impact. The Fabian failures are in one sense British failures. First, they had little sympathy or interest in the working class. It is relevant that, given the rapid growth of TUC membership in the early 1900s, they had no firm links to the union movement. Second, they were intolerant of the policy process. For example, on learning of the 1911 proposals, Beatrice Webb wrote in her *Diaries* that invalidity insurance was a major error because the workers 'ought to be conditioned on better conduct' and 'that the state got nothing for its money' if workers had unconditional compensation.[110] As with the early Victorian utilitarians, policy had an inexorable logic. Third, there was the shadow of oppressive policymaking in most of their proposals. In commenting on early pension plans, Sidney Webb wrote, 'the maximum justifiable expenditure for anybody is that amount which keeps him in the fullest working efficiency.'[111] The Webbs do not appear to have learned the lessons of J. S. Mill and they were sadly out of tune with the view that a wealthy society could afford to protect the disadvantaged and poor, even if the best means were open to dispute.

The intellectual fermentation of the Edwardian period was not wasted because it provided the setting, if not the policies, that

[109] Norman and Jean MacKenzie, p. 358.
[110] Quoted by Clarke, p. 119.
[111] Quoted by Clarke, p. 38.

were to launch the British welfare state. Yet it is difficult to see
how these ideas ever connected with the policies that emerged in
1911 and in the interwar period. What Briggs calls the 'middle
class Marxists' were in some ways more objectionable than this
bland rebuke suggests. They did not understand the impact of the
industrial revolution and they had little respect for the ordinary
voter who had struggled for a century to be recognized in British
democracy. They formed exclusive clubs such as the Rainbow
Circle or the 'Coefficients' to formulate policies without giving
much attention to the people who would live with the results.[112]
These groups, including the Fabians, remained primarily intellectual clubs, moved by the inquiries and problems of the period,
but not seeing the political implications of these demands and
needs. The new liberals languished for many years, but they were
unable to capture the Liberal Party after its moment of glory. The
Conservative Party went its cautious way and managed to guide
Britain through the difficult inter-war years. The Labour Party
enjoyed its moment of victory in 1923 and floundered in 1931,
but was unequal to the task. All accepted the major social role of
the state, but none saw that it had implications for governance.
As we shall see, the politics of social reform in Edwardian Britain
changed little to the present day.

If the attempt to redirect liberalism was so unsuccessful, how
did the government learn about the proposals and problems that
were being discussed in so many quarters? For one thing, government was still managed by a relatively small elite at the turn of
the century. Much communication took place at dinner parties,
over country weekends and in the small circles of ambitious
reformers and their political friends. Perhaps more than today, the
press was an instrument of informed opinion and many of the
discontented became editors of newspapers or journals. Still,
government was mobilized in a relatively short period of time if
we recall that in 1906 the Liberals had no formed views about
social policy. The critical link between ideas and policies was
administrative, and a more complete account will be given in
Chapter 3. A large number of those who actually made policies

[112] The 'Coefficients' were a small circle involved with the efficiency movement
in 1902 and dissolved after about six years. See Gilbert p. 80. The Rainbow
Circle lasted thirty years. See Clarke, p. 56, and Freeden, *The New Liberalism
. . .*, p. 256. Both groups were based on the new liberal thinking. For details on
their later activity, see Robert J. Scally, *The Origins of the Lloyd George Coalition.*

passed through the London settlement houses, often Toynbee Hall. The settlement movement began with Canon Barnett who looked to religion to heal the growing divisions among the social classes.[113] Assembling his reformist Anglican friends at Oxford, Arnold Toynbee, Alfred Milner and Jowett, the Master of Balliol, he raised funds for a direct attack on the misery of the poor.

The settlement houses, especially Toynbee Hall, became the crossroads for officials who would administer the liberal version of the British welfare state. Beveridge was a teacher at Toynbee Hall and he carried out some of his earliest research there.[114] Sidney Webb met his future wife, Beatrice Potter, at dinner at Toynbee Hall. Hammond's wife, Barbara Bradford, worked there, as did Tawney.[115] Others had their direct exposure to poverty in different circumstances. Beatrice Potter went into self-imposed exile in rural Lancashire and Octavia Hill worked in the London slums. Though there had been an accumulation of social legislation throughout Victorian Britain, the idea that the state should massively intervene came rather suddenly. Unlike most of Europe and the United States, within a decade the social agenda became part of the parliamentary agenda. The liberal welfare state in Britain was in many ways not a product of politics, but a product of political opportunity that exploited the reflection and research of an entire generation. This is not an argument against its results, but an observation on the political circumstances of its creation. The major actors were gripped with their diverse experiences of grinding poverty. They are not to be blamed that they had much less experience in politics, nor that British politics made it relatively easy to circumvent the tedious political struggle surrounding the creation of welfare states in the rest of the democratic world. But what the new liberal experience also shows is that the British welfare state was legislated without the popular support and the political coherence that can be found in other democracies.

[113] See Gilbert, *The Evolution of National Insurance* . . ., pp. 41–2. For more details, see Henrietta O. Barnett, *Cannon Barnett, His Life Work, and Friends*, London; 1921, 2 vols, 3rd edn.
[114] Jose Harris, *Beveridge*, pp. 44–63.
[115] MacKenzie and MacKenzie, p. 138. Gilbert, p. 421, notes that in addition to Beveridge and Llewelyn Smith there were six clerks working on the 1911 Act with Toynbee Hall backgrounds. On the interlocking circle of social reformers, politically and intellectually linked to Toynbee Hall, see Asa Briggs and Anne Macartney, *Toynbee Hall: The First Hundred Years*, London; Routledge and Kegan Paul, 1984, pp. 25–90.

Converting ideas into policies is not a simple task, particularly when reformers must run the gauntlet of democratic politics. A combination of historical and political reasons made it possible for many of the early twentieth-century British reformers to avoid the political hurdles, in no small part because they were already living on the fringes of the ruling class. To some extent, the rapid developments of 1906–11 were the product of being the first democratic state, leaving aside Germany, to launch a welfare state. First, the reasons for the early initiative also revealed its weaknesses. Edwardian policymakers did not have to deal with the problems of complex government. Second, nationalization of social policy could not be effectively resisted, as we shall see in more detail, by other political groups. Third, party alignments were fluid, if not confused by other issues. And fourth, the most common reason for passing major legislation, the injustices and inadequacies of the Poor Laws, overpowered their perception of the problem. It is no discredit to the liberal welfare state in Britain to observe that its creation was not the product of a critical election or of organized pressure outside government, but reform was strangely apolitical. British politicians and intellectuals had been helping build a case, if not a rationale, for the welfare state since the 1880s. But what remains different from most democratic countries, particularly in the light of the widespread debate and inquiry, is that their work had such vague political purpose and such ambiguous political consequences.

FRENCH LIBERALS SEIZE THE STATE

Unlike British liberalism, French liberalism never had a distinct political manifestation. The political turmoil of nineteenth-century France was not conducive to the clear alignment of doctrines and party identities that was possible in the more orderly British system. French liberalism, like French socialism, took on confused and diverse forms as it was compelled to adjust to tumultuous political events, and confronted with the unwieldy diversity of French society. The result is that strands of liberal thinking are taken up by various political tendencies, shaped to fit political realities of the day and then discarded as political objectives are realized. As the social legislation debates from 1890 to 1910 demonstrate, the translation of ideas into policies was an evolving and dynamic process, never far removed from defining a concept of the state, but never able to limit the state to a single political creed. The effect was that, for each legislative battle, French politicians devised new ways to reconcile policies with the Revolutionary assumptions of the French state. On the other hand, France, like other European countries, achieved what Britain failed to do, that is, social legislation became part of a developing and expanding idea of the state. Though the benefits of the welfare were slower to materialize, in both a political and conceptual sense the foundations were more solid.

In linking new ideas to policies, a number of circumstances required a more laborious intellectual effort than took place in Britain. First there were no unchallenged champions of liberal thinking who approached the influence of the early Victorian utilitarians or the turn of the century new liberals. French liberals were divided by the same frustrating political divisions that arrested the growth of democratic government. There were monarchial liberals, Catholic liberals, conservative liberals and republican liberals, each with their own political organization and with their particular links to French society. Second, French liberalism never accepted the unrestrained individualism of British, and, in a different historical context, American liberalism. Through the variety of liberal ideas there was the common strand that collective authority required a higher purpose than simply maximizing individual utilities. For some, such as the Catholic liberal, Le Play, this meant resurrecting the family, and, for others, such as the turn of the century republican liberal, Léon Bourgeois, this meant constructing a workable notion of social solidarity. As a result, collective authority as expressed through the state is never far removed from the formulation of new policies. Third, there were a number of unfavourable external circumstances which doctrinaire liberals could not reverse. The French economy was not highly competitive nor was France a world trader for whom classical liberal economics made sense. Capitalism and the state may have had an uneasy partnership, but its roots extended to the *ancien régime* and so a simple linking of politics and economics in the classical liberal mould was excluded.[116] Just as the small scale of French industry in the 1960s retarded de Gaulle's plans to develop

[116] See Kuisel, *Capitalism and the State in Modern France*, pp. 1–30.

a competitive economy, so also the eight million *patrons* of turn-of-the-century France[117] found unbridled liberal economics as much a threat as a solution.

The effect on the political development of the French welfare state was clear. As Hatzfeld writes, social security 'does not appear as a creation torn from the great battle of the working class and as a damning, as one says, of the ever increasing flood of pauperism.'[118] Thus, France escaped the close association of social assistance with poverty and urban misery that was so frequently felt in Britain. Though not progressing as fast as Britain, the favourable result was concern with the interdependence of social legislation and an awareness of social reform as an expression of the republican democracy. Monod, for example, was lavish in his praise of Théophile Roussel, over the 1880s the tireless advocate of protection and benefits for children.[119] The 1893 legislation permitting *bureau de bienfaisance* to provide free medical care to the poor became a precedent for the law on assistance for the aged and disabled. The principles of the 1898 law on accident compensation were revived in the social insurance debate.[120] However imperfect the results, the long debate of the 1920s on social insurance echoed the ideas and principles that were expressed before the war.[121] The overall effect in terms of the development of ideas is strikingly different from Britain because of the continuity of argument and development of underlying justifications for an expanded social assistance system.

The liberals could never fashion a persuasive case against social reform because they were themselves so deeply involved in trying to fashion an effective democratic government. The political realities of Louis Napoleon's coup in 1851, of the German defeat and the Paris Commune in 1870–71, of Boulanger and later Dreyfus, meant not only that social legislation was retarded for reasons that

[117] In the 1901 census, 8 million French classified themselves as *patrons*, nearly as many as the 11 million workers, and more than the 7 million artisians. Fifty-eight per cent of the firms employed 10 or fewer people; 27 per cent a single person. Hatzfeld, *Du pauperisme* . . . , p. 259.
[118] Hatzfeld, p. 263.
[119] See Henri Monod, *L'Assistance publique en France en 1889 et en 1900*, Paris; Imprimerie Nationale, 1900, pp. 19–22.
[120] H. Derouin, A. Gory and F. Worms, *Traité et practique d'assistance publique*, Paris; Sirey, 1914, v. 1, p. 305.
[121] See *Journal Officiel*, Chambre des Députés, séance du 9 avril 1930, Annexe No. 3187, pp. 500–643. Hereafter the Rapport Anotelli.

went beyond partisan political interests, but also meant that as social issues reached the political agenda they were inescapably merged with the political developments of the day. Until 1905, much the same immediate political concerns affected socialist debates on social legislation. The overall effect was to amalgamate social legislation with the democratic development of state.

The most important political consequence for social policy was that need alone never seemed an adequate rationale for French social legislation. At times, French social benefits are more generous than the Anglo-Saxon principles of utility and self-reliance would permit, and at other times, more frugal because the same benefit could not be provided to all citizens. Need is the point of leverage for a liberal interpretation of social assistance, but it rarely dominated the French debate. In one of the earliest debates on social insurance, in 1901 Léon Mirman, a Socialist Deputy and later Director of Public Assistance, was repelled by the possibility that France might be divided into the insured and the assisted. Proclaiming that 'the moral value of saving is not measured arithmetically'[122] Mirman, like most French social reformers, wanted assistance to go to anyone in trouble. Rather than concentrate on uniformity of treatment, the state must promise universality of access.

Thus, the development of the French welfare state could never be separated from the development of the French state itself. With the exception of the liberal economists, the theme of collective responsibility for all persons suffering from social or economic failures of the state runs through all the early versions of social reform. In most of these initiatives there is also the view that social assistance and social action are interdependent, that is, that attempts to alleviate misery and poverty must be accompanied by the mobilization of the victims. For the Catholic right, the major spokesmen were Count Armand de Mun and Marquis de la Tour du Pin. Though wary about the secularizing force of democracy, they supported the organization of worker 'chapels', the extension of social reform and education to the workplace, free Sundays (*la semaine anglaise*), and limited working hours. As with most reformist movements, there was an elaborate network of voluntary discussion groups and pastoral clubs, the 'Oeuvre des Cercles,' to carry the

---

[122] *Journal Officiel*, Chambre de Députés, Débats parlementaires, session ordinaire 1901, séance du 6 juin 1901, p. 1267.

Church's social mission to the congregation and the people.[123]

Like nearly every political movement in France, the movement for Catholic social action was internally split. In this case, the division corresponds to the historic distinction between the Church hierarchy, adamantly opposed to developing the Church's social mission until Pope Leo XII pronounced the encyclical *Rerum Novarum* in 1891, and the pastoral or village church of the *curé*. Léon Harmel became the organizer of social action among workers in the 1880s, and advocated family supplements, school assistance, worker training programmes, voluntary insurance (*caisses de prévoyance*), and factory councils. By 1888 there was a small group of Catholic socialist deputies in favour of pensions, accident insurance, restriction of labour abuses (*travail noir*) and the formation of a Ministry of Labour to inject worker interests into government. The social mission of the Church and its social works was sufficiently successful to stimulate their secular rivals, the freemasons, to launch their own programme of social education and social works.[124]

From early in the nineteenth century the Catholic social movement developed ideas that would have seemed radical and strange to British church organizations in late Victorian Britain. In 1833 the Society of Saint-Vincent-de-Paul was founded to work toward reconciling royalist Catholics with democracy. A few years later, in 1840, the Jesuit Society of Francis-Xavier was created to assist the 'fallen' – criminals, vagrants, and drunks – by providing instruction, materials and shelter for them to construct useful lives. Melun was active in the Society of Social Economy and advised Napoleon III on the formation of mutual insurance societies in the 1850s.[125] He founded the Society of Charitable Economics and started publication of the *Annales de la Charité*.[126] The Society's

[123] Dansette, *Histoire religieuse de la France contemporaine*, pp. 185–208. See also Benjamin F. Martin, *Count Albert de Mun: Paladin of the Third Republic*, Chapel Hill; University of North Carolina Press, 1978.
[124] See Mildred J. Headings, *French Freemasonry Under the Third Republic*, Baltimore; Johns Hopkins University Studies in Historical and Political Science, 1948, **56**, pp. 177–86.
[125] Jean-Baptiste Duroselle, *Les débats du Catholicisme social en France jusquà 1870*, Paris: Presses Universitaire de France, 1951, pp. 510–12. Actually, Melun probably gave more conservative advice than necessary, for Louis Bonaparte was thinking of making membership obligatory. Melun also favoured excluding consumer cooperatives from the advantages given mutual societies.
[126] The *Annales* became the *Revue d'Economie Contemporaine* in 1860 and later was called *La Contemporaine*.

report on social reform of 1860 contains many principles of modern French social legislation: direct management, half by workers and half by *patrons*, and direct contributions from the workplace. The Society also favoured ending the ban on union organization, creating a Chambre Syndicaliste d'Ouvriers to compete with the influential Chambers of Commerce and Agriculture, and legislation to encourage cooperative insurance against unemployment and sickness.[127] The inability of the Catholics to unite around the Third Republic doomed most of these experiments, and even conservative republicans, such as Thiers, found the corporatist element in Catholic social ideas suspect.

Without question, the scholar and leader who most ably defined liberal Catholic social thinking was Fréderic Le Play. His contribution is of particular interest because his view of social harmony as integral to the well organized state continues throughout the social policy debate in France. Social harmony for Catholic liberals was analogous to social solidarity for the left. Many social theories of the French state were generated by ardent Catholics, but perhaps more salient in transmitting ideas to policymaking levels is the fact that so many of them were *polytechniciens*. While German idealists provided inspiration for a better society through state action, and British positivists such as Spencer and Hobhouse provided mechanical models of society, many French social thinkers tried to state explicitly how social reform conformed to their concepts of the state. The ranks of social reform thinkers are filled with graduates from the Ecole Polytechnique and the Ecole des Mines: Philippe Buchez, the leader of the Atelier movement in the Second Republic; Frederick Le Play, advisor to Napoleon III and founder of the Society of Social Economy; Emile Cheysson, the energetic advocate of voluntary insurance (*prévoyance*) at the turn of the century and founding member of the Ligue de Prévoyance; and Paul Guieyesse, the actuary of the Ministry of the Interior whose 1901 report on pensions became a keystone in the following debates.[128]

Like many conservatives in late nineteenth-century France, Le Play admired the stability of British society, but his rationale

---

[127] On the social report of 1860, see Duroselle, pp. 632–40.

[128] The Ecole Polytechnique was by no means staunchly republican, but there was a progressive group in the school. See Terry Shinn, *Savior Scientifique et Pouvoir Social: L'Ecole Polytechnique, 1794–1914*, Paris; Presses de la Fondation Nationale des Sciences Politiques, 1980, pp. 101–31.

for social reform was among the clearest statements of Catholic liberalism.[129] In effect, it was to combine respect for property with the sanctity of the family. To achieve this end, his critique of republican France, meaning the Revolution, was that discontinuing primogeniture dispersed the resources of families, and produced both the moral and material decline of family life. The family serves as the model for the state and for industry, where the bonds of affection and respect of the strong family should be reproduced. The social aims of political and economic life are to extend the harmony and morality of the devout family to the entire society. Because Le Play was an esteemed advisor to Napoleon III his ideas had little chance of being accepted as republican France emerged during the Third Republic. Among his many distinctions, he was President of the Universal Exposition of 1855, which included discussions of social reforms and became the model for the international Congres d'Assistance Publique that continue into the twentieth century. But his impact on social thought in France is more accurately judged from his journal, *Réforme Sociale*, which he founded in 1856 and which continued to publish until 1912. Throughout these years it attracted a wide variety of authors on social reform, not so much because they were Catholic, but because the underlying notion of family solidarity was clearly an important justification for the French welfare state. Nearly half a century later, the republican Monod would pay tribute to Le Play at the annual meetings of the Congrés International d'Assistance Publique et de Bienfaisance Privée. Quoting Le Play's famous maxim, 'No theory justifies abandoning those who suffer,' Monod drew applause from the audience.[130]

Catholic liberalism in the Second Empire was naturally an anathema to the republicans who took control of the Third Republic. Once the radical republicans were ascendant in the Bloc de

[129] The full statement is found in M. F. Le Play, *La Réforme sociale en France*, Paris; Plon, 1846, v. 2, pp. 166–236, the chapter on the family entitled 'Family, the True Social Unit.' True to his faith, Le Play blames the decline of Ireland on British imposition of division of heritages under the law of 1703, while the English maximized the beneficial effects of their exploitation by preserving primogeniture, p. 119.

[130] See Monod's speech, *'L'Assistance publique en France en 1900,'* *Recueil des Travaux du Congrès International d'Assistance Publique et de Bienfaisance Privée*, Paris; Secrétariat Générale du Congrès, 1900, p. 18. The Congress itself was an offspring of the social reform sections organized by Le Play for Paris expositions of the 1860s and met with some regularity from about 1890 to 1910.

Gauches, the religious basis for social reform came close to treason. When conservative republicans, many of them good Catholics, used the example of the Petites Soeurs de Pauvres, a women's order devoted to social works, as a defence for voluntary agencies in the debates of 1903, they were derided by the radicals and the socialists.[131] The importance of the Catholic liberals, unlike the new liberals in Britain, is how much their concept of social harmony and social peace as the aim of welfare survived despite the bitter religious feelings among the republican majority. The radicals and socialists wanted a wholly secular foundation for the welfare state, but the sanctity of the family and the protection of children were accepted. Most important, the notion that the state had a social obligation united republicans, liberals and socialists, something that British politics rejected.

Although the republican view of social injustice and social protection bears many similarities to the voluntarist approach to the state and its services found in other countries, the rapid transformation of the republicans over the life of the Third Republic propelled them toward acceptance of the welfare state. But several circumstances unique to French politics delayed their full commitment. There was, first, the political instability of the Third Republic itself which exacerbated their relations with socially-minded Catholics and eventually drove them to the severe anti-clericalism of the Combes government. The bankruptcy of French liberalism as a guide to social policy appears most strongly in the late 1890s as the republicans tried to renew their political appeal. For moderate republicans, such as Waldeck-Rousseau, the Church was objectionable as a rival power to the state and the Dreyfus affair a scandal because of the abuse of the law and the judicial procedures. The moderates were prepared to make substantial social concessions, most notably the 1884 law recognizing labour unions.

Waldeck-Rousseau is a key figure in tracing the breakdown of traditional French liberalism in the shift of power from the moderate republicans of the 1880s to the radical republicans of the Bloc des Gauches. A devoted Catholic from Brittany, his political

---

[131] *Journal Officiel, Débats Parlementaires*, 8e legislature, session ordinaire de 1903, séance de vendredi 29 mai, p. 1788. The derision was 'small sisters of the rich' beause many sisters in the order were the daughters of wealthy Catholic families. Membership in the Petites Soeurs doubled during the Second Empire, and was particularly visible to the anticlerical republicans.

career and his ideas reveal how the early republicans saw the state and society as inextricably interlocked, and, unlike the British, consciously used social legislation to make this relationship stable and harmonious. As Minister of Interior in 1881, he worked to bring government into contact with the nascent unions, still virtually untouched by Marxism, while still holding to the liberal tenet that such relationships must be voluntary and contractual.[132] Like many leading radicals, he felt the socialists were no threat because they were 'unable to leave the domain of abstract metaphysics,'[133] but he agreed that a fundamental redirection of the state was needed. Nevertheless, he brought the Socialists into government under his Presidency of the Council in 1899 and encouraged Millerand to increase contacts with unions, to organize regional Labour councils and to devise an effective arbitration system.[134] Even the more traditional liberals of the Third Republic accepted the state as the initiator of social reform although they could not accept the ardent laicism of Combes and the virulent attack on the Church in 1904. Despite the zealous attack on the Church,[135] it provided a bridge between moderate and advanced liberal ideas that never clearly emerged in British politics.

Second, liberalism stagnated because anticlericalism reinforced radical republican dependence on the peasants and rural society, the groups least willing to accept the costs of expanded social protection and least sensitive to growing problems of urban workers. The most controversial public debate about national intervention in social problems over the 1890s was not about social insurance, but about rural fire insurance. Private companies charged farmers high rates and Léon Bourgeois gained his progressive reputation from his attack on fire insurance monopolies in 1894. The struggle between private and public social insurance that continued through the 1920s was fully rehearsed in the fight

[132] Pierre Sorlin, *Waldeck-Rousseau*, Paris; Colin, 1966, pp. 258–69.
[133] Sorlin, p. 376.
[134] Sorlin, p. 472–80. For a more detailed account of Millerand's policies see J. Stone, *In Search of Social Peace* . . ., pp. 123–59.
[135] There is little doubt that the extreme measures originated with the bitter hostility of the Freemasons toward Catholicism. The Léon Bourgeois government of 1895, for example, included 8 Masons in a cabinet of 10. Mesureur, the leader of the Grand Lodge of the Masons, was prominent in founding the Radical Party in 1901. With a membership of only 32,000 at the turn of the century, Masons dominated high office throughout the Third Republic. See Headings, *French Free Masonry* . . ., pp. 71–86.

over state-supported mutual societies to insure farmers in the
1890s.[136] The radicals played on the theme of social solidarity,
most importantly Léon Bourgeois, who for rhetorical purposes saw
the relation of social equality to republican ideas. Indeed, the
essential fiscal instrument for expanding welfare, the income tax,
was accepted in 1895, fifteen years before Lloyd George's budgetary adventures in Britain. Over the 1890s there were two major
studies undertaken by radical leaders, one on relations between
employers and employees by Felix Faure, and an elaborate inquiry
into the costs of social insurance by Guiyesse. Within the Ministry
of Commerce, the Office du Travail was expanded and a Direction
of Social Insurance created. Ten propositions for invalidity, old age
and retirement insurance came before the Chamber of Deputies.[137]

Third, many liberal reformers were rigidly bound to constitutional restrictions on collective action. The constitutional
reconciliation of individual and collective action plagued French
government throughout the nineteenth century, and made it difficult to define and organize new programmes. Though many
republicans wanted to see Revolutionary ideas of equality manifested, they were susceptible to the historic problem that all com-
binations outside the rubric of the state were a threat to democracy.
This was, of course, one of the primary objections to privileges
enjoyed by the Catholic Church. The *loi le Chapelier* lived on in
the fierce controversies over fashioning a law on associations.
Compromises had been devised for business and agriculture by
erecting the Chambers of Commerce and Agriculture as partially
national agencies. The principle had been further breached by
Napoleon III in his law on mutual insurance societies of 1850.
To conduct their war against the Church, the radical republicans
proposed a new law on associations in 1889, which eventually
emerged as the 1901 law on associations, creating *établissements
publics* or agencies able to share the legal and moral authority of
the state.[138] The political aim was to permit the state to compel

[136] For details, see Louis Schnoll, 'Le monopole des assurances,' *Revue de Prévoyance
et de la Mutalitié*, November 1911. There were two important books, one in favour
by Dr Charles Levassort, *Le Monopole des assurances*, Paris; Marchal and Billard,
1910; and against by William Lambert, *Le Monopole des assurances*, Berger
Levrault, 1910.

[137] Georges Hamon, *Histoire Générale de l'Assurance en France et à l'étranger*, Paris;
Journal d'Assurance Moderne, 1896, p. 305.

[138] See Conseil d'Etat, *La Réforme des établissements publics*, Paris; Documentation
Francaise, 1971. The same dilemma retarded the growth of municipal socialism.

the registration of secondary schools under rules that would deny
Catholic, and particularly Jesuit, schools a legal existence. But
having constructed a legal solution to associational activity, little
was done to extend the rationale to social and economic activities.

The liberal economists were able to enter directly into the policy
process. Foremost among them was Paul Leroy-Beaulieu, a Deputy
and member of the Institut de France. In the development of ideas
about social reform, his importance is the remarkable success that
his very orthodox classical liberal economcis could have so late in
the development of French democracy. To him the salary was a
'most natural and useful contract.' The steady growth of workers'
purchasing power over the nineteenth century made its value
self-evident.[139] He was not opposed to increased leisure, worker
involvement in factory management or wage supplements for specific needs, but the wage agreement took on a sacrosanct quality
excluding all forms of social insurance. His convictions seemed to
have no limits: public utilities were 'a menace to public liberty'
and public pensions a form of 'pillage'. Though he did not deny
that some services might be more cheaply provided by the state,
such intrusions were dangerous and to be kept to the very
minimum. Indeed, he comes close to abandoning his republican
beliefs in his condemnation of the 'noise and uproar and confusion'
of elections, and the ever present threat of 'the momentary infatu-
ation of the majority of the nation.'[140]

His pronouncements would be less amazing were they not so
blatantly reactionary. As the debate on social insurance unfolded
in the 1890s, he could proclaim 'By its nature obligatory insurance
in many areas would weaken the drive (*grand moteur*) of civilization,
that is, the individual effort, that frees man.'[141] In fact, the French
economy was already intermingled with the state. Unlike Britain,
every effort to enhance social protection received state support and
privileges, in particular the mutual societies. Voluntary insurance
had been encouraged by the government since the Restoration,
but it was during the Second Empire that they made extraordinary
growth. In 1852 there were 2,438 societies with about a quarter
of a million members, and in 1872 there were 5,793 societies with

[139] Paul Leroy-Beaulieu, *Essai sur la répartition des richesses et sur la tendance à une
moindre inégalité des conditions*, Paris; Guillaumin, 1881.
[140] Paul Leroy-Beaulieu, *The Modern State in Relation to Society and the Individual*,
London; Swan Sonnenschein, 1891, pp. 104–5.
[141] Quoted in Hamon, *Histoire Générale de l'Assurance . . .*, p. 143.

800,000 members. By 1892, they had multiplied to 9,600 with 1.5 million members, and by 1902 to 13,677 societies with 2 million members.[142] The moderate republicans reinforced the law on mutual societies in 1898, and created a Conseil Supérieur des Sociétés de Securité Mutuelle. For the liberal economists the societies were the alternative to social insurance, and they were active in the Ligue Nationale de Prévoyance et de la Mutualité in order to propogate their views. The League attracted a number of leading radicals, Jules Siegfried and Georges Berger, and for many years Waldeck-Rousseau presided over its legal committee. Much as in the case of the British Friendly Societies in 1911, the mutual societies were able to impose compromises on the 1910 and 1928 laws for social insurance.[143]

The liberal economists were naturally unopposed to voluntary savings, but this too relied on the state in France. Napoloen III encouraged the growth of the Caisse d'Epargne or popular savings, and these efforts were continued by the republicans. When another law reinforced popular savings, in 1881, the Caisse had 541 regional and 2,000 local offices throughout France with deposits of over 1.5 billion francs. The system prospered in the Third Republic and by 1904 there were 12 million accounts with 4 billion francs in deposits. Popular savings were by no means a purely middle class precaution. Levasseur calculated that a third of the deposits were held by miners and a quarter by other workers.[144] The offices were concentrated in the more industrial regions of the Seine, Rhone and Nord. Thus, the appeal of the liberal economists did not necessarily fall on deaf ears or even only bourgeois ears. They had considerable evidence to buttress their

---

[142] These figures are taken from Eugéne Rochetin, *Les assurances ouvrières mutualités contre la maladie, l'incendie et le chômage*, Paris; Guillaumin, 1896, p. 73. Slightly different figures and an account of the new legislation appeared in Levassuer, *Questions ouvrières* . . ., pp. 790–6.

[143] The important difference is that the Friendly Societies realized that they were not able to provide full benefits and, while extracting concessions from Lloyd George, knew that state insurance was essential. In both cases the compromise was similar, enabling the cooperative insurance groups to continue to act as agents for the state.

[144] Levasseur, pp. 770–85. The contrast to Britain depends on the different institutional emphasis of the banking system. British banks remained heavily oriented to commercial and industrial financing and took less interest in popular savings, that were more often deposited as postal savings.

view that social protection could be achieved without disturbing the labour market.

Leroy-Beaulieu's protégé on social reform was Emile Cheysson, who was active in the Ligue de Prévoyance and secretary to the Political Economy Society, founded by Leroy-Beaulieu to promote liberal economics. Cheysson wrote widely during the social debates of the 1890s and as Director of the Musée Social was often consulted by parliamentary commissions studying social problems.[145] Like other liberals he realized that strong republican government was a threat to sound fiscal insurance principles. He wrote, 'By the law of voting these humble, once disinherited, persons have suddenly become masters and will not forget it.'[146] In some ways he displays a keener sense of the political limits of economics than do the British new liberals, for he realized that parliament would not be able to resist passing more social legislation and he saw that imperialism would only substantiate more claims to social protection. He was aware of society's 'social debt' to workers and he was not opposed to unions, but, like most liberals, he resisted 'imposing virtue by decree' by which he meant obligatory social insurance. But his disapproval of 'subsidized liberty' is less dogmatic than in the case of the turn of the century British social reformers because the French were not facing a problem of urban poverty of similar dimensions, nor were they labouring under the onerous social assumption of the Poor Laws. All this made the liberal plea for self-supporting and voluntary insurance more feasible. But, as happened in Britain openly and the United States quietly, liberal economic principles for social insurance were quickly abandoned once laws were passed. It is not the lack of social conscience or social awareness that doomed the liberals as a political force, but the inadequacy of their economic principles.

Like Britain and Germany, in the turbulent international situation between the wars France had little time to develop social

---

[145] Emile Cheysson, *L'Assistance des ouvriers contre les accidents*, Paris; Guillaumin, 1888; and *L'Assurance rurale et le regroupement des communes*, Paris; Guillaumin, 1886. On his services to parliament, see E. d'Eichtal and C. Brunot, *La Solidarité nationale* . . ., Paris; Picard, 1903, pp. 128–38; and Clark, *Prophets and Patrons*, pp. 109–11. On the Musée Social, see J. Stone, *The Search for Social Peace* ..., p. 52 and 61; and Sanford Elwitt, 'Social Reform and Social Order in Late-19th-Century France,' *French Historical Studies*. **11**, spring 1980, pp. 431–51.
[146] This and the following quotes are taken from Emile Cheysson, *L'Evolution des idées et des systèmes de retraite*, Paris; Society of Political Economy, 1902.

policies, and compared to these two countries much less need. But the political factors were also important. As the French Radicals and Radical Socialists drifted toward the right, the reservations of Catholic liberals and secular liberals among the republicans seem to have slowly merged. The clearest spokesman was Edmond Villey whose work pays tribute to Le Play, and whose ideas stress moral education.[147] His work is more important in the setting of this study as evidence of how liberal thinking in France, as in Britain, seemed to mark time for twenty years. Like most of middle class France, Villey disapproved of the general strike, the income tax and social insurance. As with most of the liberal thinkers, what is lacking are positive proposals on how to solve growing social problems. The liberals had very clear economic principles, but they had no way to link them to political issues.

Though it does not directly enter into the politics of social reform, it should be added that the interwar period saw the blossoming of French economics, which in many respects marks the final schism between liberal-inspired social thinking and the politics of social policy. Two figures loom above the others, Clément Colson, who is regarded as the founder of micro-economics in France, and Jacques Rueff, who lived on as the conservative economic adviser to French governments until the Fifth Republic.[148] As leaders in establishing modern economics in France, they were active in the resistance to the 1928 social insurance law, largely because they regarded unemployment insurance as economically impossible. Citing the disastrous effects of British unemployment policies of the 1920s, Colson led the fight to show that unemployment is an uninsurable risk and argued that shifting the costs to wealthier workers and *patrons* 'is an inequity, and encouragement to carelessness and misconduct, and a cause of general ruin.'[149] Rueff echoed the arguments but for monetary reasons.[150] As we shall discuss further in Chapter 4, the

---

[147] See Edmond Villey, *Les Périls de la démocratcie française*, Paris; Plon, 1910, and *Le Progrès social*, Paris; Presses Universitaires de France, 1923.

[148] Rueff was de Gaulle's personal economic adviser. See Jacques Rueff, *Combats pour l'ordre financier*, Paris; Plon, 1972.

[149] Clement Colson, 'L'Assurance contre le chômage,' *Revue Politique et Parlementaire*, **127**, 1926, pp.5–18.

[150] Jacques Rueff, 'Les Conditions du salut financier,' *Revue Politique et Parlementaire*, **123**, 1925, pp. 5–11.

fight over unemployment insurance became the Waterloo of liberal economics.

The more direct link between ideas and social policy in France is largely due to the critical role of the Ecole Normale Supérieure. The late development of a modern civil service in Britain, its domination by the privileged elite that still controlled Oxford and Cambridge, and the ease of directly placing the new crop of socially aware officials in top jobs relieved them from fully developing their ideas. The Oxbridge tradition gave the privileged access to power and a rationale for change that required little justification by means of competitive politics or parliamentary deliberation. Reconciling the new liberalism with party platforms, packaging it to make new electoral appeals and, perhaps most important, public engagement in major political disputes could be neatly circumvented in the still privileged world of British policymaking. This was not the case in France. The Ecole Normale was almost a microcosm of the struggle for democracy. Numerous 'normaliens' had been active in the Second Republic and many went into temporary retirement rather than take the oath of loyalty to Napoleon III.[151] Unlike the more aristocratic Ecole Polytechnique, the Ecole Normale prided itself on discovering the best of French brains. Through school inspectors and lycée professors trained at the Ecole, it made no secret that it preferred dedicated students of modest origins.[152] Though all of its students were by no means political activists, it provided an institutionalized centre for rethinking the political and social assumptions of French democracy.[153]

[151] On the Ecole Normale prior to 1870, see Robert J. Smith, *The 'Ecole Normale Supérieure and the Third Republic* . . ., pp. 5–18. For a glimpse of how the Directors dealt with political turbulence, see the excerpts from their correspondence with the Ministry of Education in C. Bouglé, ed., *L'Ecole Normale Supérieure: D'où elle vient – où elle va*, Paris; Librairie Hachette, 1934, pp. 1–44.

[152] Unmistakable evidence has been assembled by Robert J. Smith, *The 'Ecole Normale Supérieure and the Third Republic* . . ., pp. 30–55. In this respect, the Ecole Normale differed substantially from the Ecole Polytechnique which continued to recruit most of its students from conservative, upper–middle class, Catholic families. See T. Shinn, *Savoir Scientifique et Pouvoir Social* . . . , pp. 65–99.

[153] The main competitor for political power was the Ecole Libre des Sciences Politiques where many politically-inclined normaliens took courses. The Ecole Libre seems to fill a fascinating intermediary place between the more conservative Ecole Politechnique and the more progressive Ecole Normale. See Pierre Rain, *L'Ecole Libre des Sciences Politiques, 1871–1945*, Paris; Fondation Nationale des Sciences Politiques, 1963.

Unlike the individually-sponsored and discreetly privileged products of Jowett's Balliol, the normaliens were intimately involved in reshaping French political thinking, in translating new ideas into workable education programmes and in providing a new philosophical justification for democracy. Distinguished professors from the Ecole such as Emile Boutroux and Henri Bergson became the conduit for German idealism into French philosophy. Amidst the shifting sands of the early Third Republic an intellectual current developed that stressed 'individual freedom, action and will.'[154] Among the translators of political idealism into political action, perhaps the most successful was Lucien Herr.[155] Librarian of the Ecole Normale for nearly forty years (1888–1926), he pressed bright young students such as Jean Jaurès and Charles Péguy to learn German philosophy and to develop the peculiar brand of French socialism that is influential to the present day. A key figure in organizing the Ligue de Droits de l'Homme to defend Dreyfus, Herr helped construct the vision of republican socialism that Jaurés, whom Herr recruited into the Socialist Party, espoused throughout his career. From the prolonged struggle of ideas fostered in the Ecole grew a new perspective of the nature of the French state whose traces can be found throughout the course of French social legislation.

The intellectual impact of the Ecole Normale can be traced along various lines. First, it was the *grand école* responsible for school inspection and staffing the higher levels of secondary education. Contrary to Crozier's less favourable view of the grip of the elite *grands corps* on French society and politics, the influence of the Ecole Normale was transmitted throughout the educational system to defend more democratic forms of education and to help redefine

---

[154] Smith, p. 64.
[155] There were two biographies of Herr written by his friends, Charles Andler, *Vie de Lucien Herr (1864–1928)*, Paris; Reider, 1931, and Paul Dupuy, *Lucien Herr, 1863–1926*, Paris; 1927. A more critical account was later written by another friend who became disillusioned with socialism, Hubert Bourgin, *De Jaurès à Léon Blum: l'Ecole Normale et la politique*, Paris; Fayard 1938 (Reprinted by Gordon and Breach, 1970). The best account of his influence over the development of socialism is Daniel Lindenberg and Pierre-André Meyer, *Lucien Herr: Le Socialisme et son destin*, Paris; Calmann-Lévy, 1977. For a somewhat Marxist account see Jean Francois Sisrinelli, 'The Ecole Normale Supérieure and Elite Formation and Selection in the Third Republic,' in J. Howarth and P. Cerny, eds, *Elites in France*, pp. 66–77.

French democracy itself. In the Ministry of Education two normaliens, Jules Ferry, who had been banned from teaching under
the Second Empire, and Jules Simon set out to modernize French
education. The permanency of the high officials linked to the
school was of great help. Georges Perrot, the Ecole Director from
1883 to 1903 had close links to the moderate republican reformers.
Louis Liard, architect of the modernized Sorbonne for thirty years,
came from the Ecole and helped construct strong links between
the two institutions. Brilliant pupils of the Ecole were active in
politics, among them Jaurès, who never broke his close association
with the Ecole, as well as Leon Blum, Simone Weil, Edouard
Herriot and Raymond Aron.[156] Through the network of key
officials, leading socialists and political figures, the Ecole Normale
provided a 'new republican nobility.'[157]

Second, the Ecole provided an intellectual thrust to French
socialism that has yet to be dissipated despite the eclipse of the
French Socialists through most of the Fourth Republic. Herr and
his pupils believed that unlike Germany where socialism was
imposed from above by a disciplined party, France could develop
an 'integral socialism' blending the best of French revolutionary
and democratic history.[158] Distrustful of the vulgar Marxism
emanating from German socialists and advanced in France by the
socialist labour leader, Guesde, and less consistently by Vaillant,
the new generation of French socialists wanted to build on the
tradition of Proudhon and Brousse to free workers of both parliamentary and Jacobin constraints.[159] Though he later became
an ardent Catholic and strongly nationalistic, Péguy, whom Herr
regarded as his most brilliant pupil, most fully developed the idea
that an activist, worker-led socialism could be reconciled with
French democracy. Though often misinterpreted as no more than

[156] See Smith, pp. 104–31.
[157] See Smith, p. 103.
[158] The phrase comes from Lichtheim, *Marxism in Modern France*, New York;
Columbia University Press, 1966, pp. 30–3, whose book is probably the best
account of how French socialist theory developed at this time. On the conflict
with the revolutionary tradition, see Jolyon Howorth, *Edouard Vaillant: La creation
de l'unité socialiste en France*, Paris; Syros, pp. 129–91.
[159] See Lindenberg and Meyer, pp. 71–2. Jaurès shared Herr's distrust of Germany as recorded by George Lefranc, *Jaurès et le socialisme des intellectuels*, Paris;
Aubier-Montaigne, 1968, p. 46. On Brousse's influence over French socialism,
see Carl Landauer, 'The Origin of Social Reformism in France,' *International
Review of Social History*, **12**, 1961, pp. 81–107.

another version of revolutionary Marxism, Sorel's syndicalism was another effort to link political action among workers to the formulation of a new form of humanistic socialism. The struggle to define socialism in French terms may account for inability of positivist thinking to dominate French socialism, an intellectual failing of British socialism that helps explain the pallid version of Marxism that developed in Britain.[160]

The critical link between the intellectual ferment of the *Ecole* and the intense socialist debates bearing on social policy was Jean Jaurès. Like other socialists favouring a parliamentary strategy, Jaurès came to the Party after some years as an independent, loosely aligned with the radical socialists. Elected to the Chamber of Deputies in 1885 at only 26 years of age, Jaurès was part of an amorphous group of 'opportunists' on the left who had no firm party allegiance. He was disillusioned by the radical policies of the 1880s which he considered reckless, vague and, above all, uncertain about the social goals for a republican regeneration of France. The fiery republicanism of Gambetta had cooled because the moderate radicals, like Liberal politicians in Britain, were unable to construct a positive programme from their mixture of anticlericalism and imperialism. Gambetta himself proclaimed in the 1880s 'there is no social solution because there is no social question,' and Ferry accepted the sanctity of private property. Jaurès later wrote, 'when I entered politics in 1885, I knew only two things – the Republic on one side, and the royalist-clerical reaction on the other'. His first parliamentary speech was on increased local control of schools, but he soon took a leading role in the debates over accident compensation for miners and introduced one of the first pension bills.

Both his confidence in education and his devotion to the Republic suggest the brand of 'republican socialism'[161] that Jaurès hoped to cultivate. Similar to Edmond Maire and the CFDT of the Fifth Republic, Jaurès suspected orthodox Marxism because of its

---

[160] Noel Annan, *The Curious Strength of Positivism in English Political Thought*, London; Oxford University Press (L. T. Hobhouse Memorial Lecture, No. 28), 1959.

[161] The phrase comes from Lindenberg and Meyer, *Lucien Herr . . .*, p. 161. On the parliamentary climate during Jaurès' early years in the Chamber see Harvey Goldbert, *The Life of Jean Jaurès*, Madison; University of Wisconsin Press, 1962, pp. 34–9, from which the material in this paragraph comes. See also Max Gallo, *Le Grand Jaurès*, Paris; Laffont, 1985.

narrow view of how workers might progress. Under Lucien Herr
at the Ecole his thesis was a blend of idealism and materialism,
attempting to reconcile Marx and morality. But as Goldberg
notes,[162] he was always a normalien or humanist for he was
equally concerned with Voltaire, Rousseau and Condorcet, writers
who saw the diffusion of education as the way to achieve full
development of human capacities, and, in this way, the foundation
of vigorous democracy. Jaurès never accepted historical determinism, which helps explain why within parliament he was able
to cooperate with Vaillant, whose revolutionary Marxism yielded
to the necessity of using every possible parliamentary device to
inform and to mobilize workers. It also helps explain why Jaurès
could never commit himself unreservedly to the militant Marxism
of Guesde whose 'worker Jacobinism' reduced workers to instruments of a class struggle. Jaurès believed that only 'the intellectual
equality of all will make social equality tenable,'[163] and that
democracy had a vital part to play in liberating workers.

The comparison between the intellectual struggle of the French
socialists and the pragmatic socialism of the nascent Labour Party
in Britain exposes the very different climate of ideas at the time.
Both parties worked with the liberal parties of the period, but the
French Socialists played a more important role. There were some
links between the two parties. Herr sent his close friend, Charles
Andler, to Britain to discuss the future of British socialism
with Annie Besant, one of the Fabian founders, Hyndman and
Burns.[164] But the political context for the development of socialist
influence was completely different in the two countries. Despite
the lukewarm Marxism of the British socialists, they had little
influence over social policy in Edwardian Britain. Given the institutional limits on minor parties in Britain, there is no reason to
think that even a more militantly Marxist Labour Party would
have been more influential in party and parliamentary politics

---

[162] Goldberg, The Life of Jean Jaurès, p. 85. On Jaurès' thesis, see Goldberg, pp.
77–93. Jaurès' brilliant thesis was ranked just beneath that of his classmate,
Henri Bergson. Durkheim was in the Ecole class behind Jaurès.
[163] Goldberg, p. 86. The phrase 'worker Jacobinism' is from Daniel Lindenberg,
Le Marxisme introuvable, Paris; Calmann-Levy, 1975, p. 105.
[164] Charles Andler was Herr's closest friend, an avid student of Nietzsche, and
took the first French aggregation in German studies. From 1894 he was maitre
de conferences at the Ecole. See Lindenberg and Meyer, p. 135. Andler's career is
an interesting demonstration of how socialist intellectuals drifted into many nooks
of French life, see Lefranc, Jaurès et le socialisme ..., pp. 107–18.

in Westminster which provided neither the opportunity nor the incentive to question the nature of British government. Although tactics were a major cause of internal schisms and personal bitterness among French socialists, the vital political problems of the Republic gave them a vehicle for their ideas and, in turn, put them in close association with the transformation of the French state under the radical republicans.

The paradoxical result was that even though the French socialists were excluded from power for most of the inter-war period, their contributions to the debate over social policy from roughly 1890 to 1910 became a major contribution to the French welfare state. The British Labour Party did not have a decisive voice in either the social legislation of 1911 or in the disconnected efforts to respond to major social questions in the inter-war period. Numerous reasons can be produced for the relative success of the French socialists but among such reasons their skill in extracting concessions from the more cumbersome policy process and in maximizing their influence as partners in radical socialist governments looms large. Despite internal party wrangling and ideological conflict they were consummate politicians. Much of the credit goes to Jean Jaurès who managed to make the socialist parliamentary group effective and became the critical translator between socialist thinking, the republican state, and the policy process. Behind him stood Herr, Andler and Gabriel Monod, a leading radical socialist professor at the Ecole. Once the Dreyfus affair exploded, Lévy-Bruhl, professor at the exclusive Lycée Louis le Grand and an Ecole graduate, and Péguy joined them. The result was that the early debates on social reform in France were directly reinforced by sophisticated philosophical minds, for whom the future of the French state and Dreyfus affair were interlocked.

The juxtaposition of the Dreyfus scandal and social legislation gave Jaurès a political opportunity to press for reform while defending the Republic. He used his chance with extraordinary political skill. Jaurès' conversion to socialism in 1892 was followed the next year by the socialist electoral victory of 1893, giving them 50 seats in the Chamber. Rumours of the Dreyfus scandal were then common, but Jaurès was too busy defending socialists in court to give great attention to Dreyfus.[165] The orthodox Marxist, Guesde,

---

[165] Lindenberg and Meyer, p. 142; when Herr asked Blum what were his views on Dreyfus, he did not know who Dreyfus was.

initially viewed the Dreyfus affair, as he did the Boulanger threat, as a bourgeois quarrel which should not be allowed to deflect the organization of the workers.[166] It was Herr who mobilized his students and colleagues of the Ecole over 1897, and finally, five days after Zola's explosive charge, *J'accuse*, the leading socialists, Guesde, Jaurès, Millerand and Viviani, signed a manifesto on behalf of Dreyfus. The Dreyfus affair set the stage for a new attempt at socialist unity, and gave additional influence to Jaurès' Parti Socialiste Francais (PSF), even though his group was reduced to 38 deputies in the 1898 elections, and to 36 in the 1902 elections.

As in Britain in 1906, the return to power of the French radicals in 1895 under Léon Bourgeois offered the socialists new parliamentary opportunities and revived hopes for social legislation. After the bitter debate on income tax in 1896, which passed the Chamber with socialist support only to be blocked in the Senate, the government fell. After the interregnum of the Méline government, another opportunity arose with the Waldeck-Rousseau government of 1899. Although Guesde persuaded the 1899 Socialist Congress to vote that the class struggle does not permit supporting a bourgeois government, Jaurès defended the socialist 'ministerialists' who felt that the Dreyfus scandal demanded national unity and who saw chances of obtaining basic social reforms. The progress of the left in 1902 and 1906 offered new possibilities, but by then the socialists were beginning to withdraw even though Jaurès continued to use the PSF to support social legislation. Under the influence of the German Social Democrats, the Amsterdam Congress of the Second International took an anti-parliamentarian stance, and in 1905 the union of the socialists in the Section Française de l'Internationale Ouvrière (SFIO) forbade official participation in cabinets.[167]

Our immediate concern is that, for practical purposes, internal feuding and the split of international socialists neutralized their influence until the 1940s. Many of the most capable leaders left

---

[166] Lindenberg and Meyer, p. 152; Lefranc, *Le Mouvement Socialiste. . .*, pp. 102–3.

[167] For details on these events, see Goldberg, pp. 253–342. See also the assessment of Lefranc, *Le Mouvement Socialiste*, pp. 134–59, on the links between the PSF and the Masons, who wanted to back Jaurès against the militant Marxists. According to Lindenberg and Meyer, pp. 186–99, Herr and his group were sure that Jaurès would overcome the Guesdists.

the PSF after it was absorbed into the SFIO. Millerand and
Viviani decided to remain with the radicals. Briand became Minister of Education in 1906, and President of the Council in 1908.
Although the socialists had strength in the Chamber of Deputies
in the 1906 and 1910 elections,[168] their refusal to take political
responsibility left the field to the jumble of radical and radical
socialist politicians who held power until 1936. In reflecting on
socialist experience, Blum later wrote that the pre-war internal
bickering destroyed socialist unity after the high hopes of 1899.[169]
But the political debacle is not the only test of socialist progress.
What the French socialists achieved from 1890 to 1910 was in
many ways more lasting and more constructive than what the no
less divided socialists in Britain were able to achieve.

The definition of the French welfare state that took shape around
the turn of the century was not the result of an orderly political
process, but was the product of an unusual convergence of policy
interests. Though constructed amidst political uncertainties, the
consensus is more like the policy devised by the Swedish Social
Democrats in the 1930s than the partisan politics of Britain or
the autocratic politics of Germany. The radical socialists and the
socialists made curious partners. Blum later wrote that socialist
complicity in the intense anticlericalism of the early 1900s diverted
them from their socialist goals.[170] Léon Bourgeois is correctly
regarded as an opportunistic radical, but he may have been unjust-
ly treated by those who have less interest in policymaking. As President of the Council in 1898 he had his Minister of the Interior,
Barthou, request that the Conseil d'Etat make the first serious
study of the constitutional and legal problems of establishing
obligatory insurance. The report became the foundation of the
debate over social insurance for the next thirty years. Bourgeois
and Barthou were convinced that those 'physically unable to work
for the necessities of life' should be cared for by the state.[171]

---

[168] In the 1906 election, 54 Socialists were returned plus 13 independents; and
in 1910, 76 Socialists and 22 independents. Thus, Socialist strength in the
Chamber far exceeded Labour strength in the House of Commons before World
War I.
[169] Lefranc, p. 133, from Blum's *Le Problème de l'unité*, Paris; Librairie Populaire,
1945.
[170] Lindenberg and Meyer, pp. 190–4.
[171] From the tribute to Bourgeois and Barthou in Henri Monod, *L'Assistance
publique en France . . .*, p. 31. See also Lawrence A. Minnich, Jr, *Social Problems*

Barthou wanted communes and labour unions to have the right to organize social security funds, a means of generalizing local commitment to improved social assistance.[172]

The second group of persons who helped make the link between the social ideas of the day and policy were the defected socialists, the 'ministerialists' who drifted away from the socialist movement. They too have had rather a bad press for their infidelity to socialist principles, but their cumulative effect within government has been neglected. Most prominent among these persons was Alexandre Millerand, the socialist who joined the Waldeck-Rousseau government in 1899. Using his position as Minister of Commerce, he enlarged and reorganized the Conseil Supérieur du Travail and tried to spread the notion of labour conciliation throughout the country with subordinate local labour councils. He created the Office Nationale de Statistique et de Placement in 1900, predating similar official efforts to collect reliable information about workers in Britain by roughly a decade.[173] He brought other moderate socialists into the administration, such as André Fontaine and Léon Mirman, who became Director of Public Assistance in 1905. In Chapter 4 we shall have reason to return to the contribution the group made to initiating early industrial relations policies. Compared to Britain the early transformation of reform ideas into policies was a remarkably bipartisan effort.

FALSE STARTS AND PERMANENT DIRECTIONS

In a general sense, all the industrial democracies were moving in the direction of the welfare state by the turn of the century. The early evidence of the ravages of industrial cities, the waste and deterioration of human potential, and the brutalizing effects of unemployment were unmistakable. Mass democracy and the early

and Political Alignments in France 1893–1899: Leon Bourgeois and Solidarity, Ithaca, NY; Cornell University, September 1948, doctoral dissertation.
[172] These policy options were excluded in Britain. Local authorities were distrusted because of the long history of Poor Law problems. Under the 1911 law unions could organize collecting societies, but few did.
[173] Martin Derfler, *Alexandre Millerand: The Socialist Years*, The Hague; Moton, 1977. See also Raoul Persil, *Alexandre Millerand (1859–1943)*, Paris; Société d'Editions Françaises, 1949, pp. 24–34, a not very good biography.

labour organizations set in motion political forces that even the most conservative politicians had to recognize. Resistance to social reform was not so much because liberals were bound to abstract capitalist principles, but because they had difficulty imagining how the state could play a constructive role in solving problems. There was no well articulated 'growth theory' of social justice though it was perhaps implicit in the imperialist response of British reformers following the Boer War disaster.[174] Excessive reliance on interpreting the progress of social reform with predetermined socio-economic models, Marxist or quantitative, distorts the origins of the welfare state. Reading history backwards is no less difficult than reading our future.

In this case, what eludes us is perhaps the most important transition of modern state systems. As suggested in Chapter 1, institutional analysis helps to reveal the continuities of policy-making over long periods of time. An essential part of such an exercise is to see where new ideas were coming from and how new thinkers managed to inject their ideas into policy process. The claim is not that ideas alone determine political and social change. The transformation of new thinking into policy of any kind is a two-step process. In Britain, the Webbs, the new liberals and the conservative radicals all worked within political and institutional constraints. In France, the Catholic liberals of both the right and left, the secular radicals and radical socialists, and the socialists all operated in a particular democratic tradition, one that happened to be under severe threat during much of the period when social reform was under discussion. Even though social need may have been less in France than in Britain at the turn of the century, it is important to see that the concept of a welfare state was well developed, in some respects linking the redefinition of the French state to social change more effectively than did the British. Measuring social reform only by results can be politically misleading. The results in France were meagre until 1945, but the direction was quite clear in 1910.

As we shall examine in more detail in Chapter 3, the critical political question in all these transformations was the social services bureaucracy. As perhaps most dramatically illustrated by

[174] Both the political and social implications are well described in Robert J. Scaly, *The Origins of the Lloyd George Coalition*, and by Bernard Semmel, *Imperialism and Social Reform: English Social Thought 1899–1914*, Cambridge; Harvard University Press, 1960.

the charity movements in Britain and America.[175] By 1900 the liberal voluntarist solution had been thoroughly tested and found wanting. Similarly in France, the local *bureaux de bienfaisance*, which were closely linked to local charity and the Church, were under attack. The political issue in extending the formidable French bureaucracy to wider social needs was building the *bureaux d'assistance publique*, the keystone to Henri Monod's plans. The critical political difference is, of course, that in France both agencies were part of the state structure so that the conversion of ideas into policies was a less abrupt change in the organization of the state than was the construction of an entirely new central administrative machinery to replace the Poor Laws. From a policy perspective, constructing the British welfare state was a two-step process: the national government had to establish its claim, and then organize itself. This may seem paradoxical given the history of Poor Laws, but in a policy sense the central feature of late Victorian social reform was universal rejection of the Poor Law system. There could be no better evidence than the ease with which the report of the Royal Commission on the Poor Laws was cast aside. Somehow, for policy purposes a century of experience was worthless.

France may be condemned to having strong policymakers and a weak parliamentary system, but the notable characteristic of the social debate at the turn of the century was that many basic characteristics of the French welfare state as finally accomplished in 1945 were remarkably well defined. Leaving aside of course the ultraconservatives, the agreement extends across changes in government and embraces the right and the left. There is first the theme of social solidarity, that is, that the state is responsible for maintaining a minimum living standard for all those who cannot work. Mirman constantly reiterated the social obligation of the state in the debates on insurance for the sick, disabled and aged from 1901 to 1903. At his insistence, and supported by the radicals and socialists, article one of the proposed law was changed from 'All French have the right to assistance' to 'All French have the right to social solidarity instituted in the form of obligatory assistance under this law.'[176] To the 'wild applause' of the Chamber,

---

[175] On the early nineteenth-century charity in America, see Blanche D. Coll, 'Public Assistance in the United States: Colonial Times to 1860,' in E. W. Martin, ed., *Comparative Development in Social Welfare*, London; Allen and Unwin, 1972, pp. 128–58.

[176] *Journal Officiel, Débats parlementaires*, session ordinaire du 1903, séance de vendredi 29 mai, p. 1783.

Monod outlined how the richer departments and communes have an obligation to support those unable to organize local insurance funds.[177] The law was passed by 552 to 3, but blocked in the Senate.

That social solidarity was more than political rhetoric is borne out by the repeated claim that social insurance required redistribution among local areas and among social classes. In 1903 the Mirman study showed that the state would contribute about 100 million francs, though estimates varied widely and were used to help delay the bill. In the 1930 debate on social insurance, the principle of *fonds de majoration et de solidarité* was again approved.[178] While the Ministry of Finance bridled at the expected cost, it was expected that the state would contribute through general taxation to support those who could not contribute. Even the more orthodox Dr Chaveau, who led the Senate resistance to the 1928 proposal, admitted that social protection was for the family, not the individual, and accepted higher charges for single, high-paid contributors.[179] When France finally achieved a national social insurance plan in 1945, the *fond de solidarité nationale* remained a charge against all contributors so the state could provide benefits for those without incomes. The principle of self-financing social insurance was never popular in France, while every effort was made to avoid Treasury responsibility in the British 1911 law and the principle of individual self-financing was maintained as late as the Beveridge national insurance scheme.

Third, from the earliest debates there is a continuity in thinking about how to organize social insurance. In the 1860s the Comte de Melun favoured localized insurance funds managed equally by workers and *patrons*. As we have seen, in the 1903 debate Vaillant wanted worker majorities on local insurance agencies though he did not get his way, and Aynard, the spokesman for the right, pointed out the dangers of having insurance wholly in the hands of state administrators.[180] The laws of 1928 and 1930 were based on mutual insurance plans to be managed by all the contributors, and the 1945 laws finally put in practice the concept of national

[177] *Journal Officiel*, 1903, p. 1843.
[178] *Journal Officiel, Rapport Anotelli*, 1930, pp. 526–9.
[179] Dr C. Chaveau, *La loi sur les assurances sociales à la portée de tous*, Paris; Librairie Générale de Droit et de Jurisprudence, 1930, pp. 63–83.
[180] *Journal Officiel, Débats parlemenatires*, Chambre de Députés, séance du 12 juillet 1905, p. 2884.

social insurance managed by tripartite committees of contributors, both workers and *patrons*, and government officials. Thus, in three important respects the shape of the welfare state was foreshadowed: state and society had a common concern expressed in the theme of social solidarity; the state had an obligation to protect everyone against social risks; and the contributors as citizens had a right to manage their own contributions.

In short, there was a convergence of ideas and policy proposals in France from the turn of the century, but it took the political system nearly half a century to make them into reality. While this is surely a negative comment on French politics, it is not necessarily a negative critique of French policymaking. That France could anticipate the future without having the political means to enact reforms is more to be lamented than praised. But it also suggests that the concept of the state, being more clearly articulated in France than in most democracies, induced political thinkers and social reformers to organize their ideas. One could not think about the welfare state without also thinking about the state. Almost the reverse was the case in Britain. While it does not impugn the motives or the results of the early advance of the welfare state in Britain, British policymakers paid surprisingly little attention to the array of social reformers and social policy advocates that appeared on all sides in late Victorian Britain.

There were many reasons why the British had difficulty getting their ideas into focus, but one reason must surely be that neither the elusive British constitution nor the discipline of parliamentary and cabinet governance placed a premium on such qualities. One cannot argue that a generation that read the flood of proposals from Sidney and Beatrice Webb, Bernard Shaw, J. A. Hobson, Graham Wallas, J. L. Hammond, C. F. G. Masterman and Joseph Chamberlain lacked ideas. At best, what Britain devised was a 'stark collectivism'[181] which benefited little from the new liberal critiques and which was virtually untouched by socialist thinking. At the same time, the readiness of Parliament to act after 1906 does not allow us to say that political will was weak. The problem is more one of how the British political system is geared to the conversion of ideas into proposals. The simple answer to this question is that the welfare state conversion takes place within the administrative system. More than ever in the past, the welfare

[181] Marquand, *MacDonald*, p. 88.

state relies on paid officials to simplify social and other policy problems so that political solutions can be found, and on their ability to anticipate and to remedy the weaknesses of experimental legislation. How the administration served as a bridge or a barrier in the conversion of ideas into policy is the subject of the next chapter.

3

Organizing Welfare

The political and administrative changes in the interwar period are essential to understanding how welfare states were reconstructed in 1945. With varying degrees of success and certainty, the European states made irreversible steps toward accepting social responsibilities from 1890 to 1914, and in doing so compromised the classical liberal values that buttressed the early development of democratic government. There followed the confused and confusing interwar period, ending with the surge of new social legislation in France and the United States in the 1930s, the collapse of German democracy and the long struggle against unemployment in Britain. In the midst of the unparalleled realignment of world power and search for an enduring peace, social policy took on a new significance. Indeed, it is tempting to argue that the interwar years are the most crucial in the development of the welfare state. There are very few changes in social policy since World War II that cannot be traced to initiatives and problems that became apparent in the interwar period.

At first glance, one might consider the interwar period as singularly unpropitious for the development of the welfare state. The social programmes devised before World War I languished in parliaments, faltered under the economic pressures of the depression, and in Germany succumbed to the appeal of national socialism. If anything, the political and administrative debates surrounding the future of social programmes and social protection were more tedious and prolonged than at any previous period. Political leaders were constantly distracted by international shock waves as the edifice assembled at Versailles crumbled, as old colonial structures were shaken by nationalism, and finally as the fascist powers forced them to put aside all other concerns.[1] The desperate efforts to build a new world political order were closely linked to the problems of building a new world economic order, and the national economies were, in turn, highly unstable. Social policy may have been low on the political agenda, but it was never off the political agenda. For the first time, the major economies experienced massive unemployment. Though the efforts to protect the unemployed were often as contrived and experimental as the prewar efforts to protect the poor and sick, by force of circumstances, if not by intent, the democracies began to devise unemployment policies. Democracies confronted the dreadful choice between protecting jobs and providing benefits. In the progression of the welfare state as a policy problem, the critical link between wage and social policy became apparent.

Not only were the institutional structures to deal with unemployment laid down between the wars, the early welfare states underwent their most severe tests. If the positivist accounts of the development of welfare states are read in reverse, these changes often appear as an extension of major class conflicts, the decline of capitalist economies or inevitable progress toward some new social order. As we shall see, at the micro-level policy choices were seldom that clear nor were the early social gains ever seriously challenged in the political arena. In an historical context, the political significance of the interwar period is quite different. With remarkably little effective resistance the major obstacles to the complete nationalization of social policy were pushed aside. First, the liberal refuge of private or charitable assistance proved totally inadequate. Second, the private insurers learned, even if they reluctantly acknowledged, that many serious social problems exceeded the capacity of actuarially sound insurance. Third, and perhaps most important for post–1945 developments, professional groups were gradually co-opted into national social security programmes. Fourth, the agricultural sector first received the protection of the state and its established interests had to be preserved, sometimes enhanced, before substantial aid went to urban dwellers. In effect, the major private and local actors, who might be expected to resist most fiercely expansion of welfare states,

[1] To grasp the free context of policymaking, the memoir of P. J. Grigg, *Prejudice and Judgment*, London; Jonathan Cape, 1948, is instructive. He was private secretary to five Chancellors of the Exchequer, and his recollections are primarily of delicate international problems.

learned to live with welfare states so that its full nationalization after 1945 proceeded with very little controversy.

WAGE AND BENEFIT INTERDEPENDENCE APPEARS

Welfare states could not advance toward a social democratic solution without meeting a number of important conditions. At the policymaking level, unemployment was less a vague manifestation of Marxist doom than an event which bankrupted established ways of dealing with poverty and neglect. These choices were not made in the framework of Marxist or liberal views of economic relations but in the context of governments struggling with dimly understood, monumental problems. For one thing, it became clear that even modest solutions to unemployment exceeded local resources and capabilities. But governments differed greatly not only in when such acknowledgement occurred, but in how new policies were implemented. Simply lubricating the labour market, as done with the prewar development of labour exchanges in Britain, France and Germany was perhaps the limiting liberal solution to this problem. Once governments intervened directly in the labour market, there were new problems of organizing fiscal and budgetary responsibilities, most often within the framework of earlier fiscal and budgetary practices of each state. Lastly, the state acquired enhanced tax powers. Only Sweden, a late welfare state developer, could generate a new institutional framework to consider these problems. For the other democracies, entry into the labour market was not nearly as simple.

If one applies the rule of recognized interdependence of social and wage policy, one might consider the interwar period as the time when the foundations of the modern welfare state were laid. The accomplishments of the period are even more amazing if one recalls that, for most of the period, governments of the right were in power. Nor is it any clearer for the interwar period than for the prewar period that the left, distracted by the split in the socialist movement, had better or different policies to suggest. Perhaps because the steps toward a fully developed welfare state were so cautious, the political and administrative preparations of the 1920s and the 1930s were remarkably durable. In any event, the debate on obligatory social insurance continues in France from 1922 to

1930, displaying substantial consistency with the designs and procedures of earlier accident insurance and protection for aged, sick and incurable. In Germany, the autocratic welfare system of Bismarck continues to operate, but the enormous inflation of the 1920s left little room for improvement. Perhaps the most momentous event was Hitler's seizure of social insurance funds to finance rearmament, a lesson that was not lost on the Social Democrats and German unions as Germany was rebuilt after the Second World War. In the late developing of welfare states of Sweden and the United States, political forces accumulated to bring about the massive policy changes of the 1930s.

As we have seen, in the ordering of ideas and justifications for the welfare state, Britain remains something of an anomaly, in part due to circumstances and in part due to policy choice. First, as it would do again in World War II, World War I forced the British into mobilizing their entire economy around the war effort. As early as 1913, mobilization plans extended to postwar issues, and the early proposals were followed by the accumulation of powers under Lloyd George's Ministry of Munitions, the experience of the War Cabinet, and the work of Reconstruction Committee.[2] By the end of the war, there had been detailed studies of not only those areas subjected to severe dislocation for war purposes, such as agriculture, shipping, mining, electricity and railways, but further studies of future policies for health, housing, taxation, and industrial relations. But by 1921, nearly all the new proposals had been put aside, and the entire battery of wartime powers dissolved.[3] Why Britain failed to move ahead with the numerous reforms designed between 1914 and 1920 is a subject of historical dispute, attributed to causes as diverse as concern for 'business as

[2] See in particular the excellent description in P. Ford, *Social Theory and Social Action*, pp. 205–97.

[3] See Kathleen Burk, ed., *War and State: The Transformation of British Government, 1914–1919*, London and Boston; Allen & Unwin, 1982; David French, *British Economic and Strategic Planning 1905–1915*, London; Allen & Unwin, 1982; and Arthur Marwick, *The Deluge: British Society and the First War*, Boston; Little Brown, 1965. For three excellent accounts of the Reconstruction Committee and its work, see Peter Fraser, 'The Impact of the War of 1914–1918 on the British Political System,' in M. R. D. Foot, ed., *War and Society: Historical Essays in Honour and Memory of J. R. Western 1928–1971*, London; Paul Elek, 1973, pp. 123–39; Robert J. Scaly, *The Origins of the Lloyd George Coalition*, pp. 348–56; and Philip Abrams, 'The Failure of Social Reform: 1918–1920,' *Past and Present*, **24**, 1963, pp. 43–64.

usual' and the breakdown of the wartime Coalition government with the Labour Party. In any event, it was entirely imaginable that Britain might have made sweeping social reforms twenty-five years before 1945. The lesson was not lost on Labour Party leaders after World War II.[4]

Secondly, because Britain experienced more severe unemployment than any other democracy, policies concentrated on the single issue of unemployment. The paradoxical effect was that the persistent issue of the Poor Laws lingered on until 1929, when public assistance was assigned to local government. No sooner had this historical problem been resolved, but the depression hit new depths, forcing central government to establish a new system of national public assistance, and in doing so perpetuating many of the objectionable characteristics of the Poor Law in the new assistance system. The labour market was further disrupted because Britain lost large portions of its income from shipping and manufactured exports, while, as during World War II, its industrial plant deteriorated and technology stagnated. Coupled with desperate, and some think ill-advised, efforts to protect the pound at the price of severe deflation, unemployment took a devasting toll after World War I. After a series of improvised and largely ineffective efforts to provide unemployment insurance over the 1920s, to be analyzed more fully below, the world depression hit with full force in 1930. To relieve the devastating effects of long-term unemployment, the Unemployment Assistance Board (UAB) was devised to provide assistance to the growing numbers of poor. As in the Edwardian period, it is not that the political will was lacking, but that the policy process seemed unable to grasp the first signs that social welfare had become a much more complex task than heretofore imagined. As we shall see in more detail in Chapter 5, the Beveridge Plan was in many ways designed to meet the problems of the 1930s, no small accomplishment, yet far short of the challenge of the modern welfare state.

But whatever the shortcomings of the British political process, in Britain and in most of Europe and America, the governmental

---

[4] The seminal article is by R. H. Tawney, 'The Abolition of Economic Controls, 1918–1921,' in J. M. Winter, ed., *History and Society: Essays by R. H. Tawney*, London; Routledge and Kegan Paul, 1978, pp. 129–86. The article was published in shorter form in the *Economic History Review*, **13**, 1943. The historical irony is that the preservation of wartime controls until the early 1950s contributed to Labour's defeat in 1951.

and political compromises appeared that made the welfare state all but reality. The missing necessary condition was, of course, massive public funding which only became possible after 1950. From a policy perspective, what is essential is the extent to which the potential political obstacles to a fully-developed welfare state were eroded away. First, and perhaps most important, democracies became accustomed to big government.[5] In Britain, for example, the proportion of the active labour force in the public sector changed little from 1851 to 1891. The mid-nineteenth-century social service agencies were, by modern standards, miniscule: the Poor Law Board employed 84 persons, the Board of Trade 103 and the General Board of Health 30.[6] But from 1902 to 1914 social services employment in Britain doubled to over 5,000 persons, and by the end of World War I over 15,000 persons were employed in social services. The major postwar expansion was in the Ministry of Pensions, expanded to 24,000 persons by 1920. The next surge came in the late 1930s as the UAB was organized with an additional 8,000 staff. Thus, social service employees roughly doubled from 1914 to 1933; and in the period from 1933 to 1950, they almost quadrupled. Of course, national figures may underestimate social service employment because some large services, such as health and housing, remained localized between the wars. In 1931, for example, localities employed 126,000 health staff, and, as now, all the teachers.[7]

Few other democracies established social service agencies on the scale of Britain, but France was no stranger to big government and, in fact, her bureaucracy grew more rapidly over the nineteenth century than did Britain's. Employment by the national government nearly tripled over the nineteenth century, from 130,000 in 1839 to 220,000 in 1871; and to 350,000 by 1911.[8]

---

[5] In this respect, the rate of growth of governmental services and social spending often exceeded that of the high spending 1970s and 1980s, but the early political and administrative leaders were not accustomed to such activity. Compare with Richard Rose, *Understanding Big Government: The Programme Approach*, London; Sage Publications, 1984.

[6] Moses Abramovitz and Vera F. Eliasberg, *The Growth of Public Employment in Great Britain*, Princeton; Princeton University Press (for the National Bureau of Economic Research), 1975, p. 18.

[7] The figures in this paragraph come from Abramovitz and Eliasberg, pp. 17–27, except the local health figure, found on p. 77.

[8] The figures are taken from Walter Rice Sharp, *The French Civil Service: Bureaucracy in Transition*, London; Macmillan, 1931, pp. 16–19.

By World War I, another 100,000 persons had been added, and by the end of the war, the French civil service stood at slightly over 600,000 persons, roughly where it remained for the interwar period.[9] But the scale of national government has rarely deterred French reformers from pursuing their ends, and public employment was a commonly accepted means to extend services. In 1927, there were 146,000 teachers on the national payroll as well as 145,000 postal workers. Although the nascent Ministry of Labour stood at only 2,068 persons in 1927, it should be remembered that many French social services and much social insurance were organized through various local and semi-public agencies. Indeed, the main reason it is hard to label French government 'liberal' is that new national agencies have always been erected with relative ease.

In considering the official effort to respond to social needs, it would clearly be misleading not to allow for the huge organizational effort needed to conduct the war and to rebuild the country. To a remarkable degree, the after effects of World War I mobilized France as a social service state, even though social insurance and social assistance remained modest. Even more than in Britain, France could not ignore the devastating social effects of the war.[10] Although only six per cent of French territory was occupied during the war, it was the richest part of France, containing 14 per cent of the industrial population. The human toll was enormous, the 1.5 million dead and the 3 million wounded being roughly twice the British toll. In 1919, the state undertook the retraining and rehabilitation of the veterans, and in 1920 a Ministry of Pensions was established to administer war disability payments and veteran pensions. During the war, a Ministry of Food (*Ministère de Revitaillement*) was created, and the disarray of agriculture with the huge mobilization helps account for the substantial effort devoted to protect agriculture over the 1920s.[11]

---

[9] There appear to be discrepancies in various accounts of the size of government. M. Long and L. Blanc, *L'Economie de la fonction publique*, Paris; Presses Universitaires de France, 1969, pp. 38–9, arrive at about 390,000 permanent national civil servants plus about 300,000 local employees. After levelling off through the 1920s, government employment grew by 36 per cent from 1927 to 1941.

[10] It is interesting to note that like Britain, France thought that World War I would be short. Leroy-Beaulieu predicted six months for an allied victory. See Pierre Legendre, *Histoire de l'Administration: De 1750 à nos jours*, Paris; Presses Universitaires de France, 1968, p. 405.

[11] For a good account of the interwar activities of agricultural groups and their

In addition, France recovered Alsace-Lorraine, and a major programme was launched to reintegrate the lost departments into France. In these and other ways, France was well accustomed to forceful and embracing governmental initiatives well before the modern welfare state emerged in 1945.

Second, the democracies became accustomed to large social service budgets and the growth of social spending as a normal pattern of government operations. Though rates of growth of social spending did not reach the phenomenal levels of the 1970s and 1980s, in Britain, for example, between 1914 and 1950, the percentage of public spending devoted to social services doubled roughly every 20 years.[12] In 1905, British total social spending exceeded its rival champion spender, defence, for the first time. By 1913, social spending was a third of all public spending and, after the interval of the war, regained its predominance by 1921. Largely due to high unemployment, Britain was the first country to establish high social service budgets. From 1930 until 1950, Britain spent about half of all public funds on social services, well before the large surge of social spending in most other democracies which only began after World War II.

In France, as one might expect, the transformation of national finances was more intricate. Much to the distress of Britain, a world trader trying to regain its international position, France took a protectionist stance. At what were ultimately to prove very high costs, jobs were protected, and, in turn, social spending demands reduced. Even so, the economic plight of France was severe. Between 1919 and 1936, the national product declined by 10 per cent. The debt burden of World War I was enormous, amounting to over 40 per cent of state expenditure in 1926, which explains in part the intransigent role of France in extracting war reparations from Germany in the post-war period. From 1872 until 1938, over half of the national budget went for defence and veteran benefits.[13] Within these tight constraints, it is remarkable that social spending increased as much as it did. In 1907, social services accounted for slightly over three per cent of the state budget,

benefits, see Robert Delorme and Christine André, *L'Etat et l'economie: Un Essais d'explication de l'évolution des dépenses publiques en France 1870–1980*, Paris; Editions Seuil, 1983, pp. 309–29.
[12] See Table A–15, Peacock and Wiseman . . ., pp. 186–7.
[13] For the figures on national budget changes, see Delorme and André, pp. 36–45.

increasing to over four per cent as the early social legislation was implemented, not including educational expenditure. Though small compared to Britain, social expenditure was the most rapidly increasing expenditure in the interwar period, reaching six per cent of the national budget by 1938.[14]

But the aggregate figures conceal a third and more important change that was occurring in most democracies between the wars. For the first time, ministries of finance throughout the democratic world were being geared to new activities. Although it is correct, as Ursula Hicks observes, that 'economics and finance remained much as they had been for generations,'[15] this does not take into account the defensive measures of the British Treasury or the French Ministry of Finance that set the stage for later developments. There was widespread agreement that the British Treasury must exercise more strict and reliable controls over public spending. In 1914, the Royal Commission on the Civil Service had recommended more power to the Treasury, and these views were echoed by the Parliamentary Select Committee on National Expenditure in 1917. In 1919, both the Haldane Committee on the Machinery of Government and the Internal Treasury Committee of Inquiry of Sir John Bradbury, the Joint Secretary, who at 41 years of age was responsible for the massive financial operations needed to pay for the war, confirmed these views. As a result, the organizational setting for the continuing struggle between financial and budgetary authority and the welfare state was put in place.[16]

The Treasury accomplished most of its objectives by 1920. In 1919, the Establishment Department was created placing the Head of the Civil Service in the Treasury. The following year the Prime Minister acquired the power to approve all top civil service appointments, which in effect gave full powers to the Head of the

---

[14] Delorme and André, pp. 56–7. Educational spending remained at approximately 9 per cent of the national budget throughout the interwar period.
[15] Ursula Hicks, *The Finance of British Government 1920–1936*, London; Oxford University Press, 1938, p. 2.
[16] The basic structure for Treasury domination of postwar events was in fact well in place before the war. See the Royal Commission on the Civil Service, *Report* (Appendix: Evidence), London; Parliamentary Papers, 1912, cd. 6210, p. 37, where Sir Robert Chalmers, the Financial Secretary, made a spirited defence of Treasury practices. The Haldane Report or Machinery of Government Committee, *Report*, London, Parliamentary Papers, 1918, cd. 9230, pp. 17–21, did not ask for any major changes in Treasury control.

Civil Service. Also, in 1919, the Treasury was able to close the important loophole in civil service recruitment that, for example, allowed Morant's Board of Education to develop independently before the war and the Ministry of Labour to grow during the war. Ambitious ministries could no longer hire large numbers of outside experts. With billions of pounds of debt to balance on the international market, largely through financial operations of the J. P. Morgan Company of New York, the Treasury was able to successfully demand full control of spending proposals. After 1919, ministers could no longer directly engage their colleagues in cabinet-level horsetrading for new expenditures, as had been the practice in the past. All bills obligating the government to new spending had to undergo Treasury scrutiny before cabinet discussion.[17] The crowning achievement was to have a single head of the Treasury bureaucracy, a Permanent Secretary. Sir Warren Fisher took on the job in 1919 and for twenty years was the most powerful man within Whitehall.

Similar to the growth of state officials over the nineteenth century, France developed important state organizations for financial and investment needs well before the welfare state emerged. The Caisse des Dépôts, an agency to manage public savings, was created in 1816 to manage the debts from the Napoleonic wars.[18] The French Treasury dates from 1822, long before modern ministries of finance were imagined, and in 1862, a *Direction Générale de la Comptabilité Publique* was created under the Second Empire, the forerunner of the influential *Direction du Budget* of the French Ministry of Finance.[19] France also became accustomed to using semi-public banking structures for social needs. The Crédit Foncier was established in 1854, largely to help finance Haussmann's vision of Paris, and the Crédit Agricôle received generous infusions of state monies in the 1890s and 1920s to revive agriculture. Though none of these public finance agencies were primarily concerned with welfare activities, the interlocking structure of state or state-supported financial institutions to meet social needs, such as mutual insurance, were well established long

---

[17] See Kathleen Burk, 'The Treasury: From Impotence to Power,' in Burk, ed., *War and the State* . . ., pp. 84–107.
[18] On the origins and activities of the Caisse des Dépôts, see Roger Priouret, *La Caisse des Dépôts*, Paris; Presses Universitaires de France, 1966.
[19] Legendre, *Histoire de l'Administration* ..., pp. 363–79.

before 1945.[20] The elaborate system of funds (*caisses*) established in 1945 only eluded the elaborate network of French financial institutions for a few years.

Thus, the stage was set for the struggles between spending pressures and financial restraint that we have become accustomed to in the era of the advanced welfare state. In fact, these contests began in interwar Britain. As the depression worsened after 1921, the Treasury sought cuts of roughly a fifth of the national budget and organized the Geddes Committee to find them.[21] The Committee was ruthless in its treatment of social services. It recommended abolishing the newly formed Ministry of Labour; slashes in spending for Labour Exchanges, so laboriously constructed by Beveridge before the war; the sale of local public housing, an effort was just beginning; and similar cuts in education, pensions and public works. When the depression again hit Britain in 1930, another Treasury committee, the May Committee, was appointed to repeat the Geddes exercise, this time with the support of Labour Party ministers.[22] Despite the occasional inroads into Treasury orthodoxy made by Keynes, Tawney and a few others between the wars, the Treasury established strong controls over social spending. Indeed, one of the most dramatic contrasts between the interwar and postwar British welfare state is the loss of Treasury control over social spending after 1950. For many similar reasons, France too underwent a series of severe budget cuts from 1926 to 1929 as Poincaré reduced French deficits.

The fourth important organizational transformation of the interwar period was to raise doubts about local government as an agency of social protection and social service. As we shall see, the bulk of social legislation between the wars relied heavily on local government. Perhaps the most dramatic political change associated with the emergence of the modern welfare state after 1945 was the nationalization of social programmes of all kinds, but prior to

[20] On the early linkage between mutual insurance and the state, see Eugène Rochetin, *Les Assurances ouvrières: mutualités contre la maladie, l'incendie et le chômage*, Paris; Guillaumin, 1896.
[21] P. Ford, *Social Theory and Social Action*, p. 280. The full report is *First Interim Report*, Committee on National Expenditure (Geddes Committee), London; Parliamentary Papers, 1922, cmd. 1581. The *Second Report* appears in late 1922, cmd. 1582, and the *Third Report*, 1922, cmd. 1589.
[22] Financial Secretary to the Treasury (May Committee), *Memorandum of the Measures Proposed by the His Majesty's Government to Secure Reductions in National Expenditure*, London; Parliamentary Papers, 1931, cmd. 3952.

1918, local government was the fastest growing public sector. In France, for example, until 1912, local government, including departments and communes, accounted for 30 per cent of national public expenditure. The war accounts for the sudden drop to about 20 per cent because localities had neither the organization nor the resources to undertake the reconstruction of France.[23] Contrary to the contemporary interpretation of France as a highly centralized state, until World War I France was decentralizing in budgetary and organizational terms. From 1872 to 1912, local budgets increased more rapidly than either the national product or the national budget.[24] Moreover, public assistance remained a local function. In 1904, the departments provided 25 per cent of public assistance; in 1929, 32 per cent; and in 1950, 48 per cent.

The steady decline of British local government as an effective voice in national policymaking is a long and intricate story,[25] but in Victorian Britain the localities provided more social assistance than did national government. In 1890, nearly 40 per cent of local expenditure was for social services, and so it remained until 1955.[26] The key to centralization, which we shall examine in more detail, is that localities could not raise sufficient funds, and became increasingly dependent on national grants, which, in turn, brought new national demands and regulations. From 1920 to 1940, roughly half of local social spending was provided by grants from Westminster, and by 1949; such transfers exceeded local tax contributions. In effect, the government smothered local government with social grants, but in doing so extracted an enormous price in local autonomy and initiative.

Though we often think of the period from 1920 to 1940 as a dormant interlude in the transformation of modern democratic states, if we examine policy changes closely, there are many reasons for thinking otherwise. This is perhaps more the case for social policy than for any other area of state activity. Partly stemming from the prewar legislation and administrative changes, and partly

[23] See J. C. Thoenig, 'Local Subsidies in the Third Republic: The Political Marketplace and Bureaucratic Allocation,' in D. Ashford, ed., *Financing Urban Government in the Welfare State*, London; Croom Helm, 1980, pp. 119–41.
[24] The figures in this paragraph come from Delorme and André, *L'Etat et l'economie . . .*, p. 35 and p. 75.
[25] See Ashford, *British Dogmatism and French Pragmatism*, London and Boston, Allen & Unwin, 1982.
[26] The figures come from Peacock and Wiseman, Table A–25, pp. 206–7, and Table A–18, p. 194.

from the mobilization of World War I, governments had been radically changed by 1920. Often unintentionally, three essential preconditions for the rapid expansion of the welfare state were met: governments developed budgetary and financial operational capacities that could easily be turned to social issues; governments began to develop both the organization and the staff who saw social problems as their main administrative interest; and the local capacities for providing social services proved inadequate or had insufficient resources to meet new social needs. Thus, the major structural prerequisites to the development of the welfare state were well defined by 1940, and, as we shall see, they heavily influenced both the political debate and the political setting for the future transformation of democratic states.

Though the turbulence of interwar politics cannot be recapitulated here, it is reasonable to ask why the political will and political motivation to expand many of the social reforms generated before and during World War I were lacking. First, and perhaps most important, more abstract theories about the transformation of modern states fail to portray how the horror and destruction of the war impressed the leaders of the day. Most European states did not recover their pre-World War I levels of production until the late 1920s, and the two most powerful European countries, Britain and France, had very different economic interests and economic strategies for the recovery.[27] However controversial the reconstruction of Europe after 1945, there was no intact and highly productive economy to play the role of the United States in rebuilding Europe in the late 1940s. Easy as it may be to imagine the controls of wartime redirected to social purposes, much as Titmuss hoped to do after World War II,[28] there is little evidence that business or labour wanted such a transformation. In a policy framework, it should also be recalled that ministries of finance had neither the staff to conduct such an operation nor was there conceptual equipment to make such an effort intelligible.[29]

---

[27] See Charles S. Maier, *Recasting Bourgeois Europe: Stabilization in France, Germany and Italy in the Decade after World War I*, Princeton; Princeton University Press, 1975.
[28] Titmuss' ideas about converting wartime solidarity into social solidarity will be discussed in Chapter 5. They appear in his official social history of the war, *Problems of Social Policy*, London; HMSO, 1950.
[29] There was no clear economic concept of how to assess or to allocate social costs until Pigou's *Economics of Welfare* was published in 1921.

Second, the disarray of the political parties at the close of World War I must be taken into account. In Britain, both the Conservative and the Labour Parties were internally divided by the war, by Ireland, and by trade policy. The divisive tactics of Lloyd George and his repudiation of Asquith left the Liberal Party in a shambles. In France, the war left the radical socialists and the socialists dispirited and divided so that except for the short-lived Cartel des Gauches, like the impotent minority British Labour government of 1924, was unable to initiate major legislation.[30] In Germany the Social Democrats were in even more desperate straits. In 1914, the Party had enormous influence, having been elected to 110 seats in the Reichstag, nearly 3,000 city councils and some 9,000 rural councils.[31] But in 1919, the Social Democratic leader, Wilbrandt, wrote, 'There was not the least idea of what one should do. No one knew how to do what needed to be done.[32] Even so, the Social Democrats gained 112 seats in the first democratically-elected Reichstag of 1920. Quite apart from the awesome economic problems facing a defeated Germany, with a third of the Social Democratic functionaries in the Army and split by a pacifist faction, the Social Democrats were unprepared to govern in 1918. The rapid deterioration of the economy and the uprisings against the Weimar Republic soon reduced their chances to press for new social reforms. Underlying these debilitating political circumstances, in all these countries, parliamentary rule was eroded during the war. Reconstruction strengthened administrative power, just as the initial social legislation had done prior to the war.

[30] On the experience of the Bloc des Gauches, see J. N. Jeanneney, *Leçons d'histoire pour une gauche au pouvoir. La faillite du Cartel (1924–1926)*, Paris; Editions du Seuil, 1977. Jeanneney argues that the Bank of France helped precipitate economic problems to defeat the left-centre government. But at the time it was common for national bank directors to criticize governments as did Lord Norman Montagu, the Director of the Bank of England, for most of the interwar period. On the political confusion in France, see also Maier, *Recasting Bourgeios Europe* . . ., pp. 88–109 and pp 355–420.
[31] The standard study of the indecision and isolation of the Social Democratic Party is Guenter Roth, *The Social Democrats in Imperial Germany: A Study in Working Class Isolation and National Integration*, Totowa, NJ; Beminister Press, 1963, who discusses the postwar scene pp. 285–303. See also Karl Schorske, *German Social Democracy 1905–1917: The Development of the Great Schism*, Cambridge, MA; Harvard University Press, 1955.
[32] From George Lefranc, *Le socialisme réformiste*, Paris; Presses Universitaires de France, 1971, p. 21.

Third, the political links between the parties of the left and the labour movement remained uncertain and fragile. In Germany, the revolutionary uprisings of Liebnicht and Luxembourg derailed rebuilding strong union organizations and with devastating inflation social relations remained explosive well into the 1920s. Many of the social gains of 1918 were postponed, and, as Maier notes, the Social Democrats had little choice but 'to contain social tension on conservative terms or not to contain it at all.'[33] The alliance of the left and labour that was to propel democracies into the welfare state was no more effective in Britain and France. Although French unions made considerable inroads in organizing the public sector, Confédération Générale du Travail (CGT) membership among railway workers, for example, fell from over 300,000 in early 1920 to 100,000 by the end of the year.[34] In Britain, union membership soared to over 8 million workers in 1920, and the Triple Alliance of miners, transport and railway workers presented a formidable political force to the government. But with a million workers idle during the 1920 coal strike, the miners yielded without consulting their allies, while the Labour Party as yet had few trusted leaders from labour ranks. After the failure of the general strike of 1926, union membership steadily declined to about four million members in the late 1920s, and the slow process of linking the Trade Union Congress (TUC) to the Party only began in earnest over the 1930s.[35]

In assessing the slow material progress of the welfare state in the interwar period in socio-economic terms, we ignore the political uncertainties that in one form or another made social progress disappointing. Throughout Europe, one might expect more results because both the leaders and the reforms of the prewar period opened so many possibilities. Few democratic leaders foresaw that their anticipated six-month war would extract such a terrible toll of death and destruction. Many of them realised that war would delay rather than enhance social reform. In a typically prescient mood, Churchill noted that 'all the world is changing at once,'[36]

[33] Maier, *Recasting Bourgeois Europe* . . ., p. 385. For his discussion of the uncertainties, political and economic, see pp. 356–403. See also Richard N. Hunt, *The Social Democracy, 1918–1935* . . ., pp. 1–26.
[34] See Georges Lefranc, *Le Mouvement syndical sous la IIIe Republique*, Paris; Payot, 1967, pp. 329–50.
[35] See Eric Wigham, *Strikes and Government 1893–1974*, London; Macmillan, 1974, pp. 37–55.
[36] Read, *Edwardian England* . . ., p. 255.

but neither he nor any other democratic leader could foresee how political stability might be restored. The new liberals and the Liberal Party, the critical link between the political influence and policy aspirations of the left, were destroyed. A melancholy Hobson would write in 1921 of 'a world breaking away from all settled laws of life and plunging into chaos.'[37] In France, the changes were in many respects even more debilitating because under Clemenceau the radicals and radical socialists could rest on the laurels of their defence of the Republic. Assassinated by an Alsatian nationalist in 1914 for his efforts to avoid war, Jaurès was no longer there to heal socialist schisms and to lead the parliamentary struggle of the left. For the first time, the SFIO vote exceeded a million votes in 1910, giving them 76 seats in the Chamber of Deputies, and in 1913 the Party won 103 seats. But the international division of the socialist movement and internal fights over the war left them weak and ineffective.[38] Nonetheless, the social debate continued in parliament throughout the 1920s. Even so, 'the peculiar liberal balance of social solidarity and mutual interest,'[39] which enabled prewar French liberals to support reforms at the turn of the century, continued and provided a continuity for the nascent welfare state in France that Britain, plagued by depression and unemployment, could not achieve.

SUBORDINATING BRITISH LOCALITIES

The welfare state could not develop unless national governments were able to nationalize the social policies dispersed among local governments, assigned to localized charities and left to local religious institutions. The struggle between levels of government began some decades before national governments agreed to take on social responsibilities, and so both the duration and the intensity of the struggle are important clues to the political development of the welfare state. The controversies are historically rooted in the territorial tensions inherent in modern democracy and therefore

[37] Quoted in Clarke, *Liberals and Social Democrats* . . ., p. 205, from Hobson's *Problems of a New World*, London; 1921.
[38] See Jean-Jacques Fiechter, *Le socialisme francais: De l'affaire Dreyfus á la Grande Guerre*, Geneva; Librairie Droz, 1965, pp. 165–222. On the internal divisions of the Labour Party, see Marquand, *Ramsey MacDonald*, pp. 136–237.
[39] Freeden, *The New Liberalism* . . ., p. 233.

pre-date even the rudimentary turn-of-the-century welfare state by many years. Each liberal democracy had its own strategy for dealing with the resistance of localized power to the early formation of national democracy. The structures and organization put in place during the struggle later become part of the context for forming welfare bureaucracies and organizations. Modern welfare bureaucracies do not acquire political power of their own until much later, when the new framework for social administration has sufficient autonomy and scope to challenge directly traditional administrative habits, in most countries not until 1945 or later. The nationalization of local powers involves three important political changes: the restructuring of local capacities to mobilize politically; the transfer of tax resources to the centre or the limiting of local tax powers so the state can control taxation; and increased authority of national over local administration. The outcome of these changes depended heavily on the historical compromises made to achieve liberal democratic governance in the eighteenth and nineteenth centuries.

The mobilization of local political interests is virtually inseparable from the historic struggle to achieve liberal democracy. Compared to most democracies, the struggle in Britain was extraordinarily extended, and indeed continues well after the first major step toward a national welfare state in 1911. Though we often think of Britain as a territorially compact nation, her history is riddled with major domestic political crises over territorial problems. Over the nineteenth century, both her physical isolation from the power struggles within continental Europe and her military supremacy made it possible to ignore internal territorial conflict in ways that were not permitted countries having a more precarious political existence and less reliable political control of their peripheral areas. Ireland is, of course, the dramatic illustration. A festering source of civil discontent, parliamentary obstruction and eventual civil war that no continental power could safely tolerate, Ireland is not without influence on the development of the British welfare state. After the victory of 1906, the Liberals began to lose by-elections and were dependent on Irish nationalist votes in Parliament, thereby curtailing their ability to reverse the Tory educational reforms of 1902 with their protection of religious educational institutions. It is interesting to recall that, in his waning years, the leading new Liberal, J. L. Hammond, reflected on how the Irish war may have been at the root of Liberal failure.[40]

Local democracy was the cornerstone of liberal democracy in all the democratic states, but countries vary enormously in their patience and skill in circumventing locally-held powers. The British strategy was, and remains into the 1980s, a particularly ruthless one. From the wave of Whig reforms in the 1830s, ambitious national policymakers have found local government deplorable and unreliable. The first illustration is the 1834 Poor Law Amendment Act itself, which was the product of Benthamite distaste for local inefficiency. In his report on the Poor Law administration, Sir Edwin Chadwick heaped scorn on the outmoded local welfare agencies, which was not too difficult to do, but often ignored the innovations some were making to alleviate the expense and inadequacy of poor relief.[41] Though Chadwick's arrogance soon made him distasteful to even Conservative governments of the day, the strategy for local reform remains essentially unchanged to the present day. The 1834 Act simply erected outside the local structure a machinery of government that Parliament could manipulate independently if it so chose. The 600 new Poor Law Boards of Guardians were elected, but on a narrow, property-based franchise, and their tax powers or rates were separate from local tax powers. Thus, there was no risk that overzealous local authorities might expand their tax powers to provide overly generous social services, as had happened in Speenhamland,[42] while the power of inspection under the nationally appointed 'Three Wise Men of Somerset House', the Poor Law Commission, was to enforce utilitarian justice.

The capacity of the localities to resist the nationalization of social security in Britain was further reduced, largely inadvertently, by

---

[40] Clarke, *Liberals and Social Democrats*, p. 279. See also Hammond's *Gladstone and the Irish Nation*, London; 1938.

[41] On the 1834 Act, see Derek Fraser, *The Evolution of the British Welfare State*, pp. 28–50; and S. E. Finer, *The Life and Times of Sir Edwin Chadwick*. Parliament refused to give the Assistant Commissioners or inspectors the powers Chadwick wanted, and declined to make Chadwick the secretary to the Poor Law Commission. Under the prevailing Tory administration of the country, most Poor Law Boards refused to build the additional workhouses needed to enforce Chadwick's 'less eligibility' principle.

[42] In 1795, the Berkshire village decided to increase Poor Law benefits to the price of bread, thereby making a living wage roughly equivalent to poor relief. See also this chapter, n. 77.

the retarded political development of local government. After the
revolution of 1688 national and local government were virtually
synonymous in the eyes of the landed aristocracy and, in the
gradual evolution of parliamentary government over the eighteenth
century, aristocratic manipulation of their local fiefs was expected.
Because the parliamentary boroughs were the basis of a highly
corrupt system of representation, the system could be used effectively to exclude the urban areas from Parliament. Indeed, the
political development of local democracy in Britain was substantially behind that of many less democratic continental regimes.
The first reform of 1835, the Municipal Corporations Act, kept
rural Britain under the appointed Justices of the Peace and limited
the number of urban local governments that could be formed.
Until the Reform Act of 1832, the growing urban centres of
Manchester, Leeds and Liverpool, had no parliamentary representation at all, while aristocratic rural preserves, such as
Cornwall, sent dozens of MPs to Parliament. As a further guarantee that local councils in the few urban boroughs would not yield
to political temptations of increasing local services, a third of the
councils were lifetime aldermen. Not until the Local Government
Act of 1888, fifty years into the slow march toward universal
franchise in Britain, did all local governments have elected
councils, but their potential enthusiasm for social reform was
further dampened by Tory legislation over the 1890s establishing
urban and rural districts to divide the powers of the new local
authorities.[43]

The ease with which Parliament could paralyse local government was, and remains, rooted in the blanket power of *ultra
vires*, but such constitutional limitations were hardly needed in so
fragmented a structure. Even if the localities had tried to mobilize
social services, the functional dispersion of local powers in Victorian Britain bordered on chaos. There were over 80,000 different
local authorities, including 600 Boards of Guardians supervising
poor relief, 4,600 school boards outside local government, 290
prisons and 228 asylums under the Justices of Peace, and 182
independently organized local boards of health.[44] The Local
Government Act of 1888, a Conservative bill, like every reform of

---

[43] For additional details of the substantial political constraints, see Douglas E.
Ashford, *British Dogmatism and French Pragmatism*, pp. 33–84.
[44] D. C. Roberts, *Victorian Origins of the Welfare State*, p. 278.

British local government to the present day, erected disparities of size and resources that virtually prohibited using local areas as the basis for social programmes. Aristocratic reserves, such as Rutland with its 21,000 inhabitants, were protected, while the sprawling industrialized regions, such as Yorkshire, were forty times larger. By reducing the permitted size of urban authorities from the 150,000 recommended in the bill to 50,000, a conservative Parliament added further assurance that zealous urban government would not unleash a tide of welfare spending. Although London acquired the status of a county council in 1888, the intricate system of vestry government and Conservative-controlled London boards permitted conservatives to resist social legislation well into the twentieth century.[45]

In many respects, the resource controls become the key to understanding the paralysis of British local government as social services expanded in late Victorian and Edwardian Britain. The Whig reforms of the 1830s may be best viewed as a collection of laws to assure the landed aristocracy that the local rates or property taxes could not be increased. Perhaps the best demonstration of Mayer's hypothesis concerning aristocratic powers[46] is the regularity with which an aristocratic Parliament bought off local resistance to local political and social and political reform with subsidies, or, more accurately, the way in which the common concerns of the aristocrats in Parliament and in localities converged to keep local taxation low. Poor Law reform was acceptable to the Tories because it promised, as it did, to limit local poor rates. Corn Law repeal in 1846 was made acceptable when Peel, against his better judgement, drew on the Contingency Fund to provide local tax relief lest cheaper food force localities to increase taxes. From 1870 there was absolutely no doubt about the growing disparities of urban and rural resources, as the detailed studies of Sir George Goschen, later repeated in 1891 by Sir Henry Fowler, made

---

[45] For four years after the 1902 Education Act, London refused to implement the law. On Tory control of London see Ken Young, *Local Politics and the Rise of Party: The London Municipal Society and the Conservative Intervention in Local Elections 1894–1963*, Leicester; Leicester University Press, 1975.

[46] Atho Mayer, *The Persistence of the Old Regime*, New York, Patheon, 1981. Though not the point of his book, Mayer does not recognize how vulnerable this made the aristocrats once social needs became unmistakable, thereby leaving no option but central control. In effect, the Conservatives burned their bridges behind them.

crystal clear.[47] Like every Prime Minister since his time, Gladstone refused to give localities a more flexible tax even though a local income tax was recommended by his able financial adviser, Goschen. The Local Government Act of 1888 was eased through Parliament with tax relief on land of two million pounds, and the creation of districts in 1894 made palatable by de-rating land of half its tax value. In 1817, land taxes provided two-thirds of local revenues; by 1891, only fifteen per cent.

The formula for controlling potential local excesses remains unchanged in the twentieth century. Although they can be traced back to the conditional grants to improve prisons and asylums of the radical Whigs of the 1830s, each social reform impinging on localities has been accompanied by major increments in local subsidies, which protected property owners from paying for new social services and, in turn, provided new grounds for centralization. We have already seen how the system was used by Sir Robert Morant to implement educational reforms in Edwardian Britain. The turn of the century Royal Commission on Local Taxation could find no better solution to local plight than to increase grants.[48] The Local Government Act of 1929, the next major reform of local government after 1888, fully de-rated agricultural land and provided a block grant that by 1930 was a third of local revenues. Though sometimes viewed from afar, especially by Frenchmen, as a peculiar virtue of British local government, the local subsidy became a political football after World War II, eventually escalating to nearly two-thirds of local revenues and easily permitting the Conservatives to impose the harsh controls of the 1982 and 1984 Local Government Acts. The Thatcher government only made a bludgeon of what was always a rigid and arbitrary control.

[47] Goschen's 1870 report is reprinted in his *Reports and Speeches on Local Taxation*, London; Macmillan, 1872, pp. 2–51. Fowler's report appears in the *Parliamentary Papers*, vo. 58, 1893. For a summary, see Douglas E. Ashford, 'A Victorian Drama: The Fiscal Subordination of British Local Government,' in D. Ashford, ed., *Financing Urban Government in the Welfare State*, London; Croom Helm, 1980, pp. 71–96.
[48] Royal Commission on Local Taxation, *Report*, Parliamentary Papers, 1901, cd. 638. For a more detailed account of the grants, see Ashford, *British Dogmatism and French Pragmatism*, pp. 251–307. Trade-offs between grants and local services became more complicated after World War II. If a grant is calculated in respect to total local spending, including separate accounts for housing and paid services, the grant reached about 40 per cent of total local budgets.

With such a formidable array of policy instruments at its disposal, it is hard to imagine how British policymakers, had they wished an alternative to nationalized social reform, might have found one. The Achilles heel of Parliament, if there was one, was that British cabinet government and administration does not have the means to implement its policies. The strong central administration was able to manoeuvre its way around Parliament and even ministers, as in the case of some Morant's policies, but it never had the integrated field administration of France or the ponderous state bureaucracies of the United States or Germany to carry out central initiatives. There was neither the administrative loyalties of the French *grands corps* nor the bureaucratic self-interest of the American states to enable the ever growing British local civil service to seize the inititative as the welfare state expanded, even though until 1945 most social and health services were implemented at the local level. The main reason was that at the turn of the century the expansion of welfare services, Poor Law administration, health and education, were accomplished with minimal local involvement. The dismal performance of the Local Government Board persuaded all the Edwardian reformers that local dependence would be fatal, and there were no political reasons to make local compromises.

The negative image of the Local Government Board requires some explanation for it contrasts sharply, for example, with the leading role taken by the French Ministry of the Interior in the 1880s under Henri Monod to convert local social services to national purposes. At that time, more than half the British countryside did not even have elected government. Again, one must examine the Victorian roots of welfare administration. Until 1951 there was no ministry identified with the interests of loal government. The first step in this direction was the Local Government Office Act of 1858, created by Parliament as a reaction against the excesses of public health administration rather than as a mobilizer of local political interests.[49] Given the confusion of local social and health services of mid-Victorian Britain, and the

---

[49] See Royston Lambert, 'Central and Local Relations in Mid-Victorian England: The Local Government Act Office, 1858–1871,' *Victorian Studies*, **6**, 1962, pp. 122–39. The Treasury undermined the power of the Local Government Board in much the same way as the Board of Education and Ministry of Health were handicapped years later. See Roy M. MacLeod, *Treasury Control and Social Administration*, London; Bell (Occasional Papers on Social Administration), 1968.

inability of a still nascent national civil service to supervise local
services, the Local Government Board was formed in 1871. Much
of British modern social administration actually emerges from the
formation of national boards to deal with local problems that
either exceeded administrative capacities of Whitehall or frustrated
parliamentary government. But in the early development of welfare
state administration in Britain, the Local Government Board
became the weak sister to the Board of Trade, which rapidly
developed under dynamic ministers, such as Lloyd George and
Churchill, to take the initiative in labour legislation, and the Board
of Education of 1899 that came under the masterly control of Sir
Robert Morant.

The history of the Local Government Board is a series of
accounts of frustrated social reform. In 1871, the Board inherited
a collection of functions, including public health and Poor Law
supervision, and was in a key position to become the crucial agency
linking national and local government.[49] But the Board was the
captive of conservative local politics, not an agent of change. In
the 1870s, the newly established Board reacted against the public
health reforms being gradually assembled by Sir John Simon.
Over twenty years, Simon had organized modern health services,
starting as a medical officer for London in 1848 and, from 1855,
as Britain's Medical Officer under the Board of Health.[50] Like
Morant and others to follow, Simon was adroit in using temporary
appointments and finding dedicated young civil servants to pursue
his aims.[51] Under the 1866 Health Act, he acquired the power of
inspection over crowded housing and sanitation, never debated in

[49] See Royston Lambert, 'Central and Local Relations in Mid-Victorian England:
The Local Government Act Office, 1858–1871,' *Victorian Studies*, **6**, 1962, pp.
122–39. The Treasury undermined the power of the Local Government Board
in much the same way as the Board of Education and Ministry of Health
were handicapped years later. See Roy M. MacLeod, *Treasury Control and Social
Administration*, London; Bell (Occasional Papers on Social Administration), 1968.
[50] Though it is tangential, public health services developed rapidly in mid-
Victorian Britain in response to appalling cycles of cholera and diptheria
epidemics. Nineteenth-century local government legislation is sometimes characterized as the history of 'standpipes and sewers.' Chadwick's second famous
report was the 1842 *Report on the Sanitary Condition of the Labouring Population of
Great Britain*, but as in the case of the Poor Law reform, his arrogance made him
suspect to a then stronger Parliament, and he was not selected to implement the
law. For background, see Fraser, *The Evolution of the Welfare State*, pp. 51–71.
[51] On the growth of Simon's power, see Royston Lambert, *Sir John Simon. . .*, p.
386.

Parliament, that Chadwick, the early advocate of centralized public health control, had never been able to achieve.[52] By appointing a jealous and narrow-minded political colleague to be the first secretary of the Local Government Board, Gladstone made life unbearable for Simon, and he resigned in 1876.

The second political blunder of the Local Government Board was to become the defender of Poor Laws as the pension debate developed in late Victorian Britain. It is the habit of ministers to guard their powers fiercely, but in the isolation of British cabinet government these instincts can run wild. Of course, the plight of the Local Government Board was compounded because governments had little taste for the politically unrewarding tasks of reforming local government, and no ambitious minister wished to be brushed with the tar of the Poor Laws. Though there were Presidents of the Local Government Board, such as Joseph Chamberlain,[53] whose vision might have made the agency more influential, its future was sealed by John Burns, who oddly began his political career as a militant in the left wing of the labour movement.[54] On achieving ministerial rank as part of the Lib-Lab compromise of 1906, Burns became the irrepressible advocate of Poor Law principles. When Asquith announced his pension plans in 1908, Burns sought an amendment to make the aged poor with more than 20 years on poor relief ineligible, and, with the support of the reactionary Charity Organization Society, he wanted to have strong local committees to review applicants to be sure that 'malingerers' did not receive full pensions.[55] He testified in support of the Poor Law before the 1905–9 Royal Commission. Although local government still accounted for half of all public spending in

[52] There was an embittered exchange between the aging Chadwick and Simon, in part over whether infection was carried by air (suggesting small sewers and closed sanitation) or by water (suggesting larger sewers and simpler sanitation). But basically Chadwick adhered to the Benthamite, and later Webbian, view that there had to be total and centralized control *before* making changes; Simon, like the famous Edwardian civil servants, was more diplomatic and more circumspect.

[53] Chamberlain made his switch to the Conservative Party on the condition that a major local government act, the Act of 1888, he brought forward. He was President of the Local Government Board for a few months, and had he remained there, the history of British local government would likely read very differently. His national fame was based on his huge success as an advocate of municipal enterprise as Mayor of Birmingham.

[54] See Kenneth Brown, *John Burns*, London; 1977.

[55] Gilbert, *The Evolution of National Insurance in Great Britain*, pp. 220–1.

1905,[56] Burns had little new to offer the new breed of ministers
and civil servants. Between 1890 and 1914, local spending slightly
more than doubled (to £46 million), but national spending nearly
multiplied by seven (just under £55 million). National government
was overtaking local government, and neither the locals nor their
feeble minister had anything to say.

Even if the ambitious Liberal leaders, Lloyd George and Churchill, had been prepared to share the limelight with the old Labour
leader, it is doubtful if the new cohort of reformist officials would
have consented. Sir Arthur Newsholme, the Chief Medical Officer
of the Local Government Board until 1918, clearly remembered
the betrayal of public health administration by the Local Government Board and opposed the merger of health and Poor Law
inspectors under the 1871 formation of the Board.[57] Taking up
Simon's conviction that Britain must have a united health ministry,
Newsholme detested the 1,727 health authorities that complicated
the advance of national health programmes. He was to hope in
vain for the 'root and branch reform of local government'[58] that
was to him, and many others, the keystone to national health
reform.

As we saw in Chapter 2, local government was no less distrusted
by Whitehall for the great variations in the quality of education.
Sir Robert Morant constructed an educational system that brought
localities under national rules, but in doing so also built the
prototype of British national organization for social purposes.
Morant's political acumen in avoiding the morass of local politics
became the hallmark of the successful civil servant. His ability to
use indirect means to accomplish a 'guidance of brains' over an
unwieldy and often reluctant local government system brought
him acclaim.[59] The 1902 Act allowed him to use local taxes
to support his educational reforms.[60] By adept manipulation of

---

[56] Hay, *The Origins of the Liberal Welfare Reforms*, pp. 40–1.
[57] Sir Arthur Newsholme, *The Ministry of Health*, p. 22. At this point, Newsholme
cites Simon's advice that a single, expert authority was essential to public health.
[58] Newsholme, *The Ministry of Health*, p. 51 and p. 138. His full report can be
found in the *47th Annual Report of the Local Government Board*, Supplement Containing the Report of the Medical Officer, London; Parliamentary Papers, 1918,
cd. 9169.
[59] Allen, *Sir Robert Morant*, p. 26.
[60] Actually a second act was passed to deduct school expenses from local grants
where local authorities refused to levy new local taxes. With diplomacy, Morant

ministerial powers he then set out to assemble a formidable coalition of national and local power: the school inspectorate effectively monitored local education; school lunches were a natural sequel to expand social services; and school medical inspection laid the groundwork for nationalized medicine.[61] Morant's success might be viewed as the exception that proves the rule. By stealth the second-ranked Board of Education developed an organization that was no less influential than a French ministry. Against the wishes of the Treasury, and most civil service reformers, he assembled his own *grands corps* without officially having one. The Board of Education, and its successor, the Ministry of Education from 1945, became the model of effective national supervision of local services.

The remaining pillar of local administration was, of course, the Poor Law Boards of Guardians, the albatross of the early British welfare state. There was no greater cause of suspicion among all policymakers than that directed at the Poor Laws. As in the case of British local reform, the unappealing politics and the complex administration of public assistance repelled the Edwardian reformers in the civil service. Within government, everyone was prepared to use the infamous laws to justify social reform, but few were prepared to propose alternatives. Outside government, only Beatrice Webb, who deeply resented the rejection of her recommendations by the 1905–09 Royal Commission, made Poor Law reform her mission in life. During World War I, she worked with both a subcommittee of the Ministry of Reconstruction and on the MacClean Committee to see them demolished. In fact, the most onerous provisions of the Poor Laws were being diluted from the 1870s. In 1876, as part of the first educational reform, local beneficiaries were exempt from the most odious of pauper punishments, disenfranchisement, if their children received educational benefits from local taxes. In 1885, this exemption was

agreed that London might have a county rather than a borough level school authority, the origin of the justly famous London Educational Authority that even survived the Conservative 1963 London Act.
[61] In 1907, the Board of Education formed a Medical Department with Sir George Newman as Chief Medical Officer. He became the first Permanent Secretary of the Ministry of Health in 1918. Newman was favoured by Morant and the Webbs over the disappointed, but less diplomatic, Newsholme, Medical Officer of the abolished LGB.

extended to those receiving medical assistance from Poor Law facilities. Another breach was the Education (Provision of Meals) Act of 1906, which allowed Poor Law Boards to feed needy children without stigma. An even greater compromise, no doubt made to avoid complications, was Asquith's decision to soften discrimination against paupers in the 1908 Pension Act.

But as we shall see in more detail in Chapter 4, the Local Government Act of 1929 did not succeed in eliminating the stigma of poverty. Under the highly adverse conditions of the time, it was necessary to create local Public Assistance Committees (PAC) in 1931 to provide means-tested public relief for the long-term unemployed. The experience of the PACs replays the Victorian history of local government in so far as ministers did not want the burden of administering relief, yet feared that the localities would be too generous. In an effort to reconstruct unemployment assistance in the mid-1930s, means-testing was made a national function under the Unemployment Assistance Board (UAB), thereby imposing the stigma of poverty on unemployment relief.[62] Under the threat of war, the UAB took over the responsibility of administering assistance to pensioners in distress under the new title, the Assistance Board, only to resurface again as the National Assistance Board under the Beveridge Plan. Whether viewed as administrative convenience or administrative necessity, the effect was to transmit the stigma of poverty into the modern British welfare state.

CIRCUMVENTING FRENCH COMMUNES

The fundamental political difference between British and French local government in the development of the welfare state is that the French *collectivités locales* were never imagined as instruments of social policy, but as part of a common struggle by state and society to build a stronger and better France. The French com-

---

[62] The most detailed account of the UAB's activity is found in a report by Tony Lynes, *Low Incomes: Evidence to the Royal Commission on Distribution of Income and Wealth*, London; Department of Health and Social Security, Supplementary Benefits Commission, Paper No. 6, HMSO, 1977, pp. 33–58. Unavailable at the time was Lynes' book on the UAB, *The Unemployment Assistance Board*, London; Croom Helm, 1985.

munes and departments have a legitimacy that probably exceeds that of local government in any modern democracy. France is the only major democracy where local government was not brutally consolidated over the 1960s and 1970s to facilitate the redistributive tasks of the welfare state and to conform to whatever concepts of administrative efficiency leaders of the time thought would advance the interests of national government. The reasons for the sense of mutual dependence, and, more important, the sharing of national goals, run deep in French history, and could not be simply swept aside as France began to build a welfare state.

As Weber's magnificent study of the peasantry shows,[63] until roughly 1870 the countryside remained politically incoherent and large areas of France were inaccessible to democratic politics. In the Third Republic, Gambetta and other republicans learned to orchestrate radical and revolutionary sentiments among peasants and farmers. Many of the moderate republican leaders, such as Jules Siegfried and Waldeck-Rousseau, were provincial notables. To them local government was integral to republican France and until 1914 localities were the main building blocks of their social policies. In contrast, the Victorian policymakers, no less concerned with property, were highly suspect of local government. From the earliest Reform Bill of 1834 until the turn of the century, the aim was to use county government to perpetuate landowner privileges.[64]

The French tactic was quite different which may explain why it seemed more natural to work with communes and departments. Local government was institutionalized at the national level in the Senate, often called 'la grande maison des communes de France.' Though a thoroughly unrepublican and undemocratic institution, the Senate's opposition and delay was accepted as a fact of French territorial politics. But unlike the House of Lords, it was not a resting place for venerable politicians and social privilege. While the House of Lords rejection of Lloyd George's 1909 budget was an affront by an archaic institution, Senate procrastination was an exercise in forming republican unity. Once compromises on social legislation were reached between the Chamber of Deputies

---

[63] Eugen Weber, *Peasants into Frenchmen: The Modernization of Rural France, 1870–1914*, Stanford, CA; Stanford University Press, 1976, pp. 241–77.
[64] For historical background on the reasons for reform in the nineteenth century, see Douglas E. Ashford, *British Dogmatism and French Pragmatism . . .*, pp. 33–84.

and the Senate, most social laws were passed unanimously.[65] Social progress was an affair of state which even Senate conservatives could not ignore and which even socialist Deputies, like Jaurès, took seriously.[66]

Despite the slow pace of social legislation in the Third Republic, political institutions, both national and local, were able to play a constructive role throughout the early development of the French welfare state. Of course, social conditions helped because France never developed the culture of poverty which was institutionalized by the British Poor Laws and which was perpetuated by the need for massive public assistance between the wars. The politics of class might have intruded more strongly on French social legislation had not the political right so thoroughly discredited itself in the early years of the Third Republic. Naturally, the rich disliked social legislation, but their interventions in the political debates are derisory complaints compared to the prestige and influence still given the conservative interests of the Charity Organization Society and the defenders of the Poor Laws as Britain built her welfare state. For example, one finds the Baron Xavier Reille charging in 1903 that extending public assistance funds to hospitals and hospices under the new public assistance law would lead to 'obligatory internment.'[67] To the great amusement of the Chamber of Deputies, Jules Auffray opposed benefits for destitute children because they would 'destroy the difference between marriage and free love' to which the left replied with inexorable political logic that these inequalities would be worked out as the young did their military service. But the difference was more profound than the outworn tactics of the right. The right was politically discredited by the 1890s, and the charity movement could not escape being swept away by radical republican religious fears.[68] By 1890, the classical liberal view of Thiers that collective efforts threatened the Republic

[65] See J. Stone, *The Search for Peace* . . ., p. 60, for additional details on legislative organization. The law of 1905 was passed in the Chamber by 552 to 3 votes; the 1910 pension law by 280 to 3 in the Senate and 560 to 4 in the Chamber.
[66] See *Journal Officiel*, Débats Parlementaires, Chambre de Députés, 1905, seance du 12 juillet 1905, pp. 2890–1. Jaurès yielded because he feared that leaving the legislation to the next session would defeat it (national elections were coming up) and because he placed more priority on establishing the 'right to pensions'.
[67] *Journal Officiel*, Débats Parlementaires, Chambre des Députés, séance du 4 juin 1903, p. 1836.
[68] *Journal Officiel*, Débats Parlementaires, Chambre de Députés, séance du 29 mai 1903, p. 1786, and Hatzfeld, *Du Paupérisme à la securité sociale*, p. 67.

was no longer meaningful in French politics. The intense political difference within the Bloc des Gauches was over the application of the laws of association against the Church as a form of political tyranny, not over education itself.

Whereas the national conflict over local reform, and implicity over the social role of local government in Britain was polarized between counties and boroughs, in France it was over the social status to be afforded assistance at the local level throughout the country. The British centralized because they distrusted local government; the French centralized to achieve republican goals. The debate over the *bureaux de bienfaisance* and the *bureaux d'assistance publique* makes this unmistakable. Within a year of passing the 1905 law on state-administered public assistance for the aged and disabled, 644,000 persons were receiving aid and over 106 million frances were being spent. In addition, by 1912 over a million persons were receiving free hospital care under the 1893 law and 133,000 pensions under the 1910 law.[69] All these laws involved territorial organization through the departments and communes. Much as one may distrust the French administrative state, it was used then and now to achieve uniformity of service within the larger context of the state itself. The republicans, the Gaullists and even the Socialists of 1981 are alike in seeing the localized structure of the state as integral to policymaking.

As we shall see in more detail in Chapter 4 the sense of collective obligation attached to the French state helped overcome working class as well as localized objections to the welfare state. The left and the unions could accept the legislative compromises of 1905 and 1930 because there was much less doubt than in Britain when a right to state protection had been established. The fact that these 'rights' were less generous than benefits in Britain should not hide the equally important fact that the constitutional and legal foundations of new state activity were clear to political groups regardless of class. For example, when the Marquis de la Ferronnays intervened against the public assistance law of 1905 to complain that it would place intolerable burdens on small communes and destroy family obligations, Millerand had the ready, if inadequate, response that Ferronnays' objection could be met only by revising the Family Code. The socially aware Millerand

---

[69] John Weiss, 'Origins of the Welfare State: Poor Relief in the Third Republic,' *French Historical Studies*, **13**, Spring 1983, pp. 47–78.

had been the *rapporteur* of the Council of State study of obligatory public assistance when Léon Bourgeois was Minister of the Interior, and could demonstrate that no more than one in sixty-three French persons would qualify for public assistance, not an unreasonable burden on small communes that often had no more than 500 inhabitants.[70] Thus at a very early stage in the welfare state, territorial arguments were minimized, in part because the scale was small, while in Britain local intransigence remained the great unsolved problem of early social legislation. Local reform always lagged behind social legislation, keeping the localities in a subordinate, reactive situation.

In the 1903 debates, the crucial role of the communes in providing social and public assistance was never questioned. The Mayor, for example, was to make a list of eligible persons. Deputies agreed that in small communes he might consult with the *bureau de bienfaisance*, the object of radical suspicions for its links to the Church and outmoded forms of charity, because the poor were well known in small communes and the quality of the hospices public knowledge. But in larger communes the Mayor could be expected to work through the new *bureau d'assistance publique*. This kind of practical political compromise was always difficult to forge in Britain because, as we have seen, long before the Victorian welfare state emerged, the localities were paralysed by an antiquated tax structure and an archaic organization that made policy compromises impossible. The same kind of Gallic logic influenced the decision on joint administration with prefects. The state administration, contrary to contemporary interpretations, was not feared but assisted in implementation. One Deputy noted that the aged, poor and disabled were at a great disadvantage in small communes because peasants 'have no pity on those who do not work,' and 17,000 small communes did not even have a *bureau de bienfaisance*.[71] Given a more flexible field administration, the problem was neatly resolved by also having canton committees in these areas which would consult with charitable organizations and other mayors. As was to prove the case during the rapid urbanization of France in the 1960s, the French had alternatives to overcome the small scale system.

[70] *Journal Officiel*, Débats Parlementaires, Chambre des Députés, séance du 29 mai 1903, pp. 1788–91.
[71] *Journal Officiel*, Débats Parlementaires, Chambre des Députés, séance du 4 juin 1903, pp. 1826–31.

The argument over financing the early public assistance law is in many respects the most revealing for it demonstrates how intergovernmental sharing of social costs has always seemed a natural consequence of social legislation. Maurice Sibille, the defender of Catholic privileges and charity, objected to the basic formula, still roughly adhered to in modern French *aide sociale*, of dividing costs with about a fifth paid by communes, and two-fifths by departments and the state respectively. He pointed out that the new law would provide funds to care for about 153,000 persons, while estimates showed that over 400,000 persons would be eligible for public assistance. Clearly, the 11 million francs collected by private charities would be needed to supplement the 13 million francs to be raised by the communes. The intent was similar to the tactic of C. S. Loch, who hoped that British national insurance might be turned to the support of private charity. A compromise of administrative and partisan politics, common to French policymaking, was made. The *rapporteur* of the law, the radical Bienvenu Martin, agreed that the prefect would appoint charitable organization representatives to the new *bureau d'assistance publique*, and that leaving private contributions to local discretion (*prestations forfaitaires*) had failed miserably in advancing the 1893 law on health care.[72]

The relation of the communes and departments was substantially altered after World War I. In fact, compared to Britain, the centralization of French local government is relatively recent. But even social insurance, an easily centralized activity, left a role for local *notables*. The critical difference between the Senate and the Chamber versions of the proposed law was the role of departmental *caisses*. Insurance funds were to be assembled at the departmental level, so the point of discord shifted to control and supervision at that level. In part, this was because, even in the 1920s, national capabilities to operate national insurance were severely limited. While there was to be an Office National d'Assurance under the Ministry of Labour and a Conseil Supérieur d'Assurances Publiques, national staff to run the system was limited to 173 employees, 12 inspectors and one accountant,[73] a far cry from the state bureaucracies built after 1945 to run the modern social

---

[72] *Journal Officiel*, Débats Parlementaires, Chambre de Députés, séance du 12 juin 1903, pp. 1930–43.
[73] *Journal Officiel*, Rapport Anotelli, p. 518.

security system, and clearly at odds with the view of France as an administrative state.

The main controversy was not over the social aims of the law but over the role of the mutual insurance companies, themselves organized at the departmental level and, roughly comparable to the Friendly Societies in Britain, the instrument of a self-reliant middle class and benevolent employers. While the fight was, as always, over costs, the issue was defined politically, that is, how the interested parties would be represented on the departmental *caisse* committees. As often happens in the political development of the welfare state, the struggle to preserve middle-class concerns inadvertently worked to hasten full national control. In the Senate revisions between 1928 and 1930, many of the departmental powers were removed, the *caisse primaire* or single fund was broken up, and efforts were made to shift the full costs of non-contributors (the aged and poor) to national government. In the final compromise between the two chambers, a complex system of interdependence among the different funds was arranged, the participation of the self-employed was made voluntary (*facultative*), and the equal participation of employers and employees on the fund committees was guaranteed.[74] As we shall see in more detail in Chapter 6, all these complications were perpetuated in the complete nationalization of social insurance after the war.

But the most distinctive feature of the early social insurance law in France, never fully reproduced with such clarity in any other social insurance schemes, was to make the charges for both social needs and public assistance a social obligation. In most countries, the costs of public assistance were initially shifted to local governments without strong national intervention or, as in the case of Britain, shifted to localities *with* national controls. In some respects, the aims of the radical socialists and socialists of the pre-war period, outlined in Chapter 2, prevailed, even in the period of uninspiring and cautious government of the 1920s. The state had a responsibility for *solidarité*, that is, for the condition of society as a whole that few leaders rejected, even if they disliked the burden. Thus, even a conservative Senate could agree in 1930 that there

---

[74] Rapport Anotelli, p. 576. These reservations were the work of Dr C. Chaveau, the representative of the mutual societies. See C. Chaveau, *Les assurances sociales*, Paris; Payot, 1926. See also the continuity with earlier reservations, Maurice Jourdain, *De l'intervention des pouvoirs publics en matière d'assistance par le travail*, Paris; Rousseau, 1901.

must be *fonds de majoration et de solidarité* or a solidarity fund to which the various *caisses* were obliged to contribute. The solidarity fund was to be used to provide insurance contributions for invalids and the aged poor, to reimburse the funds for family benefits and shortfalls in worker pension benefits, to assure full sickness benefits for low income persons, and, of course, in a wartorn France, provide for widows.[75] From a Marxist perspective, these arrangements may be seen as a way of shifting social costs to the state as capitalist society declined, but this would be gross misinterpretation of how it was thought about in France and a serious distortion of the intent of policymakers. For France, more than any other democracy, social protection took on independent meaning and cut across local interests, class divisions and financial concerns. As the radical and socialist philosophers and sociologists had argued since the 1880s, individual and collective morality was not neatly compartmentalized.

The transformation of the liberal into the welfare state was much too intricate a task to be reduced to simple class arguments. This is not to say that the rich willingly provided for the less fortunate in any democracy, but that the political means for making the transition were different in every democracy. The different scenarios are most readily visible in the politics of local reorganization as the welfare states developed. In France, there was, and remains, an institutionalized identity of national and local interests. The identity of state and society made consolidation of local governments, and thereby their ease of national manipulation, less essential. To be sure, there was resistance from all levels of government, but levels of government as such were not seen as a barrier to achieving social reform, as was the case in Britain. French territorial politics was more articulated than in Britain, but the localities were not as distant from national concerns nor did national government set out to exclude them. This is not to say that class differences were not salient in developing the French welfare state, they could hardly not be so in such a determinedly *bourgeois* society. But class differences were, if anything, more uniformly distributed across local government and more equally affected by the concept of *solidarité*, making it more difficult to make communes and departments the scapegoats of social failure.

<hr />

[75] Rapport Anotelli, pp. 526–9.

Unintended consequences play an important part in understanding the development of the welfare state. For example, conveying British local policy interests to the national level were, in fact, virtually isolated from national policymaking until very recently. On the whole, British counties and boroughs valued their isolation from national politics until the complications of policymaking in the 1950s, in part a function of the growth of social services, forced them to adopt new practices. From its formation in 1872 until 1944 the Association of Municipal Councils (now the Association of Metropolitan Authorities) was the instrument of two men, father and son, who were masters at getting private bills through Parliament in order to achieve individual local authority needs in a piecemeal fashion. They were privy to national legislation and able to separate local demands from national politics. As Keith-Lucas and Richards note, the major local government associations were 'almost part of the constitution, with an accepted right to be consulted on both policy and detail of proposed legislation and in almost daily contact with senior civil servants, or with ministers themselves.'[76] The arrangement was a mutually convenient one, for it relieved Parliament from struggling with intergovernmental complexity, while enabling MPs to return to their constituencies with political rewards. Thus, the intergovernmental structure, no doubt unintentionally, insulated local government from national politics. Unlike localities in any other democracy, British local government remained aloof as the welfare state emerged and had little political incentive to take the initiative. The result, as we have seen, is that it was politically easy to circumvent local government as social policies multiplied and administratively convenient to design policies that eluded effective local political control. Even though localities were constantly required to meet new standards and provide new services, as a political event the welfare state somehow passed them by until Britain had to wrestle with the realities of intergovernmental politics after World War II.

Admittedly, French social reforms advanced at a slower pace than in Britain, but communes, departments and Paris were at least marching to the same music. As intergovernmental conflicts over social policies appeared in Britain, there was little alternative

---

[76] Brian Keith-Lucas and Peter Richards, *A History of Local Government in the Twentieth Century*, London; Allen & Unwin, 1978, pp. 180–221.

but confrontation. The first of these was the Poplar incident, when a Labour borough of London refused to implement economies in Poor Law benefits in 1921.[77] Whitehall invoked national audit powers, and the mayor and 29 councillors trooped off to prison to the accompaniment of their enthusiastic supporters. As in many intergovernmental conflicts in Britain, zero-sum tactics failed, and eventually the government gave way. The same non-political formula was tried again in 1972, when another Labour borough, Clay Cross, refused to implement public housing rent increases.[78] In these ways, central-local politics were polarized in social policy-making, as in many other areas of common concern. In no other political system could national government so easily ride rough-shod over local preferences. Paradoxically, neither could Britain build a modern welfare state without localized programmes, but the Beveridge Plan left little room for local government, which had been a suspect partner in welfare state activities since the turn of the century.

The Poplar incident deserves some elaboration for it helps explain why reformers between the wars were nearly as suspicious of local government as a vehicle for social reform as were the Edwardians. As we have seen, there was no formula for redistribution of revenues from the highly unequal local tax bases, but there was one important exception. A Metropolitan Poor Fund had been established so that within the rubric of Poor Law administration, not local government as such, London boroughs shared poor relief expenses. By 1922 Poplar had actually borrowed roughly a fifth of the entire fund, and insisted on paying poor relief at a higher scale than did other London boroughs. The problem might have alerted a more responsive administration to the pending crisis of unemployment insurance, for it was caused more by the unemployed poor than by the aged poor. The Ministry of Health was outraged by the occasional payment of poor relief in addition to unemployment benefits to especially needy

---

[77] For an account of the Poplar conflict, see Brian Keith-Lucas and Peter Richards, *A History of Local Government in the Twentieth Century*, London; Allen & Unwin, 1978, pp. 650–91. The Speenhamland conflict is described by Mark Neuman, 'Speenhamland in Berkshire,' in E. W. Martin, ed., *Comparative Developments in Social Welfare*, London; Allen & Unwin, 1972, pp. 85–127.
[78] On the Clay Cross conflict, see Austin Mitchell, 'Clay Cross,' *Political Quarterly*, **45**, 1974, pp. 165–77.

families.[79] The Ministry had expected that their efforts to expand unemployment relief with the 1920 Act would lower poor relief, especially in London, and it appears to have been baffled by the growth of public assistance in parts of London, even among similarly stricken East End boroughs. For example, Poplar had nearly 21 persons per thousand on poor relief, compared to Bethnal Green with 8 per thousand.[80] What was actually happening was that in the areas of prolonged unemployment, some localities refused to apply 'less eligibility' rules and used public assistance funds to provide payment at the higher levels given the 'eligible' unemployed. In the fifteen Poor Law Unions with the highest rates of benefits one found about seven per cent of the population, but a remarkable 22 per cent of all the paupers in Britain. By 1924, the Exchequer had been forced to loan £2 million to the Metropolitan Poor Fund, one-fourth of which went to Poplar.[81] Thus, it cannot be argued that British politicians and high civil servants were unaware of the real effects of the policies in the 1920s, although, as we shall see in more detail in Chapter 4, no major new policies were forthcoming until the mid-1930s.

Territorial politics impinges very differently on the social security and welfare structures of other democracies. In the United States, the 1935 Social Security Act made specific provisions to permit states to influence social policies. One reason to question the interpretation of Lowi and others of the development of the American welfare state is that well into the postwar era American territorial politics more nearly compare to European policymaking in the mid-nineteenth century. Nor could the entrenched federalism of German politics be excluded from the early organization of German social benefits. In the early organization of sickness insurance funds (*Krankenkassen*), Bismarck failed to achieve the total nationalization of the system that he preferred. As in the case of unemployment insurance, a complex semi-public organization grew within the legal framework of the Imperial Insurance Code (*Reichsversicherungsordnung* or RVO) to reconcile professional, local

[79] *Third Annual Report*, Ministry of Health, London; Parliamentary Papers, cmd. 1713, pp. 79–81.
[80] *Second Annual Report*, Ministry of Health, London; Parliamentary Papers, cmd. 1446, 124–5.
[81] *Fifth annual Report*, Ministry of Health, London; Parliamentary Papers, cmd. 2218, 1925, pp. 94–8. With nearly as high a rate of unemployment, Stockton still had only a third the rate of pauperism in 1922, *Third Report*, p. 81.

and client interests outside the governing framework.[82] Within a single national organization the intricate system of over 1500 sickness funds was organized in a semi-public organization, the Federal Association of Sickness Funds (*Deutsche Ärztevereinsbund* or DÄV) whose 239 member groups had enlisted roughly two-thirds of the German doctors by 1894. Thus, the DÄV followed the corporatist model of many German organizations dealing with social problems and until 1974 was easily dominated by the employers and unions.[83] As in most countries, public assistance remained a local responsibility although it came under increasing scrutiny during the severe inflation and unemployment of the 1920s. Public assistance did not become a legal right (*Sozialhilfe*) until the Federal Social Assistance Act of 1961.[84]

Although the small scale of Swedish government means that local government was not likely to become an obstacle to developing new social policies, several political circumstances of Swedish development made this even more likely. First, in the years before the rise of the Social Democrats the Liberal Party never developed the strong rural roots of liberal parties in many other countries. In a still primarily agrarian country, the educated and urban Liberals held little appeal for farmers and, as proven more difficult in larger European countries, the Liberals were eliminated with relative ease.[85] Thus, local government never had the political power to become the viable advocate of more cautious social reform as it did in the larger democracies. Second, the Social Democrats skilfully maintained an alliance with agrarian parties, in part because the Swedish lumber industry was undergoing modernization as Sweden herself industrialized. The possibility of an influential rural class developing apart from social democracy was

[82] On the historical background to the organization of German sickness insurance, see Deborah Stone, *The Limits of Professional Power: National Health Care in the Federal Republic of Germany*, Chicago; University of Chicago Press, 1980, pp. 34–54.

[83] The account of the rebellion against blue-collar (DGB) and white-collar (DAB) domination of the employee quotient of representation can be found in Henry A. Landsberger, *The Control of Cost in the Federal Republic of Germany: Lessons for America?*, Washington, D.C.; Department of Health and Human Services, Public Health Service (DHHS Publication No. (HRA) 81–14003), 1981, p. 9.

[84] Germany has not avoided the complications of localized welfare services. See in D. Grunow and F. Hegner, *Welfare or Bureaucracy?*, Cambridge, MA; Oelgeschlager, Gunn and Hain, 1980, pp. 143–61.

[85] Douglas Verney, 'The Foundations of Modern Sweden: The Swift Rise and Fall of Swedish Liberalism,' *Political Studies*, **20**, 1975, pp. 42–59.

avoided because in the 1930s agrarian interests appeared best served by aligning themselves with the Social Democratic politics.[86] As a result, the political complications of 'country versus city' so common in British local politics or the self-reliant agricultural class evolving from the French peasantry never became a barrier to the early implementation of a more advanced form of the welfare state.

BLUNTING THE FRENCH PRIVATE SECTOR

Because modern welfare states and their services are usually studied in the context of developments since 1945, a second major hurdle in the political transformation of modern states may be neglected. Because public and private forms of assistance were differently institutionalized, judging the welfare state solely in relation to social and economic differences may oversimplify political questions of major importance. In many ways, the nineteenth century is our best guide to the reconciliation of private and public interests in the welfare state because most early social reformers and policymakers did not imagine radical change in the economic order. Those who did were not credible, and soon lost their political influence. Moreover, the basic structures of economic production and economic organization were well in place by 1900. Much of the political skill and ingenuity exercised in the transition from liberal to welfare state was actually about forging acceptable compromises with private insurers, mutual insurers and various independent worker organizations for social protection and self-improvement. In each country, these groups were of course themselves the product of historical forces and had found their place within the constitutional and institutional framework of each country well before welfare states were imagined.

For a number of reasons, crude Marxist interpretations of how private interests were reconciled to the welfare state are not very persuasive. First, the relationship between the socialist parties and the labour movement varied greatly from country to country so that the left had to consider their internal political divisions as well as their presumably historic role as defenders of the working

---

[86] See Gösta Esping-Andersen, 'Fifty Years of Social Democratic Rule: Single Party Dominance in Sweden,' 1984, mimeo.

class. Second, differences in industrial structure and economic development affected how and where labour movements developed political interests in welfare. Both these questions will be analysed further in Chapter 4. Third, a number of private interests, not the least insurance companies, found the unburdening of unprofitable risks on the state highly desirable,[87] and employers did not uniformly oppose social benefits. Some industries, such as the Lyon silk manufacturers and Lever Brothers in Britain, were leaders in devising social benefit schemes for their employees. Fourth, assuming that the societal dilemmas of the capitalist state are primarily a function of the industrial working class leaves out agriculture, which, as we shall see, had, and still has, an important voice in determining the shape of welfare states. Fifth, and perhaps the most serious political complication of class interpretations of the welfare state, governments of the right have often been the villains in persuading the private sector to make concessions to the welfare state and in designing schemes that place social costs on private industry.

These questions become indeterminate in Marxist language. For our purposes, the main difficulty is that Marxist theory, like many liberal macro-economic theories, tells us very little about political processes. The controversies surrounding the funding, contributions and benefits of early social insurance programmes were one of the testing grounds for those hoping for ideological solutions. Whatever its abstract economic uniformity, the property issue arose in very different political forms and contexts, and unavoidably arose in ways that differed greatly with the historical development of industry, agriculture and labour in each country. With the exception of Britain, in the early stages of the welfare state, few policymakers saw socialized property or even nationalized industry as closely related to social policy. If anything, their arguments were the reverse: social insurance would protect workers and enable them to achieve the dignity and leverage of self-reliant employers and the self-employed. On the whole, as we shall see in more detail in Chapter 4, they were right, though this change

[87] This is the central hypothesis of James O'Connor, *The Fiscal Crisis of the Capitalist State*, New York; St Martin's Press, 1973. As will be explored further in Chapter 5, the problem is that with the development of advanced welfare states over the 1950s and 1960s, many of the severe political problems were *within* the public sector.

was not, and even today is not, without political risks for workers and unions.

What might be called true 'capitalist' intervention in social security operations came much later, as financial and industrial leaders saw the immense funds being accumulated by governments. Intervention at this later stage was nearly always self-defeating, as, for example, with the 1939 amendments to the American Social Security Act by Hans Morgenthau to index social benefits with inflation in order to minimize the potential impact of social security funds on the capital market.[88] In any event, the sectoral differences over building welfare states could not be phrased in abstract definitions of property, but had to be fought out over the ways various categories of property owners and diverse private interests related to social policies within each democracy. Though by no means wholly 'private' in an economic sense, there were perhaps four main political groups aligned with private sector interests, who had to be appeased. They were the farmers, the doctors, the mutual or voluntary insurance companies and the private insurance companies. Only the latter group had unmistakable private market foundations though even the huge private insurers, such as Prudential in Britain or the 'Pru' as it was affectionately called, were coming under government regulation.

As an industry subject to immense technological changes and rooted in each country's historical pattern of land ownership, agriculture had been subject to severe economic risks well before the welfare state emerged. Because farmers and peasants were often the backbone of early democratic rule, agriculture had long been successful in transferring risks to the state. Many of these habits were simply adapted to the welfare state. The experience of mutual insurance companies was very different. Often the product of the early, self-reliant labour movements and heavily middle-class and blue-collar, they were the main focus of political conflict. By 1900, it would be incorrect to think that either agriculture or mutual insurance were 'capitalist' endeavours because both were already dependent on the state, though they did defend private ownership of land and individual self-reliance for social protection. For professional reasons, the doctors presented a different kind of political problem.

[88] See Bruno Stein, 'Funding Social Security on a Current Basis,' in D. Ashford and E. W. Kelley, eds, *Nationalizing Social Security*, Greenwich, CN; JAI Press, 1986.

In all the democracies, farmers displayed special talent in organizing themselves so that it should come as no surprise that they were one of the most skilful groups in exploiting the development of the welfare state. Indeed, it is misleading to assume, as many contemporary commentaries on the welfare state do, that agriculture had little to do with expanding state capacities, which, in turn, could be used to see that farmers acquired maximum social benefits with minimal contribution. Their success in using the social institutions of the state may be less visible because the social protection that farmers wanted, and usually obtained, was income maintenance through price supports, protective tariffs, cheap credit, substantial capital subsidies in the form of roads, flood control, irrigation, storage facilities, electrification, etc. Quite independently of patterns of land ownership, type of product, and size of rural population, by the late nineteenth century, farmers everywhere seemed able to fashion corporatist organizations, usually having the Ministry of Agriculture at its head,[89] and often reinforced by state-supported agricultural colleges, extension services, disease control agencies, etc. In a way, farmers fashioned their own rurally oriented welfare state distinct from the industrially based welfare state.

Unlike Britain, where the landed aristocracy dominated agriculture, at the turn of the century France still had a large peasant population. Their strong republican tradition provided an identification with the state, but they might have obstructed the development of the French welfare state had they not received many benefits for their loyalty. In fact, the social debate began in the 1880s when Léon Bourgeois used the monopoly of agricultural insurance to gain a foothold for his social policies. The Méline tariff of 1884 was in part a reward for the wide support given the radicals and radical socialists by farmers in the 1880s, and organized in part by agricultural professors of the state education system. From 1897, the Bank of France began making direct subsidies to Crédit Agricôle,[90] and in 1900, as part of the development of

[89] On the corporatist structure of the Ministry of Agriculture and its clients today, see John T. S. Keeler, 'The Corporate Dynamics of Agricultural Modernization in the Fifth Republic,' in W. Andrews and S. Hoffman, eds, *The Fifth Republic at Twenty*, Albany, NY; State University of New York Press, 1981, pp. 271–91.
[90] Crédit Agricole remains the largest deposit bank in France. See Jean-Claude Gaudibert, *Le dernier empire français: le Crédit Agricole*, Paris; Segher, 1977.

mutual insurance, rural mutual insurance funds were tax exempt.[91] At least visibly, French farmers were not a direct burden on the state. Their share of the national budget barely increased until the 1930s, but they benefited from a multitude of concealed supports, tax privileges and low interest rates provided outside the state budget.[92] When social insurance was debated over the 1920s, the farmers were not strongly opposed, in part because the conservative resurgence in French politics provided over 200 million francs in agricultural relief in 1930.

Though clearly capitalist insofar as private land ownership defines economic self-interest, the farm population of France became one of the most favoured beneficiaries of the welfare state. They received special treatment as pension plans developed over the 1950s, and partial medical coverage in 1961. By then, their tax exemptions were valued at 2.8 billion francs. Even so, the funds collected by their own organization, the Caisse de Mutualité Social Agricôle, were unable to provide benefits at the prescribed levels and received a subsidy of over 3 billion francs.[93] Agricultural contributors were paying no more than a fourth of the cost of their social security benefits in the 1960s, and their relative position steadily deteriorated as young persons left the countryside and the rural population aged over the past twenty years. The ratio of contributors to beneficiaries became impossible, and, by the 1970s, there was only one contributor to three beneficiaries for many of the insured social risks.[94] Not the least of political paradoxes in the development of the French welfare state is that the social group most worried over the growth of welfare became one of its most lavish beneficiaries.

As in the case of most economic sectors in France, they were also politically split in France. The Société des Agriculteurs de France was founded in 1867 under the Second Empire, and by

[91] On the early history and politics of the mutual insurance societies, see George J. Sheridan, 'Aux origines de la mutualité en France: le développement et l'influence des sociétés de secours mutuels, 1800–1848,' *La Revue de l'Economoie Sociale*, July–September 1984, pp. 17–25.

[92] Most of the statistics in this and the following paragraphs come from Delorme and André, *L'Etat et l'économie*, pp. 303–65.

[93] On their special treatment after World War II, see Francis Netter, 'Annexe', Comité d'Histoire de la 2è Guerre Mondiale, Colloque sur l'Histoire de la Securité Sociale, Caen, 8–9 April 1980, p. 236.

[94] See Gilbert Guillaume, 'Agriculture,' in P. Laroque, ed., *Succès et faiblesses . . .*, pp. 179–218.

1914 had about 750,000 members. The state-within-the-state was reinforced by the radical republicans when the public assistance law debate took place in the first decade of the century. Partly to counterbalance the Société des Agriculteurs, composed of larger landowners, the radical republicans encouraged the formation of the Federation nationale de la mutualité et de la coopération agricôles in 1910 to further cooperation among smaller farmers. As a result, most farm owners were able to purchase a variety of services, including social insurance, at reduced rates and did not need to play an active role in the early social security debates. Farmers could be insured under the terms of the 1928 and 1930 laws, but under a voluntary scheme that reduced their contribution. With the exception of agricultural workers, who were not insured until 1947, French agriculture did very well with its own organization. Once the modern welfare state emerged after World War II, farmers could pretty well define their own terms of participation and demand their individual system of social protection within the national system. But the very success of their organization meant that French farmers, unlike the rurally influential in Britain and the United States, had little reason to constitute a political opposition to increasing the social role of the state.

As in Britain, the real political fight over developing social insurance arose from the small, voluntary or mutual insurance companies. In 1821, the Société de Bienfaisance was allowed to form a Grand Conseil des Sociétés de Secours Mutuels. The council acquired the most traditional of political powers, the powers of certification, inspection, and audit.[95] As part of the classical liberal stimulus to French government in the Second Republic and early period of the Second Empire, laws of 1850 and 1852 gave mutual insurance companies special privileges and special protective legislation. Legally, the voluntary sociétés de secours mutuels were never wholly private organizations like the British Friendly Societies, and so the public–private distinction was, as is so often the case in France, blurred by state support and state regulation from the earliest development of private insurance. The early mutual insurance companies received their first infusion of state funds from

---

[95] See Hatzfeld, Du paupérisme à la securité sociale, pp. 206–8. There was also a Société protestante de Prévoyance et de Secours Mutuels in Paris and a Société Lyonnaise de Secours Mutuels in Lyons from the Second Republic. These organizations also served as political meeting grounds for republicans during the political repression of Napoleon III.

10 million frances from the confiscation of Orléanist property.[96] At the turn of the century, the mutual insurance companies were receiving a state subsidy of over a million francs per year. Though they did not multiply until later in the century, mutual insurance companies had an independent existence in France well before similar activities developed in other states. French mutual insurers were never independent of state institutions, which helps explain both their durability and their influence as modern welfare institutions developed in the twentieth century.

As Hatzfeld argues,[97] the central political issue over development of mutual insurance was not unlike that of any group trying to establish its identity within the French state. Though one might translate the struggle into socio-economic terms, the issue was much more the long-standing republican dilemma over how to create associations. Though economic liberalism was evoked much later to defend private insurance, especially over the 1920s, the initial battle was whether the mutual societies might be endowed with public authority as semi-official institutions. It was not the politics of the market place that complicated the growth of French mutual societies, but the politics of the state. The same complication arrested the development of business and labour groups. The continuity within the political debate is characteristic of the French state, and sets it apart from the shifting grounds for political favours and political rewards that are part of the Anglo-Saxon welfare state. In any event, the republicans of the Third Republic were enthusiastic supporters of the mutual insurance, and the law of 1898 bestowed a semi-official existence on them.[98] Insofar as there was a protest over their invigoration, it was overriden. Over a hundred of the hundred and eleven Chambers of Commerce in France and 1,500 agricultural unions voted against the 1898 proposal.[99] But the reform was part of the Léon Bourgeois social programme and basic to the early radical republican vision of France.

The political arm of the voluntary insurance movement was the

---

[96] E. Levasseur, *Questions ouvrières* . . ., p. 790.
[97] Hatzfeld, pp. 192–4.
[98] The reform was actually planned by Léon Say in 1884. See Emile Cheysson, 'L'imprévoyance dans les institutions de prévoyance,' *Réforme Sociale*, **6**, no. 2. July–September 1888, pp. 273–80.
[99] For additional details, see Louis Schnoll, 'Le monopole des assurances,' *Revue de la Prévoyance et de la Mutualité*, November 1911, pp. 11–23.

Ligue Nationale de la Prévoyance et de la Mutualité, the republican social welfare analogue to the more famous Ligue d'Enseignement that produced the radical education reforms of the 1880s. The Ligue de Prévoyance predates the surge of social reform activity in Britain, and, in many respects, was a more formidable political organization than anything constructed by the Webbs or the British new liberals. Waldeck-Rousseau was chairman of its legal committee; Paul Guiyesse, the actuary who made the first major study of the costs of social insurance in 1901, was an active member; Emile Cheysson, the champion of self-financing insurance, was president of its technical committee,[100] Emile Levasseur, the venerable historian of French welfare and member of the Collège de France, often participated; and there were numerous republican leaders among its officers, such as Bourgeois, Ricard, Siegfried and Berger.[101] In general, they linked to the *polytechnicien* stream of nineteenth-century social reforms, described in Chapter 3. The annual conferences of the mutual societies was a major political event. In 1905, 24,000 societies attended the Paris congress when a banquet for 50,000 persons was served on the Champs de Mars, and the President of France gave the official address.[102]

All this suggests that the mutual societies were not to be treated lightly by politicians. In addition, their sickness and death benefits were an important social contribution to the early welfare state in France. At the dawn of the Third Republic in 1869, there were about 2,600 societies with 289,000 members; by 1902, there were 13,677 societies with about 2 million members. Levasseur estimated that they paid about a fourth of the sickness costs of their members, often through plans sponsored by *patrons*, as in the case of the Lyon silk workers and the railway workers. But like the Friendly Societies in Britain, they were not run on a 'scientific' basis, requiring the same contribution regardless of age, promising full pensions without actuarial knowledge, and not carefully separating the various risks which they insured against.[103] Some of the

[100] Cheysson seems to have been hypnotized with the economic effects of compound interest and never tired of telling how one franc invested under Louis XI would now be a billion francs. Better yet, a millime invested under Charlemagne at 5 per cent would provide 6 billion annually. See his article cited above.
[101] For details, see Georges Hamon, *Histoire Générale de l'Assurance* . . ., pp. 111–12.
[102] Levasseur, p. 796.
[103] Figures and critique for Levasseur, p. 793 and p. 797.

insurance plans for public employees were also operated as mutual insurance plans. All this helps to explain their political survival, for they were seen more as appendages to the state than as competitors for insurance. Long after the British Friendly Societies were forgotten, one finds a no less critical figure than Amboise Croizat, the Communist Minister of Social Security in 1945, defending the role of mutual societies and reassuring the left-coalition government then governing France that the Societies would be represented in the new social security organization. When the modern French welfare state was designed, the precedent of the 1898 law was used to justify the legal foundations of state insurance, not to attack voluntary insurance.[104]

Unlike Britain and the United States, the large private insurance companies in France never had great influence in designing social insurance. Again, the difference is not so much that France lacked entrepreneurial talent but that banking, like the private sector as a whole, grew in close association with the state. While the Anglo-Saxon countries encouraged small individual savings through the Post Office and public institutions,savings were not identified with the objectives of the state except in time of war nor were they channeled though specialized state institutions. As part of his never completed liberal reforms, Napoleon III encouraged the Caisse d'Epargne to expand, and it achieved enormous popularity under the republicans and later the radical republicans.[105] By 1881, the Caisse d'Epargne had over 2,000 offices scattered throughout France with deposits of over 1.5 billion francs. Between 1881 and 1904, deposits more than doubled, and depositors grew in number to over 11 million persons, roughly a fourth of all Frenchmen. Like the mutual insurance societies, public saving was not a purely middle-class phenomenon. About a third of the deposits were from miners, and the Caisse was particularly strong in working class areas in the industrial west and north.[106]

In France, as in most democracies, the private insurers were a

---

[104] See the Rapport Buisson, *Journal Officiel*, Documents de l'Assemblée Consultative, séance du 24 juillet 1945, Annexe 554, pp. 725–38.

[105] French nationalism has always permeated French saving habits. The German indemnity of a billion francs in 1871 was paid off in one year. The Caisse des Dépôts was formed in 1816 to assure prompt and reliable payment of occupation costs of the Napoleonic wars. These habits help explain why France took such a hard line on payment of German reparations after World War I.

[106] See Levasseur, pp. 779–85.

paper tiger in opposition to social insurance. In 1910, no more than half a million Frenchmen held private insurance, most of it through cost sharing plans in some 320 different plans sponsored by benevolent *patrons*.[107] In France and elsewhere, the real Achilles heel of private insurance plans was that they were run on an actuarial basis, paying relatively small benefits after thirty years or more of participation. Thus, the attack of private insurers had to adjust to financial and political realities. Along with Dr Chaveau, representing the mutual insurance societies, the leader in the attack on the 1928 and 1930 laws was Robert Pinot,[108] the insurance specialist from the Union des Industries Métallurgiques et Minères (UIMM), the successor to the famous, and sometimes infamous, Comité des Forges of the nineteenth century. The UIMM was, as it is today, the central agency managing private industrial insurance plans, and from the 1920s to the present acts as the bargaining agent for industry as social insurance is designed and implemented. The central argument of industrial insurers was that risks must be separated, a principle that was used successfully against postwar plans to have a *caisse unique* for all social insurance and was revived in the 1967 reforms of French social security. While one might argue that the private insurers had a measure of success, the internal divisions of the modern French social security system, to be elaborated in Chapter 6, are the product of the incremental construction of social insurance. An unavoidable problem in any political context is the insistence of early savers, many of them public employees, that their *droits acquis* be protected. Thus, it would be incorrect to see the partial success of the UIMM as a purely private sector ploy but, more accurately, as the clever use of the state against the state by making a political appeal to a wide range of insured persons.

But the political conditions for a simple polarization of private and public approaches to insurance never existed in France. As early as 1889, the radical republican Minister of Justice, Ricard, who conducted many of the studies set in motion by Léon Bourgeois, saw that social insurance contained a fatal political flaw

[107] Hatzfeld, p. 39. His discussion of Pinot's role in the 1920s is found on pp. 156–71.
[108] Pinot was a respected insurance expert and not simply a private sector lobbyist. See Robert Pinot, *Les oeuvres sociales des industries metallurgiques*, Paris; Colin, 1924.

where 'one would vote on one hand for increased benefits (*indemnités*) and, on the other hand, for reduced premiums (*primes*).'[109] Simultaneously, like all good republicans, Ricard was determined that there should not be 'privileged categories' of beneficiaries in any public system, a preoccupation that was much less in evidence in the development of British and American social insurance. To be sure, leaders in other countries saw the political contradictions of a dual insurance system, but most often tried to resolve the differences by compartmentalizing insurance. The French approach was basically different. Even the earliest advocates of social insurance confronted the implicit political contradictions and worried that social insurance would divide rather than unite the French nation. Although the liberal economists, such as Leroy-Beaulieu, would continue their exhortation for self-reliance and self-supporting insurance plans throughout the 1920s, it was no more than a holding action.

If there was any successful political coalition built on private interests, it was the short-lived resistance to accident compensation, legislated in 1898 and 1899. In a politically fragmented France, accident risks enabled widely divergent political actors to converge because neither large employers, small employers nor farm owners wished to contribute. More important, accidents are a form of risk where mutually advantageous political deals could easily be made. In the early legislation, large employers achieved their goals by making proof of negligence a legal burden of the employee, a condition that effectively neutralized the laws. Small employers got a voice for *patrons* in the management of the fund, assuring them that the political power of small businessmen and merchants would be felt. The farm owners were the most successful, getting full exemption for farm accidents unless they involved machines, which, of course, were relatively rare at the turn of the century. Many a rural Deputy achieved oratorical heights explaining how a person stupid enough to be kicked by a horse had no right to compensation. The same rule applied to forestry workers, presumably because no sensible forester would let a tree fall on himself.[110] Over the 1920s, accident compensation was extended to all of agriculture and the defeating negligence procedure overturned. But once again, the inadvertent equalizing

---

[109] Quoted in Hamon, p. 145. See also Henri de Moly, 'L'assurance obligatoire et le socialisme d'Etat,' *Réforme Sociale*, **6**, no. 55, April 1888, pp. 706–19.
[110] See Hatzfeld, pp. 282–8, for full details.

effects of political greed appears. Employers did agree to accept full responsibility for paying valid accident claims, and this concession was repeatedly used to defend the development of the French welfare state.

One of the main reasons why simple socio-economic interpretations of the welfare state are politically misleading is that, as social protection and social insurance developed, there also developed distinct professional interests whose ability to mobilize widespread popular resistance was limited. Health insurance is, of course, the most dramatic illustration, and the experience of the French doctors over the 1920s anticipated the fragmenting of political interests as the welfare state developed a more intricate organization. Although Hatzfeld is right to argue that there is a basic similarity in the values of private business and private medicine, he acknowledges that there is a substantial difference between the political concessions to the welfare state as they affect personal incomes, as in the case of doctors, and the rules of the marketplace as they affect entrepreneurs.[111] In any event, the politics of medicine and health are seldom as simple as the common socio-economic generalities. Dr Chauveau, as we have seen, waged a successful battle in the 1920s to protect private medical interests, but by the 1950s the system absorbed 8 per cent of French consumer income. As in Britain, the quotient of doctors in public employment steadily grew, including about a tenth of all doctors by 1950. A further complication is the relation of doctors to the hospital system, and over a third of hospital beds were in the public sector by 1958. With about 12 million Frenchmen subscribing to additional medical insurance through mutual insurance companies in 1961, the demand side of medical care is not simple either. By 1957, about 70 per cent of the population was receiving public health benefits, and when agricultural workers and farmers were added that year, coverage rose to 85 per cent of the population.[112]

In summary, taking the edge off unruly capitalism in France was seldom as ideological an issue as partisan versions of French politics suggest. Unlike the more abrupt and politicized development of welfare state organizations in Britain and the United States, there was an institutional and moral continuity in the

[111] Hatzfeld, pp. 288-94.
[112] Details in this paragraph from Henry Roson, 'Santé,' in P. Laroque, ed., *Succès et faiblesses. . .*, pp. 71–101.

growth of the French welfare state that often persuaded political contenders of all colours that change was needed. The nature of this continuity was pointed out early in the century by Levasseur,[113] though he does not develop its political foundations. There were three overlapping concepts of social assistance and social protection in France: *prévoyance*, or individual effort against risks as in all liberal approaches to the welfare state; *patronage*, or combined individual and group (*mutualité*) efforts to provide protection; and *assistance* or *solidarité* as developed by the radical republicans, radical socialists and socialists. The progress of social legislation in France is slow compared to Britain or Germany, but from its inception incorporates the steady progression from a simple liberal view of welfare and social equality to the values of the advanced welfare state. The more developed concept of a state in French politics made it difficult for any major political actors to evade the full consequences of their decisions. It was, therefore, more difficult than in other democracies to isolate society from the state, while the state itself could not as easily ignore threats to the solidarity of the French people. As we shall see in Chapter 6, the deep interdependence of social and political values meant that once the welfare state acquired full recognition in France in 1945, it grew at an alarming pace.

SUBMERGING THE BRITISH PRIVATE SECTOR

Compared to most welfare states, the historic compromises worked out between economic liberalism and the needs of modern democracy in Britain were timid and tentative. The reasons for this run deep in British history: a financial community, the City, which was able to preserve a remarkable degree of autonomy from the state; a banking system that thrived on world trade and therefore was protected by its identification with British imperial and defense needs; a landed aristocracy that was not adverse to profitable intermarriage with the rising industrial class; the concentration of 'smoke stack' industries and workers in the north of England and in Scotland, where they were much less visible, and less effective in making their needs known to government; a new

---

[113] Levasseur, p. 778.

middle class that aped the rich and powerful, to name only a few. The curious result is that, although the rich and poor were more divided than in most democracies, class differences were less easily mobilized to affect the emergence of the welfare state. The political corollary was that the very wealthy felt less need to fight against the emergent welfare state, in part because their economic interests were insulated in British sectorial politics.

The way in which the political struggle with the landed aristocracy overlaps the emergence of the welfare state is a political peculiarity of the British system. Even the politically dominant Junkers were at least identified by their political dependence on Prussia and the army. Their blatant manipulation of German democracy through the three-class voting system was therefore more readily attacked. In contrast, the power of British landlords spread across rural and urban areas. In the cities, powerful figures such as the Duke of Westminster made millions on land development and, in the countryside, the prestige of the landed was virtually untouched until late Victorian reforms of local government, public health and education. Defining rich landowners as those with land values over £50,000, Offer estimates that they owned half the agricultural land. One per cent of the owners held 30 per cent of the land in terms of value.[114] A rural population of 320,000 tenant farmers farmed 88 per cent of the land. Over a million acres were put aside as hunting playgrounds for the rich, where beating badgers, hunting foxes and dragging down deer may have diverted the upper class from the real social changes going on in British cities, but their power was immense.

The depoliticization of the land question is an integral part of the launching of the British welfare state, though usually omitted from less political accounts of the British welfare state. There are two political circumstances of great importance. First, Labour intellectuals came overwhelmingly from London, and their main concern, with good reason, was the brutally exploited and chaotic problem of 'casual labour' on the London docks. As we shall see in more detail in Chapter 5, the Webbs and the young Beveridge considered an orderly organization of the labour market through Labour Exchanges the prerequisite to employment reforms. The

[114] These figures come from the superb study of Avner Offer, *Property and Politics 1870–1914*, Cambridge; Cambridge University Press, pp. 113 and 130. An early study of land inequality was J. Bateman, *The Great Landlords of Great Britain and Ireland*, London; 1883, 4th edn.

famous studies of Booth and Rowntree were of urban poverty,
though the latter was aware of rural poverty and later worked on
the problem for Lloyd George. While the nascent Labour Party
had its strongholds in the north, London was their big political
prize and later their political showcase.[115] The inadvertent effect
was to distract the Labour Party from the land reform and from
rural poverty. Second, the political controversy over recovering
land 'rent' or accrued value for public purposes was broached well
before the Labour Party was formed, and, to some extent, was
pre-empted by the Liberal Party. In 1888, the Liberal Party
committed itself to recovering 'ground-rents' or increased land
values, and, as will be recalled from above, Lloyd George's 1909
budget shocked the Tories more because of its mild land taxation
clauses than for its social benefits.

The political dynamics of the land question are crucial because
over nineteenth-century Britain, and even well into the twentieth
century, increased land values were an obvious source of funds for
the social services and an unmistakable source of social inequalities. Political thinkers of every hue were preoccupied with the social
injustice of economic rent: Ricardo, Bentham, Bright, Cobden, J.
S. Mill and T. H. Green. Oddly enough, it was an American,
Henry George, who mobilized these discontents with his best-
seller, *The Irish Land Question*, in 1881, and his name was said to
be second in familiarity only to Gladstone.[116] George's proposal
anticipated later schemes for nationalizing industry. He proposed
a 'single tax' that essentially would buy out landowners and eventually entrepreneurs with their own profits. The early effort to

[115] Preoccupation with London runs through the history of the Labour Party
and is embodied in the career of Herbert Morrison, The Labour victory in
London in 1934 was a crucial step in reconstructing the Labour Party after the
1931 debacle. See Bernard Donoughue and G. W. Jones, *Herbert Morrison: Portrait
of a Politician*, London; Weidenfeld and Nicolson, 1973, especially pp. 189–210.
Ironically, as Labour recovered, Morrison's devotion to London became a political
handicap for him and in many ways diminished his chances of becoming Party
Leader. Essentially, the weaker the Labour Party becomes, the more influential
London politics becomes, which, in turn, deflects the recovery of the Party from
other national problems, a kind of self-perpetuating imbalance readily visible in
the early 1980s.
[116] As the title of George's book suggests, the land question overlapped with the
Irish question where compensating British landlords was a major obstacle to
reform, and helped paralyse Liberal interest in land reform. See Roy Douglas,
*Land, People and Politics: A History of the Land Question in the United Kingdom
1878–1952*, London; St Martin's Press, 1976.

provide public housing was also essentially a problem of how to find land. The Royal Commission on the Housing of the Working Classes of 1884 was a strange compendium of political interests, including the Prince of Wales and Lord Salisbury for the Tories and Sir Charles Dilke for the Liberals, and was a non-partisan attempt to neutralize the agitation that Henry George spread across Britain.[117] As we saw in the first section of this chapter, the threat of increased local taxes, and therefore enhanced local social services, was, first, an issue over increasing land taxes and, second, transferring them to urban areas. But the politial power of the landed was preserved and further protected by diminishing local property taxes, and thereby further handicapping localities as agents for the welfare state. Land was 'de-rated' by half in 1896 and fully exempt in 1929, both decisions by the Tories.

The rapid progress of the British welfare state from 1911 owes something to effective neutralization of the landed interests, achieved by granting them protection from local taxation and by isolating the land issue from politics. In this respect, 1911 was a replay of the repeal of the Corn Laws in 1846. With his uncanny political intuition, Lloyd George saw the issue clearly, but after World War I never again had the power to renew his attack. In 1913, Lloyd George hoped to win the coming election by an appeal to rural voters in the Tory seats in the countryside. He appointed Rowntree to make a Land Enquiry on rural poverty, but typically made his own proposals before the study was completed![118] In 1925, he paid for the preparation of *Land and the Nation* or 'Green Book', a study of 600 pages that would have nationalized growing land values. But Conservative domination between the wars meant that no strong legislation was possible.

---

[117] It is interesting to note that Sir George Goschen, the expert on resource inequities among local authorities, was a dissenter on the Royal Commission. In fact, the Royal Commission approved a tax of 4 per cent on land improvement which Offer, *Property and Politics* . . ., pp. 186–7, concludes would actually have been an appropriate rate given increased land values in late Victorian Britain. The Royal Commission on Local Taxation of 1901 again considered a tax on land, but refused to make increases.

[118] See Offer, pp. 372–85, for more details. See also Bentley B. Gilbert, 'David Lloyd George: The Reform of British Land-Holding and the Budget of 1914,' *Historical Journal*, **21**, no. 1, 1978, pp. 117–41. Liberals were also aware that despite their social insurance bill, spending on education and housing was declining before World War I. Having opted for social insurance, funds for other social reforms had to be found elsewhere.

Although the Labour Party was committed to land nationalization, its weak governments never had the power to force through such controversial legislation, nor was land a very attractive electoral issue to the battered Labour Party.[119] After the war land policies were mired in the interministerial rivalries, the complexities of housing, and the priorities of building new towns.[120] Thus, what had long been recognized as the most serious social injustice of the British welfare state eluded politics, but in doing so separated what might be the only true capitalists, the big landowners, from the politics of welfare.

Perhaps the best demonstration of how difficult it is to make simple generalizations about the relation of class politics to policy-making comes from the second private sector critic of the welfare state, the voluntary insurance companies or Friendly Societies.[121] Unlike the landowners who were adept at protecting their interests from welfare state requirements until well into the 1920s, the Friendly Societies were on the forefront of the political struggle even though the political outcome was never in serious doubt. Although they performed much the same service for middle and low income groups as the French mutual societies, their political resources and their political objectives were entirely different. They were seldom the instrument of benevolent employers, like many French societies, nor were they as middle class as the French voluntary insurance companies were. The Friendly Societies protected the self-reliant worker and lower middle class against the two most fearful risks of Victorian industrial life: a pauper's grave by providing a death benefit sufficient to purchase a plot and pay for a funeral; and the poor house by providing a widow's benefit to relieve the loss of the family wage earner. Hence, the Friendly Societies have a distinctly British origin in the oppressive history

---

[119] Labour Party proposals to resolve the land issue were never pressed, but Snowden, the Chancellor of the Exchequer in 1931, did propose a land tax which was then repealed by the Tories in 1934. For the most part, their concern was with labour colonies in the countryside to receive the London poor, a particular favourite of George Lansbury, but hardly a progressive, or very effective, measure.
[120] There is an excellent study of the political hash made of land reform since World War II. See Andrew Cox, *Adversary Politics and Land: The Conflict over Land and Property Policy in Post-War Britain*, Cambridge; Cambridge University Press, 1984. See also the helpful book of John Ratcliffe, *Land Policy: An Exploration of the Nature of Land in Society*, London; Hutchinson, 1976.
[121] See P. H. J. H. Godsen, *The Friendly Societies in England*, Manchester; Manchester University Press, 1961.

of the Poor Laws,[122] while the mutual societies arose from the slower and more dispersed evolution of an industrial France. The curious political fact concerning the Friendly Societies was that though they more distinctly focused on a social class than their French counterpart, they behaved contrary to the long-term interests of their clients and did their best to cripple the 1911 Act.

In contrast to the landowners, the Friendly Societies' political influence was clearly the product of political change rather than political privilege, in particular, the spread of the franchise and organization of mass parties. Their political organization held the most austere Victorian politicians in awe. In 1900, they had between 70,000 and 80,000 agents who visited over four million members every week or so to collect the small weekly insurance premiums. Gilbert estimates that about half the entire adult male population of Britain was contacted. The two largest, the Manchester Unity of Odd Fellows and the Ancient Order of Foresters, had over 700,000 members.[123] The solidarity of the members was reinforced by the fraternal character of the societies. As we shall see in more detail in Chapter 4, the failure of the British labour movement to insist on more participation in managing social security is largely due to the demise of the Friendly Societies, combined with the distraction of unions with more pressing concerns between the wars. In France, a more militant and weaker labour movement insisted from the earliest social legislation that social insurance funds have a quotient of union representatives, a condition embodied in nearly all major social legislation and fully institutionalized by the postwar French welfare state. But in the age of British craft unions, themselves often of a semi-fraternal nature, the 'badge of respectability,' membership in a Friendly Society, helped isolate the labour movement from the welfare state.

One of the reasons to distinguish between the economic and political significance of changes in the welfare state is that many conservative welfare organizations survived well beyond the period of their usefulness. This is clearly the case with the Friendly

---

[122] On the similarity between the position of the Friendly Societies and the traditional poverty views of the Charitable Organisation Society, see James H. Treble, 'The Attitudes of the Friendly Societies Towards the Movement in Great Britain for State Pension, 878–1908,' *International Review of Social History*, **15**, 1970, no. 2, 19, pp. 266–99.

[123] B. Gilbert, *The Evolution of National Insurance* . . ., p. 167.

Societies as Gilbert shows very clearly.[124] First, because they developed when the active life span of a worker (and most others) was shorter, their actuarial estimates, when used at all, were deficient. At the turn of the century, they often still used life tables devised between 1838 and 1854, and so as workers lived longer the societies went bankrupt. Second, with the full development of industrial society toward the end of the century, birthrates declined, and they could not renew their membership and premiums with more members. Third, rising rates of interest toward the end of the century concealed their deteriorating financial condition, and their records were so poor that many did not even know what their reserves were. Fifth, and partly because of their fraternal character, they fought bitterly among themselves, against public pensions and for the strict imposition of a means test on any social insurance, thereby aligning themselves with the archaic forces supporting Poor Law principles.[125] Rooted in working class self-reliance, they opposed the development of social insurance and inadvertently excluded workers from a role in its future development. There are few greater political paradoxes in the development of the British welfare state.

Regardless of their economic vulnerability, the Friendly Societies had to be taken seriously in designing the 1911 Insurance Acts. Their opposition could kill it, and Labour members of the Asquith government defended them. Although Lloyd George was constantly changing his mind over tactics as the bill progessed, he consistently favoured the idea that if Friendly Societies, and later other organizations, were incorporated as collecting agents, then the contributors would have physical evidence in their pockets in the form of their stamped booklets which would ease the resistance to compulsory contributions. The government was well aware that the administrative costs of the societies were often over a quarter of their collections, but hoped this might be reduced by official supervision.[126] The 1910 actuarial study for the 1911 Act showed

---

[124] These arguments are presented in detail in Gilbert, pp. 170–4.

[125] Asquith secretly cleared his 1908 Pension Act with the Friendly Societies who agreed not to oppose it because the pensions were small, means-tested, and funded by the Treasury (assuring that subsidies would be minimal). B. Gilbert, *British Social Policy 1914–1939*, Ithaca, NY; Cornell University Press, 1970, p. 256.

[126] In fact, Treasury fears of excessive administration costs were well grounded. In one of the first audits of the new insurance system, administrative costs of £2 million were incurred in distributing benefits of £7.6 million. See Fourth Report

that only about £10 million could be acquired by taking over the societies.[127] Nonetheless, Lester Stead, the secretary of the Ancient Order of Foresters, was consulted throughout the preparations, and appointed to the English Insurance Commission in 1912 when the Act was implemented. Stead was a key supporter of the of the principle that there should be no 'state guarantee' or assured national responsibility to repay losses of collecting agents. Unlike France, where the notion of social solidarity made the state a partner from the beginnings of social insurance, in Britain both officials and the societies could agree that a guaranteed state minimum was too 'socialist', would conflict with the contributory principle (used in exactly the opposite way in France in order to justify state support), and would encourage 'malingering', that is, excessive benefit claims, an old Poor Law preoccupation.[128]

Thus, the 1911 Act was in some respects a way to ease voluntary insurance toward a peaceful demise, but the large, private insurance companies ('industrial insurance' in British terms) were not as easily reconciled. Again, the situation differed substantially from France, where private insurance was not particularly popular, and private savers looked to the state. Lloyd George had, in fact, hoped to avoid coming into conflict with the private companies, but once it was decided that contributors' widows could hardly be denied some benefit from their spouse's death, the issue had to be faced. The large companies insured about 30 million persons for death benefits for widows and children. The total value of the

of the Work of the National Insurance Audit Department, *Report*, London; Parliamentary Papers, 1917, cd. 8977, p. 15.

[127] Though no reflection on the ingenuity of disarming the Friendly Societies by making them the collecting agents, the idea came to the main official involved in drafting the bill, William J. Braithwaite, in the bathtub. He recalled it from Canon Barnett's Victorian pension scheme. Lloyd George also came back from his German visit with serious reservations about a state-run fund. See W. J. Braithwaite, Sir Henry N. Bunbury, ed., *Lloyd George's Ambulance Wagon*, London; Methuen, 1957. Bunbury edited the book from Braithewaite's diaries twenty years after his death. It is a fascinating account of daily policymaking under Lloyd George, but coloured by Braithwaite's huge disappointment at not being appointed chairman of the Insurance Commission in 1912. Morant, who had stepped down from the Board of Education over a minor scandal, was selected over Braithwaite, and for a year they violently quarrelled. Braithwaite resigned and spent an uneventful life in Inland Revenue, one of the few great Edwardian officials never to achieve distinction.

[128] Braithwaite, pp. 77–89, for details. Like most officials, he regarded the Friendly Society people as well-intentioned, but a 'thick-headed crowd'.

insurance was £285 million. The largest of these companies, Prudential or the 'Pru', was the largest property holder in Britain, the largest shareholder in the Bank of England, and one of the largest lenders to local government. Though it was well known that they made huge profits, it was clear to Lloyd George and his advisers that if he jeopardized private insurance the Tories would fight the bill clause by clause.[129] Unlike the Friendly Societies, the private companies were also nationally organized to fight together through their powerful pressure group, the Association of Industrial Assurance Societies, which was well represented in Parliament by sponsored MPs.

A true political fox, Lloyd George at first hoped to use the voluntary companies against the private companies, but it soon became apparent that the private companies, some of whom were even then bailing out poorly run Friendly Societies and improving their shoddy management, were much better placed to spread alarm among their smaller brethren. Contrary to more radical views of political life, politicians seldom wish to be dead heroes. Lloyd George arranged to meet secretly with the adroit lawyer of the private companies, Sir Henry Kingsley Wood. Lloyd George agreed to drop the widow benefits in exchange for Wood's support, against the interests of his ally, the Friendly Societies, to extend the sickness benefit period. The politics of survival are seldom attractive. In return, Wood lined up pledges of support from 490 of the 670 MPs, which gives some idea of the formidable powers of the 'Pru'. Lest one jump to the conclusion that this is unmistakable proof of the power of concentrated capital, it should be noted that extending the sickness benefit had more significance in enlarging the role of government in the British welfare state than did the concession to private pensions. Public pensions were to grow under political pressure in any event. As Gilbert notes, what Wood really helped to do was to nationalize one of the private sector's most natural allies, the medical profession, and justify an even greater intrusion of the state into individual choice.[130]

---

[129] See Gilbert, *National Insurance* . . ., pp. 318–24. As we shall see, the bitter resistance from the conservative spectrum of opinion came largely from the doctors, when the closure had to be invoked.

[130] The information in this paragraph comes from Gilbert, pp. 318–40. The historical irony is even greater because Lloyd George was trying to minimize the influence of the Webbs and Morants over the bill, all of them advocates of a centralized health scheme. To complete the historical twist, Wood became Min-

To understand the situation of the doctors in the 1911 Act, the fourth pivot of potential private sector influence over the British welfare state, one must regress to the expansion of public health services from the turn of the century, and even earlier. Sir John Simon proposed a unified medical service in 1871.[131] Long before other states began to consider reforming medical and health care, Britain made substantial advances using the ever vulnerable local government system. In 1866, local public health inspection became obligatory and was reinforced in 1872. In the familiar sequence of national subsidies following national demands, parliamentary grants to pay half the salaries of these local officials followed in 1873. The Local Government Act of 1888 required a county medical officer with full medical training, and the Local Government Act of 1894 gave these officials unlimited tenure of office lest they run foul of local politics. With the addition of pension and salary guarantees in 1922, the local medical officials were in an unassailable position.

From a comparatively early date, the British government also employed a large segment of the medical profession, and a long line of top administrators wanted to unify private and public care. Simon's enthusiasm for a national medical service carried over to Sir Arthur Newsholme, the medical officer of the prewar Local Government Board, who regarded the 1911 sickness insurance, as did many other leading Edwardian administrators, a setback in achieving their ultimate objective.[132] In fact, by 1917, in one guise or another, the government employed nearly half the 26,000 doctors in Britain. There were over 7,000 Poor Law doctors, nearly 3,000 public health doctors, almost 1,300 within the school medical service, and 350 working for local mental hospitals. In addition, 308,688 hospital beds were in public hands, almost 170,000 under the medical facilities needed for public health, 94,000 to provide care for paupers, and almost 45,000 beds in

ister of Health in 1937 and proved an able manager of national insurance in a difficult period. He then served as Chancellor of the Exchequer from 1940 to 1943 while the Beveridge Plan was being written!

[131] See Lambert, *Sir John Simon*, p. 487, and Newsholme, *The Ministry of Health*, pp. 35–8.

[132] Newsholme, *The Ministry of Health*, p. 259. His strong views on the matter, plus the influence of the Webbs, help account for the Chief Medical Officer of the Board of Education, Sir George Newman, rather than the more senior Newsholme, being chosen as CMO of the newly founded Ministry of Health in 1919. Newsholme was also discredited by influenza epidemics during the war.

the 'voluntary' sector, hospitals run by local governments, but identified with public health care.[133] All this is not to detract from the momentous decision to nationalize medical care in 1948, but only to show that, compared to most countries, Britain had moved substantially toward public medical care thirty years before the law was passed.

As pressures within government multiplied to nationalize medicine, the doctors, the potential fourth pivot of privately based resistance to the welfare state, did not realize that they were to be victims of conflicting official strategies rather than of their own intransigence. The British Medical Association achieved power as a result of opposition to the 1911 Act, but was not well organized a decade before. Though now forgotten, thousands of doctors served on health panels of Friendly Societies, and, at the turn of the century, general practitioners were poorly paid. But government rejected the strategy of Morant and the Webbs, namely that a strong national organization should be first established, preferably through local health committees that the bureaucracy could manipulate, with health and medical services extended to the general population later. The reformers detested Lloyd George's strategy because it involved too many political uncertainties and promised only minimal medical care to those below the poverty line. No doubt more direct controls of the medical profession would follow, though these minor details neither satisfied the administrative reformers nor deterred Lloyd George from following the most opportune political route.[134] The effect was to squeeze the doctors between allying themselves with the local authorities against the Morant plan or with the insurance companies to protect, at least for the immediate future, their professional autonomy. For the long term, it was clearly a Hobson's choice for they were certain to come under increasing public control no matter which course they took. Though they disliked the Friendly Societies, they disliked local government more.

Despite the devious route that bureaucrats planned to achieve nationalized medical care, one can empathize with the frustrations the Edwardian officials must have felt with their situation. Before

---

[133] Newsholme, pp. 245–8.
[134] The strategies are outlined most clearly by Frank Honigsbaum, *The Struggle for the Ministry of Health, 1914–1919*, London; Bell and Sons, Occasional Papers on Social Administration, No. 37, 1970, p. 18.

the 1929 local reorganization, there were 1,727 public health authorities in England alone. In addition to these scattered medical services, there were doctors involved with 318 local education authorities and over 300 voluntary agencies.[135] One hardly needed a Morant, dedicated to the concept of a 'directive brain centre,' to see why simplification was appealing. In 1906, 124,000 children under one year of age died. For every nine soldiers lost in France in 1917, twelve babies died at home, giving rise to the saying that it was more dangerous to be born in England than to fight in France.[136] Under the Board of Education Morant had done everything within his power, and some things clearly not within his power, to lay the groundwork for a national medical service. The Elementary Education (Provision of Meals) Act of 1906 allowed local authorities to voluntarily use their rates to improve health, made compulsory in 1914. The Education (Administrative Provisions) Act of 1906 provided for local medical inspections in schools, made compulsory in 1909. The Local Education Authorities (Medical Treatment) Act of 1908 allowed local school authorities to provide treatment. Much of this legislation went through Parliament almost unnoticed.

Thus, the development of medical and sickness benefits under the 1911 Act presented the doctors with a dilemma. Were they to follow the lead of the Board of Education, and be subjected to local authorities, or were they to follow the lead of the Insurance Act, and be subject to the Friendly Societies' discretion? Their distaste for the inefficiency and politics of local government inclined them toward the social insurance solution. In particular, the practitioners disliked the poor quality of many local public hospitals and shared the public distaste for Poor Law facilities. The specialists ('consultants') also wanted nothing to do with hospitals that were poorly designed for primary care. As part of the long public health tradition of Victorian Britain, local hospitals were often no more than isolation hospitals to control epidemics, tuberculosis, etc. None of the doctors wanted to be submerged in the Poor Law institutions and their inferior care of the sick poor. Given these circumstances,the doctors had little alternative other

---

[135] Newsholme, p. 51; and Honigsbaum, p. 13.
[136] Honigsbaum, p. 13. On the growth of medical legislation, see Gilbert, *National Insurance* . . ., pp. 102–57.

than confrontation, seldom a successful political tactic.[137] Lloyd George's solution was similar to that used by Bevan thirty years later.

A report by the British Medical Association (BMA) showed that few doctors were getting more than six shillings for patients on their panels with the various voluntary health insurance schemes. They asked and received over eight shillings per listed client. Lloyd George also used the Bevanite tactic of playing the specialists against the practitioners. His speech to the Royal College of Surgeons was a great success. The consultants were already being cultivated by Morant who provided money for medical research, and Lloyd George adopted this tactic by deducting a small share of sickness insurance contributions for research. In addition, the practitioners were given Local Medical Committees to protect their professional interests before the local insurance committees, where they were also represented. While it is correct that the doctors won most of the concessions they wanted, it was a typical case of battles won and wars lost. Their 'strike' of 1912 spread panic within the government, but it could not hold and within a year 25,000 of the 26,000 doctors had signed on with the new plan.[138]

Thus, it would be a serious error to see the 'success' of the doctors as some version of private interests towering over the state. As events transpired, many of them unforeseeable by the doctors or anyone else, the move toward a Ministry of Health was irresistible. It was almost entirely the work of internal administrative politics, and in many ways foreshadowed the entire shape of the British welfare state. Like Titmuss a generation later, Addison was inspired by 'war socialism' and his stint, not entirely successful, in the Ministry of Munitions seems to have inspired a radical vision of the future, which may account for the cooling of his relationship with an ever cautious Lloyd George.[139] But even in

[137] Though put in various forms, this is the principal reservation of most British analysts to Harry Eckstein's, *The National Health Service*, Cambridge, MA; Harvard University Press, 1958.

[138] Lloyd George asked his political ally, Christopher Addison, to handle negotiations with the BMA. Another part of the compromise was to limit medical benefits to those with incomes under £160 in order to protect private practices. See Kenneth and Jane Morgan, *Portrait of a Progressive* . . ., pp. 13–19; also Sir George Newman, pp. 391–403.

[139] Kenneth and Jane Morgan, *Portrait* . . ., p. 33. Of course, by 1913, Lloyd

1914, the momentum for a ministry could not be stopped, and the many advocates within government could act more freely as political leaders were preoccupied with war preparations. The Chief Medical Officers of the Board of Education and the Local Government Board (LGB), Newman and Newsholme, respectively, were both committed to forming a ministry, and, in turn, in close touch with Morant and the Webbs. While the old dilemma of choosing between first erecting the structure or extending services persisted, there was no doubt about direction. In 1914, Morant and Newman helped Addison prepare a memo to the Prime Minister advocating the immediate creation of a Ministry of Health. As President of the LGB, following the retirement of Burns in 1914 (much to the relief of all the reformers), Addison was free to cooperate with the Board of Education. Though relations were not always smooth, a system of maternity grants was devised using 600 health visitors and 600 maternity centres devised (illegally) by the Board of Education.[140] In 1914, the National Insurance Commission was moved from the Treasury to the LGB, and the pauper hospitals brought within the orbit of the nascent medical benefit system. Thus, administrative politics took its inexorable course, only temporarily deterred by objections from private medicine.

Like social insurance in the 1906 election, the question of creating a Ministry of Health was not on the Liberal manifesto for the 1918 election. As the Central Medical Officer (CMO) of the Board of Education, Newsholme's final reports of 1917 and 1918 clearly outlined the framework for nationalized medical care.[141] It was only a matter of time. The main obstacle in the final stages of creating the ministry was not private medicine, whose concerns had been worked out in confidential negotiations by the ubiquitous Wood, but from forces within government itself. The National Insurance Commission felt that its functions would

George had moved on to his land reform campaign and was busy undermining his Prime Minister, Asquith. After the war, Lloyd George had little time for the Ministry of Reconstruction, then under Addison.

[140] The account of the negotiations over maternity benefits can be found in Honigsbaum, pp. 20–3. Lloyd George asked his friend Haldane to negotiate the conflict and Haldane, following the old preferred path of his friends, the Webbs, gave control to the LGB.

[141] Newsholme makes very clear the interdependence of sickness and poverty. By 1918, it was clear that about a third of poverty could be attributed to sickness. See *47th Annual Report of the Local Government Board*, Supplement, pp. xiv–xvi.

be jeopardized. Addison's unhappy stint as Minister for Reconstruction brought him together with Morant and Newman. They were assisted by Lord Astor, then private secretary to Lloyd George, and organizer of the Unionist Social Reform Committee.[142] In the strange ways of policymaking, the radicals were aided by Addison's friendly relations with the Conservative Leader, Bonar Law, a friendship formed over the chess table. As finally thrashed out within government,the insurance advocates again got their way, partly because of Wood's skill in forming an unbeatable coalition of unions, Friendly Societies and anti-Poor Law forces, all favouring 'a Ministry of Health (with) almost dictatorial powers.'[143] Though taken off the Cabinet agenda four times over 1918, the bill was finally passed with Addison as first Minister, Morant as Permanent Secretary (he died in 1920), Astor as parliamentary secretary, Wood as private parliamentary secretary, and Newman as CMO. There is probably no better illustration in the entire history of the British welfare state of how an administrative coalition excluded party politics and dominated the private sector. The doctors, as always, got some consolation for the Medical Consultative Council, an advisory body on medical benefits, was dissolved and put at the disposal of the BMA.[144]

Though we shall have reason in Chapter 6 to return to the complexities of organizing medical care after World War II, the politics of building the National Health Service (NHS) were in many respects a replay of the politics of forming the Ministry of Health. As Klein states, the postwar legislation built a unified medical service, not a unified health service.[145] This meeting of minds, which was to open the NHS to severe criticism over the 1960s and 1970s, is as old as the strange alliance of the BMA, the Liberals and the Labour Party in 1918 who, for very different reasons, agreed there should be no interference in the control of practices and no comprehensive health centres. The result was that for administrative reasons three separate services were built

---

[142] Astor's role is a throwback to aristocratic politics. His family had experienced several serious tubercular illnesses, and he became a fanatic on the improvement of tubercular care. Improving tubercular care was also a minor provision within the 1911 Act.

[143] Honigsbaum, p. 39.

[144] Honigsbaum, p. 55.

[145] Rudolf Klein, *The Politics of the National Health Service*, London; Longman, 1983, p. 18.

into the new national system and soon proved to have serious deficiencies. Actually, the doctors had outlined the terms for their agreement in 1920 in the Dawson Report.[146] They too favoured a complete reorganization of health services, using the practitioners at the community-level for basic care, and having a second-tier service of specialists, the entire structure focused on primary care. The role of government was established. What remained to be achieved, and this became one of Bevan's main problems, was to reconcile the practitioners and the specialists, a wholly professional problem that, like so much of the advanced welfare state, simply eluded democratic politics.

Because the NHS so clearly differentiates Britain from other modern welfare states, it is important to see how political interests affected its development in the interwar period. There were so many influential persons, the Webbs, Newman, Newsholme and others who had no doubts about a totally nationalized health care that the source of political resistance is often overlooked in functional accounts of British welfare. In the eyes of policymakers, and particularly the Treasury, it was a case of how to make available resources outside government pay for increased benefits. Because of the huge war deficit, and after 1921 because of the soaring unemployment, the most important roadblocks were not erected by interested parties outside government, but by internal procrastination and indecision. It is important to recall that the 1911 Act compromise with the Friendly Societies began to plague government even before the war. In 1914, there was an elaborate investigation into the rising costs of sickness benefits that had already strained the Friendly Society funds, and those of the other 'Approved Societies' administering the benefits.

The 1911 Act had been in effect only fourteen months when claims increased nearly a third above estimates, much of it accounted for by increased claims by women. Some notion of the intricate administrative forces already involved in the British welfare state may be gleaned from the size of the report, over 1700

[146] *Interim Report of the Consultative Council on Medical and Allied Services* (Dawson Report), London; Parliamentary Papers, 1920, cmd. 693. The Dawson Report is a remarkably detailed plan, providing organizational charts for the new tiered structure, full descriptions of types of health care at each level, and outlines of how hospitals and doctors would operate at each level.

pages in three hefty volumes.[147] Perhaps the most interesting testimony was from Sidney Webb, who dogmatically insisted that the Insurance Committees must enforce stiff standards, and if they would not, be forced to do by government.[148] The only problem with this Benthamite advice was, first, that national administration did not have such a capacity, especially while depending on local authorities and committees for revenues and implementation, and, second, that it violated the historic principle of the British civil service to avoid direct involvement in policy implementation. Naturally, the war put many of these issues aside, and by 1922 health spending was the most rapidly increasing social expenditure. Health costs of national government had grown from half a million pounds in 1914 to 29 million in 1922; local health expenditure had doubled from slightly over 15 million pounds in 1914 to 28 million in 1922.[149]

An ironical twist of the war was that the foundations of the British economy were further eroded while many social services appeared to be in relatively good condition. In 1921, the Friendly Societies had over 12 million members receiving benefits under the 1911 Act. Due to the same relief that allowed the Unemployment Insurance Fund to grow to £20 million and highly profitable investments during the war, their financial reserves were restored. In 1921, they paid out £8 million in benefits, though their administrative costs were an appalling £2.5 million.[150] Once economic

---

[147] *Report of the Departmental Committee on Sickness Benefit Claims*, London; Parliamentary Papers, 1914, cd. 7687. The three appendices, cd. 7688, cd. 7689 and cd. 7690, were each about 500 pages.

[148] *Report of the Departmental Committee* . . ., v. 2, pp. 381–439. Webb had a particularly revealing exchange with Walter P. Wright, Grand Master of the Imperial Order of the Odd Fellows, and an officer of the Manchester Unity Friendly Society, over the poor distribution of doctors. In Stoke-on-Trent there were one to nearly 9,000 persons; in Hampstead, London, one to 500 persons. The national average was then one to about 2,000 persons. Clearly the Friendly Societies knew that Webb was their relentless critic.

[149] Geddes Report, pp. 103–4. The Committee noted the Friendly Societies' reserve and that £150,000 of this reserve were actually Treasury transfer payments, p. 134.

[150] *Second Annual report*, Ministry of Health, London, Parliamentary Papers, 1921, cmd. 1446, pp. 150–3. A detailed table also appears of Friendly Society and other membership in insurance schemes. By 1921, membership in old Friendly Society plans and in the expanding private insurance plans was about equal, indicating the growing dependence of the old organization on the large modern insurance companies. The administrative costs are given in Appendix IX, p. 207.

disaster struck in 1921, the rules of the game were changed. The Treasury had its eye on social service reserve funds outside government, which by 1922 were still an impressive £14 million for the Friendly Societies. Benefits had soared to £20 million and administrative costs seemed to have been restrained to a mere £3 million.[151] Nationally-funded social policies have a way of collapsing in unison so that the most desperate need was to restore a workable system of unemployment insurance. A Royal Commission on National Health Insurance was reported in 1926.[152] The changing political context of social policymaking is denoted by the appearance of new social service pressure groups. For example, the Society of Medical Officers testified on 'the need for genuine coordination of all the medical agencies in every area.'[153] The British Medical Association gave strong support to health insurance. The controversial Friendly Societies naturally gave enthusiastic support, but noted the 'highly wasteful and inefficient' practice of the complex organization of medical services. The Commission could agree on little more than the need to pool Friendly Society resources, a position no doubt strongly advocated by the ubiquitous John Anderson, the member with strong Treasury connections. The Commission noted the Friendly Societies' reserve and that £150,000 of this reserve were actually Treasury transfer payments.[154] But the Commission was too divided to make a substantial impact and of course by this time Neville Chamberlain, as Minister of Health, had his own plans for restructuring social services and local government.

In summary, of the four groups who had material reasons to delay the development of the welfare state in Britain, only the landed aristocracy were partially successful. But their success is measured less in terms of their effective resistance to social insurance than in terms of their political skill in influencing resource distribution between national and local government. Their ability to use this kind of political leverage pre-dates the

---

[151] *Third Annual Report*, Ministry of Health, London, Parliamentary Papers, 1922, cmd. 1713, p. 107.
[152] *Report*, Royal Commission on National Health Insurance (Napier Report), London, Parliamentary Papers, 1926, cmd. 2596.
[153] Royal Commission on National Health Insurance, p. 56.
[154] Royal Commission on National Health Insurance, p. 236. The Treasury had also been casting its eyes on the Friendly Societies' reserves as a way of subsidizing the local voluntary hospitals.

welfare state by fifty years, if one wishes to date the British welfare
state from the Whig radicals of the 1830s. By the turn of the
century, they had little defence. In fact, in Victorian Britain, the
Tories took the politically wise course of passing the 1902 Education Act, and the Tory tactic of judicious concessions to the
welfare state continued. The unintended consequence of protecting
landowners was to dampen conservative resistance in the twentieth
century. Reform of education, public health, labour relations and
eventually medical care were all justified because of the chaotic
state of British local government and territorial fragmentation that
landowners did so much to preserve. It is intriguing to speculate
whether the rate of change of social policy in the first twenty years
of the century would have been as rapid had this not been the
case. Everyone, including the private insurance lawyer, Wood,
could always raise the Poor Law 'taint' to justify more national
intervention.

Thus, the large landowners bought protection by helping centralize the British state, but oddly enough few modern private
interests were very effective in resisting the welfare state. The
voluntary insurance companies were economically weak by 1900,
and persisted until the reforms of the 1940s only because of their
political organization, the failure to terminate the Poor Laws
and, to some extent, their usefulness as political allies of private
insurance. Although the private insurers were threatened by social
insurance, they made compromises, most of which were managerial
and therefore did not seriously blunt the aims of social insurance.
As for the doctors, in 1911 as in 1948 they were internally divided,
had different vested interests in the accumulation of public medical
care, and did not try to extend their reservations beyond their
professional interests. Perhaps the most curious aspect of the gath-
ering momentum of the British welfare state was that few politicians took a lively interest in wage policy and labour relations,
as we shall see in more detail in the next chapter. For the moment,
it is only important to note that the first measure to relieve
unemployment, the Unemployment Act of 1905, was a weak
Tory law and depended on Local Distress Committees for its
implementation. Labour politics was not central to political
reforms at the turn of the century, but labour conflict was very
much in evidence and the power of the craft unions recognised.
In contrast, the socialists and the unions in France and other

continental countries had relatively clear claims to make on their nascent welfare states, and many of the principles enunciated from 1920 to 1945 reflected demands of the Labour movements. Though a declining party, the Liberals continued to take the policy initiatives until 1930, while Labour, for reasons not entirely of its choosing, had few workable policies to make social equality a reality. Thus, the party best placed to rethink social policy had little new to offer in the 1920s or the 1960s and ultimately was itself the victim of disastrous labour and wage policies. Unlike the social democratic movements in Germany, Sweden and, in modified form, even France, the British left was curiously unimaginative as a policymaker.

Several important political and administrative features emerge from the early intervention of the British state in social affairs. First, to a much greater extent than recognized in conventional accounts of social welfare in Britain, it depended on localized, if not local, support. Both Parliament and Whitehall were acutely aware that they could accomplish little without local organization and local resources. They resolved the issue by continually increasing local grants as national requirements became more demanding. Second, as is particularly the case with the 1911 Act, it became more common to arrange bipartisan support for major reforms. As we have seen, by 1914 Parliament, if it ever had much direct interest in social policy, was virtually excluded from critical decisions. By the 1920s, important decisions were almost always made within the administration, under the strict eyes of an increasingly powerful Treasury. Third, from the 1920s, social policies were often designed and directly supervised by the Treasury. Although its limited administrative capacity meant that new functions were transferred to new social ministries, funds and finances were Treasury business. This would not have been possible were the Treasury less confident of its ability to control social expenditure. In 1913, the Treasury established separate social 'returns' or accounts alongside their traditional debt and defense accounts. Tightening the grip of the Treasury was mainly a post-World War I event, though in principle it had always been strong. Without a field administration to provide reliable controls on local excesses and confronted with a growing body of official big spenders, the Treasury worked to centralize the British welfare state, and in doing so made its rapid growth after 1945 much easier.

ADMINISTERED POVERTY

Although socio-economic explanations of poverty are correct in arguing that the poor readily fit into a class-based vision of society, class politics does not uniformly fit the political and administrative response to poverty. The political risk seldom loomed as large as the social injustice. At the policymaking level there were different assumptions, different strategies, and different objectives once modern states decided that poverty was a potential threat to social and political institutions. Once poverty was recognized as a threat to democracy, the early responses are important pre-conditions for the formation of advanced welfare states in the mid-twentieth century. These assumptions, methods and goals were institutionalized in particular ways in each political and administrative system. It is not that the socio-economic explanations are wrong, but they are inadequate to understand how and why the politics of welfare varies so widely among modern democracies. From a policy perspective, the critical decision, then as now, was how to split the poverty problem into manageable parts. Unless one proceeds on the utopian assumption that poverty can be totally eliminated at a single blow, politicians and administrators first had to decide what to do.

As we have seen in the preceding section, there were two competing strategies in Edwardian Britain. One was to follow the Victorian precedent, however poorly managed, and attack poverty through charity and minimal pensions. The approach has its origins in the earliest realizations of the misery of the poor in mid-Victorian Britain. Indeed, the time needed to convert the early agreement about the plight of the aged poor into public policy provides another reason to question how rapidly the British welfare state really advanced.

Nearly sixty years elapsed between Henry Mayhew's sensational *London Labour and the London Poor* of 1851 and the 1908 Pension Act. There were no contributory national pension plans until 1925. Thus,it is hard to argue that Britain rushed into constructing income protection for wage earners, much less the poor and disabled. The competing strategy was Lloyd George's persuasion, formed in part for political convenience in 1911, that attacking invalidity and sickness would be best. His view made sense because it was known by 1910 that half the aged poor were sick or disabled. As he put it, 'Poverty was the evil sickness caused, but for these groups sickness was the evil that poverty caused.'[155] His argument might be considered the first version of the poverty cycle theory that gained popularity in the 1960s and 1970s among such differently inclined politicians as the ultra-conservative Sir Keith Joseph in the Heath administration and the poverty specialists surrounding President Johnson. Which view is correct has yet to be determined, but the important political effect was that neither the left nor the right in British politics ever formed a clear policy position on poverty, and could, therefore, reverse themselves at ease as political circumstances seemed advantageous. There was no conspiracy to preserve the Poor Laws because none was needed. The curious result was that in the most stable of democratic systems, the social question that had the clearest social roots was politically neutralized.

Politicians did find momentary reasons to intervene, but the unintended effect was to give the administration a virtual monopoly of the emerging welfare state. As was the case with local government reform,[156] administrative decisions predominated throughout the early development of the British welfare state, making the British civil service more crucial in the development of welfare than in any other state, including the supposedly administrative state of France. Asquith's 1908 Pension Act was designed in secrecy by a few close advisors and Treasury civil servants. The 1911 Insurance Act was written, or one might say patched together, by Braithwaite and a hastily assembled group from the Treasury, while Lloyd George manoeuvred his way around political pitfalls.[157] The main critics of these plans, the Webbs and their cohorts, had only an administrative strategy to differentiate themselves from either Liberal or Conservative proposals. In trying to use poverty, or any other reform, to reorganize totally the British state, they managed to offend everyone, rather like Sir Edwin Chadwick a century before. Unless one wishes to consider the Royal Commission on the National Health Service of 1979 a social security measure (and ignore its political utility as a way of

---

[155] Quoted in Gilbert, *National Insurance . . .*, p. 315.
[156] See Douglas E. Ashford, *British Dogmatism and French Pragmatism*.
[157] Parliamentary procedure encouraged such concessions to the bureaucracy. When closure was invoked on the 1911 Act, nearly 40 of its 114 clauses had not been debated and were left to later Treasury regulations. Braithwaite, *Lloyd George's Ambulance Wagon*, p. 225.

delaying decisions and of protecting the administration), the last open debate about the British welfare state was the Royal Commission on Unemployment Insurance of 1930. The immense influence that Titmuss had over social insurance and welfare policy in the 1950s and 1960s is only imaginable in a system where administrative policymaking is effectively centralized. Largely because of the administrative complexity of welfare, it was easy to pull bureaucratic blinders over its progress, but nowhere as easy as in Britain.

Put in more political terms, the poor became a class that was easy to neglect. The paradoxical effect was that the Poor Law mentality, as well as the Poor Law machinery, survived relatively intact, if increasingly inadequate, until 1948. The first universal pension plan proposed by Canon Blackley in 1878 was backed by a strong national organization, the National Providence League, but the political costs were immediately escalated by the combined resistance of the Friendly Societies, the Charitable Organization Society and the old craft unions. Joseph Chamberlain proposed another national pension scheme as part of this Radical Programme of 1885, but Gladstone had no time for it and Chamberlain joined the Conservatives a year later. The alarming poverty studies of Booth produced yet a third plan for non-contributory pensions which did attract many of the early leaders of the left.[158] Political tactics were never excluded. Gladstone, faced with defeat, appointed the Royal Commission on the Aged Poor in 1892, but included both Booth and Chamberlain which assured stalemate. Lord Salisbury was finally moved to appoint a Select Committee on the Aged and Deserving Poor (the Chaplin Committee) in 1899, but its recommendations preserved the stigma of poverty through a thrift test, and would have covered only a third of the aged over 70 years.

In many respects Asquith's opportunistic law of 1908 made good sense: pensions had to be universal or they would omit the

---

[158] An interesting territorial dimension to the early pension agitation eludes most functional strides of the welfare state. The Conservatives were responding to strong demands from northern cities, where they were weak. The Booth studies, though not Rowntree's, were of London and so tended to focus poverty concerns on the capital city where the Labour Party had much to gain. How much this distorted the problem of poverty is difficult to judge, but London's poverty was by then compounded by crime, acute long-term unemployment on the docks and elsewhere, and of course the sharp social differences that differentiated East End politics from the rich areas of the city.

most needy; pensions had to be supported by national taxation or they would be at the mercy of unreliable local governments; and paupers could be included from the time of the law as a workable compromise to gradually erase the Poor Laws.[159] The debate anticipated the politics of the welfare state. Balfour had no strong disagreements with the bill, and the Conservative tactic was to try to make the law so generous that it would collapse.[160] Within the confines of his cabinet, Asquith accomplished what took politicians of most states years to learn. He made 'free' pensions seem possible, partly because a budget surplus caused no fierce resistance from the Treasury. The results were by no means insignificant for the number of persons on 'indoor' relief diminished rapidly in the next few years, which made it easier for Lloyd George and Churchill to put the Poor Law question aside to pursue their own policies. But it was never a budgetary bargain. The spending commitment to those over 70 years soon reached £12 million, while previously total government spending on this age group was £2.5 million. What Asquith gained was a more precious political commodity, time to devise a new approach and some new ammunition for electoral purposes as Liberal strength slipped in by-elections. These lessons were not lost on the young Churchill, who organized contributory pensions in 1925 in total secrecy in the Treasury as part of his 'all-in' insurance scheme. The provision of widow and orphan pension rights was not even discussed in the Cabinet.

What may escape our perception of the transformation of the British welfare state is the extent to which it was the product of the Treasury. Unlike the small band of social reformers from the Conseil d'Etat that could use the *grands corps* to plot the expansion of the French welfare state or the adroit band of progressive social insurance experts from Wisconsin who formed the basis of the American Social Security Administration, macro-economists, and not particularly progressive ones at that, took control of the British social insurance system. In 1908, Asquith used the power of the

---

[159] These are Gilbert's observations, pp. 215–17. Gilbert also points out, p. 160, that the failure of the Tories to exploit this opportunity was one of their most serious errors. In what seems a typically British view of improving social protection, Hay, *The Origins of the Liberal Welfare Reforms*, p. 203, disagrees.
[160] Read, *Edwardian England* . . ., p. 170

Treasury to hasten through his scheme, and even declared it a money bill in order to avoid a possible veto from the House of Lords. The 1911 Act, we have seen, was almost entirely the product of a small band of Treasury officials, relying heavily on Sir John Bradbury, head of the Inland Revenue Service, Sir Robert Chalmers, a high Treasury official but no friend of Lloyd George, and Masterman, Financial Secretary of the Treasury, to smooth the way. Sir Warren Fisher, Permanent Secretary of the Treasury from 1919 to 1939, first established his reputation as an able young Treasury civil servant working on the bill.

The idea of extending social insurance to dependents in 1921, thereby making it nearly universal except for agricultural workers, domestic servants, and the self-employed, could be launched because the Treasury found that the immediate postwar boom left the surplus of £20 million in the National Insurance Fund. Treasury power was such that Neville Chamberlain was considered a rather foolish young man in 1924 when he preferred the Ministry of Health to the Exchequer. Treasury officials always sat on the Joint Commission administering the fund, and their distrust of social spending was shared by many other top civil servants such as Sir John Anderson (later Lord Waverly). Naturally, financial ministers of every democratic government closely watched the growth of social spending, but in no other country did they assume as prolonged operational control. As we shall see in more detail in Chapter 5, Treasury control backfired in a strange way for it made it possible for one person, Beveridge, to plan the renovation of the entire system. The Treasury officials working with him withdrew once they saw the scope of his plan, but Beveridge was only using an exclusive policy process that had been well established by the same officials between the wars. Little wonder then, as Harris writes, that 'Beveridge's policy had an almost Gladstonian ring of old-fashioned financial orthodoxy.'[161]

The inadvertent effect of Treasury control on the British welfare state can hardly be exaggerated. The Treasury continued to play a more direct role in social policy throughout the interwar period than in any other democracy. A price of more rapid, if not always fully considered, advance was that the Treasury needed a veto over zealous officials' proposals. Under the 1920 Unemployment

[161] Jose Harris, *Beveridge* ..., p. 358.

Act, and the subsequent improvisations during the 1920s, the Treasury was the lending agent of the Unemployment Fund, and it ultimately went into debt as the official borrower of the Fund when the British economic situation deteriorated. From the Treasury's perspective, any solution was preferable to fixed claims on national revenues which, in turn, encouraged both the perpetuation of Poor Law principles for the poor, thereby shifting the burden onto local taxes, and improvising unemployment schemes after World War I. As we shall see in more detail in Chapter 4, the various forms of transitional support devised by the Treasury postponed more serious thought about the reforming social policy. From 1931 to 1935, for example, those receiving transitional assistance grew from 66,000 to 222,000 persons.[162] Unintentionally, the British created a new pauper class while trying to avoid the stigma of the Poor Laws.

In France, and for different reasons on most of the continent, it was not as easy to divorce political rhetoric from political deeds. In Sweden, the politics of poverty never had much chance to achieve prominence. The Social Democrats acquired dominance as rural society was converting itself into an industrial society. The uniformity of social change provided less opportunity for severe poverty to occur, an important reason why, as we shall see in more detail in Chapter 4, the Swedes could move more swiftly toward consideration of the wage implications of the welfare state. German industrial prosperity postponed the severe poverty of Britain until the 1920s, but under the severe dislocations of inflation and unemployment, many poor turned to fascism for survival. The formation of a 'lumpen-proletariat' assisted fascism just as the severe British unemployment of the 1930s assisted Sir Oswald Mosley in Britain.[163] The critical political difference, of course, was that a weak Labour Party in a stable political system was able to reject national socialism and its authoritarian solution

---

[162] Eveline Burns, *British Unemployment Programs 1920–1938*, Washington, D.C.; Social Science Research Council, 1921, pp. 115–16.
[163] Not to diminish the importance of Mosley's expulsion from the Labour Party in 1930, but the reason seems to have had much to do with very traditional institutional concerns. His plan would severely curtail the power of ministers to run their own show. Snowden, the Chancellor the Exchequer, was a dedicated defender of Treasury privileges and to him, as to future Chancellors, the subordination of the Treasury to a national plan was abhorrent. Mosley was replaced at the Duchy of Lancaster by the rising Clement Attlee. See Marquand, *Ramsay MacDonald*, pp. 534–9.

to poverty. In France, the fascist solution to poverty and unemployment was not a central feature of the Croix de Feu, and it was in fact defeated by a coalition of the left in 1936. Despite the slow progress of the French welfare state between the wars, resistance to anti-democratic movements in France was easier because the poor were not irrevocably differentiated from the self-reliant.

A number of circumstances contributed to the difficulties of divorcing poverty and pensions in France. For one thing, France prided herself on being a self-sufficient nation and so incomes were better protected, though at enormous economic cost in terms of industrial development. When Britain was in the depths of depression and experiencing new forms of poverty between the wars, André Siegfried chided Britain about the risks taken by countries that did not first protect the economic well-being of their own citizens.[164] Beneath these concerns, there were fundamentally different concepts of the meaning of aging and its relation to social class. As Stearns puts it, the function of social class was 'to prepare a differential response to aging.'[165] As in Britain, the local relief of poverty was inadequate, but the French population as a whole was aging and the plea of social solidarity could, in principle if not in fact, become the basis of a policy. From a Marxist perspective, there was a perverse effect because the large firms more often initiated pension plans and thereby protected many of the most vulnerable from the effects of poverty.[166] In addition, government was a 'softer touch than industry.'[167] The history of French pensions is in large part the constantly enlarged claims of the public sector or segments of nationally dependent industries, such as mining, railroads and merchant seamen. Thus, the politics of poverty was less central to social and political change in France than in Britain, first, because it was more difficult to insitutionalize their separation from the state, and, second, because protection was extended to economically vulnerable segments of the population. All this provided a cushion against poverty that was on the whole less well developed in Britain.

For purposes of this study, the crucial difference was that the

[164] André Seigfried, *England's Crisis* (trans. H. H. Hemming), New York; Harcourt Brace, 1931.
[165] Peter N. Stearns, *Old Age in European Society*, New York; Holmes and Meier, 1976, p. 42.
[166] Levasseur, *Questions ouvrières* . . ., pp. 111–21.
[167] Stearns, p. 58.

institutional and political dynamics in France were very different from Britain. When French public pensions were first discussed in the 1890s, neither workers nor the nascent socialist party felt that it was a critical decision. The Marxist assumption that caring for the aged and poor was a purely capitalist problem left the policy in the hands of the state in a way that was never open to British policymakers. When pension legislation was under consideration in 1910, the militant spokesman of the CGT, Paul Lafarque, argued that since only 8 per cent of the workers lived long enough to be included, they should ignore the issue.[168] Their economic fatalism left the question to government, but on crucial votes in the Chamber the socialists often found reasons to support change. The CGT supported the formation of a Fédération des Retraites in 1930, and a Communist Minister of Social Affairs conducted government policy as the post-war reforms were introduced. But after World War II, neither the Socialists nor the Communists found pensions a sufficiently exciting issue to include them in their electoral programmes.[169] The argument is often made that if only the Labour Party and the British unions had been militant Marxists in the 1930s, the course of British social policy would have been different. The French experience suggests this view is too simple. By isolating themselves from policy change for doctrinaire reasons, the French left was in a position to support the best that was offered with less political risk and to use the state structure to best advantage as political opportunities appeared.

The early organization of the welfare state helps explain the disinterest, and at times the hostility, of the left toward its policies. But in France the first Socialist minister, Alexandre Millerand, built on the Office of Labour in his ministry, the Department of Commerce, to advance the concept of social peace that had been launched by Waldeck-Rousseau in the 1880s and developed into a vague, but unifying, concept of solidarity by Léon Bourgeois. The Director of the Labour Office, Antoine Fontaine, helped build the administrative superstructure that produced much of the legislation of the late 1890s.[170] The administrative foundations changed little until 1945. Likewise, persons such as Llewellyn Smith and Morant built new administrative structures on the

---

[168] Stearns, p. 50.
[169] Stearns, p. 52.
[170] See J. Stone, *The Search for Social Peace* ..., pp. 50–75.

Whitehall model. Indeed, Llewellyn Smith's organization of the labour studies section of the Board of Trade and Morant's research for the Education Committee of the Board of Education became the key agencies in advancing social policies in Edwardian Britain.[171] With the formation of the Ministry of Labour in 1916 and the Ministry of Health in 1918, plus national insurance held closely to Treasury requirements, the basic structure, and the inherent rivalries and battles of the interwar period were imprinted on British government. The administrative capacities of the emergent welfare states 'were more or less fixed by 1918.

In comparing Britain and France, the point is not so much that one country centralized more than the other, this was implicit in building welfare states, but it is that they centralized within different administrative and political constraints. Quite apart from the trials of labour unrest and unemployment between the wars, France achieved a remarkable measure of continuity. While certainly not yet showing signs of social democracy, the interlocking nature of social benefits and wages was recognized. As we shall see in Chapter 4, under the direction of Cahen-Salvador, Parodi and Laroque, who designed the 1945 welfare state, France never lost grasp of the relationship between labour and social policy. If their reasons were not ennobled by socialist justifications, the result was still more constructive than the intense suspicions generated between government and the TUC between the wars which ultimately persuaded the TUC, like their Victorian predecessors owning land and business, to use Parliament as their main weapon of reform. Continuity, as well as continued dialogue, was difficult to achieve in Britain because the Whitehall model of policymaking made the new social ministries easy victims of Treasury power. The Ministry of Labour, as we shall see, was nearly decimated in the early 1920s.

Like states, organizations have their internal logic. The British rules of the game made rethinking the direction of the welfare state difficult, but the direction was clear in the ideas of most early social reformers. The Fabians wanted to permeate the elite and few British leaders, including Haldane, Beveridge and Morant saw things differently even if they disagreed with the Webbs. In a more

[171] On the internal rivalries affecting educational reform, see Peter Gordon and John White. *Philosophers as Educational Reformers: The Influence of Idealism in British Educational Thought and Practice*, London; Routledge and Kegan Paul, 1979, pp. 114–38.

savage administrative world, they remained vulnerable and most of the Edwardian aspirations were easily wiped out after World War I. The French administrative state gave more autonomy and more security to top officials. If France did not progress materially as fast as Britain, there remained a unifying concept of how social policy related to the state that was quite distinct from the heavily bureaucratic social agencies of Germany or the macro-economic balancing act of the early Swedish welfare state.

In summary, the welfare state, and very likely any future version of the welfare state along social democratic lines, cannot escape institutional and historical precedents. In so far as the positivist models of welfare states overdetermine the limits of change, and possibly misconstrue the object of change, they blind us to the cumulative nature of institutional change. One result is that we may place too much emphàsis on specific obstacles to change, such as an archaic local government system, the power of privately provided care and insurance, and the influence of professionals. As we have seen in this chapter, the easily identifiable protagonists to welfare states were dealt with rather easily. Indeed, the favourable reputation of the British welfare state may be a function of concentrated power in Parliament that could so ruthlessly sweep away institutional obstacles to ministerial designs. To the extent that leaders in other countries had to redefine the direction of the state in order to justify social reform, they were more likely to see some of the future complexities of welfare states, including the interdependence of wages and benefits. Political and administrative complexity has its virtues at the policymaking level because more open and more polonged policy debate has a better chance of discovering future difficulties. Perhaps the best illustration is the tortured effort of Whitehall to deal with unemployment between the wars compared to the tentative consideration of major reorientation of welfare states along social democratic lines in most continental countries.

4

Wages and Welfare

Under the early liberal state the political and economic assumptions between wages and welfare remained relatively distinct. The political distinction fell away as the property qualification for voting gradually disappeared in the late nineteenth century. In effect, political equality advanced more rapidly than economic equality. As we have seen, progressive liberals and early socialists made this difference the keystone to their attack on the state in the nineteenth century. The most extreme attack was of course launched by Marx who equated the two objectives. The political controversies and political movements that developed around socialist ideas have clouded over the extent to which liberal democrats themselves perceived the problem, and, as outlined in Chapter 2, how the old democratic order began fashioning social legislation to alleviate the most serious economic and social disadvantages. Social policy became the leading edge of the regeneration of democratic government and the early welfare state a confession that old values of private charity and individual self-reliance were no longer adequate policy guidelines.

The socio-economic models of the welfare state leave little room for the political complexity of the changing policy role of the left in the interwar period. In effect, the political forces of the left faced a dual task. First, they had to achieve some agreement between labour movements and socialist leadership. Second, there was a process of learning about democratic institutions, how to influence policy-making and how to organize support. Emphasis on the social and economic dimensions of the welfare state rests on a political simplification, namely, that once socio-economic problems were recognized, the policy solutions would be available

to any rational person. But there are many reasons why institutions, not to mention parties, leaders and publics, do not always
react in objectively rational terms. Most important, for real actors
the values attributed to social and economic objectives are not as
easily distinguished from political rewards and motives as more
abstract models might suggest.

Treating the social and economic complications of modern states
as independent variables within state structures omits what were
perhaps the most severe tests of democratic loyalty which the left
had yet to endure in 1914, and underestimates the importance of
the cruel test of loyalties imposed by World War I.[1] To these
political problems must be added the internal problems of the left
as it reeled before the demands of Leninist Russia and was torn
apart by the demolition of the Second International. Not only
were socialists detracted from their new democratic roles, but
the conservative right was supplied with plentiful ammunition.
Nonetheless, progress toward unquestioned legitimacy was the
major advance of the left between the wars. The Social Democratic
Party (SPD) led the troubled Weimar Republic for five of the
fourteen years of its brief existence. With only a plurality the
British Labour Party led the government in 1924 and achieved a
parliamentary majority in 1929 only to flounder in 1931. The
French socialists briefly returned to power under the Cartel des
Gauches in 1924, and triumphantly returned to power in 1936 to
rescue the Third Republic. When the democracies turned to the
full institutionalization of the welfare state in 1945, there was no
doubt about the democratic reliability of the non-Communist left.

But the left was limited in its new institutional and policy role
by the reliability of labour support. Only in Germany were the
links between the SPD and the German Confederation of Workers
(ADGB) unbreakable, and even there important differences in
priorities appeared from time to time. But Legiens, the ADGB
leader, had actually appeared with the German Minister of the
Interior during the war to announce labour conscription, and the

---

[1] The British Labour Party was heavily involved with international talks to avoid
the war, especially the pacifist MacDonald. See Marquand, *Ramsay Macdonald*,
pp. 207–37. Jaurès was a key figure in the liaison between continental socialist
pacifists and was assassinated by an Alsatian nationalist for his efforts. See
Feichter, pp. 205–22. In Germany, the SDP was torn apart, but finally voted
for war credits. See Carl Schorske, *German Social Democracy 1905–1917*, Cambridge,
MA; Harvard University Press, 1955.

turbulence of Weimar left little time to argue over SPD–ADGB differences. In France, the independent unions under Jouhaux were closely involved with government, and amidst the contortions of Stalinist rules imposed on Communist workers, even the Communist segment of the labour movement rallied to the Republic in 1934. Over World War I, a leading British labour leader, Arthur Henderson, joined the wartime cabinet with two of his colleagues, and shared responsibility for the detested regulation on labour.[2] Though the left was not responsible for many important policy initiatives between the wars, its political presence was established. Between the wars socialists acquired policymaking experience, which heavily influenced their views of the 1945 welfare experiments.

The aim of this chapter is not to try to explain why democracies encountered such severe social and economic problems between the wars, but how this experience affected the incorporation of the left into democratic institutions, and later, affected the demands the left placed on the newly-formed welfare states of 1945. Those who may see the interdependence of welfare and wages as primarily a social or economic problem may underestimate how difficult it is to imagine, construct and evaluate the institutional superstructure of more advanced versions of the welfare state. The institutional and administrative conditions needed to articulate how the welfare state affects incomes, and how incomes and productivity, in turn, enhance or impede the aims of the welfare state, do not appear on a *tabula rasa*. Even within the left there remained important institutional arguments over the reconciliation of socialist goals and democratic political institutions. Although the British Labour Party for example, seldom had less than a third of its members from the working class,[3] it was among the most cautious of socialist parties to accept the interdependence of wages and welfare.

Indeed, the socio-economic argument can be easily reversed in the light of prevailing economic and social conditions. Britain, the least willing of countries to devise a new relationship between wages and welfare, experienced the most severe unemployment

[2] Henderson resigned in 1917 because Lloyd George forbade him to attend a socialist conference in Sweden on the war settlement.
[3] James Hinton, '*The Rise of a Mass Labour Movement: Growth and Limits,*' in C. J. Wrigley, ed., *A History of British Industrial Relations, 1905–1914,* Amherst; University of Massachusetts Press, 1982, p. 37.

between the wars. At several points unemployment was over two million, at a much lower standard of living than today. Unemployment peaked at 3.4 million in 1932 and averaged about a million workers for nearly twenty years with only 60 per cent of the workforce insured.[4] The experience made the British Labour Party and the TUC enthusiastic advocates of the welfare state, but it produced nothing that compares to the Swedish concept of wage solidarity or even to the more differentiated French system of occupational claims on welfare that make social benefits a visible aspect of wage bargaining. In short, there are numerous historical and institutional conditions that intervene before any rational logic of wages and welfare can be enshrined in national policy. As we shall elaborate more fully in Chapter 5, the institutionalization of the welfare state from 1945 to 1950 was a product of institutional constraints and limited understanding of the ultimate aims of welfare states.

WELFARE AND THE AMBIGUITY OF THE LEFT

Given the Marxist assumptions of the left until World War I, the failure to participate in the early liberal reforms of welfare is understandable. In many respects, the interwar period looms large not only because during this period the European parties of the left learned to work within parliamentary constraints, but because they began to see how the welfare state might be used to advance social equality and social justice. The turn of the century socialists were no more prepared for the advance of the welfare state than were the nineteenth-century liberals prepared for its early growth. Few persons on either end of the political spectrum foresaw the interdependence between welfare and wages that would become the hallmark of the advanced welfare state. As we shall see in Chapter 5, the odd result was that after 1945 most welfare states were institutionalized in very conventional ways and with little controversy. For a number of reasons the continental socialists

[4] The economist Pigou called this the problem of the 'intractable million'. On Labour Party uncertainty see Robert Skidelsky, *Politicians and the Slump: The Labour Government of 1929–32*, London; Macmillan, 1967. Also David Marquand, *Ramsay MacDonald* ..., pp. 543–637.

were better prepared to move their cause forward by using the welfare state than was the British left.[5]

There are, of course, important national differences in the perception of the relationship between social needs and politics. But designing a strategy of social reform for the left was immensely more complicated because the early socialists initially saw little hope of rebuilding socialist societies without revolutionary change of existing institutions. In no country were these internal schisms more pronounced than in France, where the socialism of Adolfe Blanqui survived as the most influential socialist doctrine well into the Third Republic. Ranged against the Blanquists were the revolutionary views of Jules Guesde, for whom neither the Boulanger crisis nor the Dreyfus affair were adequate justification to rally to the Republic. If the French socialists were readily dismissed in French politics of the late nineteenth century, it was because ideological discord could so easily shatter their precarious unity. Nearly a decade of tedious ideological debate went into forming the tenuous rapprochement of 1898, only to see the invitation of the socialist leader, Millerand, to join the Waldeck-Rousseau government plunge the socialists into chaos once again.[6] In the elections of 1902, there were two socialist parties, the *Parti socialiste française* (PSF) of Guesde and Vaillant and the *Parti socialiste de France* (PSDF) of the anarchists. Indeed, as Lefranc observes, the ultimate unification of the French socialists in 1905 in the *Parti socialiste, section francaise de l'Internationale Ouvrière* (SFIO) was achieved only under strong pressure from the international socialist movement.

But the reactions of the left to growing demands for more elaborate social policies at the turn of the century should not be seen wholly in terms of the ideological splits of socialist parties. Such internal divisions were no less prominent in Britain and Germany, though more successfully overcome in order to pursue parliamentary strategies. What differentiates France from other

---

[5] Only recently has there begun to appear more detailed studies of the confusions and disputes within the left over the 1930s. On Britain, see Ben Pimlott, *Labour and the Left in the 1930s*, Cambridge; Cambridge University Press, 1977; and Elizabeth Durbin, *New Jerusalems*, London; Routledge and Kegan Paul, 1985.

[6] Tensions between the 'ministerialists' and militants exploded when Gen. de Gallifet, a leader of the bloody repression of the 1871 Commune, was made Minister of War in 1898. See Georges Lefranc, *Le Mouvement Socialiste sous la Troisième République*, Paris; Payot, 1977, pp. 105–10.

countries are the severe problems of making a reliable alliance between the socialists and the labour movement. The CGT was founded in 1895 under the leadership of a fiery anarchist, Emile Pouget,[7] who saw the role of unions to be the disruption of bourgeois society by means of the general strike, boycotts, and slow-downs. For the early CGT, social policy was a device to promote working-class solidarity, which explains their interest in the *Bourses de Travail* (labour exchanges) and more generally in direct worker control over social policy. In France this long and complicated process continues, as can be readily seen in the unmanageable division of unions among the Communist Con-féderation Générale du Travail (CGT), the independent-minded but socialist Confédération française démocratique du travail (CFDT) and the conventional labour politics of the Force Ouvrière (FO). We shall return to the weaknesses and strengths of national labour movements as social policy advocates in Chapter 5, but for the moment it is important to recall the intense revolutionary and anti-parliamentary stance of the early French labour movement.

The key transitional figure in reconciling the hostility of the French labour movement with parliamentary change was Edouard Vaillant. The direct heir of Blanqui and a Communard of 1871, his career embodies the important transformation of distinctly French working-class values into a strategy to use social policy to advance labour's interests. Although credit for keeping the parliamentary role of the socialists alive goes to Jean Jaurès, it was Vaillant who justifiably has been called the 'grandfather' of French social security.[8] No less revolutionary than the more doctrinaire Guesde, and aligned with his faction, Vaillant favoured the organization of labour exchanges, the development of munici-pal socialism, and was a strong advocate of national insurance. He favoured the formation of a Ministry of Labour, actually accomplished in France in 1906, more than a decade before similar recognition in Britain. He proposed a law in 1896 to organize a Conseil Supérieur du Travail with departmental branches. When the formation of the SFIO took place under the harsh restrictions

[7] The CGT was linked more closely to the anarchist strain of French socialism. See Christian de Goustine, *Pouget: Les Matins noirs du syndicalisme*, Paris; Editions de la Tête de Feuilles, 1972.

[8] Maurice Dommanget, *Vaillant: Un Grand Socialiste 1840–1915*, Paris; Table Ronde, 1956, p. 161. Also Jolyon Howorth, *Edouard Vaillant: La création de l'unité socialiste en France*, Paris; Syros, 1982.

on parliamentary activity that Guesde insisted upon, Vaillant helped construct a workable compromise with Jaurès in order to preserve the credibility and a measure of flexibility for socialist Deputies.[9] Of course, all these policies were part of his tactic to develop working-class consciousness. As he said of national insurance, 'it creates an appetite and pushes them (workers) toward a creative and rich (*fécund*) struggle, a sense of solidarity against the *patron*.[10] His proposals in the Chamber of Deputies were designed to achieve this end. In 1903 he was a leader in the debate over a law to transform French public assistance into a national insurance programme. He wanted social insurance organized at the communal level to enhance worker participation, but coordinated nationally by an Office National d'Assurance with two-thirds of its directors from the CGT.[11]

Contrary to the widely accepted image of the French socialists as estranged and remote from the development of social policy, they had clear goals and, compared to the British left, enjoyed parliamentary influence well before the establishment of the British Labour Party. During the republican resurgence of the 1880s, the Socialists were able to gain a number of seats in the Chamber of Deputies. With nearly 50 socialist Deputies, Guesde himself was elected in 1893, but retained his revolutionary posture, which was to erode his relations with Jean Jaurès. Guesde wrote, 'Parliamentary action is revolutionary, whatever the policy, by fighting from the high tribune of the Chamber to recall the discontents of the workshop, the countryside and the factory and by cornering capitalists by denying or weakening their satisfaction.'[12] As the quotation suggests, the difficult problem in explaining the relation of the French left to social policy is why they cooperated as much as they did. Their proposals were quite specific and their contributions to the political debates at the turn of the century well conceived, though naturally demanding much more than might be expected from a liberal government. In the legislative elections of 1902 the PSF held 37 seats and the PSDF 14 seats,

[9] Lefranc, *Le Mouvement Socialiste* . . ., p. 123.
[10] Dommanget, *Vaillant* . . ., p. 167
[11] *Journal Officiel, Débats parlementaires*, session ordinaire de 1903, 8è legislature, séance de vendredi 29 mai 1903, pp. 1777–81, for the debate on Vaillant's amendment. See also his book, *Assurance sociale*, Paris; Imprimérie Centrale de la Bourse, 1901.
[12] Lefranc, *Le Mouvement Socialiste* . . ., p. 56.

and in the 1906 elections, as a precariously united SFIO, they continued to hold 51 seats with nearly 900,000 votes.[13]

Because British institutions defined the basis of political legitimacy so clearly, the British socialist movement, much to the dismay of its continental Marxist critics, could simply fit their views into an effective and reliable electoral and parliamentary structure. They did this with remarkable success. Under the skilful guidance of the secretary of the International Labour Party (ILP), Ramsey MacDonald, the nascent socialist party had over 700,000 members by 1902, merely nine years after its foundation.[14] By cooperating with the Liberal Party, the Labour Representation Committee (LRC) had rapid success in acquiring parliamentary seats, growing from 2 MPs in 1900 to 42 by the second 1910 election. Their actual strength during this critical phase of the early social policy debates in Britain was less than their French counterparts, but they shared strength in a formidably powerful parliament.

The early Labour Party leaders had few plausible social policies. The Webbs worked diligently to create their particular version of a socially just state, but policymakers were cautious. The critical political features of Fabian social reform were, first, its unrelenting elitist quality and, second, its heavy reliance on administrative manipulation and centralization. It is no disrespect to the energetic Webbs to note that social proposals of all parties share these qualities in Britain. The Webbs made little secret of their sceptical view of mass democracy. In contemplating their tireless efforts to refashion the London County Council, Beatrice Webb considered it 'a machine for dodging democracy (in a crude sense) by introducing government by a select minority instead of rule by the majority.'[15] As the self-appointed 'official archangels' of the welfare state,[16] the Fabians were in fact remarkably unsuccessful in bringing about major changes in British social policy. Like their Benthamite predecessors of the early nineteenth century, their

---

[13] Lefranc, *Le Mouvement Socialiste* . . ., p. 146.

[14] David Marquand, *Ramsay MacDonald*, London; Jonathan Cape, 1977, p. 75.

[15] Quoted In W. H. Greenleaf, *The British Political Tradition: The Ideological Heritage*, London; Methuen, 1983, p. 398.

[16] The phrase was coined by H. G. Wells, who, like many other younger intellectuals of the Edwardian period, found themselves uncomfortable with the Webbs' elitism. Both Cole and Tawney had difficulties accepting the Webbs' political strategy.

highhanded ways and stringent administrative demands offended
many of their potential political supporters. Many of the austere
Edwardian politicians realized that their demands were excessive,
including a young and ambitious minor minister, Winston
Churchill.

Lest we blame the Webbs too unmercifully for the political
curiosities of the British welfare state, it should be noted that the
paternalistic strain within British social policy can be traced to
the early Victorian period.[17] The political argument is simply that
the institutional stability of British parliament generated a kind of
self-confidence among British socialists that continental socialists
rarely enjoyed. In addition, around the turn of the century, ideological struggles were not as crippling as those among continental
socialists. With the possible exception of MacDonald, most of the
Labour Party leaders of the inter-war period had few radical
social ideas. For example, their proposals to relieve the high
unemployment between the wars were well-known, modest proposals from the Edwardian period. If anything, the Keynesian
views incorporated into the programme of the dying Liberal Party
in the 1929 election were the most daring response to the issue
that dominated British social policy from 1920 until World
War II.

The intricacies of social policy, particularly during the persistent
and crippling period of unemployment between the wars, were
hardly the stuff on which political leaders could concentrate. Mac-
Donald himself was distracted by his concern for the international
socialist movement and squabbles with the ILP.[18] Bound to a
testy Chanceller of the Exchequer, Philip (later Viscount) Snowden
who fervently espoused Treasury caution at every move, and to a
jealous Arthur Henderson, who often made no secret of his feeling
that MacDonald had cheated him from becoming Prime Minister,
MacDonald, even if he had the temperament for poring over
the complexities of social reform, had little encouragement or
inspiration from his own colleagues. The National Government of
1931 to 1935 introduced an entirely new generation of Labour

---

[17] See David Roberts, *Paternalism in Early Victorian England*, London; Croom Helm,
and New Brunswick; Rutgers University Press, 1979.
[18] MacDonald never succeeded in healing the split within the ILP organization
over shifting to a more revolutionary posture. See Marquand, *MacDonald . . .*,
pp. 450–557. The disastrous defeat of 1931 silenced the more militant socialist
wing of the Party until the rise of Aneuran Bevan.

leaders. The disastrous election of 1931 reduced the Party to its proportions of 1910.[19] Concern naturally focused on political recovery rather than social reform. The political situation made the Party even more dependent on the TUC, most notably Ernest Bevin, and thereby further tied Labour's social agenda to the immediate interests of the unions.

Most of the critically important questions affecting the British welfare state in 1945 were mapped in the 1930s and within the political and institutional setting of Parliament. The immense increase in social benefits in Britain following World War II involved few major political adjustments. Perhaps the most important point of agreement was that wage and social policy would remain formally separated. There is little evidence that the Attlee government, distracted by the immense problems of reconstruction, gave much thought to the future complications of the Beveridge Plan.[20] For the moment, it is important to underscore how the strength of organized labour in Britain inhibited original thinking within the Labour Party. In a few words, the British welfare state is admired for the wrong reasons. It is not unique because of its initial generosity or breadth, but because political and institutional conditions enabled Labour leaders to proceed more rapidly than continental socialist leaders who were constantly forced to reconcile their policies with disunited and weak labour organizations.

The importance of forging a new political alliance between labour movements and socialist parties should be clear. The right could rely on its pre-war strategies, but the left had only begun to enjoy parliamentary success in the decade preceding World War I. Their ability to devise new policies and to respond to unemployment was in large part dependent on the ability of their leaders to work in concert. In redefining the nature of democratic governance, the concessions that conservative parties made to business are much less indicative of the future direction of democratic politics than was the ability of the labour movement to work

[19] On the internal stresses and strains of the Labour Party over the 1930s, see Ben Pollitt, *Labour and the Left in the 1930s*, Cambridge; Cambridge University Press, 1977; and James Jupp, *The Radical Left in Britain 1931–1941*, London; Cass. 1982.
[20] See Kenneth Morgan, *Labour in Power, 1945–1951*, Oxford; Clarendon Press, 1984, pp. 142–87; and Henry Pelling, *The Labour Governments, 1945–1951*, London; Macmillan, 1984, pp. 97–118.

within the framework of democratic politics. The importance of these explorations into the labour market and wage policies can only be fully appreciated if we see how little was known about the problem itself. However clear policy options might be in terms of abstract models of society or the economy, innovation and resourcefulness was needed on a scale that has probably never been equalled in the history of democratic governance. Indeed, not all democracies survived the challenge.

In the late nineteenth century, officials and academics had only a dim idea of what unemployment meant. As Jose Harris writes, unemployment was seen as a voluntary condition and 'for the most of the nineteenth century inadequacy of income as such, whether caused by low wages, irregular employment, or even by sickness, was not considered a legitimate object of state interference, beyond the conditional subsistence granted by poor relief'.[21] Until the early industrial depressions of the 1880s in most European countries real wages increased over the century. For the most part, nineteenth-century union leaders, like Marx, subscribed to the Malthusian view that there was a limited amount of wages. For liberals the task of the state was mainly to see that poor relief was provided when demands on this pool were excessive. For Marxists, the political problem was to abolish all other claims on the wage pool. Understandably, Marx detested Lasalle, the German labour leader of the 1860s, because he subscribed to the Iron Law of Wages, which remained official SPD doctrine until 1891.[22]

The leading British economist of the day, Alfred Marshall, had little interest in unemployment as such, although as we have seen he did speculate before the Royal Commission on the Aged Poor that it might be cheaper to provide jobs than poor relief. Joblessness was of course a much less acute problem in France than in other European countries, which may in part explain why revolutionary syndicalism could have the success it did. If everyone is unemployed, revolution loses its political rationale, but France was not in dire straits until the 1930s, and even then unemployment never exceeded 800,000 persons. In the United States, Gompers of course remained the defender of capitalism and craft unions, while, as we shall see in more detail below, the Swedish

[21] Harris, *Unemployment and Politics. . .*, p. 35.
[22] Moses, *Trade Unionism in Germany* . . ., p. 23–41.

unions simply skipped the political controversies over the meaning of unemployment.

Though it seldom enters into the socio-economic models of the welfare state, devising policies to deal with unemployment was technically and conceptually a more demanding problem than were earlier proposals to improve education or basic security for the disabled and poor. These problems, their effects and costs, are relatively easily measured. Even if not overly generous, the classical liberal policies of charitable relief and religiously-endowed education had the rough dimensions of the new social problems in hand. In many respects, the political issue in launching the welfare state around 1900 was how to revise obsolescent liberal policies concerning the poor and the less educated. Unemployment was an entirely new problem for the democratic states.

Regardless of Marxist or liberal inclinations, the task remained of translating essentially descriptive studies into policies. No doubt early industrialization goes a long way toward explaining why Britain developed unemployment policies from the 1911 Act onward, but it is also important to note that policy was devised in a comparatively short period of time. Often accompanied and supported by the young Beveridge, the key figure in this development in Britain was Sir Hubert Llewellyn Smith who developed a labour research group within the Board of Trade. From this effort emerged a number of detailed studies of the cost of living of workers, earnings and hours of work in numerous industries, etc.[23] Much the same had been done by Sir Robert Morant in the Inquiries Section of the Board of Education, one of his first innovations in educational policy. At about the same time, Beveridge's first book, *Unemployment and Industry*, appeared as did Hobson's *The Problem of Unemployment*. Foreshadowing the future complexity of unemployment policies, Beveridge became committed to improved organization of the labour market, while Hobson more prophetically saw that unemployment had multiple causes that might be characterized as underconsumption. More important to the policy process, the precedent was established for government to assemble its own data and to conduct its own studies so that unlike Germany and Sweden, where the labour movements developed their own research and policymaking capacities, much of the

[23] Read, *Edwardian England* . . ., p. 154; and Gilbert, *The Evolution of National Insurance* . . ., pp. 267–9.

detailed materials on British policies remained, shrouded by the secrecy rules of Whitehall.

The British experience of centralizing wage studies and labour legislation was much less an intentional tactic to deprive the labour movement of a voice in social policy than a simple continuation of a fundamental constitutional characteristic of British politics and policymaking. The Edwardian policymakers had little more respect for the new industrial elite than they did for the erratic and sometimes emotional union leaders. The incentives as well as the opportunities for the labour movement to participate in the construction of the early welfare state were therefore heavily influenced by the ability of both business and unions to link their wage policies to the state. Contrary to Marxist interpretations, Whitehall had little interest in dealing directly with either group when social questions arose. Industrialists did not begin to play a central role in policymaking until the pressures of the war, when production rather than social policy was the main concern.[24]

LABOUR ACCEPTS DEMOCRACY

Compared to other European countries, unions, industrialists, bankers and commercial groups had little experience in public policy. Until about 1918 Whitehall and great civil service barons were isolated from both labour and business and for the most part wanted it that way. Indeed, when Lloyd George introduced a battery of 'outsiders' into the war government in 1917, he sent shudders of alarm through Whitehall. Among the new arrivals were a shipowner appointed to the Insurance Commission, a grocery wholesaler made Food Controller, a Duke's land agent on the Board of Agriculture, as well as the industrialists in the Ministry of Munitions and a labour leader, Arthur Henderson, as a member of the War Cabinet.[25] Both the industrialists and unions detested the strict controls of the Ministry of Munitions, in particular Ernest Bevin to whom the task of rebuilding the TUC fell over the 1930s.

---

[24] The Federation of British Industries was not formed until 1916 and the National Council of Employers' Organisations in 1919. See Keith Middlemas, *Politics in Industrial Society*, London; André Deutsch, 1979, pp. 120–51.

[25] Peter Fraser, 'The Impact of the War', in K. Burke, ed., pp. 135–6.

While the disastrous course of British industrial relations over
the 1920s tempts one to see the isolation of social policy from
wages and other industrial policies in socio-economic terms, and
obviously lends itself to a Marxist interpretation, none of these
explanations take into account the extent to which the policy
process itself, a construct of British institutions and politics, shaped
these issues as they did nearly every major policy problem between
the wars. To an extent that would be unimaginable in France,
Germany or Sweden, the policy interests of government, business
and labour were compartmentalized. The question is not so much
that each group did not individually pursue its political advantage,
but that each became an image of the British parliamentary model,
self-sufficient, aloof and insulated from 'outsiders'. Wages and
welfare were separated in Britain not because of a failure of
imagination, but because nothing but the Westminster model made
sense. To a remarkable degree, this remained the case after World
War II.

Unlike Britain, where the unions were fragmented at the turn
of the century, the German unions had developed a much stronger
central organization as defence against the hostile German political
environment. As the internal divisions within the SPD multiplied
before World War I, the ADGB found its collaboration with
socialists increasingly difficult. In 1906, for example, the ADGB
forced the SPD to comply with a union federation decision to
accept a strike settlement for the Hamburg masons after the Party
had refused to expel the recalcitrant workers.[26] Although the
Gotha Program of 1896 included Party recognition of the need to
obtain more protection for workers, the eight-hour day and shop
closings by 8 p.m., the SPD was less and less able to press for social
legislation and, as Nettl describes, became a 'non-participating
opposition'.[27] Both organizations were of course still burdened by
their exclusion from German political life, but from about 1900
their strategies to acquire political legitimacy diverge.

As Moses describes the problem, 'Both polarized sections of
German society hoped for positive integration of the other, but on

[26] Moses, *Trade Unionism in Germany from Bismarck to Hitler, 1869–1918*, Totowa,
NJ; Barnes and Noble, 1982, pp. 142–5.
[27] Peter Nettl, 'The German Social Democratic Party 1890–1914 as a Political
Model', *Past and Present*, **30**, April 1965, pp. 65–95. Nettl also argues that the
extent to which the ADGB became the political arm of the Party contributed to
the immobilization of the Party.

their own terms.'[28] For a time the war seemed an opportunity for
the left to gain the respect of the German political and industrial
elite. Legien, the ADGB leader, knew that the German army had
a plan to totally repress unions if war came, and so, without
consulting the SPD, negotiated with the Ministry of the Interior
to protect union funds and preserve unions during hostilities.
Rather like the enthusiastic social planners within the Lloyd
George government during World War I, the unions saw war
mobilization as a way to simultaneously achieve social equality
and political acceptance. Legien distanced himself from the intense
ideological debates of the Party during the war in order to pursue
his own version of war socialism (*Kriegssozialismus*), and turned his
scorn on the 'phraseturners' (*Phrasendrescher*) within the Party. In
one more futile attempt to acquire respect, during the war the
unions dispensed their huge strike fund of 88 million marks to
relieve workers.[29]

For a number of reasons, the immense potential influence of the
SPD and the early union federation (ADGB) never achieved its
promise. Their many disappointments have produced a complex
literature on German socialist and labour history from both Marxist and liberal viewpoints. Despite Bismarck's repressive laws
against socialists, the ADGB had assembled a powerful organization by 1890, including 59 nationally-organized unions with
over 200,000 members, by far the largest labour movement in
continental Europe. By 1903 the SPD had 81 seats in the Reichstag, one of the largest socialist parliamentary groups among the
European socialist parties and the second largest party in
Germany. Perhaps it was the great strength of both movements,
paralyzed by the immovable institutional obstacle of the German
state, that, in turn, engendered the divergence and suspicion
between the SPD and the ADGB. Under enormous political uncertainties, the union leadership built a strong, centralized organization to withstand political rejection and hostility, while simultaneously pursuing every opportunity to demonstrate to German
conservatives and industrialists that the unions were loyal to the
state. The unions continued to develop a *Sozialpolitik*, but the
political circumstances meant that neither spokesman for the left

[28] Moses, p. 180.
[29] For a full account, see Gerald D. Feldman, *Army, Industry and Labor, 1914–1918*,
Princeton; Princeton University Press, 1966.

was able to make a major new departure in the inter-war period.

The political result was that in the least stable of all democratic experiments, the Weimar Republic, the unions turned to their own vision of economic democracy. Article 165 of the Weimar Constitution provided the legal foundation for equal status of unions and employers, and amid the chaos of Weimar the ADGB worked to build a system of worker councils. There were important gains for labour, the Works Council Act of 1920 and the Unemployment Act of 1927, but the Party and the unions never acquired the respect of the German elites. The laboriously negotiated alliance of business and labour (*Zentralarbeitsgemeinschaft* or ZAG) never materialized and the National Economic Council, the crowning corporate body to govern the works councils, met only once. Weimar only served to deepen the hatred of labour among most German industrialists and the tragic internal political divisions of German society remained for fascist exploitation. Theories to explain the permanent schisms of German politics and society abound, worker alienation, *embourgeoisement* of the party and the unions, organizational centralization, mindless political tactics and the economic disaster of the Versailles Treaty,[30] but the pertinent fact for the development of German welfare state was that democracy was not fortified by the autocratic social reforms of Bismarck.

Whether effective unemployment relief might have stabilized German democracy in the 1920s seems doubtful. There had been a federal unemployment insurance plan since 1918 although there was a means test and no legal rights were provided. In face of soaring unemployment in 1923, Streseman allocated a small percentage of land welfare expenditure to the system. In fact, neither the SPD nor the ADGB seemed to attach high priority to unemployment insurance.[31] When a national plan was agreed upon in 1927 only the political extremes, Communist and Nazi, voted against it, but in the economic and political chaos of the late 1920s the political effectiveness of comprehensive social protection was barely tested.

[30] Alienation was strongest in the Communist faction of the workers. The *embourgeoisement* view was expounded by Weber as part of his postwar fears of bureaucratic domination, which were later extended by Michels. See Moses, *Trade Unionism in Germany from Bismarck to Hitler* . . ., pp. 299–304.

[31] See Daniel Levine, 'Social Democracy, Socialism and Social Insurance, Germany and Denmark, 1918–1933,' in R. F. Tomasson, ed., *Comparative Social Research: The Welfare State, 1883–1983*, Westport, CT; JAI Press, 1983, pp. 67–86. Also Wolffsohn in Mommsen, ed.

The remarkable ability of the Swedish socialists and unions to merge their policy objectives between the wars was not as easy as retrospective accounts of the Swedish model sometimes suggest. Because we are easily preoccupied with the progress of the Swedish welfare state in the 1950s we may overlook that relations between the union confederation (LO) and the Social Democratic Party (SAP) were controversial. Many policy compromises preceded the formation of parliamentary government, but were not defined or implemented until much later. In terms of the transformation of welfare states, the critical intervening factor was that strong political links that developed between the SAP and the LO in the first decades of the century.

Unlike most democracies, their alliance was formed in the process of obtaining universal suffrage and parliamentary supremacy early in the century. Social and economic policies were still unclear. But as early as 1922 the LO also indicated that it preferred 'wage solidarity' over conventional, competitive wage bargaining.[32] By this was meant wage agreements that would diminish wage differentials primarily in agriculture and forestry.[33] Unlike the older democracies, agreement over wage policy preceded the development of more generous social benefits. Incorporated in this major compromise and essential to its acceptance by employers, there was agreement that industry would remain in private hands. This political difference between the Swedish and British cases suggests that Heclo's argument concerning the similar development of social policy in the two systems needs to be considered with reservation.[34] British unions spent most of the 1920s fighting for wages with weak support from a distracted Labour Party.

The peculiar political course of Swedish democracy can be directly linked to the strikes of 1902 that built the momentum leading to universal suffrage in 1918. The SAP leader, Branting, initially made the Party organization co-determinous with union districts in 1900. The failure of the 1909 general strike persuaded the SAP and LO leaders to separate the two organizations, but the political links are much closer than those found in turn-of-the-century France, Britain, or even Germany until 1890. While leaders of the left had to compete for recognition in most democracies,

---

[32] See T. L. Johnston, *Collective Bargaining* . . ., pp. 32–5.

[33] Though the standard sources on Sweden do not elaborate this point, LO concern for low agricultural wages appears consistent, if not motivated by, the 1930 alliance of the SAP and the Peasant Party.

[34] Heclo, *Modern Social Policy in Britain and Sweden*.

history made the Swedish left an integral component of democratic development that the older liberal democracies had achieved well before the welfare state emerged. In 1912 80 per cent of SAP members were also LO members.[35] Once democracy was established the entire left could immediately concentrate on translating its aims into workable public policy. As many commentators on Sweden note, Sweden never experienced political pluralism.

The Swedish Employers' Association (SAF) was also a nationally-organized and powerful body well before employers in other countries began to organize to fight unions, in part because of the concentration of ownership of Swedish business and in part because late industrialization required a highly-organized private sector. For some years Sweden was on a disastrous course. From about 1910 to 1930 Swedish industrial relations were a shambles with the SAF able to conduct well coordinated lockouts to humble the LO. Important as Sweden's military and economic vulnerability may be in explaining agreement over the 1930s, for over a decade labour and business had been locked in a political combat that could have easily destroyed the country. Once the SAP abandoned their Communist support after the 1928 election defeat, the political grounds for industrial peace were established.

With weaker labour movements and more autonomous agricultural sectors, socialist parties elsewhere faced more difficult political problems. Diverse industrial structures in other European states meant workers, however well organized, could not duplicate the Swedish political situation. The political opportunity for Sweden to fashion a compromise between wages and welfare did not depend simply on the power of the left, but on a governing alliance with farmers in the Peasant Party whose political payoff was agricultural protection. The political alliance is remarkably similar to the Junker alliance with agriculture in Bismarck's Germany, but with the opposite political effect. For the older European economies, these compromises had been made by liberals many decades earlier.

Although the Basic Agreement between the LO and SAF of 1938 is certainly the cornerstone of the Swedish welfare state, linking wage and social policy was not without political difficulties. In the early 1930s the SAP remained committed to orthodox economics and was uneasy over the risk that LO wage proposals

[35] See T. L. Johnston, pp. 26–31.

would aggravate inflation. Sweden had high unemployment (reaching 23 per cent in 1933) but the SAP was also opposed to deficit finance.[36] Nor was it entirely clear that the LO could elicit agreement with its policy from its own members.[37] In a series of adroit moves the SAP snatched victory from the jaws of defeat. First, the 1933 budget increased public relief for the unemployed and raised the minimum wage to solidify lines to the LO. Second, the Riksdag appointed the Nothins Commission with the intent of forming a new wage policy, clearly signalling to both the LO and the SAF that were they unable to settle the issue, parliament would step in. Third, the LO overcame internal opposition to a devaluation that the SAP considered essential to its new departure, thereby relieving pressure on the SAP for deficit financing.[38] Although voluntary employment insurance was established in 1934, like other social policies to follow, it was not central to the policy aims of either the LO or the SAF. Both the LO and the SAF were under enormous political pressure to construct the Basic Agreement (Salsjobaden Agreement) of 1938. Had the LO failed, it would have meant increasing public assistance and thereby shelving its favoured policy of wage solidarity, plus the threat of increased differentials creating dissent among the member unions in the future. For the SAF the attractions of autonomy were obvious, but were sweetened by conceding generous corporate tax benefits in 1932.

Considering the weakness of the French labour movement, including the crippling effects of the split of the CGT into three unions in 1921, the left still moved toward incorporating their ideas in the slowly evolving French welfare state. Although the anarchist and revolutionary strands of the labour movement prod-

---

[36] On the early employment policies of the SAP, see Gustave Moller, 'The Unemployment Policy,' *Annals of the American Academy*, 197, 1938, pp. 47–71. Moller was Minister of Social Affairs.

[37] Johnston, p. 36. The incident involved two unions voting against mediation during a strike in the building industry. The LO did not have powers to discipline member unions until 1941.

[38] The interpretation followed in this paragraph is based on the doctoral dissertation of Henrik Jess Madsen, *Social Democracy in Post-War Scandinavia: Macro-economic Management, Electoral Support and the Fading Legacy of Prosperity*, Cambridge, MA; Harvard University, 1984, pp. 131–40. Madsen couples this argument with evidence of the instability of Swedish government compared to Denmark and Norway.

uced political rhetoric that might alarm the most sanguine of liberals, in the convoluted pattern of French politics the socialists and the CGT managed to support, often decisively, the social reforms that emerged between the wars. Spared the German problem of acquiring legitimacy and unsympathetic with parliamentary politics, the French labour movement tried to steer a middle course while supporting the social reforms that emerged before World War I. Indeed, compared to the distracting struggles of the stronger ADGB and TUC, the continuity of social demands by the French left was impressive.

Though controversial for his moderation, Léon Jouhaux, who at 30 years of age became the secretary general of the CGT in 1909, kept alive worker interest in social reform. His delicate compromises permitted union supporters in the Chamber of Deputies to vote for social legislation, while publicly rejecting the inadequacies and injustices of these laws.[39] In addition, the CGT had to guard itself against the remnants of anarchist workers and the Communist splinter union (CGTU) whose tactic of penetration (noyautage) of CGT locals constantly drained away CGT energies. From the mid-1920s the revival of Catholic trade unions presented a third division within the labour movement.[40] Though the unions were seldom in a situation between the wars where they could provide decisive support for social reform, Jouhaux continued the tradition of the left of supporting social legislation.

Thus, despite the predominance of conservative governments in France over the 1920s, the left and the labour movement remained consistent in their demands. The CGT's 'Minimum Program' of late 1918 included union participation in the Versailles negotiations, recogniation of public sector unions, the eight-hour day, a National Economic Council, the nationalization of national

[39] On his life see Bernard Georges and Denise Tintaut, Léon Jouhaux: Cinquantes années de syndicalism, Paris; Presses Universitaires de France, 1962, 2 vols. For example, Jouhaux linked the issue of supporting the 1910 law for the aged and disabled with the question of division of contributions (répartition) and age of eligibility.

[40] Figures vary on the size and strength of the unions. Saposs, The Labor Movement in Post-War France, p. 166, puts the peak CGT membership of 1919 at 1.6 million; Henry Ehrmann, French Labour from the Popular Front to Liberation, New York; Oxford University Press, 1947, p. 51, suggests 5.1 million in 1937 after the Popular Front. But membership fluctuated wildly and at times the CGT fell to 100,000 members.

resources and more social legislation.[41] Even with the fragmentation of the labour movement, some progress was made in
all these directions by 1940. In close contact with the Ministry of
Labour, the labour movement developed relatively specific ideas.
The two CGT specialists on social problems, Aimé Rey and
Georges Buisson, wanted social security based on universal participation, the unification of all social funds (*caisses*), tripartite
contributions, and increased benefits for nearly all areas of social
insurance.[42] With more success than British unions, the CGT also
initiated its own mutual insurance scheme, insuring over half a
million workers for sickness by 1939.[43] Anticipating the tripartite
management of the post-war French welfare state, the Popular
Front encouraged the unions to join with business[44] to form the
Comité d'Action et de Prévoyance Sociale. Though Blum was
unable to expand social insurance, the discussions of the late 1930s
provided many of the ideas incorporated in the French welfare
state after World War II.

Perhaps because of their numerical and organizational weaknesses, a foothold in the policy process was and remains attractive
to French unions. From their earliest rivalries, French unions have
found official recognition in public agencies a way to acquire
advantages over other unions. When the Cartel des Gauches, for
example, created a National Economic Council in 1925, the CGT
seized all the union seats on the Council. Similarly, the unions
looked upon the Bourses de Travail (Labour Exchanges) with
suspicion, but where socialists were strong were not inhibited

---

[41] Saposs, p. 44 fn. The insistent demands were the 40-hour week and paid
vacations, acquired in the 1936 Matignon Accord.

[42] Georges Lefranc, *Les Expériences syndicales en France de 1939 à 1950*, Paris; Editions
Montaigne, 1950, pp. 310–13. The CGT created its own Bureau d'Etudes in
1934 and became increasingly committed to 'planisme' under the influence of
the Belgian socialist, Henry de Man. René Belin, the secretary of the CGT, and
the young Pierre Laroque, then working with Parodi, were active in these
discussions. See Georges Lefranc, *Les Expériences* ..., pp. 314–28, and *Essais sur
les problèmes socialistes et syndicaux*, Paris; Payot, 1960, pp. 127–47.

[43] Lefranc, *Les Expériences* ..., p. 313.

[44] Unlike Sweden and Germany, where well-organized business groups opposed
the labour movement from its earliest years, French business was slow to organize.
Until World War I the main opposition was the Comité des Forges, reconstituted
later as the UIMM and including some 7,000 firms. A weak organization of
other business was started in 1919, the Confédération Générale de la Production
Française, reorganized in 1936 as the Confédération Générale des Patronats
Français, in 1936. See Ehrmann, pp. 10–14.

from taking full control. In Lille, the CGT made the Bourse its headquarters, and excluded competing unions from its offices and from sharing minor benefits.[45] Unlike Britain and the United States, where public sector unions were weak or compliant, the CGT used its public sector strength to advantage. One of its main advances was to obtain permission from the Cartel des Gauches to organize public employees, and in 1928 it extracted governmental endorsement of its plan to exclude the Communist CGT faction from recruiting among public employees. Saposs estimates that by 1921 80 per cent of government workers were organized.[46] They were not to achieve similar importance in British and American labour movements until the postwar period.

A complete history of the progress of the French labour movement between the wars has yet to be written, but its entry into social policy questions was never plagued by the hostility that characterized British industrial relations over much of the interwar period. The acceptance of labour as a partner in governmental decisionmaking began before World War I. In 1911 a minimum salary for household workers in the clothing industry was approved virtually without debate.[47] The law was an important turning point in negotiating with unions, providing joint participation of workers and owners in fixing salary levels, paving the way to extend minimum salary legislation after the war, and shaping public expectations. In 1913, the CGT acquired equal representation in the Conseil Supérieur du Travail. The war had a more lasting impact than in Britain. In 1914 a *Fond du Chômage* of 20 million francs was established to provide for dislocated workers and the families of men sent to war as well as an expanded

[45] Saposs, pp. 292–305 and pp. 161–3. Unlike the shadowy political existence of similar corporatist groups formed in Britain and Germany over the 1920s, the Prime Minister presided, the Council formed its own agenda, decided its own electoral procedures, and, important to the unions as a sign of official recognition, had its records published in the *Journal Officiel*. It was the precedent for the Economic and Social Council of the Fourth Republic.

[46] Saposs, p. 126. Ehrmann, pp. 23–4, estimates that in 1935 about half the union members were government employees, while at that time no more than 6 per cent of private sector employees were unionized.

[47] William Oualid and Charles Picquenard, *Salaires et tarifs, conventions et grèves: la politique du Ministère de l'Armement et du Ministère du Travail*, Paris and New Haven; Presses Universitaires de France and Yale University Press (For the Carnegie Peace Foundation), 1928, pp. 281–3.

programme of labour placement.[48] Critical to these decisions was
the Ministry of Armaments where Millerand's protegé from the
independent socialist faction, Albert Thomas, was minister and
used the war to advance his concept of labour peace. The momentum carried over to the postwar law on collective bargaining,
which remains the bedrock of French labour legislation. Despite
intense opposition from owners, it was passed unanimously by the
Senate in 1919 making consultation between the *patrons* and,
significantly, 'national worker organizations' obligatory.[49] It was
followed by the 1920 law regulating the eight-hour day or forty-
eight hour week which like so much French legislation was
implemented by an intricate organization of departmental and
regional committees. More than the labour movements of Britain
or Germany, the French unions were rewarded for their efforts in
World War I.

French labour acquired the aura of political legitimacy which
constantly eluded the German labour movement and which
remained a heated dispute in Britain until World War II. Business
considered the Matignon Accord of 1936 a capitulation to radical
interests, but it remained a milestone in the collaboration between
the labour movement and government. Next to Swedish developments it is the most substantial political advance that any
European labour movement made between the wars.[50] In addition
to large pay increases, the unions acquired the right to appoint
shop stewards, a 40-hour week without loss of pay, paid vacations
and the promise that firms could no longer refuse collective bargaining. However difficult the divisions of social class and socialist
ideology, by 1940 French unions had a claim on French national
government that propelled them into becoming major actors in
the organization of social security after 1945. Their desire to have
an institutionalized claim on the French state is a major difference
from the labour movements in nearly all other democracies.

Considering the early development of social legislation in Britain

---

[48] According to Oualid and Picquenard, the departmental committees of union
and owner representatives continued to be active after the war and, unlike the
British Trade Boards, made important local decisions, especially concerning the
application of the eight-hour day.
[49] Qualid and Picquenard, p. 324.
[50] My account relies heavily on Saposs, pp. 36–59. See also the numerous
histories of the Popular Front such as Georges Lefranc, *Histoire du Front Populaire,
1934–38*, Paris; Payot, 1965.

and the long history of the labour movement, the relationship between British unions and the state is perhaps the most difficult to understand. Compared to the fierce struggles in France, Germany, Sweden, or even the determined pluralist setting of American politics, the British unions seem never to have found a comfortable and productive way to link the interests of workers to the British state. On the contrary, in the most stable of democracies unions stood apart from social reforms. Politial parties, in particular the Labour Party, remained distant from the TUC. There are of course many explanations for the 'failure' of British unions,[51] but the explanation is not likely to be found in examining unions or the Labour Party in isolation.

In contrast to the continental labour movements, British unions never questioned the fundamental institutional assumptions of British politics. The Marxist explanation of their failure to develop revolutionary principles would be a more convincing explanation were it not that similar isolation from Whitehall and Westminster can be observed among many groups in Britain. In the late nineteenth century, every other democracy was experimenting with new institutional structures and responding to major changes in party and electoral politics, including the United States. In Britain, institutional change required enormous external pressure. A policymaking correlate of an exclusive institutional structure was that unions, like other pressure groups, had few opportunities to acquire a foothold in the emerging British welfare state.

While Victorian history of British unions cannot be recapitulated, it is important to see why parliamentary legitimacy and parliamentary supremacy easily became working assumptions of British unions. The London Workingmen's Association was primarily concerned with political reforms. The early model for the TUC of 1869 was the Social Science Association, a study and educational group. The political arm of the TUC was the Parliamentary Committee under Henry Broadhurst, an admirer of Gladstone and a Liberal Party M.P. As B. C. Roberts has well described, the Parliamentary Committee saw its task, much like a compliant House of Commons Committee, to review legislation, not to develop a militant labour movement or to propose radical

---

[51] There are several fine histories of the British labour movement such as Hugh Clegg, Alan Fox and Arthur Thompson, *History of British Trade Unionism since 1889*, Oxford; Oxford University Press, 1964; and Ernest Phelps Brown, *The Growth of British Industrial Relations*, London; Macmillan, 1959.

reforms.[52] The TUC Parliamentary Committee Report of 1905, for example, mainly concerned recommendations on the threat of automated machinery, the expansion of public works and increased public employment. As Roberts notes, union ideas represented 'no real break with the past' and, much like the early Labour MPs, the TUC had little to offer to remedy the miseries of the working class but land colonies, cooperative farms, and efforts to reduce the supply of labour.[53] After the 1906 election 9 of the 13 members of the Parliamentary Committee sat in the House of Commons, but social progress was more a product of ministerial opportunism than purposeful intervention of union representatives.[54]

The exaggerated respect for parliamentary institutions that unions acquired in Victorian Britain was paralleled by similar conventional ambitions among the early socialist parties. The Independent Labour Party (ILP) was founded as a federation of worker clubs in a militantly labour city, Bradford, in 1893, but from the secret Lib-Lab electoral compromise of MacDonald the nascent Labour Party steadily gravitated toward achieving parliamentary respectability. John Burns, the hero of labour riots over unemployment in the 1880s and successful organizer of the London dockworkers, was the first Labour cabinet minister of working-class background and proved a disaster. He considered the small Exchequer grant to support the weak 1905 Unemployment Act, a voluntary arrangement to encourage local government to enlarge public works projects, likely 'to extend the virtues of pauperized dependency' and thus 'a serious blow to the morale of labourers.'[55] Against his better judgement he agreed to administer the grant through the Local Government Board, but under his strict rules only dispensed half of it. He thought the Right to Work Bill, possibly the first purely union social demand, no more than a

---

[52] B. C. Roberts, *The Trades Union Congress 1868–1921*, Cambridge; Harvard University Press, 1958, p. 169. For more detail, see C. J. Wrigley, ed., *A History of British Industrial Relations, 1875–1914*, Amherst, MA; University of Massachusetts Press, 1982.
[53] Roberts, p. 186.
[54] Roberts, p. 206.
[55] A full account of these discouraging early interventions in policymaking is set forth in detail by Kenneth D. Brown, *Labour and Unemployment 1900–1914*, London; Rowman and Littlefield, 1971. The quotes are from p. 76 and p. 86. See also his essay, 'Conflict in Early British Welfare Policy: The Case of the Unemployed Workmen's Bill of 1905,' *Journal of Modern History*, **43**, Winter 1971, pp. 615–29.

formula for 'universalized pauperism.' Indeed, the Liberal Prime
Minister, Asquith, was so embarrassed by his Labour minister
that he tried unsuccessfully to remove him from office and later
publicly disassociated himself from Burns' utterances. The inability
of the early Labour Party and unions to agree on social reform
was of course a major reason why Lloyd George and Churchill
were able to devise their own strategies for launching the British
welfare state.

Constructing a working relationship between the Labour Party
and the unions was a difficult task. In 1907, for example, a motion
was made in the Labour Party Conference to require all members
to be union members in good standing. It was narrowly defeated
by only 28 votes. Had it passed, the course of the British labour
movement might have been radically changed. Unions themselves
were undecided. The miners, for example, distrusted intermediate
bodies and fought for individual party membership until 1918. At
the time, they were the largest union in Britain with 800,000
members. As the Labour Party took shape in Edwardian Britain
there were no less than three liaison committees between the two
organizations: the Parliamentary Committee dating from 1869; a
TUC Management Committee more concerned with jurisdictional
and organizational matters; and finally the Labour Representation
Committee of 1900 which included 20 union leaders.[56] Because
of the confusion a Joint Board was formed between the Labour
Party and the TUC to rule on union affiliation with the Labour
Party (essentially to regulate union politics); to adjudicate affiliation conflicts; to discuss joint political action with the Party; and
finally to discuss labour conflicts if the TUC permitted.

These events are of interest not so much for what was
accomplished but what was not. The Lib-Lab pact, though distrusted by the union leaders, paid political dividends and overcame
alternative developments. But for a brief moment, there was the
possibility that the TUC and the Party would form more intimate
links as found in the labour movements of Sweden, Germany, and
France. Relations between the two groups were not clear until the
TUC reorganization following the war, when the General Council
was created, based on union membership. For the new generation

[56] In addition to the account of the Parliamentary Committee by D. C. Roberts,
see the account of internal negotiations in B. Gabriel de Montgomery, *British and
Continental Labour Policy*, London; Kegan Paul, 1922, pp. 251–61.

of union barons, the strength of their own unions became the first rule of politics.

The acceptance of institutional norms by British unions did not protect them from strong attacks by the courts so that their legal relationship to elections and parties was continually in doubt. These were hardly the best of circumstances to develop a socially sensitive union within the nascent Labour Party. In 1911, while the unions were under attack, the Party revised its constitution to acknowledge that it must accept 'responsibilities established by parliamentary practices,' hardly a sign of militant party support for the beleaguered unions. The prolonged crisis over union contributions to the Party began in 1905 when the Chief Registrar deleted the phrase 'Labour representation' from the charter of the Union of Patternmakers. Though later compromised by making political representation an instrument rather than an objective of the union, the issue escalated into the Osborne judgment of 1908 forbidding unions to directly allocate part of their dues to parties. While it is a mistake to interpret this decision entirely in terms of class politics or even simple partisan politics, the social costs were high. Even though unions were not forbidden to raise funds for political activities, political survival naturally became a preoccupation.

In the same way, relations between the Party and TUC changed very little between the wars, in part because of the disastrous experiment with a general strike, described in the next section, and in part because of the growing estrangement between the Party and the union, ending with the debacle of the 1929 Labour government.[57] In anticipation of a huge Labour victory in the post-war election the basic rules were formed during World War I. In 1916 the TUC Congress voted to strengthen the Joint Board and the basic pattern of TUC designation of a certain number of Labour Party candidates emerged. In return, the Labour Party programme of 1918, *Labour and the New Social Order*, included the ambiguous statement that their aim was to reconstruct 'society itself.' Its specific plans were enacting a minimum wage (acknowledged not to be a 'class' issue); democratic control of basic industries (workers councils); nationalization of financial institutions,

[57] See Robert Skidelsky, *Politicians and the Slump: The Labour Government of 1929– 1931*. Though not a sympathetic account of the MacDonald government, it is an accurate portrayal of the immense unfinished business of British policymaking.

including a capital levy to pay the war debt;[58] and vague measures to capture 'surplus wealth'. Of 361 Labour candidates in the snap election, only 57 were elected, a bitter disappointment that very likely persuaded many union leaders that they would have to achieve their objectives without relying on parliamentary support.

There are two sides to the exclusion of unions from the British policy process. On the one hand, the political elites of late Victorian and Edwardian Britain had almost no knowledge of, and very little sympathy with, unions. Did not the history of British labour legislation stretch back to the 1870s, including basic union recognition in 1871, one might more easily accept the social and economic explanations of labour strife in Britain. By the time labour protest reached crippling dimensions immediately before World War I, the British government had had nearly two generations of experience with labour problems, and legislated a battery of social insurance laws. Yet Campbell-Bannerman spoke of his 'two sops' to labour, the weak Trade Disputes Act of 1906 and the Workmen's Compensation Act.[59] Asquith certainly had more sensitivity to social needs, but it remained a paternalistic, and as in the case of the Old Age Pensions Act of 1908, opportunistic approach to social legislation. Nor were the rising leaders of the Labour Party much better prepared.

As we have seen both Sidney and Beatrice Webb were in despair over the labour movement, and wrote in their *History of Trade Unionism* that the TUC 'can hardly be said to have shown, between 1870 and 1917, at least, any development at all.'[60] Thus, while British workers did not feel the deep alienation from the state of German workers, and did not share the distrust of the state common to French syndicalism, they were in many respects effectively excluded from policymaking. With the exception of Churchill, who skilfully consulted TUC leaders to disarm their concerns over

---

[58] The first labour government of 1924 did appoint a Treasury Committee to consider the use of a capital levy to help pay the seven billion pound war debt. See *Report*, Committee on National Debt and Taxation, London, Parliamentary Papers, 1927, cmd. 2800. Their conclusion was that a levy of £3 billion would redistribute only £60 million. The best general account is by Maurice Cowling, *The Impact of Labour, 1920–24*, Cambridge; Cambridge University Press, 1971.
[59] Brown, p. 72.
[60] Quoted in Roberts, p. 360. Consistent with their view of government, their objections were that union leaders would yield to expert advice and would leave politics to the Labour Party.

Labour Exchanges,[61] few ministers had direct contact with union officials, and few wanted such contacts.

If the unions felt remote from government because of the aristocratic stance of most policymakers of the time, much the same can be said of the administrative elite. Although Britain began organizing studies of labour relations and conciliation services about the same time as France, a Ministry of Labour did not appear until 1916 and remained a weak ministry throughout the interwar period. Earlier concern with labour problems had much the same paternalistic aura that hung over most Edwardian reform. Llewellyn Smith, the Permanent Secretary of the Board of Trade from 1907 to 1916, came from a similar social background as Morant and other powerful Whitehall figures of the period. Like Beveridge, Llewellyn Smith had his brief exposure to the miseries of workers in an East London settlement house.[62] Like other Whitehall barons, his great skill was assembling statistics to demonstrate to ministers why they should follow his advice. As so often happens in Whitehall, expanding the social functions of the Board of Trade produced a scramble among ambitious ministers and officials. From 1874 to 1914 there were seventeen Presidents of the Board of Trade, almost twice the number of the more prestigious ministries.[63]

The ability of a labour movement to enlarge its objectives in order to respond to social needs and thereby acquire a credible role in social policymaking depends on two factors. First, the

[61] He did this with a simple device which was by then commonly used in France, and in different ways highly developed later in Sweden and Germany. The local officials of the Labour Exchanges were to be selected by a joint committee of three representing unions, business and government. Workers could also refuse employment offers below 'normal' wages for the area and the Exchanges were not to provide workers where labour disputes were underway. See Gilbert, *National Insurance.* . ., p. 264. With this exception, almost no later social legislation directly involved labour and business in its implementation and management. There was one TUC representative on the Royal Commission on the Poor Laws, but he later refused to join in the Webb's campaign to force poor relief reform on the government.

[62] See Roger Davidson, 'Llewellyn Smith, the Labour Department and Government Growth, 1886–1909', in G. Sutherland, ed., *Studies in the Growth of Nineteenth Century government*,London; Routledge and Kegan Paul, 1972, pp. 227–62; and J. A. Caldwell, 'The Genesis of the Ministry of Labour,' *Public Administration* (UK), **37**, Winter 1959, pp. 367–91.

[63] See Rodney Lowe, 'The Ministry of Labour, 1916–1924; A Graveyard of Social Reform?', *Public Administration* (UK), **54**, 1974, pp. 415–38.

movement must be relatively free from direct political and industrial attacks so that it may expand its policy concerns without fear
of weakening the movement. From roughly 1910 until 1945 the
TUC and its member unions were seldom free to broaden their
policy aims to encompass society more generally. Although the
unions did not live in the hostile environment of German unions
or in the confusing industrial structure of France, their political
lifeline was continually threatened.[64]

Second, the TUC and its members were not so much victims
of British class politics, or even of the severe economic dislocation
of Britain between the wars, but shared with many industrial and
governmental policymakers an inability to anticipate and to adjust
to a changing social and economic environment. The indictment
of British unions would be more serious were not the same errors
made by industry and government.

The famous 'Triple Alliance' of dockers, miners and railway
workers formed in 1914 was in a way doomed to fail, as it did,
because it was based on declining industries, all of which had to
turn to government for subsidies and eventually to nationalization
to rescue jobs. Just as early union power was concentrated in
declining industries, so too the formidable political power of the
new conglomerate unions organized over the 1920s resisted industrial modernization. The massive unions of the Amalgamated
Engineering Union (AEU), the General and Municipal Workers'
Union (GMWU) and the Transport and General Workers' Union
(TGWU) controlled the fate of the labour movement's main political force, the Triple Alliance, and continued to dominate union
strategy and industrial relations into the 1960s.

The immense political odds against the labour movement has
understandably produced numerous inquiries from a Marxist perspective. In many respects, the political explanation is more satisfactory. In all the elections from 1918 to 1935, the last election
until 1945, half or more of the Labour Party MPs were sponsored
by the TUC.[65] From its 1918 Congress onward the TUC was
determined to shape its own policies and develop its own massive

---

[64] Middlemas, *Politics of Industrial Society*, p. 156, notes how the Treasury removed
the mining subsidy of 5 million in 1921 without consulting either the miners or
the mine owners.
[65] David Butler and Anne Sloman, *British Political Facts 1900–1975*, London;
Macmillan, 1975, p. 138.

organization. The TUC was in Parliament but not part of Parliament. There is no better evidence than the career of Ernest Bevin, who helped drive home the TUC reorganization of 1918 that placed the new mass unions in control.[66]

Bevin has been both extolled and condemned because he accepted the rules of the game in British politics, but his consistent aim was to make the TUC such a powerful voice, both within the Labour Party and within Parliament, that the power of the left would be invincible. His skepticism toward intellectual Labour Party leaders, as well as toward doctrinaire socialist advisors to the labour movement,[67] was vindicated by the collapse of the Labour Party in 1931. The unintended effect was that the TUC, and even the Labour Party, were consumed with the necessities of parliamentary power. As we shall see in Chapter 5, the image of the welfare state between 1945 and 1948 was more an amalgamation of the accumulated wisdom and errors of the interwar period than a vision of a new kind of state. Launching the modern British welfare state did not involve changing British political institutions.

UNEMPLOYMENT INSURANCE: THE LEAP IN THE DARK

Unemployment insurance was a key element in the formation of twentieth-century welfare states, but its intent, organization and consequences varied greatly among the democracies. From a social perspective, unemployment insurance may be seen as a way of minimizing social protest and in an economic perspective it responds to the Keynesian principle of aggregate demand management. But the decisions to protect workers against the unpredictable rise and fall of mixed economies was in important respects a political decision, and one that was taken for many different political reasons. These differences cannot be accounted for by a

---

[66] Alan Bullock, *The Life and Times of Ernest Bevin, 1881–1960*, London; Heinemann, 1960, vol. 1, pp. 110–11.
[67] Except for his brief involvement with G. D. H. Cole's group, Socialists for Social Inquiry and Propaganda, in 1931, Bevin had no time for the more Marxist left between the wars. Citrine, the TUC General Secretary, bitterly opposed the left-wing Socialist League. See Pimlott, *Labour and the Left* . . ., pp. 48–52.

simple concept of a capitalist crisis. Many of the early unemployment programmes were passed with support from the political right and from employers' associations. There is little evidence of political conspiracy. The tremendous variation in need alone suggests caution.

While in Britain unemployment soared to over two million and was never under one million for the interwar period, at its height unemployment touched no more than 800,000 persons in France and then for much shorter periods. In addition, the industrial structures of the European nations, their vulnerability to international trade conditions, and their fiscal capabilities varied greatly. In a word, responding to unemployment was never quite as simple as might be inferred from economic and social models of the welfare state. For all these reasons, a policy perspective on the transformation of welfare states focuses attention on the institutional and political conditions of adopting unemployment insurance.

Although the creation of unemployment insurance may represent the ultimate step toward building welfare states, the motives, forms and conditions of eligibility for such insurance varied greatly among the democracies in the interwar period. Britain's rapid progress is, for example, often associated with her relatively early acceptance of unemployment insurance in 1911. But the 1911 Act was based on a particular concept of the causes and cures of unemployment that was difficult to transform into more advanced forms of wage and welfare policy in later years. Moreover, its arrival was not the occasion of bitter resistance from beleaguered capitalists as Marxist interpretation might suggest. On the contrary, there was very little debate over Part II of the 1911 Act, and it was discussed in committee for only six meetings. Beveridge noted, 'No one outside the Board of Trade knew enough to criticize it in detail.'[68] If this was the death knoll of capitalism, no one seemed to notice it. Indeed, had this fateful step been more thoroughly debated and had it aroused more interest among unions, the course of the British welfare state might have been very different.

From a policy perspective, the 1911 Act may better explain the disastrous miscalculations of British policymakers after World War I. Unemployment seems to have transfixed British policymakers.

[68] Gilbert, *The Evolution of National Insurance* . . ., pp. 283–4.

Despite the outbreak of strikes in 1912 and 1913, unemployment in turn-of-the-century Britain was seldom over two per cent. When war began the Unemployment Fund had a healthy surplus of over £3 million and, as a result of heavy contributions and few demands, by the end of the war it had a surplus of over £20 million. This surplus as well as poor economic assumptions encouraged British officials, in particular the Treasury, to recommend the 1920 Unemployment Act. As we shall see, the new scheme became totally unmanageable within a year. Without detracting from the progress of the British welfare state, employment insurance as a policy leads to very different conclusions than might be suggested in social and economic models of the welfare state. In policy terms, unemployment policies were a patchwork of improvisations over the 1920s, and in the 1930s forfeited opportunities to build a more comprehensive welfare state.

In most continental countries, the politics of unemployment protection were much more complicated. The French labour movement was ambivalent about any form of unemployment insurance until late in the interwar period. In 1910 the CGT Congress denounced the new pension law and conducted protests throughout France. A motion of support moved by the future President of the CGT, Jouhaux, was defeated by over 800 votes. Unlike the British workers who dutifully carried their benefit records, French workers considered the payment cards and stamps a control to punish unreliable workers. For Guesde, contributions in any form were a form of labour exploitation, and the accumulated fund a way of reinforcing a repressive state. But under Jaurès' prodding and using the flexibility of French coalition politics, the CGT supporters in parliament voted for the law.[69] Even though benefits were more meagre than in Britain, French unions had some specific ideas about organizing protection. Many of them were implanted in the late blooming French welfare state of 1945.

The political situation changed after World War I, in part because the CGT found it impossible to use insurance protection in its struggle against the Communist faction of the labour movement, the CGTU, whose revolutionary stance pushed the CGT toward a modus vivendi with the French state. Throughout the debate on the 1930 law, the CGT was in close touch with parliamentary leaders and officials, many of them old independent

[69] This description relies on Hatzfeld, pp. 236–48.

socialists, and carefully studied and commented on the many reports and studies. For workers, the great attraction was sickness insurance which the powerful railway and miners' unions strongly supported. Moreover, union leaders were beginning to see that the industrial transformation of France promised a stronger labour movement and more industrial concessions. From 1906 to 1926, the percentage of firms with a single employee had halved (26 to 13 per cent), while the percentage of firms employing over 1000 workers had doubled (7 to 14 per cent). As Hatzfeld suggests, by 1939 it appears that workers had lost their deep fears of insurance.[70]

There was no national unemployment insurance in France until 1958, but the unemployed were acknowledged in 1905 when the Finance Act allocated 110 million francs to subsidize local and private industrial plans. Though of much smaller scale than in Britain, the conditions for state interaction were very different. Government would provide up to 20 per cent of the cost of benefits; and in larger firms up to 30 per cent. France provided generous subsidies to local insurance schemes. By 1920 there were 97 municipal and 8 departmental unemployment funds covering 80,000 workers. The state subsidy to these plans in 1921 was 30 million francs.[71] The late appearance of a national unemployment insurance agency does not mean that unions' demands were not evolving. In many respects their demands were more faithfully imprinted on policies than in countries where urgent needs left little time to consult labour and where stronger labour movements left social planning to others.

Although Sweden had a voluntary unemployment insurance plan from 1934, it was never a central feature of the Swedish welfare state. Both the SAP and the LO skirted what is often taken to be the major threshold in building modern welfare states, further evidence that care must be exercised in using this reform as a key element in the political transformation of welfare states. Indeed, one might well argue the reverse. Where states, often for good social and economic reasons, became preoccupied with unemployment, more ambitious ideas about the relation of wages and welfare may be neglected. Unemployment in Sweden was by no means negligible between the wars, hovering around 10 per cent for most

[70] Hatzfeld, pp. 257–9.
[71] Gabriel de Montgomery, pp. 398–9.

of the period and over 20 per cent in 1933, but the political effects were moderated for a number of reasons.

First, industrial dislocations were more acceptable because Sweden was struggling to leave its agricultural heritage behind and to become industrialized. Old industrial jobs were not being abolished, but the labour market as a whole was being reorganized and shifting among sectors. Second, the SAP was going through a severe and delicate political test in the early 1930s and none of the major actors wanted to jeopardize parliamentary victory.[72] The agrarian parties were central to this achievement so that expensive programmes for industrial workers were not attractive. Third, and perhaps most important, the LO did not place unemployment insurance among its highest priorities. The LO had distrusted unemployment relief since World War I when it was used by the SAF to defend lower wages.[73] Once the possibility of wage solidarity existed after 1932, to press employers for major insurance concessions would endanger the entire scheme. All this was impossible for the other industrial European democracies, where industrial recovery and reconstruction could not be divorced from pre-war industrial and labour problems.

The depression of the early 1930s persuaded the LO and the SAP that fiscal policy, with the still unfulfilled promise of wage solidarity, should take precedence over unemployment insurance. Political instability seems to have been more important in deciding the terms of the 1934 Act than orthodox socialist fervour. For one thing, employer contributions were omitted in order not to arouse the Liberals against the government. The result was a comparatively weak unemployment insurance programme. Though it anticipated 700,000 members by 1940, in fact by then there were only 196,000 workers enrolled. The studies leading to a more complete system were not made until the socialists were in firmer control in the late 1930s and after the LO had established a much firmer grip on the labour movement. By 1942 the LO could successfully fight against a test for unemployment benefits, obtain equalization of the state contribution and link noncontributory benefits to unemployment insurance. In doing so, the divergence between unemployment and other social policies was minimized,

[72] See Sven Anders Soderpalm, 'The Crisis Agreement and the Social Democratic Road to Power,' in S. Koblik, ed., *Sweden's Development* . . ., pp. 258–78.
[73] Madsen, *Social Democracy in Post-War Scandinavia*. . ., p. 133.

and the chances of harmonizing unemployment insurance with wage solidarity were enhanced. All these developments were slow to appear in the other democracies. Unlike Britain, where additional relief was handled through a central state agency, the LO devolved these decisions to its own organization under government supervision. Compulsory contributions were not required until much later, and even then opposed by both the LO and the union welfare agency.

As in Sweden, the interwar German labour movement does not appear to have made unemployment insurance its top priority. Its plans were much more ambitious, that is, to make the ADGB an indispensable part of the national economy and in doing so to use economic policy to achieve political aims. The futility of pursuing political ends by economic means was twofold. The German employers never regarded the unions as acceptable partners and the Weimar Republic never enjoyed the stable policymaking environment that might have permitted this form of integration. Eager to achieve political acceptance, the unions never acquired a clear right to strike and relied on the Weimar Constitution. Article 165 went no further toward establishing the political power of unions than to make workers and employers 'equal' in regulating work and wages. A law of 1919 even proclaims labour to be 'the highest economic asset' of the state.

The ADGB hoped that the elaborate Works Council Act of 1920 would provide the institutional acceptance that had for so long been denied by autocratic political institutions.[74] An elaborate structure of local worker councils and local employer groups, organized at the municipal and state levels was to culminate in a National Economic Council. In theory this economic parliament could require the Reichstag to consider labour and industrial legislation, but it was never enabled to do so. Even the work councils posed a threat to the divided labour movement. As happened at the Berlin councils, they could as easily be captured by anti-democratic forces only to further embarrass the left. Nor did violence subside. The Knapp putsch forced the socialist government to call on their most detested enemy, the army, with brutal results. There was no reliable institutional foundation on which to build either respect from a hostile right or the complex economic institutions.

[74] See Moses, v. 2, pp. 291–320.

Perhaps the important lesson of Weimar for the future of welfare states was that economic democracy is no substitute for stable, strong political democracy. Failing to build its own state within the state, from 1924 the left opted for 'Democratization of the Economy', the theme of the 1925 ADGB Congress. New leaders such as Fritz Tarnow and Fritz Naphatli advanced a theory built on the feeble assumption that one might 'transfer into the economy that which has already been achieved in political life.'[75] Unlike the TUC in Britain or even the CGT in France, the ADGB had no reliable political and institutional framework. Unrestrained economic democracy could become a form of social fascism which may have encouraged the ADGB to make its brief and calamitous flirtation with Hitler's rising National Socialist Party in 1930. The goals of economic democracy were not to take durable form until the co-determination Law of the Federal Republic.

In the abstract world of German labour politics the Unemployment Law of 1927 was not regarded so much as a clear victory of the labour movement but more as one step toward a vision of economic democracy peculiar to Weimar Germany. Nonetheless, the law was extremely generous for the time, providing benefits at average wage levels; allowing 26 weeks benefit after 26 weeks of contributions; and initially imposing no means test. The plan was supposed to be able to cope with 800,000 unemployed. But the time the law came into effect, unemployment funds were nearly depleted. Rather than produce a political crisis for the unstable coalition governments of the time, the SDP and the ADGB agreed that their *Sozialpolitik* would be temporarily abandoned.[76] The labour movement acquired one of the major reforms associated with the formation of modern welfare states, but the political results were meagre. With over 2 million members unemployed in the early 1930s, the ADGB could not rely on social legislation as a defense against Hitler.[77]

---

[75] Quoted from Tarnow by Moses, v. 2, p. 358. There were roots for the new departure in Rudolf Hilferding's book of 1910, *Das Finanzkapital*, which argued that the labour movement could cooperate with capitalism to lead it in the direction of socialism.

[76] On the debates over economic democracy, see Moses, pp. 354–76.

[77] While it cannot be fully explored here, there remains an intense historical dispute over the political and economic decisions of the ADGB and SPD from 1930 to 1932. See T. W. Mason's 'Labour and the Third Reich, 1933–1939,' *Past and Present*, **33**, April 1966, pp. 112–41.

In the light of these difficulties, the resilience of British institutions is remarkable despite the improvised and ineffective British unemployment policies over the 1920s. German employment policies floundered because the left hoped to erect a new form of democracy, but British policies failed because British leaders were unable to imagine a new form of welfare state. One reason was that British policymaking assigned little importance to the views of the labour movement, and, in turn, the labour movement itself had few ambitious ideas. There was ample labour conflict, but neither unions nor government wanted to raise new questions about wages and social policy. As part of the postwar labour reforms an elaborate system of works councils, the Whitley Councils, was designed but never achieved acceptance outside the public sector.

The tentative effort to build some sort of national forum for labour, business and government was not received enthusiastically by any of the participants, and the prewar Trades Boards continued to be occupied with low-paid industries. By common consent there were no successful institutional experiments. Apparently, Llewellyn Smith's advice to the 1913 Royal Commission on the Civil Service was forgotten. He had argued that labour and 'commercial' policies could not be separated.[78] But then neither were the efforts to convert economic democracy into war socialism very successful.[79] In brief, British political institutions seemed able to protect themselves.

PROBLEMS VS PEOPLE: UNEMPLOYMENT POLICIES

The various macro-studies of unemployment insurance aside, Britain was the first country to deal directly with the enormous toll

---

[78] From Rodney Lowe, 'The Erosion of State Intervention in Britain, 1917–24,' *Economic History Review*, **31**, May 1978, p. 285.
[79] Putting aside Webb's admiration for Soviet Russia in the 1930s, there were two serious efforts to move in this direction. The first was Oswald Mosley's memo on national socialism of 1930 which MacDonald rejected, leading to Mosley's resignation and eventually to the organization of a fascist movement. See Skidelsky, *Politicians and the Slump. . .*, pp. 172–200. The second move in this direction came from intellectuals involved in the revival of the Labour Party in the 1930s. See, for example, Sir Stafford Cripps, 'Can Socialism Come by Constitutional Methods?' in C. Addison, ed., *Problems of a Socialist Government*, London; Gollancz, 1933, pp. 35–66. Compare with the very conventional list of

of unemployment while sustaining democratic institutions. The uncertainties that are revealed in British unemployment policies between the wars help us understand why the British welfare state of 1945 did not expand to broader horizons, perhaps setting the precedent for social democratic practices among the major European powers. Policymakers had great difficulty differentiating between the cyclical problems of the economy and their immediate political objectives. In a positivist framework, it is possible to discount these shortcomings as the inevitable play of class politics or inescapable failures of capitalist economies. In fact, there were many things happening over the 1920s and 1930s that occupied British policymakers: the prolonged negotiation over a peace settlement, the festering problems with Ireland, the French occupation of the Ruhr and the threat of a crippling general strike. The unfortunate effect was that ministers and civil servants had little time for the intricacies of social policy so that the country best positioned to lead the world toward a new form of welfare state had little new to say. The Labour Party did not yet have the confidence or the experience to make new departures, and the Tories had little interest in refashioning a familiar world.

There were also more specific reasons for the deficiencies of British unemployment policy. First, as Lowe writes, 'Social policy in the 1920s was not a series of defeats but a series of compromises with economic orthodoxy.[80] Compared to the searching self-doubt of the German left or the gradual institutionalization of welfare reforms of France, the British interwar period is remarkably barren of major initiatives. Perhaps the Edwardian effort had left British policymakers exhausted. Even the rising Labour Party had few new ideas until the New Fabians of the 1930s began to reconstruct the Party from the ruins of the 1931 National Government. But new proposals could not escape the grip of the Poor Laws. For most of the period, the crucial element was the ceaseless, and at times ruthless, effort of the Treasury to limit the nation's economic liabilities.[81]

unemployment remedies provided by the Labour government in 1930, *Statement of the Principal Measures Taken by H. M. Government in Connection with Unemployment*, London; Parliamentary Papers, December 1930, cmd. 3746.

[80] Rodney Lowe, 'Welfare Legislation and the Unions During and After the First World War,' *The Historical Journal*, **25**, 1982, pp. 437–41, p. 439.

[81] To be fair, the burden of 7 billion pounds debt was formidable. The Colwyn Committee reported in 1927 that in 1913–14 interest charges were only 9.6 per cent of national revenues. By 1920 interest took 21.9 per cent of revenues, and

Second, it is hard to disagree with the observation of one well-placed civil servant, Sir Ronald Davison, commenting on unemployment insurance, that 'it has never suited any political party to give a lead in the matter.'[82] The thrust of his argument was that, rather like Marxists, policymakers were unable or unwilling to differentiate the problem. The full explanation may be even more complicated than the diverse experiments which unemployment insurance suggest. The 1911 Act had focused on workers in unstable labour markets. Somehow who might be best insured against unemployment was never clearly distinguished from the historic labour problems, often involving declining industries, such as coal and textiles. As Gilbert points out,[83] Britain never even succeeded in building a good system for the half of the nation in the south where unemployment rates were by no means disastrous and where new industries were being established. In the four major regions of London, the southeast, the southwest, and the Midlands, average unemployment was 7.7 per cent; and public assistance claims a modest 100,000 persons. In the stricken areas of the northeast, the northwest, the north, Scotland and Wales, unemployment averaged 18.5 per cent and public assistance rolls carried nearly half a million persons.[84]

The economic and social distress of some areas of Britain reached such enormous proportions that we may forget that the signs of industrial decline had been evident since 1890. The explanation that officials were reacting to unprecedented problems with limited resources may be much too generous. Indeed, given the huge sums devoted to social and unemployment relief between the wars, the policy failures seem more serious. Eveline Burns raises this possibility when writing about unemployment insurance. There was never 'careful analysis of the proper place of an insurance plan in the total relief system, or of the appropriate levels of

by 1926 36.7 per cent. However, the percentages can be misleading. National revenues in 1920 were 1.2 billion, and by 1926 revenues were reduced to 758 million. See *Report*, Committee on National Debt and Taxation, London; Parliamentary Papers, cmd. 2800, 1927.

[82] Ronald C. Davison, *What's Wrong with Unemployment Insurance?*, London; Longman's, 1930, p. 4.

[83] Gilbert, *British Social Policy* . . ., p. 87. Underlying these difficulties was the longstanding British antipathy to strong regional policies which is carried over into the postwar period.

[84] Ronald C. Davison, *British Unemployment Policy: The Modern Phase since 1930*, London; Longman's, 1938, p. 123.

insurance benefits.'[85] But even her dismay is aroused largely by the inadequate organization and integration of benefits, and does not touch directly on resource and allocation problems. The Treasury acquired such great power over the new insurance system in all its aspects that even if more imaginative social policymakers had appeared, it is unlikely that they would have been able to penetrate Treasury obfuscation.

As enacted in 1911 unemployment insurance was limited to wage-earners in less stable occupations, though it is not clear why such an inappropriate choice was made. In any event, it covered only about a quarter of the British working population or 2.25 million workers. The first step toward its incoherent growth was taken during the war by the National Insurance (Munitions Workers) Act of 1916. As we have seen, the war government was having serious labour problems, especially among Clydeside shipbuilders. To pacify labour unrest and to make more strict labour regulation palatable,the government expanded the old system to munitions' workers. As Beveridge wrote, the law passed the House of Commons virtually unnoticed and 'under the guise of insuring munitions workers brought in the whole of many trades and might have been extended to every trade'.[86] In fact, it added about 1.1 million persons to the insurance lists.

In the more vulnerable wool, cotton and leather industries, all momentarily working full blast for the war effort, the workers fought to be excluded. They could not imagine the terrible unemployment soon to engulf Britain, but, then, neither did Whitehall. With scarcely more thought in either Whitehall or Parliament, there followed the Unemployment Act of 1920, expanding the system to 11 million persons or nearly all employees, of whom almost 7 million were newly covered. Unions remained free to contract out. Anticipating postwar labour problems, Beveridge had pointed out in a 1917 study that only a compulsory, universal scheme would be likely to provide sufficient social protection.

By late 1918 it was clear that Britain would soon have hundreds of thousands of men returning to the work force, while additional thousands of women left the factories. The stop-gap measure was

[85] Eveline M. Burns, *British Unemployment Programs 1920–1938*, Washington, D. C.; Social Science Research Council, 1941, p. 70.
[86] Sir William Beveridge, 'Unemployment Insurance in the War and After,' in Sir Norman Hill, ed., *War and Insurance*, London; Oxford University Press, 1927, pp. 232–3.

the 'dole' or direct government payments. These payments could not continue indefinitely so the Minister of Labour, Sir Robert Horne, who was later to spearhead the crippling of the Ministry from the Treasury, prepared the 1920 Act as an expedient solution. The preparation of the Act was poor and many of its assumptions incorrect.[87] Working from a mere seven pages of information from Horne, few MPs took part in the debate. The most controversial issue was not unemployment insurance itself, but the disparity between unemployment and sickness benefits and the fight between the TUC and the Friendly Societies.[88] If sickness benefits, in this case, particularly those for women, fell too far behind unemployment benefits, the cost of health insurance would be shifted to the unemployment scheme and become a disincentive to work. The convoluted balancing act between size, duration and kind of benefit became a major preoccupation of British policymakers for the next fifty years, in part because there were no policies linking social and wage policies.

In any event, a dozen or more unemployment laws were passed between the 1920 Act and the 1930 Act, which marks the next, and no less satisfactory, transition of unemployment policies. Although the details of this legislation are complex, they spell a dismal story whose inner workings are clearest in a table of Burns.[89] Until the depression totally unhinged British plans, unemployment remained high, about 1.2 million persons, but fairly constant from 1922 to 1930. The effect of the intervening legislation was to protect the long-term unemployed from dependence on poor relief so that when the depression hit in 1930, and continued to worsen, those calling on unemployment insurance benefits nearly doubled in one year. At the same time, the unemployed dependent on the Poor Law system steadily declined from

[87] The most serious was the assumption by the Government Actuary, Sir Alfred Watson, that the 8.5 per cent unemployment standard of the 1911 law could be reduced to 6.5 per cent. He also optimistically assumed that the 20 million surplus would provide nearly a tenth of the cost, but politicians, mainly the Treasury, soon let the fund be dispersed as the crisis heightened. The little noticed injustice of this was that funds that had been for the most part accumulated from the hard-pressed construction and steel industries were in effect used to subsidize workers and industry in other areas. See Gilbert, *British Social Policy. . .*, pp. 61–74 for details.

[88] See Noelle Whiteside, 'Welfare Legislation and the Unions During the First World War,' *Historical Journal*, **23**, 1980, pp. 857–74.

[89] Burns, *British Unemployment. . .*, p. 53. Actually, the total number of persons still under the Poor Laws changed very little, about 800,000 persons.

nearly 240,000 persons in 1922 to 59,000 by 1930. In effect, Britain was dealing with two problems as though they were one, the first inherited from 1834 and the second from 1911.

The promising finances of employment insurance in early 1920 rapidly disappeared and by 1921 over 2 million persons were unemployed. By the end of 1922 the Unemployment Fund, once the white hope of financial conservatives in the Treasury, had borrowed £15 million from the Treasury. There followed a series of laws, each well intended, but none addressing unemployment as a major social problem. Within a few months of the 1920 Act, the Unemployment (Temporary Provisions) Act of 1920 weakened the rules of borrowing and eligibility. As entire families were threatened, the 1921 Act extended assistance under unemployment provisions to dependents, thereby breaking the relationship between contribution and benefit on which contributory insurance rested. Actually, from this time, there were two benefit schemes, payments under the initial insurance principles of the 1911 Act, and 'uncovenanted payments', that is, insurance contributions paid by government so that long-term unemployed could continue to qualify for benefits.

Even if it had new ideas, the Labour government of 1924 did not have sufficient power to improve the situation. The Labour Party tried to relax the 'genuinely seeking work' rule, but this meant little when there were no jobs, and made the period of receiving uncovenanted benefits indeterminate. The new improvisations sorely tested the coalition of Liberals and Labour in the government. Using one of the pitifully inadequate checks of British government, a parliamentary motion to reduce the Minister of Labour's salary failed by only 50 votes. The next government under Baldwin had little more to offer, but appointed the Blanesburgh Committee with a broad mandate to examine the entire system. Essentially, the Committee recommended abandoning the fiction that unemployment insurance any longer operated under actuarial principles. The 1911 Act standard of no more than one week's benefit for six weeks' contributions was discontinued, and a 'transitional benefit' would be given for those unable to meet insurance requirements. These changes, supposedly to last for one year, were incorporated in the 1927 Act, but two years later there were still 120,000 persons depending on the extended benefits. The Labour government of 1929 had no better alternative than to extend this improvisation to 1931. While it should be acknowledged that the government saved thousands of persons from the Poor Law, from a policy perspective a decade had passed with no fundamental change in unemployment policies even though these policies had proved dismally inadequate.[90]

Throughout the period ministers and officials could find little reason to seek a better policy, which of course made the Treasury increasingly influential. For one thing, the Ministry of Health was busy trying to preserve sickness benefits, reform the Poor Laws and construct the new local government system of the 1929 Local Government Act. At the Ministry of Health, Chamberlain was also at odds with Churchill, then Chancellor of the Exchequer, who as so often followed his own quixotic path and feared that Chamberlain's reforms would bring new charges to the budget. The Ministry of Health was in continual conflict with the Board of Education, one of the most severely hit departments under the Geddes cuts, and of course Chamberlain's designs for a new local government structure presented another threat to the Board of Education. As many observers agree, the Ministry of Labour had the unhappy task of 'carrying the can' of unemployment. No minister wished to be tainted by its dismal problem and defended their own turf. Under these conditions, the one influential Ministry, the Treasury, hardly needed innovative officials to achieve its own conservative fiscal goals. The tragic effect was hundreds of millions spent without ever building a better policy.

At this point, one might ask why the policy process went so far astray. The social significance of unemployment was widely perceived, and the economic effort was substantial. Actual expenditure on unemployment policies nearly doubled when the first shock came between 1920 and 1921, and by 1930 had nearly tripled. By 1936 Britain was spending roughly four times the amount on these policies as in 1920.[91] First, the shape of unemployment problems was unequally distributed among industrial sectors. With national unemployment rates of about 10 per cent,

[90] The best detailed description of these changes is in E. Wright Bakke, *Insurance or the Dole? The Adjustment of Unemployment Insurance to Economic and Social Facts in Britain*, New Haven, CT; Yale University Press, 1935. See also Burns, pp. 35–51, and Gilbert, pp. 86–97. Also, the comments of the participant, Ronald Davison, *What's Wrong with Unemployment Insurance?*, London; Longman, 1930.

[91] Ursula Hicks, *The Finance of British Government. . .*, p. 194.

shipbuilding and ship repairing had over 28 per cent unemployed in 1924 and 50 per cent by 1933. By the 1930s roughly a third of the million miners were without work, even though half a million miners left the industry between the wars. About a third of the dock, port and textile workers were unemployed. The battery of unemployment legislation over the 1920s did not address these sectoral differences even though both politicians and officials lived in fear of forcing hundreds of thousands of able-bodied workers onto poor relief. Procrastination had its effect, of course, and by the 1930s many had left the labour force.

Second, there were huge territorial disparities of unemployment. Burns points out that 400 of the 630 Poor Law Unions were not experiencing large increases in poor relief as a result of chronic unemployment, while Unions containing 35 per cent of the population were providing 80 per cent of all public assistance to the able-bodied.[92] Thus a wealthy Oxford with low unemployment needed a poor rate of 7 pence, while a depressed and poor Welsh area, Merthyr Tydfil, had a poor rate of over 21 shillings. The problem was compounded by inequities in the block grant to local government. Based on percentage of local spending poor areas could levy higher rates but in proportion to their needs received less than rich areas. Of course, Chamberlain was working busily in the Ministry of Health to standardize property assessment, to revise the grant system, and to reform the local government structure,[93] but these efforts were not completed until the early 1930s.

When the dual system of relief was organized in 1934, it was learned that 30 per cent of the long-term unemployed had been without work for more than two years and 10 per cent or 25,000 had been unemployed for over five years.[94] But the Ministry of Labour did not turn to alternative labour policies until the late 1930s, in part because it was hamstrung by Treasury controls and in part because no government seemed to understand chronic unemployment. The 1911 Act was conceived as an attack on cyclical unemployment. By the late 1930s the Labour Party had

---

[92] Burns, pp. 57–61.
[93] See Ashford, *British Dogmatism and French Pragmatism*, pp. 231–50. At the root of the problem was Britain's historic antipathy to building a field administration with independent resources or a local government system with discretionary power.
[94] Gilbert, *British Social Policy*, pp. 87–9.

a more coherent battery of policies, including raising the school age, lowering retirement ages, shorter hours and public works, but even their reconstructed view of the world said nothing about industrial policy.[95] The result was that like the good public school boys that most of them were, the top officials valiantly pressed their fingers into the holes in the dyke while Britain's industrial strength went out with the tide.

As Bakke points out[96] the fundamental question was never asked. The right to a decent life in one's old age and to a basic education were relatively easy to reconcile with the liberal version of the welfare state. But how does one extend the concept of a social contract between the state and its citizens to the productive process? The British government did not hesitate to pay the costs. By the 1930s the Treasury was actually providing almost half of all unemployment support[97] and a third of all government spending was devoted to social spending. The effort and the will was not lacking which takes us back to the deficiencies of policymaking itself.

Unemployment was a more serious challenge to democracy than either socialists or liberals had imagined. Fascism cast a strange spell over both the right and left. In France, the *Croix de feu* revived the reactionary right and anti-Semitism. Following military defeat, the Vichy government blended ultra-conservative Catholicism and French nationalist resentment in a peculiar form of fascism.[98] Although not nearly as generous as British programmes, by 1933 the 1928–30 laws were reaching about 10 million persons, most of them in the industrial sector. There is an important political lesson to be learned from the inability of prewar social legislation to withstand the fascist threat.

Social and economic legislation alone could not protect democratic government. Though it could not have prevented the French defeat, Vichy exposed the fragility of the nascent French welfare

---

[95] William Mellor, 'The Claim of the Unemployed' in C. Addison, ed., *Problems of a Socialist Government*, pp. 113–49. The programme is basically the same as that advocated by Bevin in the late 1930s and undoubtedly came from the TUC, not the Labour Party. See Alan Bullock, *The Life and Times of Ernest Bevin. . .*, v.1, pp. 516–18.

[96] Bakke, *Insurance or the Dole?. . .*, pp. 87–9.

[97] Bakke, p. 89. The money was roughly equally divided between loans to the Unemployment Insurance Fund and direct payments of 'transitional' payments for the chronic unemployed.

[98] See Paxton, *Vichy France. . .*, pp. 148–68.

state. Among the democratic failures of the 1930s France is perhaps the best illustration of how easily social reform can be built to serve undemocratic regimes. Though the child and the family were always prominent in French thinking about the welfare state,[99] Pétain's combination of paternal social justice and political corporatism had an elaborate social programme, much of which survived in postwar France.[100] Less noticed, the technocratic strain in French social thinking thrived under Vichy. The meticulously detailed plans for rationing food, distributing scarce raw materials and allocating labour stimulated the technocrats who felt that a plan for social justice might reasonably precede working out its political foundations.[101]

German National Socialism is of course the best illustration of the futility of achieving social and economic hegemony of the state in the absence of effective democratic institutions. The Nazis were not particularly concerned about social programmes as such, but their ideology contained a romanticized version of a socially equal state, a national community (*Volksgemeinschaft*) subordinated to a totalitarian hierarchy. An independent labour movement was obviously an anathema to the Nazis, and the German Labour Front of 1933 marked the end of free union activity and the abolition of the strong worker organization. The specific target was to purge socialists, Jews and labour leaders from the sickness insurance funds under union sponsorship and about 4,000 officials were dismissed.[102] The intricate system of labour exchanges and unemployment insurance were completely subordinated to the military needs of the state. The implicit contractual relationship between the state and its citizens of democratic social legislation no longer existed.

[99] See Mary Lynn McDougall, 'Protecting Infants: The French Campaign for Maternity Leaves, 1890s–1913,' *French Historical Studies*, **13**, Spring 1983, pp. 79–105.

[100] Because Vichy France was a totally subject economy drastic steps were taken to protect mothers and elderly with no support. The *alloction aux vieux travailleurs salariées* of 1941 became the minimal base for supporting aged workers without pensions. The *allocation aux de famille* became the base for persons with no insurance claim.

[101] C. Gruson, *Les origines et les espoirs de la planification française*, Paris; Dunod, 1968, pp. 1–36; and Paxton, pp. 259–68.

[102] See G. V. Rimlinger, 'Social Policy under Hitler,' in Martin Rein, ed. For more details, see David Schoenbaum, *Hitler's Social Revolution: Class and Status in Nazi Germany*, New York; Doubleday, 1966.

To understand the British desperation between 1930 and 1934, it is important to see how the spectre of poverty hung over Britain between the wars. In 1921 economic decline and labour unrest had brought the Poor Law registration to over 1.3 million persons, the highest since 1863.[103] About half these persons were unemployed. In 1928, the total number on poor relief remained over a million.[104] Given the shattered state of unemployment insurance finances, there is more than a little irony that the Labour government was forced 'to grasp the Poor Law nettle' in 1930. Unemployment was at 15 per cent, the highest since 1921, and the Unemployment Fund had to dispense £110 million when its income, with little sign of change in the near future, was down to 45 million. The transitional payments scheme, estimated to cost only £4 million, was running at over £20 million by mid-1930.[105] There were four unemployment acts in 1930, but the immediate response was an Order in Council ending the 'seeking work' rule, enlarging the Fund's borrowing power, and fully transferring the cost of transitional payments to the Treasury. Essentially, Labour abandoned the insurance principles of the system, but without enough skill to restore confidence in the Labour Party.

The Royal Commission on Unemployment Insurance of 1931[106] set the terms of the debate. It recommended that the contributory portion of unemployment insurance should be restored on financially sound grounds, and that the 'right' of non-contributors to draw indefinitely on unemployment funds be terminated. There followed the Anomalies Act of 1931 which withdrew from the system the wide variety of occasional workers, such as partially employed women, the seasonally employed, the short-week workers, whose special needs had vastly complicated the entire system.[107] Next came the May Committee, a general budget-cutting exercise modelled on the Geddes Committee, that recommended increased contributions and benefit cuts totalling 35.8 million, roughly half of all the cuts to be made.[108] In August 1931

---

[103] *Third Annual Report*, Ministry of Health, p. 79.
[104] *Twelfth Annual Report*, Ministry of Health, p. 3.
[105] A blow-by-blow account can be found in Davison, *British Unemployment Policy...*, pp. 12–16. On the turmoil within the Cabinet, see Marquand, *MacDonald...*, pp. 571–603.
[106] *First Report*, Royal Commission on Unemployment Insurance, London; Parliamentary Papers, June 1931, cmd. 3872. By the time the Final Report, London, cmd. 4185, appeared in November 1932, the policy for the next few years had been determined.

talks between Labour and the TUC over imposition of means-testing broke down and MacDonald abandoned his Party. In the October election the Labour Party was reduced to 57 MPs, the smallest representation of the left since 1918. At this critical juncture in British social history, the party of the left was a total loss.

Already the welfare state was experiencing the cross-cutting aims of social policy that were to become the hallmark of the advanced welfare state conflicts after 1945. The scheme suited the Ministry of Labour because it was spared the odious job of imposing tests, while meeting the Treasury's great concern that unemployment relief avoid the unreliable hands of local government. But the price of procrastination is often that governments are left to make crucial decisions under adverse conditions. Over 1933 unemployment soared to nearly 3 million persons. The numbers of unemployed depending on public assistance doubled by the end of 1931 as the rules came into effect; by the end of 1934 there were 220,000 able-bodied unemployed on means-tested benefits, the highest number since 1922. Another effect, little noticed in Whitehall, was that the Treasury had shifted some of the burden of unemployment relief to local government, the perennial victim of Whitehall's problems.[109]

There followed the bitter Whitehall fight from 1930 to 1934 over the conditions under which Britain would accept responsibility for the unemployed. The 1934 Unemployment Act brought into focus three of the fundamental questions of transforming liberal into welfare states: national versus local control of social policies; administrative versus political (and therefore, partisan) control of

[107] See Bakke, pp. 56–67, for details. Once the system was rationalized agricultural workers were included from 1936.

[108] *Memorandum on the Measures Proposed by His Majesty's Government to Secure Reductions in National Expenditure* (May Committee), London; Parliamentary Papers, 1931, cmd. 3952, p. 2 and pp. 9–12. The cuts were severe: 10 per cent off benefits for the insured and their dependents, a ten pence increase in weekly contributions, a renewal of strict limitation of benefits to 26 weeks per year, and a means-test for the new transitional payment scheme.

[109] Burns, p. 125. See Frederic M. Miller, 'National Assistance or Unemployment Assistance? The British Cabinet and Relief Policy, 1932–3,' *Journal of Contemporary History*, **9**, April 1974, pp. 163–83. The Treasury never seemed to give up its efforts to transfer social costs to localities. In 1934 when area assistance programmes began, it proposed a levy on wealthy local authorities. The outcry forced the Treasury to provide a half million pounds in grants. See Davison, p. 29.

social policies; and the submerged issue of how wage and social policies might be coordinated.

The first issue came to a head over proposals for an Unemployment Assistance Board (UAB) which would take over the functions of the PACs, effectively nationalizing public relief. Betterton was the arch critic of a scheme which he said 'applied Poor Law methods, through a Poor Law Commission, in Poor Law language.'[110] The Ministry took the unpopular course, arguing that benefits should vary locally; that exemptions must continue; and that the real abuse was not excessive payments of some areas, but the inadequate payments in more strict and conservative local authorities. Betterton's argument was unpopular among the Tories, in particular to Chamberlain who saw the act as a rebuke to his earlier local government reforms[111] and an inroad on strict Treasury control.

Rebuilding its ranks in anticipation of the 1935 election, the Labour Party launched a bitter attack on the government. In effect, the Tories were 'simply bringing the dole to Westminster.' With an eye to the organizational deficiencies that preoccupied Conservative ministers, one Tory critic charged, 'The first assumption appears to be that Parliament has become so invertebrate and Ministers so effete that they can no longer be relied on or indeed no longer desire to discharge irksome duties of their offices without having some quasi-independent body to shield them from the worry and trouble of real responsibility.'[112] Davison's description of the UAB tells a good deal about the weaknesses of British policymaking. 'The creation of the UAB was a surprise move originating wholly in Whitehall. Not social needs, but political and financial considerations inspired it.'[113]

Cowling considers the UAB and Indian home-rule to be the two most controversial decisions in Britain in the 1930s.[114] Were not the Labour Party still badly divided internally, it seems likely that

[110] Quoted in Lowe, *Adjusting to Democracy: The Role of the Ministry of Labour in British Politics*, Oxford; Clarendon Press, 1986, p. 164. See also the full account of Eric Briggs and Alan Deacon, 'The Creation of the Unemployment Assistance Board,' *Policy and Politics*, **2**, 1973, pp. 43–62.

[111] To be fair to Chamberlain, his determination to demolish the Poor Laws is never in doubt. See *Scheme of Poor Law Reform*, Ministry of Health, PRO CAB 27/263, March 1925.

[112] The quotes are from Millet, pp. 38–9.

[113] Davison, p. 45.

[114] Maurice Cowling, *The Impact of Hitler: British Politics and British Policy, 1933–1940*, Cambridge; Cambridge University Press, 1975, p. 41–3.

the Tories would not have pressed for such a severe solution. The bill generated prolonged debate within the cabinet where ministers freely expressed their election fears.[115] One minister suggested that the sting of reduced payments for the long-term unemployed, now the charges of the UAB, be reduced by providing more milk for school lunches.[116] Distracted by the rise of Hitler and still trapped by conservative fiscal policy in the Treasury, the government essentially nationalized the Poor Laws. The unanticipated effect was to permanently imprint the plight of the poor on the British welfare state. Lacking a broader vision of how welfare affected the modern state, the Tories chose a drastic solution for a problem that was in fact starting to disappear.

In the early 1930s unemployment was not as serious as in Germany and the United States. By 1937 employment rose, unemployment insurance was paid to only 10 per cent, and the pool of long-term unemployed had been halved. But the law worked as planned. The Unemployment Fund actually showed a surplus after 1935, a fact that can be considered either Whitehall wisdom or an inability to devise legislation that accommodates a changing society, and brought a net saving to the Treasury of two million pounds. The Treasury goal was fairly clear. Any conditions that would reduce spending on poverty, where the Treasury had to carry the total cost, to unemployment insurance, where costs were shared with contributors, was a financial gain. By 1937 the Unemployment Fund showed a surplus of £62 million and as agreed in the law was paying back its debts from the early 1930s. The Treasury got its way, but paid an enormous price in imaginative thinking about the future of the British welfare state.

The futility of taking 'poverty out of politics' was quickly demonstrated. What the Minister of Labour once described as the 'national genius' for solving problems soon became a public disgrace. In the outcry over the relentless imposition of the UAB rules on benefits, the Minister resigned and the 1935 'Standstill Act' forced the UAB to reconsider its reincarnation of Benthamite justice. As a result only one per cent of the UAB decisions were

---

[115] On the cabinet debate, see PRO CAB 27/575, 20 October 1934; 20 November 1934; and 16 October 1935.
[116] PRO CAB 27/575. See also Alan Booth 'An Administrative Experiment in Unemployment Policy in the Thirties,' *Public Administration* (UK), **56**, Summer 1978, pp. 139–155.

ever appealed to administrative tribunals, and in 1936 only 41
decreases were made. The new UAB network of 6,000 officials
used its most severe disciplinary measure, condemnation to the
poorhouse, only five times over 1936 and 1937. By 1937 the new
plan appeared to be twice as expensive as MacDonald's transitional scheme. Perhaps there was no way of thinking more freely
about the nature of the British problem between the wars, but the
country had again compartmentalized poverty, the very thing that
it had spent the last fifty years trying to undo.

How unemployment became a political and institutional reality
of the democratic government had lasting effects on welfare states.
Even the truncated account of the interwar period given here
shows that electoral pressures, party politics and legislative competition had immense effects, but in very different ways. The
German Social Democrats and labour movement survived the
Second Reich only to plan for works councils and a forum of
economic democracy. Their choices were heavily influenced by
their political exclusion of nearly a century. In Sweden the increasingly ambiguous distinction between the private and public sectors
was acknowledged without political hostility and under stable
Social Democratic leadership. In France, as in Germany, the political repercussions of unemployment escalated into attacks on the
two Republics. In the long history of hairbreadth escapes, the
Popular Front rescued the French Republic. The Popular Front
established the left as an essential actor in remodelling the French
welfare state. Because the British state made the most elaborate
efforts, the inability of British policymakers to extract a new
direction from their almost ceaseless efforts from 1920 to 1934
has occupied a prominent place in this chapter. British policies
meandered for a decade and then returned to Poor Law principles,
only to be abruptly suspended, suggesting deep policymaking
problems in British politics.

The United States has not figured in this chapter because the
1935 Social Security Act, though undeniably a major turning
point in American social legislation, did not represent a major
redirection of the American political process. Indeed, the paradox
of the Social Security Act was that a law that so dramatically
changed social policy could be passed without major political
upheaval. For one thing, the American labour movement had very
little to do with its passage and its commentary on the bill added
little. Though important to the new political coalition of the New

Deal, the law did not seek a fundamental redefinition of American politics and those who might have pressed such a debate were busy with other problems. The compartmentalization of agricultural, industrial and social reform historically locates the New Deal with the early liberal reforms in Europe of the late nineteenth century. To hold hearings on the bill, Roosevelt himself selected the House Ways and Means Committee rather than the Labor Committee because he feared that more radical Congressmen might extend the scope of the bill. The Labor Department was omitted from the Committee on Economic Security in order to include the Secretary of Commerce and broaden the bill's appeal to the business community. This arrangement does not seem to have caused either Frances Perkins, the Labor Secretary who masterminded the bill, nor her Assistant Secretary, Altmeyer, any misgiving.[117] Thus, the law was a typical product of American pluralist politics, working in conventional ways among the well known pitfalls of party coalitions and Congressional politics.

Old age pensions, the most important element of the reform, might have been left out were it not for the Townsend movement. In the early 1930s 28 states and 2 territories had pension plans, but only 23 of these were mandatory. But pensions were more politically sensitive than unemployment insurance because of the huge reserves that would be accumulated by the federal government. In relation to the economic logic of social security, the parties reversed their usual positions. Alfred Landon campaigned against Roosevelt in 1936 in favour of a government contribution. A liberal Roosevelt took the conservative course because he feared that a federal financial commitment would create business objections. But business feared the more extravagent Townsend plan even more.[118] The Secretary of the Treasury, Hans Morgenthau, worked out a way to manage reserves so as not to alarm the business community and not to create public opposition by increas-

---

[117] See the accounts of organizing the Committee on Economic Security in Frances Perkins, *The Roosevelt I Knew*, New York; Viking Press, 1946; and Arthur J. Altmeyer, *The Formative Years of Social Security*, Madison; University of Wisconsin Press, 1966.
[118] The Townsend plan would clearly have increased business taxes substantially and was very popular. As late as 1939, it could muster 97 votes in the House of Representatives. Perkins, pp. 278–9.

ing the income tax. Agricultural and domestic workers were excluded for much the same reasons. Under these political constraints social security did not become a challenge to the American political process.

Compared to development in European social insurance in the interwar period the American experiment was little more than federally organized relief. The system was to be self-supporting and its fund managed by the Treasury. It was only universalized during Congressional hearings when the $250 income limit was removed. Roosevelt and his aides were careful to see that no such impression of radical change was created. Of course, the loopholes were there for the expansion of the system and eventually for government, as the lender to the system, to take a more positive role, but throughout the passage of the law the intent was to minimize the importance of the bill as a major form of government intervention. While labour obviously benefited from the bill, it did not originate from labour unrest nor was it part of a larger vision of reconstructing the labour market. If there was any 'right' proclaimed by the Act, it was that good Americans do not depend on government. The core of bureaucrats who designed and ran the system for the next thirty years were eager to sustain this myth. All this is not to detract from the immense social benefit that accrued from the law, but only to note that it was not seen and was not intended to be the groundwork for a major political change.

These things considered, outside the United States, the explorations and experiments of the interwar period become the setting for the more advanced welfare state designs of 1945. Although American welfare and insurance policies undergo no major change after the war until the Kennedy and Johnson administrations, Europe proceeded to establish elaborate national social programmes under central government. To the extent that these efforts built new institutional links and sought to overcome the liberal differentiation between wages and welfare, the democracies culminated nearly a century of change in the scope and functions of the democratic state. Essentially, the choice in 1945 was between constructing the state apparatus the democracies wished they had before the turmoil of the interwar period, or building a new framework that would take them into a new stage of democratic development.

5

The Welfare State Institutionalized

In the immediate postwar years from 1945 to 1950 welfare became an institutionalized reality. Despite the broad similarities in how demands were made and in how benefits were provided, final institutionalization of the welfare states could elude neither the interwar nor postwar politics of each country. From the late nineteenth century there had been at least two competing models: the liberal state model that hoped to exclude welfare as a primary political concern of democracies, and the socialist model which aimed at capturing the state in order to achieve a more perfect equality. The ambiguous meaning of the welfare state after 1950 is due to the diverse forms of institutionalization selected in the postwar period.

As outlined in Chapter 4, the interwar period is most significant in setting the priorities of the new welfare states, not so much because painless solutions to industrial and social problems were found but because between 1918 and 1940 governments learned that social policies are interdependent with many traditional state activities. In so far as the classical liberal state assumed that public and private interests must be kept apart, the liberal state had steadily decayed for over twenty years. The postwar policymakers were generally agreed that the simple compartmentalization of state and society, if it had indeed ever been as firm as classical and neo-classical economists assumed, was no longer workable. But there were still a number of critically important political, administrative and institutional decisions to be made. How they were made largely determined the chances, if any, of building a more ambitious social democratic welfare state after 1950. The ambiguities of social and wage benefits had become clear, the question was how national institutions might encompass so broad a challenge.

By approaching these changes in a policy context, we can see that each state applied different mixes of political pressure, elite administrative talent, and organizational resources. Moreover, the new social institutions were by no means alike nor were the same policies consistently given the same priorities. Each state had to deal in particular ways with major political obstacles to building welfare states. Governments had to devise radically new financial and budgetary practices, to train and implant a large new bureaucracy, and to apportion new responsibilities between levels of government. Social and economic conditions clearly had important effects, but there was a wide variety of purely political and administrative decisions which had little to do with these conditions or, perhaps more accurately, would almost certainly be needed regardless of the social stress and economic disruption of World War II.

The impact of World War II is one of the more complex, and on the whole neglected, factors in the transformation of the welfare states. The policy effects of major wars on policies are not easily explained, especially World War II. As during World War I, consideration of social policies was a relatively disorderly process, which once again should caution us against making simple social and economic generalizations about the massive social legislation of the late 1940s.[1] From a comparative perspective, World War II presents peculiar problems. In the case of World War I, all the parties initially believed that 'business as usual' could continue during a short war. As the war extended, their reflections about social and economic reconstruction were received in a hostile climate. The prevailing situation was radically different during World War II.

While the British enjoyed their most splendid moment in the defence of democracy, social planning was a secondary concern even though actively discussed as early as 1939. Nonetheless, there was little fundamental disagreement about the overhaul of British social legislation planned by Sir William H. Beveridge. In contrast, French policymaking during the war was a jumble of interests

[1] See, for example, Michael T. Florinsky, *Fascism and National Socialism: A Study of Economic and Social Policies of the Totalitarian State*, New York; Macmillan, 1936; and David Schoenbaum, *Hitler's Social Revolution: Class and Status in Nazi Germany 1933–1939*, New York; Doubleday, 1967.

scattered among the remnants of democratic France, eventually brought into focus by General de Gaulle in London. Within France, the Vichy regime pursued some changes envisaged by the Third Republic, but under the aegis of a strange mixture of reactionary Catholicism and fascism. The inspiration for a more socially just and economically fair French society came from the Resistance and the Free French Movement of de Gaulle, and was manifested immediately after the war. Fundamental disagreement quickly surfaced in France. By the time de Gaulle resigned in disgust over the procrastination of democratic government in January 1946, Gaullist social legislation had been seriously amended.

In the two countries, Germany and Sweden, whose politics had propelled the welfare state in advance of the other major European powers, the war had widely different effects. Under Hitler's totalitarian government social funds and social rights were abolished and merged with a totally mobilized state. While there was never much doubt that a free Germany, the Federal Republic, would reconstruct the old framework of social legislation, it took years to restore finances and to reconstruct welfare administration. Though social politics became a normal part of German politics once democracy was restored in 1951, political failure and disgrace oddly perpetuated an ambivalence about social reform reminiscent of the impasse between Social Democrats and Junker conservatives. The ideology had changed, but no one, least of all the new German leaders, could risk suspicion of restoring social assistance in the guise of fascist benevolence. At the same time, the long history of German social legislation meant that the new democratic parties had less need to innovate than did the British or French. In total disarray from persecution under Hitler, the Social Democrats were unable to shape new plans during the war so that the early reforms were directed toward reconstructing industrial relations and reviving Social Democratic ideas about economic democracy from the Weimar Republic.[2]

[2] Most of the German postwar development belongs in a planned second volume. However, the Allies did reconstitute the DGB in October 1949, and it soon had 5 million members or 40 per cent of wage earners as members. Likewise, the Germany Federation of Employers took shape with 800 member associations. The main early thrust was to develop co-determination, voted through by two states, Hesse and Wurtenburg-Baden in 1948. To prevent multiple laws, the Allied Authority suspended the law until the newly constituted Bundestag could shape national legislation. When the Bundestag reached an impasse, the Allies reinstated the two state laws in 1950. After strike votes by the metal workers

The transformation of the Swedish welfare state was delayed not only by Sweden's international dependence, but by uncertainties within the SAP and LO alliance. Important as the Salsjö-baden Agreement was as a landmark in developing a new form of the welfare state, the 1938 pact was a point of departure rather than an accomplished policy. Not until the Committee of Fifteen, a group of union elders, reported in 1941 was the future political role of the LO clear. In comparing the Swedish model with other democracies, it is important to see that the recommended course of action, and the one largely fulfilled in the post-war decade, was virtually impossible for the labour movements of Britain, France or Germany.

The recommendations of 1941 included giving the LO powers to settle (not just mediate) jurisdictional disputes among its members, to initiate (not simply to recommend) organizational changes in the LO, and to negotiate wage settlements (not finally agreed to until 1951). These arrangements were devised under some political pressure because the Communists had increased their electoral popularity during the war, winning slightly more than 10 per cent of the vote in 1944, and had conducted a five-month strike of metal workers during the war. Although the SAP won nearly 54 per cent of the votes in 1940, in the 1944 election it was reduced to its norm of roughly 46 per cent of the votes.[3] In the immediate post-war period, the Liberals enjoyed a resurgence so that the socialist scenario for Sweden was again uncertain. This drove the SAP and the LO into closer alliance and their successful handling of postwar inflation, largely due to the LO's wage restraint, made it possible to add flesh to the bones of wage solidarity.[4] In some respects, it was the only prewar innovation linking social and wage policy that survived to be developed over the 1950s and 1960s.

These few observations on events between 1939 and 1945 may suffice to show how different were the policy situations confronting the democracies at the end of the war. To compare the subsequent

and miners, the 1951 co-determination law was passed, setting the precedent for the development of labour and social policy in the Federal Republic. See Taylor Cole, 'Labour Relations,' in E. Litchfield, ed., *Governing Postwar Germany*, Ithaca, NY; Cornell University Press, 1953, p. 361–80.
[3] Sten Berglund and Ulf Lindstrom, *Scandanavian Party Systems*, Lund; Student Literature, 1978,p. 85.
[4] Johnston, *Collective Bargaining*, p. 39–41.

changes and developments in reference to external conditions or abstract models of welfare makes little political sense. Closer to the mark, each reconstructed democracy depended heavily on its interwar experience, not only in the broad sense of major social and economic changes, but in the narrower sense of how programme priorities, administrative capabilities and institutional norms changed. This is not to say that the postwar policies were totally dissimilar, but only that each state devised policies within institutional limits and around institutional norms developed prior to the war.

MOBILIZING FOR PEACE

If there is no other lesson to be learned from the gradual construction of welfare states, it is that idealism has little to do with the appearance of the new state structures dedicated to providing social services and some measure of social equality in the postwar period. Despite the speculations of those who saw the war as a demonstration of immense social solidarity, such as Titmuss, the integration of the disparate and often conflicting social policy goals of the interwar period rested with sober and cautious men. The welfare state was accomplished as it had begun, by persons with historical memories and limited knowledge. As policymakers they accepted the uncertainties of the policy process, often made strange political alliances on behalf of their programmes, and had a devastating command of the materials from which to construct new policies.

Compared to France, where administrative designs were quickly shaped to fit political demands, the British welfare state of the late 1940s was a bureaucratic product. A number of factors interacted so that a more ambitious social democratic vision never appeared. As seen in Chapter 4, in the 1930s the Conservative Party had been largely concerned with containing the costs of unemployment and the wartime Prime Minister, Churchill, had little time for social questions. In the painful process of rebuilding its strength, the Labour Party in the 1930s never considered social democratic ideas. By then Bevin had the labour movement firmly in hand and had no patience with the Party's aristocratic intellectuals. The intellectuals who were rethinking Labour's economic policies concentrated on conventional macro-economic issues.[5] Possibly the only rising leader who might have broken new ground on social policy was the young Hugh Gaitskell, but he remained in the shadow of Dalton.[6] On the left of the Party, Sir Stafford Cripps and Bevan might also have reconsidered Labour's social future, but they were consumed with the militant Socialist League and later with building a People's Front to link Russia and Britain against Hitler. Both parties were preoccupied with their traditional concerns and did so in very traditional ways. The interesting question is not over the priorities imposed by the war, but over the British failure to generate new ideas about the future of British welfare after three decades of serious social debate.

British social planning during the war was a confidential and sluggish process, soon dominated by a single figure, Beveridge. When the plan was complete it was almost inadvertently added to the postwar political agenda while serious disagreement still existed within the Cabinet. Given its undeniable popular appeal, there was no turning back once the plan was widely discussed. While the plan met with popular acclaim, there were nonetheless serious misgivings among both Labour and Conservative members of the wartime coalition. More clearly than between the wars, the process of legislation raised difficult questions about the British parliamentary structure. Much the same observation could be made about British planning in many other areas. In short, a distinctly apolitical atmosphere enveloped the legislation of the Beveridge Plan, followed by an interlude of intense, partisan politics where the rationality and comprehensiveness of the Beveridge Plan suffered badly. Politics and policymaking were in this instance, as in many other situations, not in tune.[7]

The disjointed character of British policymaking gave enormous powers to civil servants, probably more than in any other political system. One can hardly understand this phenomenon in the case of the Beveridge Plan without knowing something about Beveridge

[5] Social policy rarely entered the concerns of the prewar Labour intellectuals. See Elizabeth Durbin, *New Jerusalems...*; and in particular Ben Pimlott, *Hugh Dalton*, London; Jonathan Cape, 1985, pp. 250–67 and 385–407.

[6] Philip Williams, *Hugh Gaitskell*, pp. 61–90.

[7] As examples, see the dismal story of local government reform from 1950 to 1982, in Ashford, *British Dogmatism and French Pragmatism*; the successive upheavals of the NHS, described by Klein, *The Politics of the National Health Service*; or the successive debacles surrounding land planning in Offner, *Land and Politics*.

himself. In an age of supremely confident civil servants, Beveridge was distinguished by his arrogance. As Harris writes in her superb biography, he had a 'patronizing air, bordering at times on a suggestion of veiled contempt.'[8] Many politicians who worked with him would not be this charitable. Dalton, the Labour Party's financial expert, found him egotistical and overbearing. Attlee, seldom a harsh judge of men in public, was heard to complain that somehow Beveridge thought the war should stop so government could get on with his plan. Bevin found him quite unsuitable to work directly with labour problems and only accepted him in the Ministry of Labour when he knew he could successfully isolate Beveridge from its daily business. His exaggerated sense of self-importance is detectable in his autobiograpy. When he was fishing for a job in the wartime coalition, he noted how he wished 'to become by hook or by crook, an Economic General Staff for planning the civilian side of the war.'[9] The first year or two of war planning in Britain did not go well, but the implied assumption that he might set all problems straight suggests why he was in fact one of the last elderly senior civil servants to be called back to government.

Second, and consistent with his defensiveness, his work was in many respects unoriginal. Discussing his ideas on policy, Harris notes, for example, 'how little they were dependent upon his empirical research.'[10] If one reads the endless statistics and descriptions that Beveridge compiled for his major study of unemployment,[11] this seems a strange comment. Yet it is true in a revealing way. The Beveridge Plan was based on three assumptions: full employment, family allowances and free medical care. While it is clearly correct, as Harris argues, that the Beveridge of 1940 was very different from the Beveridge who organized Labour Exchanges in 1908, the Fabian disposition to assume that difficult issues can be unravelled by abstract models remains. The historian and Liberal politician, Ensor, noted this weakness in reviewing the first edition of Beveridge's *Unemployment*. For Ensor there was

---

[8] Jose Harris, *William Beveridge*, p. 148.
[9] William H. Beveridge, *Power and Influence*, New York; Beechurst, 1945, p. 243.
[10] Harris, p. 473.
[11] Beveridge, *Unemployment: A Problem of Industry*, London; Longman's and Green, 1910. The book was not revised, but considerably expanded in later editions, most notably *Unemployment: A Problem of Industry (1909 and 1930)*, London; Longman's and Green, 1930.

too much pure reason and too little concern about how one goes about getting politicians 'to swallow remedies.'[12] Rationality in the abstract and rationality in policymaking seldom correspond. While it is clear that Beveridge's interest in social assistance and social insurance only became central to his thinking in the mid-1930s, there is nonetheless an Edwardian simplicity in his policy recommendations.

Third, there was always an element of Victorian harshness about Beveridge's proposals. It is interesting to note that he himself wrote that his 1942 plan 'stemmed from what all of us had imbibed from the Webbs.'[13] This is a curious statement because his association with the Webbs, as with their relationship to most senior civil servants, was not one of simple subjection to Fabian models. It reflects, in part, his conversion to broad social planning in the mid-1930s, but there remained an element of compulsory justice and a reliance on rigid rules. Just as the Webbs found the early Liberal insurance proposals unsatisfactory, so too did Beveridge criticize unemployment insurance in 1911 because it neglected prevention and treated government as a 'bottomless purse.'[14]

Similarly strict views on public policy and social relationships reappear in his plan. For example, he carried on a long and futile fight to have accident compensation merged with his overall disability insurance scheme in order to protect flat-rate benefits. There was a similar insistence on standard flat-rate benefits despite the immovable fact that rents varied as much as ten times between London and the rural hinterland. Though Beveridge wanted to protect women under his plan, the deserted mother or wife got very short shrift and was left to public assistance.[15] The inherited pensioners were to have reduced benefits compared to new contributors, who would not receive their full pensions until the system was fully funded twenty years later. The plan itself was meant to be a minimal plan or a 'safety net' in a literal sense. Beveridge

[12] Quoted in Harris, p. 143.
[13] Beveridge, *Power and Influence*, p. 86.
[14] Beveridge, *Unemployment: A Problem of Industry (1909 and 1930)*, p. 294.
[15] See J. Harris, *Beveridge*, pp. 402–5. His sense of sexual equality would surely be criticized today. For example, married earners would have a separate pension, but at a lower rate of benefit than the spouse. Unmarried wives would receive the same family and social benefits, but would not receive the normal widow's pension.

had difficulty accepting that people may not assess needs 'objectively' and that politicians may not consider all benefits of equal significance.

Beveridge had immense experience in government. Even while at the LSE he participated in the Royal Commission on Coal, the Royal Commission on Trade and the Geddes Committee of the 1920s. Like any patriotic Briton, Beveridge was eager to enter war service of some kind after 1939. At this time he was Master of University College, Oxford, immersed in a study of unemployment[16] with a promising graduate assistant, Harold (later Sir) Wilson. He wrote to the Ministry of Labour, to his friends in the Treasury, and finally to Churchill himself. He turned down one job that he thought inferior to his talents, but finally accepted an offer from Bevin, Minister of Labour, to do a study of wartime factory inspection. Later he joined the erratic Arthur Greenwood, Chairman of the Production Council, to extend his manpower studies to the war situation, but Bevin appointed another, more manageable civil servant to be wartime Director of Manpower and Beveridge again felt rejected. By now Beveridge was on the verge of attacking Churchill's conduct of the war, writing letters to the *Times* and apparently leaking a story to the *Daily Mail* on the blunders being made on the deployment of civilian labour.[17] He was picked up by Dalton at the Board of Trade to prepare a plan for fuel rationing, but as he confesses he was a 'wandering voice' in Whitehall for most of the first two years of the war.[18]

Although the process involved in adopting the Beveridge Plan and its political consequences will be outlined more fully below, it is worth pausing to consider how pervasive figures, such as Beveridge, influence policymaking. His life like those of other key figures is one of the most neglected aspects of policy analysis. The

[16] His study was intended to be reply to Keynes' theory of unemployment. Beveridge thought that Keynes' theory lacked statistical content. Keynes himself accepted Beveridge's article for the March 1939 *Economic Journal*. See Beveridge, *Power and Influence*, pp. 259–60. Both men were involved in trying to reconstruct the Liberal Party over the 1930s. See A. P. Thirwall, ed., *Keynes as a Policy Advisor*, London; Macmillan, 1982.

[17] His attacks may well account for Churchill's disdain toward him. They were made at a very low point in the history of the war, when Churchill was increasingly surrounded by critics of his wartime strategy. See Beveridge, pp. 281–3; and J. Harris, p. 373–7.

[18] Beveridge, p. 290. Beveridge is again noticably piqued because Churchill did not take time to see him after the manpower report was published.

crucial blend of personal style and administrative politics remains largely unexplored. Two aspects of Beveridge's life stand out. First is the studied, formalized way in which British higher civil servants stand aloof from political pressure as Beveridge did. Second, how vulnerable are the most informed and best reasoned analyses of policy in the real world of British politics. Without depreciating the landmark importance of the Beveridge Plan, no major political figure in government trusted Beveridge's ideas. By the time the Report was on the political agenda, few trusted his political discretion. Though this result no doubt depends heavily on Beveridge's behaviour subsequent to the publication of the report, for the remainder of his life he was never again consulted on social problems. But from a policy perspective there is probably no better demonstration of the rigid boundaries between policymaking and politics in Britain, nor of the ruthless sanctions that can be brought to bear on those who violate Whitehall rules of the game.

The administrative continuity of French social policies survived the war, but the Vichy regime was another interlude in French progress toward a fully-developed welfare state. More than in Britain, the war as well as the fascist government had lasting effects on the organization of postwar social services. Reduced to poverty, with many earners in German labour camps, and with no access to foreign aid, Vichy was forced to organize and to ration social services as they never had been in France. Among the first decisions was to create a national association of doctors, the *Ordre des Médécins*, in 1940, the first major legislation on organizing medical care since 1892.[19] More influenced by Vichy's particular version of fascism, in 1941 the *Chartre de Travail* was announced, a corporatist arrangement to prevent strikes and to enlist management in labour affairs.[20] Less noticed, the *Chartre des Hopitaux* had similar importance in permitting Vichy to ration medical care, and the experiment with regional medical centres in 1943 sets the principles, if not the realities of French hospital reorganization for the next two Republics.[21] More closely aligned with reactionary Catholicism, but nonetheless connected to longstanding French

---

[19] See Monica Steffen, *Régulation politique et stratégies professionelles: 'Médicine libérale et émergence des Centres de Santé,* doctoral thesis, University of Grenoble II, Institut d'Etudes Politiques, 1983, pp. 232.

[20] Richard F. Kuisel, *Capitalism and the State in Modern France* ..., pp. 144–6.

[21] Chritian Brumter, *La Planification sanitaire,* doctoral thesis, Faculté de Droit et des Sciences Politiques, University of Strasbourg, 1979, pp. 267–89.

concerns over population decline, there was also a Ministry of the French Family, part of whose responsibility was to provide for the families left with no wage earner during the war.[22] The Vichyite *allocation salaire unique* later becomes one of the basic measures of French social assistance.

Compared to the postwar British policy process, the French were extraordinarily purposeful and yet highly vulnerable to political intervention. From this perspective, the vision of France as a relentlessly centralized administrative state requires revision. From 1945 to 1950 mobilizing support for new social policies and implementing them was protracted, prolonged and often unsuccessful. The education of high French officials may account for Cartesian indulgences, but the process itself is fraught with institutional uncertainties of a kind virtually unknown to British leaders and high officials.[23] In the case of the welfare state, it may suffice to note that the most detailed account of social legislation since the war notes that the French social security system was launched 'against the state.'[24]

First, as seen in Chapter 3, there was remarkable continuity among the officials constructing the policies and writing the laws associated with the French welfare state of 1945. Alexandre Parodi had worked with social legislation throughout the 1930s, and had recruited the young Pierre Laroque to the Ministry of Labour. The ministry itself served as a reservoir of knowledge about social problems, but the official historical memory of the interwar period was very different in France and Britain. The latter had badly bungled unemployment policy in the 1920s, and because of crippling unemployment had little time until the late 1930s to develop auxiliary social programmes. In contrast, there was an *équipe* in France whose ideas were shaped by legislation of 1928 and 1930 and whose motivation arose not so much from an abstract vision as from their own immersion in the grubby details of adapting French public law and public administration to the modest programmes of the Third Republic. Most of these men came from the Conseil d'Etat, and their status and knowledge of its operations

[22] On the progression of ministerial changes, see Maurice Bargeton, 'La formation des ministères,' *Revue Française des Affaires Sociales*, January–March, 1971, pp. 56–86.

[23] See Douglas E. Ashford, *Policy and Politics in France: Living with Uncertainty*, Philadelphia, PA; Temple University Press, 1982.

[24] Henri C. Galant, *Histoire politique. . .*, p. xvii.

provided an instititional focal point for their efforts that barely compares with the disjointed ways of accumulating influence in Whitehall.

To say there was more continuity within the French process may seem strange because clearly less had been accomplished in the interwar period. In a substantive sense, both the Laroque plan and the Beveridge plan were sharp breaks with the past. But there was more continuity in form in France and considerable continuity in terms of the content of earlier legislation. In a more precise policy sense, Beveridge scuttled the old system to build a new system. Many of the compromises and obstacles that arose after he had parted from the Ministry of Labour arose because of the ease of disconnecting intricate policy changes in Britain. Laroque had some fairly revolutionary changes in mind, but throughout the debate over the ordinance of 1945 compromises were continually made. The main report to the Consultative Assembly of 1945, the Rapport Buisson, goes to great lengths to show the connections between earlier legislation and the new plan.[25] His statement of the aim of the new law has been often paraphrased. 'We conceived social legislation as a vast palace that could contain everyone. You know what happened to that palace: a number of separate pavilions were substituted, some converted, some without roofs, some furnished and others not. We live in these small lodgings. Afterwards, we tried to install every possible comfort.'[26]

Secondly, continuity was achieved in a way that was not possible for Britain. British social security was more throroughly nationalized at an early date, in part because of the distance between social policies and the labour movement. Beneficiaries were never as intimately linked to the rising level of benefits as in France. To be sure, the magnitude of British unemployment made this inescapable, but the decision had far-reaching implications for later resistance to integrating social and wage policy. For the French the modest achievements of the interwar period, as well as many other aspects of the nascent social security system, were *droits acquisé*. For one thing, to recover from the enormous loss of population in World War I since 1918 the government had paid an *allocation de maternité* for the first child of mothers under 25 years

---

[25] *Rapport fait au nom de la commission du travail et des affaires sociales* (Rapport Buisson), *Journal Officiel*, Asemblée Consultative, 3e session, séance du 24 juillet 1945, Documents, Annexe 554, pp. 725–38.
[26] Rapport Buisson, p. 727.

or for a child born in the first two years of marriage.[27] In the 1930s, numerous company family funds began paying an *allocation mère au foyer* to assist single or unemployed mothers.[28] Under Vichy, mothers were again favoured, partly because of Catholic doctrine and partly because so many were left to the their own resources in the war. By 1943 the *allocation salaire unique* was half of all social benefits paid by the Vichy regime, though of course funds were meagre at the time. The austerity of Vichy combined with desperate need that led to the appointment of a special commission under Parodi to study social benefits, the earliest record available of a specific plan being undertaken.[29]

Third, continuity was achieved in part because of the very mixed political character of early social protection efforts. Like other privileged groups in France, by 1945 both miners and railway workers considered their special pension rights sacrosanct. The British labour movement was so powerful by 1945 that it could exercise veto power over social legislation, and in fact reversed Beveridge's scheme for accident compensation. Divided into Communist, Socialist and Christian factions, the French unions fought for their concept of social security. In a revealing comment on the problems of building the French social security system, Laroque described the problems of a labour movement, 'United by fluctuations experienced by labour organizations, by their division, their frequent weakness in confronting a rural society (*monde*) and above all a middle class strongly anchored in what it considers its privileges.'[30] The political intricacy of French democracy was reproduced by the workers. Political diversity not only prevented France from achieving the uniformity of British social security, but justified the careful institutionalization of each component of the enlarged welfare state in order to see that no group might be deprived by another and, of course, to jealously guard beneficiaries against the state itself.

French politics tends to be replicated in all her institutions, not the least those dealing with social security. The best illustration is the development and organization of family allowances. Though ideologically associated with Catholic politics, the network of

[27] Walter S. Friedlander, *Individualism and Social Welfare. . .*, p. 41.
[28] Dominique Ceccaldi, *Histoire des Prestations Familiales en France. . .*, pp. 57–9.
[29] Ceccaldi, pp. 99–101. Parodi was of course then closely involved with organizing the Gaullist branch of the French Resistance.
[30] Pierre Laroque, preface to *Succès et Faiblesses*, p. 7.

funds, contributors and firms involved in the family allocation structure by 1945 was immense. Under the impulse of *Rerum Novarum*, liberal Catholics had begun to organize family relief in the 1890s. One of the most successful groups was launched by Captain Maire, himself the proud father of twelve children![31] Benevolent employers throughout France established family funds, usually linked to the departmental *caisses* of the rudimentary social security system of the Third Republic. Just before World War I, Romanet, the Director of Personnel of Regis Joya, conducted a study showing that a worker with two children could not support his family, and the family assistance programme of the Joya firm became a model for France.[32] Further studies were made after the war by the Comité des Forges, the steel pressure group, and by 1925 there were 125 funds benefiting 1.1 million workers. Using Millerand's precedent to press reforms, in 1923 a law required firms with government contracts to have family funds. The final step was the loi Landry of 1932 creating a national family assistance programme.

The British contrast provides a vivid example of the much simpler and hence often more arbitrary politics of social policy. Shortly after World War I, an energetic and determined feminist, Eleanor Rathbone, founded the Family Endowment Society.[33] Like so many British reform efforts, it was an organization of enlightened middle-class opinion and worked through direct contacts with the political elite. Rathbone was a member of a Conservative backbench clique, the Next Five Years Group, assembled by a young, independent-minded Tory, Harold (later Sir) Macmillan. As in France, the patriotic element of family allowances appealed to certain elements in the Conservative Party and Rathbone also had strong support from a conservative spokesman, Leo Amery. But the target of the Family Endowment Society was the labour movement.

A Labour-TUC Committee on a Living Wage was appointed in 1927, but Citrine and Bevin both considered family allowances a threat to wage bargaining and in 1930 the TUC General Council

---

[31] Charles Bonnet, 'Cent ans d'histoire,' *Informations Sociales*, nos. 6–7, 1978, pp. 13–31.

[32] Ceccaldi, *Histoire des Prestations. . .*, pp. 17–18. Romanet was linked to militant Catholics in the Academy des Sciences Morales et Politiques, and in 1953, at the age of 80, was made a Commander of the Legion of Honour for his work.

[33] Eleanor Rathbone, *The Disinherited Family*, London; Allen and Unwin, 1924.

rejected the proposal. Given the interwar atmosphere, they were probably right. Before his more progressive phase of the late 1930s, Beveridge had himself advocated family allowances before the Royal Commission on Coal in order to reduce wages. But the interesting political dimension in comparison to France was the inability of a relatively well-organized and influential group to penetrate the policymaking structure. To be sure, the Treasury could and did argue that unemployment dependent allowances in 1918 and the liberal interpretation of unemployment assistance throughout the 1920s made special allowances unnecessary.[34] All this may be correct, but it also demonstrates the enormous political hurdles to linking social and wage policies in Britain.

Builders of the French welfare state could never avoid the intricate overlapping of public and private social protection. Family protection continued to grow during the difficult years of the 1930s. In 1934 benefits were paid by 162,000 firms employing 3.8 million persons; in 1938 by 450,000 firms employing 5.4 million persons, roughly half the work force.[35] As in the case of the French economy more generally, the firm family funds were linked to departmental funds, and these, in turn, represented nationally by a *caisse nationale*. The structure rested on national legislation and was subject to national regulation, but the system was the product of benevolent *patrons*, especially in the more strongly Catholic industrial areas of France. The *allocation mère au foyer* was first tried by a textile firm, Maison Leclercq-Dupine, which provided higher family allowances for families where the mother remained at home. The structure remained in place under Vichy, but with improved benefits, a stronger *tutelle* (administrative supervision) and as mentioned, the *salaire unique* for the single parent.

FIGHTING FOR NATIONALIZED WELFARE

Unlike Britain, over 1945 and 1946 France did not enjoy the institutional stability that was provided in Britain by the Parliament and the strong Labour Party majority after the 1945

[34] The material from this paragraph comes from the careful history of John Macinol, *The Movement for Family Allowances 1918–1945: A Study in Social Policy Development*, London; Heinemann, 1980, pp. 1–168. Beveridge's interest is discussed pp. 39–45.

[35] Ceccaldi, p. 51.

election. In the course of the debate over basic French social legislation there were four different institutional settings: the Consultative Assembly, a provisional deliberative body to govern until a constitution could be written; the first and second Constituent Assemblies, elected to write the constitution, and repeated because the first draft was rejected by the voters; and finally the new National Assembly of the Fourth Republic. The alleged forcefulness of French administration must be judged in the light of such institutional uncertainties. In reality, there never was a single plan as in Britain, but an accumulation of laws governing the basic structure of the system, setting limits to various kinds of protection and linking diverse interests and organizations from the past to the governmental framework. The closest thing to a full plan was the Charter issued by Conseil National de la Résistance in March, 1944, but it was more a declaration of intent than a framework for a new social policy.[36]

On his return to France, de Gaulle appointed Parodi as Minister of Social Affairs in the Provisional Government. Parodi's right hand was Pierre Laroque, who had been in London since 1942 with the government-in-exile under de Gaulle.[37] The draft social security *ordonnance* was reviewed by two bodies, the legal evaluation of the Rapport Mottin and the legislative report of Buisson. The central policymaking group was a special commission under Laroque, established in June 1945. The membership of the commission suggests how difficult it is to mobilize influence in France. Of the 32 members, 19 were from outside the government: four from unions (three CGT and one CFTC), four from *patrons*; four from·existing social security organizations; two from the semi-public family allowance organization, the Caisse des allocations familiales; three 'experts', representing the problem of reorganizing workmen's compensation; and two from Alsace-Lorraine, whose system of social insurance still contained many anomalies in relation to the less-developed system in the rest of France.[38] Policy guidance was provided by a reconstituted Conseil Supérieur des

[36] See H. Michel and B. Mirkine-Guetizevich, *Les idées politiques et sociales de la Résistance*, Paris; PUF, 1954. Of course, the National Resistance Council was itself badly fragmented between Gaullist, Communist and Catholic factions so it did not speak with an authoritative voice.

[37] To my knowledge, there are no records preserved from the government-in-exile.

[38] Galant, *Histoire politique. . .* , p. 29.

Assurances Sociales under Parodi.[39] The legal authority for this complex assortment of policymakers was the 1898 law on workmen's compensation.[40]

The Rapport Mottin of July 1945 anticipated many of the quarrels that would haunt French social security for the next forty years.[41] Like Beveridge, the French officials wanted a simple structure to manage all social insurance funds under standard rules, a *caisse unique*, combining contributions from all sources and paying out benefits to all programmes. There were two bulwarks for opposition to such severe nationalization: the family benefits organization and the accident compensation funds, which had operated since 1898 on the principle that employers alone were responsible for occupational disability. The vote on merger of the Mottin committee was a deadlock: eight persons voted in favour, including the President of the committee, the four government representatives, the two members from the CGT and one member from the Lille region. Against them were all other social groups. At this time the French Communist Party (PCF) was extending its appeal to the French people and anticipated controlling the new structure. In addition, the now Communist CGT included most of the social security employees in the government. Among the many strange alliances in French politics was the dependable agreement between Gaullists and Communists on the structure of the new system.

Second, there was an intense debate over *affinité*, which in effect meant the right of the government to compel the semi-public funds, often managed by insurance companies, firms (especially in textiles) and CFTC unions (bitterly opposed to the CGT) to be merged in a single social security organization. Third, there was an extended and inconclusive discussion of the areas of the subordinate *caisses*, another interesting example of the pervasiveness of territorial politics in France. The CGT wanted the workplace to be the location of registration and payment in order to strengthen its own industrial organization, while less organized or dis-

---

[39] Galant, p. 48.

[40] Michel Vorin, *Les origines des caisses de sécurité sociale et leurs pouvoirs*, Paris; Librairie Générale de Droit et de Jurisprudence, 1961, p. 1.

[41] I am indebted to Mme. Surzur, Secretary of the Comité d'Histoire de la Securité Sociale, for a copy of the Mottin Report, dated 9 July 1945, mimeo. Under Laroque's Chairmanship, the Committee is preparing an official history of French social security.

persed trades, such as the construction workers (*batiment*), wanted areas to be defined by residence.

The fourth, and no doubt the most politically sensitive issue, was selection of the administrative councils. Led by the CGT, there was great disagreement over occupational representation (*salariés*) and most members of the committee agreed that it should be based on the 'most representative union organizations.' This was again a concession of extreme importance to the Communists who fought throughout the debate for workplace representation, while the weaker unions wanted direct elections among all workers. Support for direct elections joined the members from the family funds, the insurance companies, the small employers and Ministry of Public Health. Against were the President of the commission, the CGT, the Ministry of Labour and the Lille regional representative. These were hardly auspicious conditions for launching a new national effort.

More critical to the future of the proposals was the Rapport Buisson, the report prepared for the Consultative Assembly debate. Already the clear definitions of power sought by Parodi and Laroque were beginning to fade. As Buisson and his colleagues saw the problem, the purpose was 'to achieve a redistribution of national income destined to appropriate (*prélever*) from privileged persons the necessary sums to supplement the resources of diverse workers and less favoured families.[42] Though never fully accomplished by the Fourth Republic, the programmes were to be coordinated by a single Director of Social Security (Laroque) under the Minister of Labour. The advisory council or Conseil Supérieur reflects the diverse interests that the new system would try to reconcile: regional and local funds (many of them already existing from earlier voluntary insurance efforts) with half the seats; the liberal professions, employees (*salariés*) and workers with a quarter of the seats; and the administration and government funds with a quarter of the seats. Direct participation in the management of the system was to be provided by an administrative council, composed of two-thirds workers, one-third employers and experts (meaning private insurers) and two doctors. As in the original plan, it was assumed that contributions would be deposited in a single fund (*caisse primaire*).

[42] Rapport Buisson, p. 725. Unless direct quotes are made, specific pages from the report will not be footnoted.

The critical administrative control, which was to become the focus of the fight over the new legislation, was the *Caisse nationale de la securité sociale* or National Social Security Fund which would be the instrument of redistribution. The scheme called for six official members of the administrative committee for the Fund including two representatives from the Ministry of Labour, one from the Ministry of Health, one from the Ministry of Finance and another from the Ministry of National Economy, and finally one from the Caisse des Dépôts which was to serve as the depository agent. In addition, there were to be eighteen elected members: three from the Conseil Supérieur, nine from regional funds (six workers and three employers), and six from family allocation funds.

As can be seen, in the space of six months since Liberation, several critical compromises had already been made. The battle with the strongly entrenched and semi-public family allocation system was conceded. More important for the future politics of the system, workers were granted a large plurality in the key management bodies, and with elected members could produce a majority. No such concessions to participant management were ever considered in Britain which is not to say that French officials were comfortable with divided control. Indeed, the politics of the system for the next forty years were to centre on how to select worker representatives and how the powers of the top management committee were to blend with official supervision or the *tutelle*.

Buisson and his friends did not conceal the basic controversies plaguing the creation of the new system. There was first the professions whose privileged position in managing the dispersed funds and allocating benefits would be preserved. In contrast to the acutely self-aware professions of France, most of them highly suspicious of the role of the state, in Britain the major private interests were reconciled to the Beveridge Plan before it was legislated. The only major British professional controversy occurred in 1948 with the nationalization of medical care. Second, Buisson raised the question of the mutual societies, but hoped that the precedent of the Department of the Seine would be followed. In this case, the Parisian mutual societies had seen fit to merge their activities in the capital region in order to facilitate handling benefits. Were this not done, as in Britain with the Friendly Societies, the disparities of benefits and procedures would have effectively crippled the system. In Britain the Cabinet itself decided that Friendly Societies were obsolete. In France, mutual societies successfully fought for control of those components of the system, mainly family and sickness benefits, where they were well organized.

Third, as in Britain, there were serious difficulties with the unions over the contributions to accident compensation funds. The 1898 law was again cited as the precedent for obligatory employer contributions and the establishment of the first truly national fund to be used in event of death or permanent disability. As Buisson pointed out, by 1945 there was a long accumulation of grievances over employer management of the local funds: worker ignorance had been exploited, controversies over compensation were drawn out while disabled workers languished, and where there was company pressure to use factory doctors.

The fourth main problem was reorganization of the family funds, but by July 1945 the Minister of Labour had already decided not to fight the issue. Undoubtedly, this was a concession to the rising liberal Catholic party, the Mouvement Républicain Populaire (MRP), which was to become the strongest opponent of the Communists in the early years of the Fourth Republic. Because these funds not only existed, but provided a variety of supplementary money for highly desirable local activities, such as sports, summer camps, etc., they were an important political prize for local parties. The Gaullists apparently decided not to take the risk that such attractive events might fall into the hands of the Communists. The possibility that family support might be localized, much less politicized, was never considered in organizing the British welfare state.

In his discussion of the specific articles of the proposed law, Buisson notes two features of the new system that differentiate it dramatically from the British and most other nationalized social security systems of the time. First, article 6 established the 'principe de répartition' or redistribution and rejected the 'principe de capitalisation'. In this way the French decided from the earliest stages of their version of the welfare state that self-financing of social benefits was impossible. Though there is no evidence that this was an intentional device to permit the rapid increase of benefits, this provision left the door open for the political escalation of the welfare state over the coming decades, particularly in the Fifth Republic. It also made it easier to delay the complex issue of pensions, which, as we shall see below, became the major source of complication of the French system as each 'social partner' fought successfully for its own privileged pension system. By this time of course the American system was also effectively, if not openly, run on a cash flow basis. In contrast, Beveridge defended self-financing for pensions, partly in order to defend himself against Treasury hostility to his plan, and accepted meagre pension payments to make them compatible with his scheme. The crucial political difference is that Beveridge and his colleagues made unworkable compromises in order to get their plan through the Cabinet and Parliament. In the more diverse and diffused political environment of France and America political compromises required fiscal generosity.

Secondly, Buisson was particularly sensitive to the importance of management by participants. Since the earliest debates over social legislation in the 1890s, parties and groups had insisted that French social security must be 'outside the state.' Moreover, Buisson underscored how effective participation would raise worker and union awareness of social inequality and social solidarity, an argument that would be instantly recognized by Le Play, Péguy, Guesde or any of the radical and socialist advocates of social protection nearly a century before.[43] Despite decades of political turbulence and defeat, the intellectual context of the new system displayed remarkable continuity. Whether effective participant control was achieved is controversial, but the point is that the French built political tensions into the social security system. In contrast, most British and American officials clearly hoped that such tensions might be excluded. Beveridge was prepared to deal with politics on the national level, though for reasons mentioned above, he was not particularly good at that, but it would have seemed strange to him, and to most reformers of the British welfare state since Beveridge, that political interests might be built into the system.

Although the Consultative Assembly did not have the prestige of a constitutionally elected body, political opposition to the Parodi-Laroque proposals was clearly in evidence. When the Assembly voted to invite the government to submit its proposals, Gaston Tessier, a CFTC leader and defender of the localized funds, led the opposition. Like the defenders of private charity in the Third

---

[43] Unlike Britain, the unions were actively involved in the early planning of social insurance. See Galant, *Histoire politique de la securité sociale en France. . .*, pp. 27–60; and Antoinette Catrice-Lorey, *Dynamique interne de la securité sociale*, Paris; Economica, 1982, pp. 35–44.

Republic, he spoke of the threat to 'free institutions' and the necessity that all active groups (*forces vives*) participate in the reconstruction of France.[44] The issue was not as clear-cut as in Britain. Tessier later pointed out in the debate on the law itself that in the labour stronghold of Pas-de-Calais the mutual funds were used to obtain coverage for nearly three-fourths of the insured. He reminded the Assembly that the Rapport Mottin showed that even the Conseil d'Etat was divided on the legality of the *caisse primaire*.[45] Political opposition is not easily ignored in France and Parodi made one of his few appearances in the Assembly to assure the Deputies that the 'singularly disorderly and chaotic' situation must be simplified if any national system is to work and to remind them that developed as accident insurance plans have become, there was no law obliging all firms to provide disability protection. Marcel Astier rose to plead for the exclusion of agriculture, which was in the main accepted. Robert Prigent, the MRP spokesman, defended the separate organization for family allowances. Amid applause, the government accepted a separate Conseil Supérieur des Allocations Familiales, while also giving the family funds representation on the Conseil Supérieur de la Securité Sociale. With these concessions, the *ordonnance* was approved.

The argument is frequently made that the French Assembly has always been a weak legislative body. Viewed as part of the policy process, the role of the Assembly is hardly negligible, nor is it self-evident that more stable lawmaking bodies have more influence in determining the content and procedures of important laws. In its debates over social security, the first Constituent Assembly provides interesting evidence of the important part played by the French legislature. Elections to the Assembly had ushered in the period of 'tripartisme', that is, almost equal balancing of Communist, Socialist and MRP groups that was to continue until the Communists turned against the democratic majority in 1947.[46] By 1946 both the Socialists and the MRP realized that they were in a difficult struggle with the PCF. After the war the CGT

---

[44] *Journal Officiel*, Assemblée Consultative Provisoire, Documents, séance du 9 juillet 1945, Annexe No. 496 and 497, pp. 608–19.
[45] *Journal Officiel*, Assemblée Consultative Provisoire, Débats, séance du 31 juillet 1945, pp. 1686–97.
[46] In the Constitutent Assembly elections of October, 1945, the Communists received 20 per cent of the votes and 159 seats; the Socialists 18 per cent and 139 seats; and the MRP 19 per cent and 150 seats.

membership had soared to 4 million members, leaving the CFTC a confessional group in only a few strongly Catholic regions. In addition, the *Confédération Générale des Cadres* (CGC) was being launched in 1944, in large part to defend the autonomy of middle class workers. In the new government, the impending split was already visible. A Communist, Ambroise Croizat, became Minister of Labour and Social Security and a MRP leader, Robert Prigent, Minister of Public Health and Population. As often found in France, policy differences were reproduced throughout the governmental structure.

At the level of parties, the democratic parties correctly perceived that the superior organization of the PCF might easily be used to convert the nascent social security system into a Communist bastion. A month after the elections, Maurice Schuman, the MRP leader, proposed a bill setting forth the conditions of autonomy that should be preserved within the system.[47] The political intricacies of social security began to appear in his bill. Disability insurance should be local rather than regional, an apparent attempt to minimize Communist control of funds. He defended the mutual societies and the presently insured. Most important, he wanted the implementation of the new law delayed until 1947. In early 1946 another Assembly report appeared on implementation of the law, this time by the Socialist Deputy, Pierre Segelle.[48] The weakness of the democratic left was exposed. The Socialist spokesman defended the planned calendar of implementation and attacked the mutual societies. But his sensitivity to emerging political differences with the PCF is visible in his defence of separate pension schemes (*régimes speciaux*) for special occupations, in particular for the miners where Socialists and Communists were fighting for members. To be sure, many of these arguments were well known, but national political differences were beginning to seep into the social security system.

At the level of the emerging social security system, new political rivalries appeared in what may seem a trivial issue, the procedure for electing the Administrative Council and some 250 regional and local committees. But this was one of the most politically sensitive issues surrounding the system and remained so through

---

[47] *Journal Officiel*, Assemblée Nationale Constituante, Annexe No. 191, séance du 22 décembre 1945, pp. 209–12.
[48] *Journal Officiel*, Assemblée Nationale Constituante, Annexe No. 698, séance du 19 mars 1946, pp. 667–70.

the Fifth Republic. In mid-1945 the Communists had favoured direct election of worker representatives to all administrative councils. Once they had achieved control of the supervising ministry, they switched to indirect elections from lists prepared by the national unions.[49] With their massive union strength, the change made it virtually inevitable that Communist representatives would control the national Administrative Council. Both the MRP and Socialist parties objected to the new tactic. The procedure was not settled until October, 1946; the electorate was defined to include not only the employed, but the unemployed, elderly beneficiaries and privately insured. The results of the first elections in April, 1947, were a resounding victory for the Communists. With over 70 per cent of the eligible voters casting ballots, an extraordinarily high turn-out, the PCF gained control of 106 of 124 committees for social security funds and 101 of 111 committees for family allocations.[50]

At the organizational level, the issue was over who would control the union of social security employees. In early 1946 the Communists had taken the lead in creating an employees' union, the Fédération Nationale des Organismes de la Sécurité Sociale (FNOSS). Outnumbering all other unions, they took control of the governing committee and made a Communist, Henry Raynaud, President of FNOSS. Only when the small, competing unions lodged a strong protest was one independent worker added to the governing committee.[51] When the Communists split from the government in 1947, FNOSS became a power-base for their attack on the government. After a bitter debate in 1950, the social security election law was revised and the CGT strangle-hold on social security employees was finally broken when a member of the CGT-FO, the new socialist union, was elected President of FNOSS. Although the Communists polled over half the votes in the elections of 1950, they controlled only 26 of the social security funds and 46 of the family funds. In the subsequent indirect elections to the three national governing bodies, their former representation was cut in half and they received no vice-presidency

---

[49] Interview, Pierre Laroque, 3 November 1983. See also Pierre Laroque, 'Problèmes posés par les élections sociales,' *Revue Française de Science Politique*, **3**, no. 2, April–June 1953, pp. 22–30

[50] Galant, *Histoire politique. . .*, pp. 117–28.

[51] Ceccaldi, p. 107.

on the Caisse Nationale.[52] The final *dénouement* of FNOSS was administered by de Gaulle in the 1960 reforms, when a new organization was created to restore government control of the recruitment, training and placement of social security workers.

BRITAIN: A RELUCTANT WELFARE STATE?

Because of the enthusiastic popular reception of the Beveridge Plan and the subsequent efforts of the 1945 Labour government to redirect the British welfare state, the postwar transformation of the British welfare state acquired an aura of consensual politics. Looking at its development through policy lenses provides a different picture. Many of the decisions as to how to proceed, how to allocate costs and how to define benefits were controversial and contested. The rational construction of a self-regulating system, intentionally protected from parliamentary intervention, was never fully achieved. The interlocking mechanisms to harmonize social assistance and social insurance worked poorly; party and group interests could still intrude on decisionmaking in arbitrary ways; and ministers seldom agreed that a comprehensive set of principles should dictate an orderly policy process or rigidly set their political agenda. Most importantly perhaps, the process policy demonstrates why it was so difficult to introduce a radically new concept of the welfare state which might have ushered in social democratic concepts of the welfare state. Despite the war and the high hopes raised by the Beveridge Plan, British policymakers continued to behave as though no radical changes had taken place in British social policy.

These failings can only be weighed in a comparative context. Germany soon revived its corporatist ideas about blending labour and social interests and France never separated competitive politics from the design and execution of social policies. The British case would be more easily dismissed as an oversight had not Whitehall and Westminster spent so much time designing a social future for Britain. The Treasury opened a file on family allowances in 1938,

---

[52] Galant, pp. 141–53. When the Communists were in power, they first hoped to have their term of office extended from three to four years. The MRP, which had strength in the family funds, wanted their term of office extended to five years! See also Catrice-Lorey, pp. 167–205.

carefully advising its officials, much as it had at every major departure in social policy since the 1911 Act, to be very cautious and to make no commitments. In June 1939, in anticipation of war, the Treasury set up a small committee under Sir Josiah (later Lord) Stamp with two prominent economists, Keynes and J. D. Henderson, to consider wages, prices and the economic planning of the war. Their general conclusion is of great interest to the welfare state for they agreed that in wartime wages must be related to family needs and they began casting about for policies that would make this possible.[53]

Indicative of the treatment the Beveridge Plan would receive in the hands of the British policymakers, the Stamp Survey evoked hostile reactions from all quarters. The Ministry of Labour attacked it as a threat to wage bargaining. The Board of Education attacked it in favour of its own well-established apparatus for providing direct services to children. The Treasury attacked in principle and only undertook more thorough investigations when ordered to do so by the Cabinet. The TUC, led by Citrine and Bevin, renewed their objections of the 1930s. The first round in the fight to establish coherent social policies, even under the pressures of war, was not auspicious.[54]

Only after two and a half years of interdepartmental bickering did the proposal for family allowances begin to take shape as a bill. The Family Allowances Act of 1945 was by no means original with Beveridge, and preparations had extended throughout the war. His interest in family allowances had always been instrumental, that is, as a useful device to manage wage policy. In the final bargaining with the Treasury, much of it mediated by Keynes, Beveridge agreed that the first child should be omitted in order to meet Treasury demands,[55] and the allowance itself was slashed nearly in half by the Treasury. Even so, he adhered to the strict principle of subsistence, wanted to have 'scientific' evidence of a child's needs, and like Victorian social reformers, worried about weakening the incentive to work and possible damage to

[53] Macinol, pp. 170–6. The committee marks Keynes' official re-entry to high-level policymaking, but his ideas were not widely accepted by the Treasury until the closing years of the war. He published his proposals in *How to Pay for the War*, London; 1940.
[54] The dispute, centering over cash payments of family allowances, is described in detail by Macinol, pp. 176–202.
[55] Harris, p. 412.

voluntary assistance.[56] Perhaps the most paradoxical resistance was from the unions because family allowances are clearly one of the most reliably redistributive of social benefits. Although the TUC approved family allowances in September, 1942, three months after Labour Party approval was given, it remains one of the more striking episodes showing the deep reservations of the British labour movement over building a coherent welfare state.

If the first foray into structural change had been disappointing, the ensuing sequel of committees, studies and reports during the war are no less revealing of the political hazards the welfare state would encounter in Britain. In many respects, the most serious obstacle was Churchill himself for he had little time for domestic problems. Commenting on the many memos on domestic problems that disappeared on Churchill's desk, Attlee remarked how they were 'gruel after the champagne of grand strategy.'[57] But to some extent, Churchill's distaste was politically justified because the wrangles over assembling a wartime government continued throughout most of the war and often reflected jockeying for political advantage in the postwar period. Many ultra-Tories still regarded Churchill as a political upstart and an unreliable Conservative.

The halting and uncertain workings of the policy process as proposals began to accumulate are aptly summed up by Addison. 'The campaign for reconstruction wore the guise of sweet reason, but it was impelled also by highly subjective and irrational motives.'[58] There was initially the War Aims Committee under a broken Neville Chamberlain, later passed on to Attlee. Irritated by the strident demands of the Party's *éminence grise*, Harold Laski, for 'socialism now', Attlee retorted the Party 'should not try to get socialist measures implemented under the guise of winning the war.'[59] The War Aims Committee was overtaken by the appointment of the Reconstruction Committee in January, 1941, under Arthur Greenwood, the popular but slothful Labour leader. The Committee only met four times over the next year or so, but it is interesting to assess its expectations against later actualities. The

---

[56] Macinol, p. 185.
[57] The best description of these multiple uncertainties is Paul Addison, *The Road to 1945*, London; Jonathan Cape, 1975. The quotes are from p. 126.
[58] Addison, p. 183.
[59] Addison, p. 182.

first meeting supported a new study of how regions related to local government, endorsed Beveridge's manpower study, discussed some vague ideas about control of the insurance business and some roughly framed ideas about reorganizing health services.[60] Perhaps the only effective action by the Committee involved land planning. It approved the idea of creating a Ministry of Town and Country Planning and late in 1941 urged that stiff penalties be imposed on abuse of land values or failure to register land.

In March 1942, the work of the Reconstruction Committee was absorbed into a new Committee on Economic Aspects of Reconstruction Problems, chaired by the Paymaster General, Sir William Jowitt.[61] With little change, this committee of the leading social ministers and the Exchequer continued until 1944, though later relabelled the Committee on Reconstruction Priorities under Sir John Anderson, Lord President of the Council. It was the cabinet committee which considered the Beveridge proposals and became the focal point for the intense debate over the costs of new social laws. As the issue became more urgent, and as party unity behind the war coalition began to flounder, another reorganization took place in November, 1944, when the Reconstruction Priorities Committee received overall command of several smaller cabinet committees, and took full responsibility for social security.[62] From early 1944 a sub-committee on full employment under Sir Richard Hopkins of the Treasury had been fighting a last ditch battle to reduce the cost of social legislation stemming from the Beveridge Plan. As was to become the normal sequence in expansion of the welfare state in the postwar period, government was becoming accustomed to spending money before it knew where it might come from. More importantly, though committed to Beveridge's ideas, the Cabinet finally began to examine its most crucial assumption, full employment itself.[63]

The cabinet debate over the full employment White Paper of

[60] First Meeting of the Reconstruction Committee PRO CAB 87/1, 1941. In fact, the rapid progress of land planning was one of the few wartime reforms that advanced steadily during the war, at least until Churchill dismissed Sir John Reith, the first Minister, in the cabinet shake-up of early 1942. See Addison, pp. 175–7.

[61] PRO CAB 87/2, 31 March 1942.

[62] PRO CAB 78/7, 30 November 1944.

[63] PRO CAB 124/204, 11 January 1944. The Committee had basic responsibility for preparing the White Paper on Employment, discussed below.

1944[64] was conducted in the light of the government's commitment to the Beveridge Plan and in anticipation of the approaching election. Perhaps these conflicting circumstances explain why Britain did not produce a more substantial bridge between its strong commitment to social welfare and its less well-defined commitment to full employment. The secret debate took place in a shifting setting with the more orthodox Keynesians located in the Economic Section of the cabinet under James Meade, himself the originator of one scheme to link social security contributions to economic conditions,[65] and the still hesitant policymakers within the Treasury, where Hubert Henderson was highly skeptical of Keynes' principles to guarantee full employment.[66] To assess the possibilities of an official policy of macro-economic management Sir John Anderson created a Steering Committee on Employment Policy, chaired by Sir Richard Hopkins of the Treasury, a self-confessed novice in wage and price policy.[67] The main political objective of the Steering Committee was to arrive at some agreement on how Britain might implement a full employment policy before the independent study then being made outside the government by Beveridge could be published. Despite the intensive efforts of the Economic Section of the cabinet, no detailed agreement was possible, in part because the Treasury and the Keynesians in the Economic Section had very different estimates of postwar income, inflation and unemployment problems.

[64] The Treasury, *Statement of Government Policy for the Creation and Maintenance of Full Employment*, HMSO, cmd. 6527, 1944.

[65] Essentially, Meade's proposal was to have variable social insurance contributions so that social insurance could be used as an instrument of macro-economic management. Meade's ideas were first advanced in 1941 and later developed in the Economic Section. See Alan Booth, 'The Keynesian Revolution in Economic Policy-making,' *Economic History Review*, Second Series, **36**, February 1983, pp. 103–23, for documentary sources.

[66] Keynes consistently favoured Meade over Henderson in the debate over probably postwar income and even warned Meade about the problems this created for a full employment policy. See John Maynard Keynes, *Activities 1940–1946. Shaping the Post-War World: Employment and Commodities*, The Collected Writings of John Maynard Keynes, Donald Moggridge, ed., v. 27, p.216 and p. 345.

[67] N. Rollings, '"The Keynesian Revolution" and Economic Policy-making: A Comment,' *Economic History Review*, Second Series, **38**, February 1985, pp. 95–100. This article is part of a continuing historical controversy over when Keynes's influence in the Treasury became substantial. See also, G. C. Peden, 'Keynes, the Treasury and Unemployment in the Later Nineteen-thirties,' *Oxford Economic Papers* (New Series), **32**, 1980, pp. 1–18. The Booth article, cited above, reviews the main contenders.

Their disagreement was only the first of many clashes between the Treasury and less orthodox official advisors over the possibilities of linking wages to social policy. In any event, on receiving an early draft of Beveridge's proposals, Keynes expressed 'wild enthusiasm.'[68] But Keynes' more theoretical mind led him to caution Beveridge that the inflation problem had been underestimated and that Beveridge's insistence on pay-as-you-go was not a primary question. More confident of the ability to control the economy, Keynes wrote that the future can be 'left to look after itself.' As Treasury concern over paying for Beveridge gained momentum over 1942, Keynes showed himself more politically astute than Beveridge, and favoured keeping the 'fiction of contributory system' rather than enter into a prolonged controversy over revision of the income tax.[69] As part of Keynes' general strategy of encouraging separate funds in order to acquire policy instruments for macro-economic management, he also wrote to Sir Richard Hopkins to support the use of special social insurance funds 'to preserve sound accounting, to measure efficiency, to maintain economy and to keep the public properly aware of what things cost.'[70] But in the press of postwar decisions, Keynes could not keep pace with all policy choices. His efforts to reduce the cost of the Beveridge Plan helped make it acceptable to the Treasury,[71] but he later resisted Meade's efforts to extend the detailed planning of social insurance to more detailed plans for full employment. Had these exchanges run their full course, the underpinning of the British welfare state might have been more coherent, even to more directly relating wage and social policy as Meade had consistently urged.

The official reception of the published report in December, 1942, was very different from its popular reception. Indeed, legislation on the Beveridge plan may be unique in British policymaking history because it was so clearly a case where popular

---

[68] John Maynard Keynes, *Activities 1940–46. . .*, pp. 204–5.
[69] Keynes, p. 223.
[70] Keynes, p. 225.
[71] The initial estimates were as high as 800 million pounds which Keynes and others thought would not be acceptable to the Treasury. Keynes worked to have about 150 million pounds removed by reducing benefits, and estimated that the cost to the Treasury would not be more than about 100 million. See Keynes, *Activities. . .*, pp. 229–55.

expectations determined government reactions, rather than following the obscure and confidential course of most British lawmaking. Its wide acceptance in principle is no doubt due to the fact that nearly all powerful critics were divided among themselves, and unlike France, institutions provided few ways for them to coalesce. The Director of the Confederation of British Industries announced 'we did not start a war with Germany in order to improve the social services,' but a group of 120 major industrial leaders endorsed the plan.[72] When Beveridge submitted his final draft to the government in October, 1942, Jowitt prepared a secret report for Churchill. Jowitt thought that an attempt to conceal the report would be damaging and Churchill, consumed by preparation for the Casablanca Conference, noted 'once it is out he (Beveridge) can bark to his heart's content.' In the following weeks it was clear that the government was quite unprepared to respond. The Minister of Information first insisted that no official facilities might be used in announcing the plan, then relented to permit a press conference and BBC publicity, and finally withdrew all mention of the plan in official propaganda, including a pamphlet already being circulated to the troops in the field.

Beveridge's apprehension that his Plan might then be sidetracked led him to publish his case independently in late 1944.[73] The Plan itself sold over 600,000 copies.[74] But it was his behaviour over 1943 that no doubt finally terminated his career in government. Beveridge had written several newspaper articles in late 1942 to publicize his plan, and then formed a group to press for adoption, the Social Security League, under G. D. H. Cole. This was clearly not done by conventional Whitehall barons. By the end of 1943, Sir John Anderson, who had inherited the problems of financing the proposals at the Treasury, instructed officials that they were to have no contact with Beveridge. Even Keynes, then immersed in postwar international finance, became cautious.[75] Beveridge himself turned to politics and was for a short time a Liberal MP only to be defeated in the 1945 election. He had crossed the Rubicon that divides politics from the British policy

[72] There are several accounts of the Plan's reception on which the following paragraphs are based: Addison, pp. 211–28; Harris, pp. 419–51; and Beveridge himself, *Power and Influence*, pp. 319–33.
[73] *Full Employment in a Free Society*, London; Allen & Unwin, 1944.
[74] One was even found in Hitler's bunker. Harris, p. 420, fn.
[75] Beveridge, *Full Employment. . .*, p. 330

process, a common act in French politics, but a fatal error in Britain. The obstinance that made his life in Whitehall uncomfortable again appeared when he formed a private committee of young, radical economists to demonstrate that his full employment assumption could work. It was of couse additional evidence of his arrogance that he thought it possible to produce a study of unemployment that might compete with Treasury views.[76]

The parliamentary debate reflected the severe tensions that the Plan generated within the major parties and is one of the earliest manifestations of the dulling political effect of large social issues. Anderson presented the government's case in Parliament in a detached manner, accepting the proposals in principle and endorsing family allowances and some form of comprehensive medical care. Of the 23 legislative proposals based on Beveridge's recommendations, only one was rejected outright (nationalization of private insurance), but reservations were made on another six. Clearly the Treasury was playing for time. The situation was uncomfortable for both the Tories and Labour. During the war a group of about 40 Tory reformers had formed a Reform Committee led by Quintin Hogg (later Lord Hailsham). They were dismayed by the government's lukewarm reception of the plan and were only brought into line with a mandatory whip. They had hoped that the government would seize the initiative and form a Ministry of Social Security. Labour was no less strained and 97 backbenchers voted against the government's motion.

One of the odd political characteristics of shifting modern states to social questions has been that these issues often more severely divide the left than the right. In the 1943 debate the Labour Party was clearly more embarrassed than the Tories. Given the strong backbench pressures, Attlee was forced to chip away at the government motion, but he was basically sympathetic to Churchill's insistence that the war was Britain's top priority. The debate provided the scene for another bitter encounter between Bevin and Morrison. Desperate not to appear disunited with an impending election (there had been none since 1935), Morrison rose to the occasion with a defence of the plan intended to rally the backbenchers behind the Party without appearing disloyal to the

[76] Even in early 1943 the Whitehall machine was mobilized to exclude him. In January, 1943, Lionel Robbins, the government's chief economist, advised Anderson against bringing Beveridge back because he was not a genuine expert on unemployment. Harris, p. 343, fn.

Coalition. Many thought his speech the best of his career, but it only won him the enmity of the left wing and later plagued his political career.[77] Bevin too was a staunch supporter of Churchill, but his reservations about the motion were rooted in his feelings about the essential autonomy of the labour movement, already apparent in his earlier rejection of family allowances and his insistence that accidents be given special treatment. He tried to soothe backbench feelings in a meeting of the Parliamentary Labour Party. It ended in an angry scene with Bevin so incensed over his critical reception that he threatened to resign from the Party and did not attend a party conference again until 1944. His loyalties were under enormous strain because Churchill refused to contemplate repeal of the 1927 Trade Disputes Act which was a major roadblock to exercising full union power over the Labour Party.[78]

The secret Treasury report on the financial aspects of the Beveridge Plan merits some detailed attention because it signals the gradual decline of Treasury influence that had been so often exercised between the wars. Essentially, the Treasury had no better card to play than a waiting game in the face of highly speculative estimates about future costs of war debts, defence and tax burdens.[79] Introduced with the caution that it would be 'prudent to avoid at this time large and continuing commitments unless there is an overwhelming case for them,' the report clung to the controversial and doubtful assumption that unemployment would remain above 8 per cent, that benefits might be recklessly increased and that the tax burden would inexorably extinguish economic growth. The report of the Reconstruction Committee was even more revealing of how far the British welfare state had yet to travel.[80] Among other things, the report lamented the loss of the Poor Law threat of prison for the unreformed unemployed, the ease of obtaining unemployment insurance, and objected to excessively high child benefits. Though not generally known to the

---

[77] Donoughue and Jones, *Herbert Morrison*, pp. 314–16.
[78] Bullock, *Life and Times of Ernest Bevin*, v. 2, pp. 221–9.
[79] Chancellor of the Exchequer, *Financial Aspects of the Social Security Plan*, PRO CAB 87/3, 11 January 1943.
[80] Committee on Reconstruction Problems, Official Committee on Beveridge Report (Phillips Committee), PRO CAB 87/3, 14 January 1943, pp. 20–2. In addition, there were detailed comments on the unworkable aspects of nearly every benefit offered by Beveridge.

public, within Whitehall the launching of the British welfare state was a stormy and controversial decision.

A few weeks later Churchill, nearly exhausted, made a speech on reconstruction about the difficulties of peering 'through the mists of the future' with no reference to Beveridge's report. What was happening was a political realignment similar in importance to the breakdown of tripartite government in France, but within the more rigid limits of Parliament. By late 1943 Labour was considerably ahead of the Conservatives in the polls, and winning important by-elections. But of particular importance in assessing the role of policymaking was the wide area of agreement actually being carved out within Whitehall. In an odd way, that was to become characteristic of policymaking in the advanced welfare state, policymakers were agreeing to a remarkable degree while politicians were struggling with their priorities and fumbling important social questions. There were two such areas of great importance, education and health.

Although education seldom aroused as intense feelings in Britain as in France, in many respects it became the twentieth century surrogate for religious politics. From a policy perspective, educational reform makes an interesting contrast with social assistance and social insurance in British politics because it was handled so differently. The bright young leader of the Tory reformers, R. A. Butler (later Lord Butler) was President of the Board of Education throughout the war, and as early as 1941 had begun to circulate his ideas about reform within the cabinet. Churchill was alarmed that a religious fight would divide the war effort, and so Butler turned to the historic British policy technique of boring from within. By the end of 1942 he had obtained general agreement from the Treasury, eliminating the obstacle that so easily plagues every British reformer.[81] A clever politician, Butler also used Labour's clamour for immediate action on the Beveridge Plan as a foil to rally Tory backbenchers to his education reform. In December, 1943, his bill went forward and became the Education Act of 1944, the most important educational legislation since 1902. It promised to raise the school age to 16, created the Ministry of Education and set in motion plans to integrate British secondary education. It also ensured that the public schools would have a place in the new system. Butler skilfully papered over the

[81] This description is based on the account in Addison, p. 173 and pp. 237–9.

question of scholarships for low income students in the public schools, and to his chagrin was forced by Churchill to reverse his claim for equal pay for women teachers. Still, it was a model of Whitehall policymaking and another tribute to a ministry that had adroitly skipped over political potholes since Sir Robert Morant.

Health has of course never enjoyed the natural clients and organizational network that an educational system provides, but it is worth noting how much progress was made during the war. As we have seen, the Ministry of Health had twenty years of experience and was no novice in Whitehall ways. As soon as the Beveridge Committee was appointed it submitted a paper to the cabinet outlining its special interests. Though the heady days of Newsholme and Newman had passed, it was in close touch with the British Medical Association (BMA). As early as 1938, the BMA had issued a report agreeing to the integration of voluntary and local hospitals and to the extension of health insurance to dependents.[82] As in other social services, the war served as a nationalizer in important ways. The Emergency Medical Service added 153,000 hospital beds to the public domain, a third of all hospital places in Britain. The Ministry established its own Committee on Post-War Hospital Policy. In 1940 a Medical Planning Committee was established with the BMA, the Royal Colleges of medicine, and representatives of the Ministry's medical officers. Although it was later to retract many of its proposals, a war-inspired BMA reported to the Ministry in 1942 that all doctors should be linked to a national medical service, that health centres should be organized with group practices, that doctors should accept part of their pay as a public salary, and that a regional hospital study should be undertaken by the Nuffield Hospital Trust. These recommendations were assembled in a government White Paper in 1944.[83]

Beveridge's assumption that his plan would only work with free basic health care was, of course, a push for the Ministry of Health. The Ministry does not appear to have noticeably changed its plans, but it seized the opportunity. The Ministry submitted a memo to the Committee on Reconstruction Priorities in 1943

[82] PRO CAB 87/1, 23 June 1941.
[83] For a summary, see Addison, pp. 179–81. A longer account can be found in Harry Eckstein, *The English Health Service*, pp. 133–63.

outlining in detail the organization of a national medical service, its areas, administration and links to the medical profession.[84] In a curious repetition of the interwar reforms and consistent with the exclusion of local government from most major British policy decisions, special care was taken to point out how local government areas were unsuitable, though the claim was still made that local authorities would have a voice in the local provision of service. When the matter arose at the cabinet level only a year later, the Ministry was still firm on the limitations to be imposed on any such arrangements. Should the local councils be aware of health matters, there must be no question of their being at liberty to discuss these matters publicly.[85] Perhaps the greatest handicap of British local government in entering into the policy process has never been its intrinsic problems, which are similar to those found in all democracies, but simply that it could not easily imitate Whitehall methods.[86] Again, there is fascinating evidence on progress toward integrated medical care made in Scotland while England searched for a solution. Though the report still adheres to the health centre scheme to organize local doctors, later virtually abandoned, it notes how Scotland had already made progress toward linking local and medical services in community health centres.

So long as education can avoid the political bog of religious differences, reforms can be made with relative ease. Its beneficiaries, the parents, are joined in a common concern for their children, its clients; and its officials generally come from the same professional background. As seen in the acrimonious debate over implementing the National Health Service in 1947 and 1948, and similarly bitter debates in other democracies, health has few of these advantages. Its beneficiaries demand the most expert and complete care; its clients are professionally divided, yet hold critical powers over the service; and debate at the highest levels readily descends to ideological polemics. In some respects, social insurance

[84] Ministry of Health, A National Health Service, London; HMSO, 1944, cmd. 6502. For the discussion of the White Paper in the Priorities Committee, see PRO CAB 87/7, 30 November 1944.

[85] PRO CAB 87/7, 27 January 1944.

[86] In an earlier report to the Priorities Committee, every ministry joins in explaining why local reorganization is undesirable. Education feared it would upset the forthcoming bill. Labour did not want to see the health plans jeopardized. See PRO CAB 87/7, 24 July 1944.

and social assistance are the most easily managed from the centre, not only for technical reasons, but because the beneficiaries are politically weak, the framework rests on autonomous organization, and top policymakers make little progress without exercising political skill and discretion. Because education ‘ and health have immediate, personal impact, costs are less controversial, while the gigantic, anonymous cost of social security can be affected politically. In the interwar period and during the war, the costs of expanded social services and social assistance preoccupied most governments. By 1945 the discussion of resources was almost entirely at the level of national government, one of the critical features in the transformation of liberal into welfare states.

In this respect, the British policy debate over funding the Beveridge Plan, or more accurately, the components of the Plan that the government wished to act on, is the first major test that many modern welfare states would experience as social security spending grew. It was not a test of intentions or even of policy choice as much as a test of whether the financial and budgetary structures that had been severely challenged in the interwar period might continue to exercise dominance over the new state structure. The political complexities of such trials easily escapes socio-economic models because the various responses are rooted in the particular development of fiscal and financial institutions. For many reasons, the early trial of strength between the British Treasury and social policymakers was an unfortunate combination of events. Britain was in this sense an unfortunate pioneer of the welfare state because she inherited enormous debts from both world wars and took them seriously.

For obvious reasons, debts permit traditional financial institutions to maximize their influence. The ease with which this was done in 1919 and 1920 has been described, as has the way in which the Treasury imposed controls on public employment in order to squash the ambitions of the early social ministries. In a couple of years, the hopes and plans of the past twenty years were simply swept away. The price of Treasury dominance was that for a decade Britain staggered from one social and economic shock to the next with almost no coherent social policy direction. Britain paid dearly for her inability to cope with the welfare state in the 1920s. An entire generation lived under the threat of poverty and the Victorian attitudes that so many wished to expunge lingered on.

The situation was not as simple after World War II, but the Treasury was still making dismally inadequate estimates. In an estimate made in 1944, the Treasury forecast that all social spending in 1945 would be £450 million, rising gradually to £831 million by 1965! The cost of pensions was to merely double in the next twenty years, and the added contribution of the Exchequer to social expenditure to be a mere £200 million.[87] With the typical cynical self-interest that characterized Treasury responses to social problems since 1919, another paper proposed that in order to achieve a pension reduction, it would be best not to provide any explanation of the reduced pension rates.[88] The utter futility of this ostrich-like attitude can only be seen by careful analysis of how the Treasury gave way. Faced with the social reality of the Beveridge Plan, the cabinet held its first full discussion of the Plan in January, 1943. Sir Kingsley Wood, the Chancellor and former insurance attorney of fame for his work on behalf of private insurers between the wars, led the attack. He accepted family allowances, but argued for larger contributions and the restriction of free medical care to low income groups. It was agreed that defence was the first priority and that the government should 'wobble', though with his customary tact, Attlee warned that this would not work.[89] At this time, the Treasury was estimating that total social spending would be about £700 million, with £265 for Beveridge programmes.[90] This was about three times 1941 expenditure so one might say that the Treasury had already lost the battle and was simply putting on a good face.

Beveridge was too much an old Whitehall hand not to realize that his Plan would have this reception, and had taken pains to arrive at a 'deal' with Keynes in 1942. As we have seen, Keynes would support the Plan in the Treasury if Beveridge worked out ways to reduce the additional costs to no more than £100 million for the next five years. The capriciousness of Treasury behaviour can only be appreciated by recalling that when the Treasury representatives on the Beveridge committee in 1942 saw how sweeping his proposals were likely to become, they withdrew to fortify themselves in the safety of their chambers. Of course,

[87] PRO CAB 87/8,'Estimated Income and Expenditure', 26 April 1944.
[88] PRO CAB 87/8, 5 June 1944.
[89] Addison, pp. 220–2. Wood's comments appear to be based on the Phillips Committee report, cited above.
[90] PRO CAB 87/13, 5 February 1943.

Beveridge was aware of Treasury hostility and made several efforts to consult them. In mid-1942, the Treasury apparently relented and offered Beveridge the assistance of Keynes and Lionel Robbins, the chief Treasury economist and its main economic planner, in order to work out 'details.'[91]

The basic Treasury position was outlined by Wood in a memo to the War Cabinet.[92] As a litany of the conventional Treasury defences of the past twenty years, it showed how little the Treasury had changed. As a revealing exposure of future vulnerabilities of social protection, it suggested how little the Treasury was thinking about the future. For one thing, Beveridge had already displayed his Edwardian fears by estimating possible unemployment at 8.5 per cent, but the Treasury thought that he may well be under-estimating it. In fact, Britain experienced a severe labour shortage after the war. Second, the Treasury viewed the doubling of employer and employee contributions with apprehension though even at this modest level the costs would be no more than 10 per cent of national income. In a few years, the costs were to be double this amount. Third, the Treasury honestly stated that cost-of-living allowances were probably too small, but offered no solutions. In the absence of more imaginative options, most states soon geared social benefits to inflation. Fourth, the Treasury correctly pointed out that the economic disincentives of contributions would fall disproportionately on labour intensive industries, but there was no discussion of new taxes that might avoid this pitfall. Perhaps the one flash of political acumen in the document is the observation that asking the five million new pensioners to pay contributions for a decade with no payments was politically unreal.

The main cabinet briefing paper on the Beveridge Plan was prepared by Sir Thomas Phillips, permanent Secretary of the Ministry of Labour. Another indication of Beveridge's problems working with others appears, for Phillips was one of the young clerks hired by Beveridge in 1909 to help organize Labour Ex-changes, but he does not appear to have either supported the Plan or to have prepared a report that would set ministers' minds at ease. If Harris' description, 'cautious, patient, unimaginative, and excellent agent of other men's ideas', is correct,[93] then it probably

[91] The material in this paragraph comes from Harris, pp. 408–12.
[92] PRO CAB 87/3, 11 January 1943, 'Financial Aspects of the Social Security Plan.'
[93] Harris, p. 375.

would not have helped had Beveridge been on closer terms with Phillips. In any event, his report makes a fascinating comparison with the broad political interpretation of the welfare state in France, Sweden and later, in Germany. In effect, Phillips did 'his Master's bidding' in the finest Whitehall tradition, and his comments anticipate the complications and problems that would divert the Plan from its original intent.

The Phillips Committee raised numerous questions.[94] It questioned how the government would enforce provisions that the self-employed contribute and expected considerable abuse of the requirement to include domestic servants. It raised the difficulties of a standard minimum of care: the means test, the variations of rents and inflation. Death benefits were left hanging largely because it looked difficult to combine the 100 million pounds of existing private policies with the national system. The strong resistance of the National Union of Miners and their advocate in the cabinet, the Minister of Fuel and Power, to integration of worker compensation in the scheme was noted. On family allowances, it advocated what became the rule, the exclusion of the first child (the Treasury wanted to exclude the first two children), and suggested cutting the family allowance nearly in half. In fear of increased costs, it defended the flat-rate pensions and specifically rejected the New Zealand scheme of variable pensions based on income. The question of whether there should be a single social security ministry was by-passed. Most damaging perhaps was the conclusion that the full employment assumption need be 'placed at least beyond the region of reasonable doubt, before the plan can be adopted.' Lastly, it accepted Beveridge's stipulation that 'the gap between income during earnings and during interruption should be as large as possible for every man.' Clearly, it was a useful document for hard-pressed ministers, but it also dramatically revealed how little had been learned over the past fifty years.

To argue that Britain stumbled into the welfare state would be excessive, but from a policy perspective it is clear that avoiding political obstacles regularly took precedence over exploring new ideas or developing national priorities in a coherent way. Few nations were able to advance forcefully, but some began to build the links between wages and welfare that were to become the

[94] PRO CAB 87/3, 4 January 1943, 'Official Committee on the Beveridge Report.'

hallmark of social democratic states. The White Paper itself was probably pushed because of the threat of demands for more benefits being organized by Beveridge and his Social Security League. Treasury economic advisors were divided over the scheme with Lionel Robbins and James Meade pressing for more recognition of Keynesian methods, with more conservative advisors, including Keynesian critics such as Hubert Henderson, holding back.[95]

Whether the scheme made economic sense is not the immediate point. Were some more coherent fiscal foundation for the British welfare state devised, including some link to industrial conditions, there might have been an opportunity to develop a clearer link to wages and prices. Ironically, Treasury apprehension, and very likely Treasury lack of skill, produced a system that was difficult to control politically and backfired to leave the Treasury vulnerable to opportunistic political intervention. Britain ended up with the worst of both economic worlds, a system with little capacity to cushion economic down-swings and with little incentive to economize in order to achieve other policy goals on the up-swings. For the moment, it is noteworthy that so few structural changes were in fact embodied in launching the Beveridge Plan.

The common political theme running through all the early British reactions to social security is the ease with which political complexity was put aside. Throughout the preparation of the laws bearing on the Beveridge recommendations, as occurred forty years earlier, the consistent message was that local government is an obstacle and a handicap to effective policy implementation. One of Jowitt's early memos on reconstruction carefully pointed to all the problems created for Whitehall by British local government.[96] The Ministry of Health prepared a report on local government reform in 1943,[97] but it never seemed to receive serious consideration. When the Ministry of Health discussed nationalizing medical care with the local authorities in 1943, it was assumed that they would passively accept the larger areas needed for the new organization. Medical distrust of local supervision was

[95] It is interesting to find Henderson, director of the Central Statistical Office, engaging in one of the most common Treasury devices to curtail ministerial appetites, under-estimating national income. Unwilling or unable to devise more delicate instruments, the Treasury was left with only blunt instruments. See PRO CAB 87/13, 13 May 1943. On that occasion, Keynes lodged a reservation.
[96] PRO CAB 87/2, 4 February 1942.
[97] PRO CAB 87/3, 11 July 1943, 'Local Government Reform.'

no less acute than it was forty years ago.[98] In early 1944 the Cabinet was still worrying about how to make sure that prying and unreliable locals did not complicate plans for national medical care.[99] Once the Labour government moved ahead with these plans, Bevan, as Minister of Health, had no time to study local government even though plans were considered.[100] Thus, it is hard to avoid the conclusion that this was, and to a large extent remains, a political system where the political complications of those outside the charmed circle of policymakers in London are most unwelcome.

Were other states doing better? As suggested in Chapter 1, what we mean by 'better' must be read against the backdrop of history and in relation to the particular political circumstances of each country. Spared the disruption of war, Sweden was able to continue on its course even though progress was not as easy as often assumed by admirers of the Swedish model. Germany had the advantage of starting afresh and with substantial external encouragement to adapt its social policy precedents to democratic institutions. Out of this complex interaction, the foundations of co-determination were layed, and with it an implicit, if not explicit, recognition that labour and welfare were inextricably bound together. The United States continued to develop the social assumptions of the New Deal, but in a confusing and halting manner that made it incomprehensible to most Europeans, possibly even to Americans. Consistency of concept is perhaps clearest in the French case. With the departure of Laroque and Parodi social security took its political knocks, but it was founded on a view of state and society that had been developed in the 1890s to defend the Republic. There was certainly a grand design in the more simple sense of top policymakers building a rational model, but this was only a pale reflection of how an expanded welfare state was to affect state structures in all the democracies.

FRANCE: A FRAGMENTED WELFARE STATE?

Abstract models of the welfare state easily overstate the extent to which launching the welfare state was a planned, coherent effort.

---

[98] PRO CAB 87/13, 28 July 1943.
[99] PRO CAB 87/5, 10 January 1944.
[100] Michael Foot, *Aneuran Bevan* . . . , v. 2, pp. 263–4.

In doing so, they also underestimate the importance of politics, and in particular make it difficult to grasp how social policy, like earlier preoccupations of the democratic states, was brought within the orbit of democratic politics. Because the politics of policymaking in France are more diffuse and competitive than in Britain, and possibly more than in any democracy, the politics of the slow process of accumulating social legislation after the war, and of the shifting political alliances that entered into this process, must be clearly understood. In some respects, fundamental agreement was even stronger in France than in Britain, but in a more highly politicized policy process there were numerous hazards to any preconceived model of a welfare state. It is politically unthinkable that France might have assembled the political forces that enabled Sweden to forge ahead despite differences between the SAP, SAF, and the LO. Given the weak and fragmented conditions of postwar German government, it was equally unimaginable that the SDP might cooperate with a conservative government such as Adenauer's to link labour participation to welfare to form a new welfare state.

The political achievements of the welfare state, as in any other area of policymaking, must be judged against the complexity and uncertainty of political forces themselves, not against an external measure or rational model of what might ideally be achieved. We have already seen how Segelle's motion in early 1946 anticipated the breakup of tripartite government. The Socialists were unhappy with the Communist manoeuvre to change the electoral procedure for administrative councils so as 'to better confine (them) to union militants' (meaning Communists) and to diminish the possibilities of using worker participation in the councils to promote social awareness among workers. The Socialists were also well aware that registration for benefits in the workplace would favour the better organized Communist workers and enhance their chances to use supplementary social funds to promote the CGT. Yet the Socialists were agreed with the Communists that the mutual societies must not be allowed to reduce the localized *caisses* to chaos and understood that the chances of generous, inflation-proof pensions were better in alliance with the Communists.[101] The situation is typical of how politics and policy interlock in intricate ways in the

---

[101] *Journal Officiel*, Assemblée Nationale Constituante, séance du 19 mars 1946, Annexe No. 698, pp. 667–70.

French political system. There were no simple partisan boundaries for the major actors nor did institutions help reduce these cross-pressures to simple choices.

The choices were by no means easier for the main centre party, the MRP. In the elections for the Second Constituent Assembly, in June 1946, the MRP surpassed the PCF in popularity with 28 per cent of the votes and held 163 seats in the Assembly, the largest parliamentary group. Although the Communist minister, Croizat, still held office, the MRP had made a claim on social policy through Prigent, Minister for Population. To the MRP the new law on family allowances was of crucial interest because of its close relation to Catholic social philosophy, but the MRP was also prepared to give a larger role to mutual societies because many of these funds had been built up by benevolent Catholic *patrons*. The Family Allocation Law of August, 1946, was in many respects the only initial proposal of Parodi and Laroque that was fully achieved, but there was the precedent of the 1932 law. As we have seen, expanding the original law was possible because of substantial concessions. The law made family support a universal payment. It included pre-natal payments for seven months, a *prime* or additional payment for the third child, a rising scale of benefits as families grew larger, and was to be paid to the person responsible for the children, not the head of the family. The cost of family allowances increased about 50 per cent, but the law was passed unanimously.[102]

As we have seen, the French did not attach as much importance to pensions as did the British. In part, this was a function of French individualism which implied that each person was responsible for his or her old age. More important, pensions raised the difficult issue of *généralisation* or universal benefit which is, in turn, linked to the more clearly defined notion of equal rights. As a stopgap measure, since 1945 the Liberation government had been paying more generous pensions to those earners covered under existing legislation, but in 1946 there were still only 1.7 million persons receiving state pensions.[103] In addition, there were about half a million government employees in various pension plans built up over the past fifty years, none of whom were prepared to give up

[102] Galant, pp. 79–83.
[103] See the report on the pension law in the *Journal Officiel*, Assemblée Nationale Constituante, Documents, Annexe No. 1215, séance du 25 avril 1946, pp. 1206–10, from which this description is taken.

their special treatment, and about half a million persons with private pension plans. The law of May, 1946, proposed that state pensions should be extended to all earners over 65 years, adding about two million persons to the state pension rolls. The reason for the small number is that both agriculture and self-employed insisted on separate plans. The supervision and organization of agricultural pensions, many of them invested in mutual insurance societies, remained with the Ministry of Agriculture. The result was that French pensions remained a complex assortment of state, mutual and private protection against old age which was not substantially changed until the Fifth Republic.

Thus, as politics returned to normal in France, by the end of 1946 there was a collection of laws: the original *ordonnance* of 1945 providing sickness and disability insurance; a pension law; a family allocation law; and a law providing assistance to the aged poor (also passed unanimously in September, 1946). After long negotiations, a system was worked out to include agricultural workers in 1947.[104] What stands out in comparison to Britain is that although the political differences in France were in many ways deeper and more ideological, so much legislation was passed with unanimous or nearly unanimous votes.

In part, the ingrained French tradition of *solidarité* was at work, but politically there was, and remains, the much closer connection of politics to policymaking in the French system. British politicians tended to concentrate on those aspects of the expanded social security system that added to their political visibility and reputations; in a more intricate political world, French politicians could not allow themselves to be seen in opposition to social reform and yet wanted to preserve the particular privileges of their constituent groups or supporters. The effect was that parties and leaders more closely identified with particular aspects and programmes of the new structure. As Galant describes, the PCF fought the MRP over the *caisse unique* and the role of private insurance; the MRP fought the PCF over politicization of the entire system; and the Socialists fought the MRP over the *caisse unique*, but wanted strong worker control. Devising the French welfare state was always at least a three-cornered political game.[105]

---

[104] See *Journal Officiel*, Assemblée Nationale, Documents, Annexe No. 1207, séance du 2 mai 1944, pp. 840–55.
[105] Galant, p. 108.

Unlike Britain, where the direction toward increased care outlined by the Beveridge Plan did not radically depart from studies
and legislation over the past forty years,the multiplication of social
legislation in France signified an abrupt departure from the slow
progress of the Third Republic. For the traditional parties, the
Radicals, Radical Socialists and other small splinter parties of the
centre, the new laws were a threatening imposition on established,
largely private or mutual, forms of protection. The first attack on
the new system came when it had been barely established. Led by
André Morice, a Radical spokesman, the opposition conducted an
interpellation or interrogation of the government in mid-1946 with
the avowed aim of overthrowing the government over several key
issues. The centre's main concern was that the *cadres*, essentially
the white-collar workers, not be forced to join the new system.[106]
In addition, there was severe criticism of the new pension law as
a threat to mutual insurance, though the real target was again to
protect the voluntary retirement insurance that more privileged
earners had placed in mutual funds. The similar debate in Britain
did not begin until the 1950s.

The same attack was made on the proposed accident compensation law. In a veiled attempt to associate the new proposals
with Vichy, Morice lashed out at 'the organization as strongly
centralized as the one so recently condemned.'[107] His motion was
to formally guarantee the autonomy of social insurance for the
cadres; to affirm the role of mutual societies in the new system; to
limit the broad representation of beneficiaries; and to declare that
a plurality of *caisses* was not inconsistent with the new plan. Other
conservative Deputies from the MRP denounced CGT control of
the administrative councils and the growing bureaucracy of the
new social security system. Essentially, the opposition wished to
undermine the key elements of the new system: popular representation,the central *caisse* for equalization purposes, and universal
contributions.

The opposition was regarded seriously for the Minister for Social
Security, Croizat, made a judicious and persuasive reply. He

---

[106] The term *cadre* is almost untranslatable. It is basically an occupational
category of more highly skilled employees, ranging from banking to engineering.
Since the war, the *cadres* had their own union, the Confédération Générale des
Cadres.

[107] *Journal Officiel*, Assemblée Nationale Constituante, Débats, séance de jeudi 8
âout 1946, pp. 3062–95.

assured his critics that the privileges of the *cadres* would be protected and that a consultative committee (*commission paritaire*) would be organized to provide direct liaison with them. As in Britain for sickness insurance in 1911, he promised that the individual concerns of doctors would be protected and that patients would have a totally free choice of physician. He reassured the moderates that mutual societies would prosper under the new system (as indeed proved to be the case) and that they would be well represented on the administrative councils. They had already acquired most of the positions put aside for experts on these councils. The dispute over the elections had escalated because the CFTC chose to boycott the 1947 elections in the face of overwhelming CGT strength. Croizat, himself a Communist, said that orders would be given to the CGT to make room for smaller unions. In conclusion, he noted the accomplishments to date: old age pensions in the Paris region had been doubled, maternity benefits had been tripled, and the state had accepted nearly all the cost of the permanently disabled. On the whole it was a persuasive performance, although in the vote of confidence the 116 Radicals and Radical Socialists still voted against the majority of 399. There followed a unanimous vote of confidence of all 426 Deputies present.

There were continued attempts to neutralize the measures surrounding the French welfare state, but the essentials were preserved. The basic differences in British and French political controversy over the welfare state bear examination. First, when the French centre attacked the system politically, it was a comprehensive and frontal attack on the foundations of the social security system. British attacks rarely led to a rethinking of the system itself, but were over details of benefits, rules and ministerial behaviour. Second, French supporters at the highest levels of government had to recognize the acquired rights and status (*droits acquis*) of earlier programmes. Those who would benefit as a class or occupation were insistent that their old commitments remain intact. Third, the French political debate was consistently about the principles of the new system, in particular preserving the political power of early contributors (both professions and unions) and insisting on a degree of elected management. In Britain it was much easier to sweep aside such criticism and political actors outside Parliament had more limited effects. The French system was organized outside the state.

Fourth, the major political concern in France was that the

new semi-public organization guard its autonomy, in part by recognizing the autonomy of ancilliary organizations. In contrast, the British political system concentrated political power in Parliament and the cabinet, though of course many organizational compromises were made with special interests. What is striking is how different the framework of political action is in the two systems: the French pushed ahead as opportunities arose and later dealt with political objections; the British preferred a model solution, leaving political complications to ministerial ingenuity or, that failing, to the undisputed supremacy of the Parliament itself.

Constructing the French welfare state depended on political mobilization and on continual political care. Much of the doubt cast on the French welfare state concerns the ebb and flow of political support. In particular, social policy advocates lament a structure which is so politically sensitive. For example, when the MRP was pressing its law for the 'economically weak' in late 1946, the PCF and the Socialists began to quarrel over their respective powers within the system.[108] None of the parties was opposed to the *allocation de vieillesse* embodied in the law, which was essentially a simple answer to the problems of the elderly poor that in the form of the Poor Law controversy had so long hampered the development of the British welfare state. Similarly, when the law on social security elections was finally debated in late 1946, the issue was not over the system itself, but how parties and politics might be reconciled with the managerial problems of the semi-autonomous system.

As tripartism began to crumble over 1947, the privileged occupations achieved their goal of separate identity and separate organization within the new system. Quite the reverse of the argument that the French administrative state is overpowering; for some months over 1947 the system worked on temporary rules and benefit schedules until a new study group, the Commission du Travail, could be assembled. British administration is rarely subjected to such excruciating demands once laws are passed. The Commission Surleau recommended that there be autonomous *caisses* for artisans, industry and commerce, professions and agricultural owners. Essentially, the social security system, as is the

[108] The information in this and the next paragraph is taken from Galant's account of the attack on the system, pp. 108–12.

case with many other landmark policies in France, became an examination of French political principles. It is not that French policymaking is 'more' or 'less' political than British, but that it is political in fundamentally different ways. To wish that this were not so is to wish that France had another kind of democratic politics.

In comparison, the politics of British policymaking left serious gaps in the new British welfare state. There was, for example, an abortive Conservative attempt to construct a more coherent pension plan in late 1943, but strong differences between the partners in the Coalition government made basic agreement impossible. As a result, it was barely noticed that the elderly poor were left with meagre support. The administrative exclusion of the Friendly Societies, the main arm of the 'Approved Societies' incorporated in the 1911 Act, was easily accomplished.[109] Britain did not endure the prolonged struggle that France had with its mutual societies, but neither did Britain debate pension issues. Not until the 1960s did the Labour Party, under pressure from Professors Abel-Smith and Townsend,[110] turn to the inadequacy of old age pensions. The effect was to preserve meagre pensions and thus to preserve means-tested supplementary support, resurrecting many of the same demeaning conditions that had been institutionalized in the Poor Laws for over a century.

NO FINAL SOLUTION: BRITISH HEALTH

Because the National Health Service (NHS) was and remains the centrepiece of the British welfare state, it deserves special attention as an illustration of social policymaking under the British parliamentary system. Although it may seem almost irreverent to

---

[109] The recommendation to abolish the Friendly Societies under Beveridge was made in early 1944. See PRO CAB 87/6, 10 January 1944. The political power of the Friendly Societies was still formidable; the National Amalgamated Society had 3 million members and the Prudential Society 4 million. PRO CAB 78/7, 15 January 1944. According to Henry Pelling, *The Labour Government, 1945–51*, London; Macmillan, 1984, p. 100, there were still 315 MPs pledged to the Societies in 1946 of whom 199 were in the Labour Party.
[110] See Heclo, pp. 263–73. The main opponent within Labour ranks was again the TUC who feared that pension reform would hurt accumulated union pension funds.

place the highly respected and until recently highly effective British health system in a policy context, it displays many of the weaknesses and strengths of British policymaking. As we saw in Chapter 2, health policies had been a central concern of British politics since the elaborate plans of Morant, Newsholme and Newman were made toward the close of World War I. Because health touched vital nerves throughout British society, the way in which nationalization took place, and its consequences, are an acid test of the British policy process. First, ordinary plans had been made by the Tory Minister of Health, Willink, prior to Labour's victory in 1945. The Conservative proposals would have preserved more autonomy for the vital actors in any health system, the doctors, the hospitals and local health services, but was cast aside. Second, so complex an activity as health care inescapably reaches across levels of government, but medical antipathy toward local government and traditional Westminster distrust of local governing capacities meant that fixed boundaries were drawn between national and local responsibilities. Third, nationalizing health required a confrontation with a strong and suspicious professional group, the doctors. Bevan's rhetoric to the contrary, costly compromises were made which placed severe constraints on how new medical services and new forms of health care might emerge over the coming years.

Judged solely by the main political objective, the NHS was an immense success. Judged in terms of the capacity of the new system to adapt to new conditions, to redefine the aims of health and to accommodate a variety of political interests, the NHS became an awkward and unwieldy instrument. Complete nationalization perpetuated difficult problems untouched. The result was three major reorganizations over the next forty years which constantly disrupted and confused policymaking for health. As in the case of the nationalized industries, 'arm's length' soon became a justification for partisan interventions in the health service that seldom produced effective solutions. The political elite of the system, the specialists, and their teaching and research hospitals in London, were carefully protected, producing new Labour attacks on the system in the 1970s. The possibilities of a more flexible national-local interface in the system was ignored, but returned to plague the system in the 1980s. The workhorse of any nationalized system, the family doctor, preserved his professional autonomy, but at the price of neglecting the reorganization of medical services at the local level and of refusing to examine the critical link between general and specialized practice. As in so many instances, the Westminster government wished to simplify its problems, making the NHS a perpetual source of political discontent.

The plans prepared by the Ministry of Health in 1943 and 1944 tried to build political intricacies into nationalization, that is, to incorporate political complexity within the policy itself. This was to be done by placing general budgeting and planning powers in Whitehall; relying heavily on local government for the execution of the plan and for the management of hospitals; and keeping a contractual link to the voluntary sector in order to relate local hospitals to the national objectives. In many respects, the basic aims and procedures had not changed radically since the plans of Newsholme and Newman were put forward. At one point the British were considering a well-developed French policy instrument, the contract, to merge the boundaries between public and private interests.[111] The early plans were not for a unified service, but more accurately for four interlocking organizations with somewhat different objectives: local joint councils, health service councils, a hospital service and group practitioner service.[112] What British policymakers lacked was a way to orchestrate a structure that might have addressed the diverse problems within a single health service. Unlike France, the notion that linkages were the core political problem was largely ignored.

Bevan benefited from much wartime preparation. His own loyal organizer from Wales, Tom Johnstone, had been closely following events in Whitehall for some time. There was the Socialist Medical Society, a group of about 2,000 socialist doctors, but their demands were eventually cast aside. In 1943, the Labour Party had endorsed a report, *National Service For Health*, calling for a salaried, public medical profession, but this too was abandoned. There was of course the not unfavourable report of the BMA from 1942, and these discussions continued during the war. Typical of Whitehall

[111] Throughout this discussion, I rely heavily on Rudolf Klein's account, *The Politics of the National Health Service*, pp. 1–30. Eckstein's book, written before official records and memoirs became available, concentrates more heavily on the BMA. For Bevan's perception and tactics, see Michael Foot, *Aneurin Bevan,* v. 2, pp. 100–215.

[112] PRO CAB 87/7 23 December 1943, 'Draft White Paper on Comprehensive Medical Service.' The Nuffield Provincial Hospital Trust had submitted a report objecting to abolition of voluntary support for hospitals, meaning totally free hospital care.

preconceptions was a report to the Reconstruction Committeee in 1944 noting that the doctors were making the impossible demand of wanting to appoint their own representatives to local councils while retaining the right to publish their independent evaluation of the new scheme. Within the iron-clad boundaries of British policymaking, the idea of such free-floating debate and discussion 'would confuse the functions of an advisory council with those of a consultative or negotiating committee' and therefore was rejected.

A great many political hurdles had been crossed while the Conservative Minister for Health, Henry Willink, was still in office. Without denying Bevan's skill and endurance in getting the Health Act through Parliament and implemented, many of the concessions that Bevan later extended and revised were no less improvised and opportunistic. Willink's concessions to the BMA were considerable. In June, 1945, the cabinet decided, first, that there would be no Central Medical Board, that is, a national governing body for the medical profession. Essentially, the NHS would have to work through a private political agent, the BMA. Second, it was decided to revive the once discarded idea of Local Insurance Committees. The forum to air medical and local interests was abandoned, though as the system developed local doctors' committees nonetheless insisted on having special status in the NHS. Third, doctors would not be forced to occupy jobs in areas with less medical care. Fourth, health care centres would be only experimental. This was in some ways the most serious compromise for it meant that individual general practice would prevail while no alternative medical organization was being built.

Lastly, and echoing Morant's tactic of making a special appeal to the specialists (consultants), the prestigious, endowed voluntary hospitals, most of them in London, would be exempt from full nationalization and keep their self-governing status as teaching hospitals.[113] These decisions are an interesting commentary on the British policy process. They were clearly intended to avoid the most serious political conflicts embodied in nationalized health, while still enabling the government to claim it was making radical reform. But the duplicity of mutual consent meant that neither aim was accomplished: the BMA still rebelled once the system was in force and the doctors did not escape partisan politics. Whatever the social and economic merits of the proposal, and of

[113] Klein, pp. 15–16.

those devised by Bevan later, the anticipated resolution of political differences over health policy was poorly imagined and poorly framed.

In any event, the unravelling of political fortunes in the 1945 election meant that the new law would be Labour's problem. Views differ over whether Bevan made a substantial change in the original plan for health nationalization. Many of the fundamental political compromises had already been made, and he did not try to reverse most of them. Perhaps the most important change did not affect doctors as much as local government for Bevan quickly decided that there should be a complete take-over of local hospitals. The ability of British politics to over-ride local concerns on health policy corresponds to similar choices in other areas. Because this is such a persistent quality of British decisionmaking, it is worth noting that Herbert Morrison, who as Lord President of the Council considered himself the 'ringmaster' of domestic policy, resisted complete takeover. The champion of London and proud of the London County Council hospital system, Morrison again offended more dogmatic minds in the Party by favouring a system of joint management.[114] In one respect, history proved Morrison right. For the next forty years the NHS would be preoccupied with how to organize hospital management.

Bevan got his bill through the cabinet in fairly short order. Full hospital nationalization was approved in October, 1945. In December, it was agreed in cabinet that the sale of practices would be terminated, but Bevan was generous in deciding compensation.[115] In fact, he made progress by using public money quite lavishly. The compliance of the voluntary hospitals was smoothed by promising to roughly double their income.[116] At first he included a salary element plus capitation fees for general physicians. The salary element might have been later extended to control their incomes. Under pressure from the BMA, Bevan jettisoned this minor control, and with it the hopes of the Socialist

[114] Klein, pp. 18–20. See also Foot, *Bevan*, pp. 132–3. Oddly enough, Donoughue and Jones make only a passing reference to the fight, p. 358. They do note, p. 369, that Bevan refused to discuss his plans with the TUC, much to Bevin's distress.
[115] PRO CAB 134/697, 29 November 1945. The average value of a practice was estimated to be 1000 pounds/year. The government agreed to compensation totalling 40 million, about twice the annual rate.
[116] Pelling, *The Labour Government. . .*, p. 104.

Medical Association that salaries would be controlled. Of course, the specialists had already preserved their additional income, as well as their privileged access to nationalized hospitals. Like Lloyd George, Bevan had the presence and boldness that seemed to impress the medical elite. As in 1911, part of his tactic was to use money to drive a wedge between the specialists and general practitioners.

By the time the bill was announced in December, 1945, Labour had foregone most of the strong controls once imagined essential to a truly national health service. The doctors had recovered their private role in the system, and their special interests were further protected by amendments in 1949. The state had accepted the professional gulf separating special and general practice and, indeed, had institutionalized it in the hospital system. Nor would the hospitals shed their private role or deny specialists private access through 'pay beds,' whose use, cost and mere existence became a thorn in the side of the NHS. The salary plan was totally ditched so that doctors continued to be paid as in 1911, and with very little supervision of the quality or organization of care beyond their own doctor committees. The costs were badly underestimated and in the first year it was necessary to return to the Treasury for an additional 153 million pounds.[117] All this is not to say that for other reasons the NHS might not be a desirable solution to Britain's medical problems. But compared to other European countries, the proposals had been seriously considered since 1920, so it was hardly a leap in the dark.

The internal political conflicts of nationalizing health itself went unresolved, most of which erupted again over 1948. Nor were the long-term political concerns of government protected. There were three major reorganizations of the NHS in the coming years. Aside from the obvious appeal to the left, it is hard to see whose political interests were satisfactorily embodied in the 1946 Health Act. Though it rests on several other bitter disagreements within the Labour Party, the final irony is that Labour allowed one of their great achievements to become the apple of discord. As Britain's economy deteriorated over the late 1940s, it was necessary to impose charges on prescriptions and dental care. Although Bevan

---

[117] See PRO CAB 134/518, 6 May 1950, 'Committee on the National Health Service.'

first accepted this necessity,[118] it rapidly escalated into a major internal fight in the Labour Party and, in turn, contributed to their political exile from 1951 until 1964. The imposition of charges was not necessarily a minor issue, but the ease with which the very party that accomplished so much descended into the most bitter internecine political warfare says a good deal about the strange divorce of politics and policymaking in Britain.

WELFARE STATES INSTITUTIONALIZED

By 1950 the modern welfare state had not only become a social and economic reality, but a political reality. Many hoped that more social protection and social equality would usher in an amended version of a socialist state, or at least a modified form of a social democratic state. Reminiscent of European fears of the mid-nineteenth century over mass suffrage, many on the right saw these changes as the end of political democracy. Like the socio-economic explanations of welfare states that rely so heavily on the quantitative measures of results, a simple partisan view of how demands were shaped by welfare states ignores the complexity as well as the diversity of the policy processes set in motion by welfare states. The design, finance and implementation of new social and economic policies to protect citizens' well-being rarely eluded established institutional practices. Decision making was rarely polarized along partisan lines nor was there much effective resistance to an enormous increase in the policymaking capacities of each democracy.

The critical political step was to achieve a degree of institutionalization of the new social policies. The interwar period has been emphasized as the crucial historical turning point because the institutional foundations for welfare states were being built between 1920 and 1940. That this could be done in the midst of political reaction, political failure and political turbulence is a tribute to the resilience of democratic decisionmaking. It is also a

---

[118] The poor financial planning for national health was in part the result of the alliance of Dalton, Chancellor of the Exchequer, and Bevan in the late 1940s. Dalton barely mentions the health service in his papers. See Pimlott, *Dalton. . .*, pp. 450–522. Bevan's attack on the party over prescription changes appears to be largely the product of his rivalry with Gaitskell. See Williams, *Gaitskell. . .*, pp. 236–58.

pre-condition of the later institutionalization of social rights and social assistance that for the most part escapes models of the contemporary welfare state that lack historical and political sensitivity. Again, the reasoning is reversed from that found in socio-economic models of the state. In some states with very advanced social policies, such as Germany, democracy crumbled.

The argument is not that Social Democrats were ill-advised to relax their social demands in the 1920s, but that even with elaborate social policies Germany failed to build a democratic framework of sufficient strength to resist fascism. The social programmes, many of them with high levels of union participation, were not part of German democracy, but part of a strategy among reactionary politicians to subdue the left. The point is not what politics did to society, but what society was unable to do for politics. The crucial intervening condition is the institutionalization of social politics *within* each democratic system.

Though we are not directly concerned with postwar development of social policies, the Occupation and the long period of conservative rule under Adenauer tended to reinstate the old structure. The initial phase of intense nationalism by the left under Schumacher made this choice much easier.[119] There was never any serious question that German workers might not recover the extensive social protection built between the wars, but it remained organizationally distinct from political institutions. In an odd way, co-determination, the effort to bring workers directly into the formation of industrial policy, reinforced the institutional distinction between the state and its components. In a repetition of history, by the time the Social Democrats came to power in 1969, the right had already reinstated the German welfare state and deprived the socialists of their natural appeal.

There were a number of outstanding issues on the Swedish welfare state agenda at the end of the war and it is important to note that their political resolution was fraught with difficulty for the SAP. The development of the 'active labor market policy' or plans for gradual transfer of industrial ownership to the state tends to overshadow the fact that many questions about social benefits that were resolved in Britain, France and other major European

[119] For a review of these events, see Arnold J. Heidenheimer, *Adenauer and the CDU*, The Hague; Martinus Nijhoff, 1960; and Gordon D. Drummond, *The German Social Democrats in Opposition*, Norman, OK; University of Oklahoma Press, 1982.

powers in the immediate postwar years were not yet settled in Sweden. Unemployment insurance was still voluntary. The plan devised in 1934 had been expected to cover 700,000 persons, but in 1940 included less than 200,000 persons. The gap was closed under strong pressure from the LO, which became the dominant force in the new unemployment protection agency, the Samsorganization.

The internal political struggle was a serious one, the LO wanted a compulsory, universal system with control resting with its own officials in the Samsorganization. The SAP preferred state-subsidized union unemployment funds with more fiscal control. The political difficulty arose, as it would in many national pension plans after the war, over the terms and conditions of price and wage indexing of state pensions. The reconciliation of these options emerged from studies done by the LO. One of the origins of the 'active labor market policy' was the work of the LO economists, Gösta Rehn and Rudolf Meidner, in the late 1940s to link the union strategy for collective industrial ownership to an acceptable compromise to pension reform.[120]

Nor had the policies for old age pensions been settled at the end of the war. As a stop-gap measure, 17 per cent of the elderly were on various forms of supplementary benefits. Again, the SAP took the more cautious approach, favouring flat-rate pensions. Their proposals were rejected in parliament and a commission appointed to draft new plans. In the commission, the LO forces were split with the Cooperative Societies against a compulsory universal system, the white-collar workers (TCO) favouring integration with older voluntary schemes, and the more militant LO representatives holding out for a compulsory system. Government indecision was costly politically. In the 1956 elections, the SAP suffered a setback. Faced with the loss of white collar support and further alienation of its Agrarian Party support, the issue was deadlocked in the Riksdag and pension reform only slipped by when one Liberal member decided not to vote.[121] Again, the SAP snatched victory from the jaws of defeat and was able to recover its position in the 1960 elections. As Esping-Anderson points out, the welfare state was always a potential threat to wage solidarity. Had the SAP

---

[120] See Heclo, pp. 127–41.
[121] See Heclo, pp. 228–53; Madsen, pp. 255–67; and Esping-Anderson, *The Social Democratic Road to Power*, Princeton, NJ; Princeton University Press, 1985.

postwar policies of linking social protection to income policy rather than to wage solidarity been accepted, it would have been more difficult, if not impossible, to pursue the more ambitious policy of an 'active labour market policy' in the 1960s.

As most experts on Scandinavian politics agree, it is not likely that the peculiar juxtaposition of social and economic conditions that enabled Sweden to move toward a more complete integration of the welfare state and wage policy are likely to be reproduced in the major democracies. Even so, SAP dominance did not guarantee that satisfactory policy solutions would always be found. The persistent search for more egalitarian policies was only possible in Sweden because of the close alliance of the LO with the SAP although even their good relations were sometimes strained. But at their worst, SAP-LO relations were never as poor as in France, where parties and unions seemed to be in perpetual opposition, and where the labour movement was ideologically deeply divided.

While one might imagine the TUC assuming such an integrative role, it was never politically possible on either the national level or within the labour movement. Nationally, the TUC was primarily concerned with union political rights, not social benefits. Internally, the TUC had always been a number of industrial fiefdoms whose barons fought among themselves as much as they fought for a vision of a new society. In contrast, by 1960 the LO membership was not only nearly 70 per cent of earners, but the LO organization was drastically consolidated from 44 to 29 union federations over the 1960s.[122] Thus, the LO's ability to steer unemployment and pension plans toward the achievement of a more equal society involved a political concentration of power that the TUC, the CFDT and even the DGB could never accomplish.

What is crucial to understanding the changing context of policy-making after the 1945 social policy reforms is that social policy had become an integral part of the institutional life of each democracy. Henceforward, countries would be arguing *about* national social security, not *whether* it should exist. Of negligible concern in most abstract views of the welfare state, it was nonetheless institutionalized in very different ways. The aggregate effects of constructing welfare states were similar across most democracies: more income for the aged; better relief from unemployment; improved

[122] Madsen, p. 236.

social services, etc. What differentiated the democracies was that the basic decision to build a welfare state was made under such different political circumstances, and, as accomplished, had such diverse institutional form. The essential political feature of the democratic welfare states was that they could respond in different ways, and could build very different frameworks to move toward social protection and social equality.

Many of these structural features were visible by 1950 although their importance in determining the future political life of the democracies was still only dimly perceived. The transformations of party and group politics was perhaps least visible in Britain because many of the groups, if not the parties, had been debating social welfare since 1890. Some important social ministries, such as education, had been skilfully mobilizing and organizing their professional clients since 1900. By 1920 the medical profession was already heavily dependent on public resources, and the BMA argued over the next step toward universal health care since World War I. What differentiates Britain politically is that few such groups actually became active participants in the organization and management of the new welfare state of 1945. Influential groups, such as the doctors, could obtain privileged positions at the top of the new welfare heirarchy, but insisted on remaining organizationally aloof at the local and regional levels. The result was that the British welfare state was perhaps the most thoroughly nationalized of all welfare states.

In France nationalization was not completed. Many of the political controversies that whirl around the French welfare state were in fact incorporated into the system. The parties could not formulate simple positions for or against welfare and were torn by the social laws of 1945 just as much as they were, and remain, cross-pressured by nearly every major social issue of French politics. The distrust of the state meant that major groups successfully insisted that they have legally defined roles in the new structure. The elections for administrative councils were soon embraced by the intense political competition that surrounds all French elections. Though still far from the social democratic image of the welfare state, the foundations for active participation and direct control were formally institutionalized. Early social service groups, such as the mutual insurance societies, succeeded in establishing a claim, reserving practically the entire agricultural population for their own care and obtaining important rights within the social security administration. The unions saw their historic claim to worker control of social security partially realized. The occupational groups, especially those already favoured by government subsidies for social purposes such as the miners, railway workers, civil servants, etc., carved out their special rights. As in the case of local government reform, the effective centralization of social policy in France may be more apparent than real. It looms in significance against the loose structure of the Third Republic but it was hardly the single structure that Parodi and Laroque had dreamed of building.

In a policy framework, the institutionalized capabilities of the two new welfare structures could hardly be more different. Relying on firm central direction, the British administration acquired strict short-term control over social spending, but very little long-term vision or design. Exactly the same problems have been observed in British economic and industrial policy.[123] Almost the reverse was the case in France. In the short term, adjustments and changes proved to be laborious and painful. But the system incorporated sufficient fundamental features of French politics to make it vulnerable to the changes in mood and preferences of French citizens. If not as nationalized as the British system, it was clearly more politicized just as labour relations, industrial policy and economic policy were. Even though organized 'outside' the French state, the social security system was closely attuned to French political realities. In contrast, the British system was more effectively located 'within' the British state. Each state found ways of reconciling a major new area of public activity with its political traditions and habits. The political differences are not apparent without isolating the context of policymaking itself

[123] See, for example, Andrew Schonfield, *Modern Capitalism: The Changing Balance of Public and Private Power*, London; Oxford University Press, 1965.

6

Democracy and States of Welfare

By 1950 the institutional frameworks of the contemporary welfare states were in place. The institutionalization of welfare policies was inevitably the product of political reactions to the dislocations and social unrest between the wars, but the unexpected growth and prosperity of the next thirty years proved to be nearly as challenging as launching social protection and social justice had been in the preceding fifty years.[1] Although it must wait for a subsequent study, the political future of the welfare state was assured. Prosperity meant that there were few departures from political realities from 1950 until roughly 1970. Less noticed amidst the recent 'crises' of welfare states is that by 1950 the major struggle over the nature of democratic values, the reconciliation of expanded social welfare with old constitutional assumptions and administrative practices, and the incorporation of social issues into the daily life of parties and groups had been accomplished.

As has been argued throughout this study, the concept of social needs and the idea of social justice varied immensely among the liberal democratic states. In one state, Germany, there were in

---

[1] The memories of the unexpected economic dislocations following World War I were still alive, and many of the young officials and economic advisors who became prominent in the 1920s were still in power. The basis for British pessimism was outlined in the Treasury economic and financial report on the Beveridge Plan. Neither Churchill nor Attlee assumed that Britain could rely on as generous support for European reconstruction as had been given to support the Allied war effort, but the harsh terms of the first American loan to rescue the British economy as inflation and shortages multiplied were not anticipated. On the 1947 economic crisis, see Kenneth Morgan, *Labour in Power, 1945–1951*. . ., pp. 330–58; and Philip Williams, *Hugh Gaitskell: A Political Biography*, London; Jonathan Cape, 1979, pp. 195–235.

fact very weak foundations in democratic precedents and capabilities. With the possible exception of Britain, assumptions of democratic viability, as well as virtually unlimited governmental capacities, no more applied at the turn of the century than they do today. If anything, from roughly 1890 to 1950 political and institutional constraints defined the course of change in the development of welfare states even more than today. It is no doubt true, as Briggs argues, that the distinguishing feature of this departure was that states began to intervene more freely in marketplace relationships.[2] But this elemental truth does not help us compare the differing ways that the liberal states went about moderating market forces, much less provide the basis for comparing the enormous differences among the early democracies in how they had already devised ways to guide economic and social forces that might threaten democratic stability well before social policies preoccupied governments.

In a comparative historical and political account of welfare states, there must be some more explicit basis for dealing with the moral dilemmas and policy risks that states actually encountered. For the predominantly liberal ethic of the early democracies, some general conception of a free market or even of social threats to democracy generated less controversy than did the key liberal political assumption, namely, that human reason could replace the hierarchical and absolute moral structure of governance of the old monarchies. The resurrection of these ethical problems in the 1980s may be regarded as evidence of moral stagnation or as proof of the underlying choices of all welfare states,[3] but from roughly 1850 to 1900 principles were often at the core of politics rather than relegated to academic retreats. As in the late nineteenth century, the recent revival of philosophical dispute about the principles of welfare states should be taken as a sign of their vigour rather than their weakness. More relevant to this study, viability of democratic political processes is revealed by the extent to which

---

[2] Asa Briggs, 'The Welfare State in Historical Perspective,' *Archives Européenes de Sociologie*, **2**, 1961, pp. 221–58. A more Marxist version with similar conclusions is Dorothy Wederburn, 'Facts and Theories of the Welfare State,' *Socialist Register*, 1965, pp. 127–45.

[3] See John Rawls, *A Theory of Justice*, Oxford; Clarendon Press, 1972, 2nd edn; Ronald Dworkin, *Taking Rights Seriously*, London; Duckworth, 1977; and C. B. Macpherson, *Democratic Theory: Essays in Retrieval*, Oxford; Oxford University Press, 1973.

the welfare policies have become commonplace in our lives even though fundamental philosophical issues remain unsettled.

Democracy might be defined as a way of living with moral dilemmas. This was certainly the case in the late nineteenth century as each democracy began a profound search for new social values that seemed consistent with their democratic traditions. Whatever the philosophical similarities of these searches, it took place under different political and constitutional conditions. For this reason, the tendency to see the emergency of welfare states as a function of socio-economic changes ignores the most challenging aspect of the change, how societies were to be linked to states in developing social policies. Democratic ingenuity and resourcefulness is somehow eliminated from a transformation where these were, and remain, essential political skills. To be sure, there is a superficial functional similarity to the policy changes as governments moved from the care of the poor to assisting the unemployed and eventually to see broad conception of income maintenance. From the initial democratic experiments of the late eighteenth century (and earlier for Britain) liberals conceded that those with no resources deserved assistance. The first chapter in the emergence of welfare states, then, was amending the rules of charity and providential help, which, as we have seen, proved to be more difficult for Britain than for any other working democracy.

Certainty about the rules of the political game and the limits of parliamentary power proved to be a handicap in devising new social policies. Important as social protest and economic dislocations were, the process of relating social and economic needs to political values took place slowly, often in ways that have no apparent link to more easily measured material problems or to more dramatic social events. As we have seen, social legislation was generally accepted by overwhelming votes so that the conflictual view of the emergency of welfare states, whether grounded in class politics or economic failure, requires some modification if we are to grasp the political complexity and the political creativity of the early social policymakers. Their talents were tested roughly in proportion to the stability and effectiveness of political institutions. If Britain does not rank as highly on an institutional scale of democratic flexibility as it may (or until recently did) on international social spending batting averages, it is because policymakers felt less need to re-examine the political and constitutional assumptions of British democracy.

In building workable links between states and societies, the first requirement was new ideas. Somehow the role of ideology has fallen by the wayside in our explanations of welfare states. The early social policymakers were quite aware that they were introducing new values, but they varied in how they anticipated these values might change democratic governance. Freeden writes, 'An ideology is judged not only by its originality but by the construction it puts on the facts and ideas it is confronted with.'[4] How policymakers perceived and formulated social policies is our only source of how social ideas changed modern politics. If Britain's achievement seems more doubtful in a policy context, it is because traditional, institutional norms were more readily isolated from the challenge of social policies. The intense moral tone of British discussions of social reform is all the more graphic because of the political ease of actually designing and implementing new social policies.

To a greater degree than in other welfare states, the values of sobriety, thrift, self-help and temperance dominated the early debates about the British welfare state. As Richter writes of Dr John Toynbee, Arnold Toynbee's father, 'he regretted suffering but never questioned the system that produced it.'[5] In other words, the 'world was divided between those who did good and those to whom good was done.'[6] This produced what Himmelfarb has called the 'culture of poverty' that is, the assumption that poverty had a moral purpose.[7] The severe moral judgments of the time are found in the records of the Salvation Army, the Charity Organization Society and the Christian Social Union. Moral fervour arose again in the 1930s with the campaigns of Archbishop Temple and in the 1950s with the unswerving moral purpose Titmuss attached to the welfare state.

Social policies are so deeply imbedded in national traditions that few countries chose to follow another's example, but the peculiar tone of British reformers was noted by Tocqueville,

[4] Michael Freeden, *The New Liberalism: An Ideology of Social Reform*, Oxford; Clarendon Press, 1978, p. 45.
[5] Melvin Richter, *The Politics of Conscience: T. H. Green and His Age*, London; Weidenfeld and Nicolson, 1964, p. 320.
[6] Richter, p. 312.
[7] Gertrude Himmelfarb, *The Idea of Poverty: England in the Early Industrial Age*, New York; Random House, 1985; see also the earlier article of E. P. Hennock, 'Poverty and Social Theory in England,' *Social History*, **1**, 1976–77, pp. 67–91.

Boutmy, Halévy, Durkheim and Jaurès. Their reservations were not about the substance of British social policies, but about the rationale the British provided. Halévy writes of the 'disinterested Machiavellianism' of British social policy[8] and there are numerous statements of leading social reformers to suggest that an apolitical tone pervaded the British welfare state at its beginnings, and may continue to do so. There are a number of possible explanations for this curious lacunae in British public policymaking. First, as Sir Ernest Barker wrote many years ago, the idea of the state is 'little grasped in England.'[9] (The fact that he said 'England' and not Britain or the United Kingdom suggests the conceptual limits the British impose on themselves.) Second, moral intensity was sometimes a substitute for empirical innovation and experimentation. Writing on the strength of the positivist tradition in British social thought, Annan notes 'the passion . . . for laying down how men ought to behave and how society ought to be organized . . . has led on to neglect the new techniques for describing how in the first place men do behave and how far organizations of society are capable of changing their behaviour.'[10] For intellectual reasons as well as political circumstances, the British brought few new organizational or implementation concepts to their version of the welfare state.

Almost to a man, the new liberal and social thinkers could be extremely brutal in their judgements on their fellow citizens. Hobhouse wrote that in a proper society 'Idleness would be regarded as a social pest, to be stamped out like crime.'[11] At the height of the new social consciousness in government circles, Sidney Ball worried about 'the moral destruction of the next generation' and a generation before Cobden had feared that social reform might 'sap forever the self-reliance of a class' (meaning the ruling class).[12] A young Beveridge thought favourably of the 'complete and permanent loss of all citizenship rights' through the judicious use of public institutions, emigration and even starvation.

---

[8] W. H. Greenleaf, *The British Political Tradition: The Rise of Collectivism*, London and New York; Methuen, 1983, p. 380.
[9] Greenleaf, p. 195.
[10] Noel Annan, *The Curious Strength of Positivism in English Social Thought. . .*, p. 18.
[11] Stefan Collini, *Liberalism and Sociology. . .*, p.139, fn.
[12] Collini, pp. 28–32.

Pigou favoured 'violent indifference' toward the 'wreckage of society'. The Social Darwinist suggestion that sterilization, exile and policing be used to create a fit society[13] had a certain appeal.

Whatever the intellectual explanation of the tenacious grip of the British 'numerical approach to happiness'[14] the conceptual foundation of the British welfare state remained individual radicalism, not a form of social radicalism. Unwillingness to confront the social role of the state is at the root of most of the continental suspicions of British social policy. The intellectual search for new social ideas was divorced from government and leading policymakers could treat social reformers in cavalier ways. Idealism was not absent, but it could not find a place in the political and constitutional structure of British politics. The weak appeal of socialism is perhaps the best demonstration of such insularity, certainly not to be explained by the absence of class politics. Socialism emerged, as Freeden writes, as 'one of the most elusive, vague, and diverse concepts in British social and political thought.'[15] Harcourt's lament that 'we are all socialists now' was not about the reconstruction of an ideology but about the pragmatic acceptance of social policies.

Individual radicalism had a long tradition in British social and political history and the continuing debate about the nature of British collectivist thought reveals a gap in British thinking that unavoidably appeared in the early conception and design of their version of the welfare state. The political effect was that the scope of the state expanded with very little re-examination of political and constitutional assumptions. The British state looked inward rather than outward. The tendency was not new to British politics. As political rhetoric and political ambitions soared in the 1880s, one detailed examination of the early development of party politics in Britain notes how 'primary interests was inevitably its own very private institutional life.'[16] The result was a policy process that

---

[13] Both quotes from Freeden, pp. 184–5.
[14] Freeden, p. 15.
[15] Freeden, p. 25. In contrast, the more profound reconstruction of social thought by Weber and Durkheim was in part motivated by their doubts over Marxist solutions to their respective national problems. In particular, see Dominick LaCapra, *Emile Durkheim: Sociologist and Philosopher*, Ithaca, NY; Cornell University Press, 1972, pp. 187–244.
[16] A. Cooke and J. Vincent, *The Governing Passion: Cabinet Government and Party Politics in Britain, 1885–1886*, Brighton; Harvester Press, 1974, p. 22.

seemed devoid of passion and ideas. The Webbs are perhaps the best example for their apolitical outlook that led them from Balfour to Stalin. Beatrice Webb once wrote 'We don't much care what persons or which party gets the credit.'[17] Like many of the early social reformers in government, the good they were about to bestow on the British people was so persuasive and so predictable that political complications and political justifications were secondary. Though it goes beyond the range of this study, the same suspicion of political competition continues in the writing of the postwar high priest of British social reform, Richard Titmuss.[18]

British political institutions made benign remove from politics possible which is not to say, of course, that the advocates of a new social state were themselves unwilling to use political ploys, flattery and even some deception to further their designs. No other major democracy was permitted such indulgences. In this respect, Heclo's comment that the 1920s was an important period of 'unlearning' is perfectly accurate as a policy statement, but applied to Britain in contrast to Sweden or nearly any other continental democracy quite misleading in terms of institutional and political change.[19] In Britain, Labour could replace the Liberals with barely an institutional tremor. Indeed, our institutional prototype of British governance, correctly or not correctly, is largely derived from the interwar period when official power, ministerial intrigue and Treasury manipulation were at their zenith. Unlike Sweden, which was to spend nearly two decades reflecting on how best to realize its vision of a welfare state, British policymakers could arbitrarily push aside policy options, pursue their political ambitions and even make some horrendous policy blunders quite undisturbed by either liberal or socialist ideas.[20]

---

[17] W. H. Greenleaf, *The British Political Tradition: The Ideological Heritage*, London and New York; Methuen, 1983, p. 380.

[18] Titmuss avoided any elaborate political justification for his ceaseless efforts to extend British social policies, yet he was masterful in working with politicians and civil servants. His political naiveté is partly revealed in his admiration for wartime solidarities as seen in his official account of social problems during the war, *Problems of Social Policy*, London; HMSO, 1950. On his distrust of the uncertainties of democratic politics, see his essay 'Welfare "Rights", Law and Discretion,' *Political Quarterly*, **42**, no. 2, April–June 1971, pp. 113–32.

[19] Hugh Heclo, *Modern Social Politics. . .*, p. 312.

[20] While it may appear unfair to British scholars, the striking aspect of much British intellectual and administrative history is the meticulous effort to identify what *was* the collectivist dimension of British politics. French, German and most continental scholars have no doubt about what collective authority means though

For the other European democracies, and in a converse way even for the development of German democracy, the formulation and implementation of new social policies was inextricably part of fundamental changes in the patterns of party politics and in the assumptions of parliamentary rule. However confused and uncertain the nascent socialist parties were in their regard for parliamentary democracy, they became a political force that set the stage for the clash of political ideas and, as democracies were threatened by facism, came to the rescue of the governments they had despised at the turn of the century. The design and implementation of new social policies, often much less generous than those in Britain, invariably provided the setting for a reexamination of basic institutional assumptions. Political instability meant that the institutional requirements and consequences of new social policies had to be closely examined. Constitutional and political realities did not permit the simple superimposition of new policy goals, new fiscal relationships or new administrative powers on old institutional frameworks.

As we have seen, the emergence of new social policies during the Third Republic was barely distinguishable from the struggle to create a workable form of republican democracy. In the 1880s the moderate republicans, most notably Waldeck Rousseau, studied the problem of extending the laws of association so that workers could enjoy the organizational rights extended to farmers, merchants and businessmen. The early reform of public assistance, the formation of *bureaux d'assistance publique*, became a republican, and later a socialist, principle. In effect, the French were struggling with their Jacobin revolutionary tradition which severely restricted group activity. To counteract this tradition, a new doctrine was devised, *solidarité sociale*, which was, to be sure, a politically opportune idea, but which was also one that Bourgeois, Millerand, and Jaurès endorsed in defence of democracy. The development of social legislation in France was not so much to remove social

of course the philosophical and moral choices are often similar. Continentals argue *about* definitions of the state, while the British more likely argue about whether there *is* a state. See, for example, early citations on the collectivist meaning of Adam Smith, Jeremy Bentham and J. S. Mill. On Mill's impatience with British government early in his career, see John Stuart Mill, *Essays on England, Ireland and the Empire* (Collected Works), John M. Robson, ed., London; Routledge and Kegan Paul, 1983. On the continuing ambiguity, see John Baker, 'Social Conscience and Social Policy,' *Journal of Social Policy*, **8**, no. 2, 1979, pp. 177–206.

pressures from politics, but to assert that each French citizen was entitled to the support needed for him or her to be a productive and active member of society.

Thus, the juxtaposition of individual and social morality was virtually the reverse of that found in Britain. Fitness to enjoy the liberties of democratic rule were not established by one's ability to avoid pauperism, sloth and intemperance. Producing the conditions for the free exercise of liberties was conceived as a responsibility of good government. Logue calls this 'social liberalism', that is, the persuasion that the 'dissolving effects (of individualism) on society were counterbalanced by the secular accumulation of social bonds.'[21] These ideas were not uniformly shared by French policymakers, but they were the driving force for the Bloc des Gauches and most coalitions of the left since the turn of the century. Social legislation was placed in the framework of achieving social solidarity.

Although admiration of German idealism among the new generation of republican philosophers was shared with their British new liberal colleagues, the semi-official philosophers of French social reform had much greater effect because their thinking coincided with the political stabilization of the Third Republic. Though many of the leading solidarist thinkers were not politicians, the emphasis of both philosophers and politicians on secular education reveals their political priorities. They worked through the French educational system, most notably using the influence of the Ecole Normale Supérieure to spread their doctrine. Alfred Fouillée, the Maitre de Conference at the Ecole Normale who influenced Durkheim, wrote that there are two social questions: capitalism and labour, and capitalism and Latin verse.[22] Durkheim himself was appointed to the vacated Sorbonne chair in pedagogy of Ferdinand Buisson,[23] the leading republican in organizing laicist education, and even when later preoccupied with his sociological explanation of solidarity Durkheim continued to teach his course on educational methods.

[21] William Logue, *From Philosophy to Sociology: The Evolution of French Liberalism, 1870–1914*, Dekalb, IL; Northern Illinois University Press, 1983, p. 207.
[22] LaCapra, p. 59.
[23] Buisson was on the forefront of the battle for laicist primary and secondary schools for thirty years, and was Jules Ferry's advisor on education in the 1880s. He later espoused Leon Bourgeoise's idea of social solidarity, pressed for female suffrage and advocated proportional representation. See Logue, pp.89–91.

The point is not that the French devised a perfect theory of society to accompany social legislation, but that the harmonious interaction of state and society became an integral part of the French concept of the welfare state. Despite the slow progress of social legislation in France, institutions were seen as the mediators between excessive individualism and societal discord. Social legislation acquired a continuity of purpose within French institutions that was perhaps unequalled by any other democracy. For Durkheim, as for many French legislators, complex institutions were a requirement of modern politics. 'Institutional pluralism'[24] meant that diverse organizations were needed to mediate relations between citizens and the state, and social organizations were part of this structure. Social policies were not simply new governmental functions, but efforts to enhance the participatory vitality of French politics, to create new associational links among French citizens, and to enable the less privileged to become fully active, responsible members of society.[25]

Possibly the most important objection to the socio-economic theories of the welfare state is their cavalier treatment of the varied conceptual responses of each democracy to social needs and social justice. Under an autocratic state, both the liberals and the socialists of Imperial Germany had much less opportunity to build a concept of the welfare state in relation to their own political problems. As we have seen, many of the political tensions between social policies and redefining the state were perpetuated in Weimar Germany. Formidable institutional barriers hampered the successful integration of social policies and democratic governance. As can be seen in both Weberian ideas and in the Social Democratic reactions, social policies became entangled in ideal concepts of the state. The rejection of the problematic nature of social knowledge and the uncertainties of democratic politics made the institutional autonomy of social reforms a desirable alternative.

In the critical effort to redefine the role of the state in society, Sweden and the United States are perhaps the polar cases. In Sweden a peculiar form of political and economic vulnerability plus

---

[24] Logue, p. 24.

[25] In so far as Durkheim expressed an interest in socialism, it was in the French tradition of Saint-Simon. The revolutionary Marxism of his day seemed as destructive as excessive individualism. On his social logic, see Steven Lukes, *Emile Durkheim: His Life and Times: An Historical and Critical Study*, London; Allen Lane, 1973.

the extraordinary patience of leading Social Democratic figures combined to fashion an entirely new framework for welfare states. Oddly enough, whether this experiment will actually work remains in question,[26] but there is no doubt that it provided a rationale for one of the most elaborate systems of social protection among the democracies. Although less has been said in this study about the United States, it is an important illustration of the institutional diversity that welfare states may take. Social security was not intended to challenge the pluralist assumptions of American politics. Given the immense social and economic diversity of the country, it was virtually impossible to shape an embracing ideology of social change so that the United States emerged as a welfare state with its liberal political foundations virtually untouched. The period of intense self-examination of political assumptions does not begin until much later than the scope of this study, that is, with the War on Poverty in the 1960s.

The institutional and political requirements of building welfare states between 1890 and 1950 had lasting effects which may be briefly noted.[27] British social politics never lost its adversarial character and social policies continue to be treated as a reserve for political and parliamentary bargaining. British institutions seemed condemned to marginal and partisan attacks on basic social and economic questions so that even some of the most notable successes, such as the National Health Service, have been constantly disrupted by political attacks from both the left and the right. As we have seen, in a perverse way the French political leaders of the Fourth Republic institutionalized many French social differences within their notion of a welfare state, but they also opened the social security system to direct participation and to direct management in ways that few other countries accepted. In a sense, the complexities of French politics were reproduced within

---

[26] The absence of clear institutional or political parameters to the Swedish accomplishment as described by Hugh Heclo, *Modern Social Politics* ..., 1974, makes the comparison with Britain less persuasive. As Heclo argues, they were both leaders in developing welfare states, but the role of the labour movements, the determination and skills of socialist leaders and the moderating role of the bureaucracies in the two countries could not be more different. Compare with Gösta Esping-Anderson, *Politics against Markets: The Social Democratic Road to Power*, Princeton, NJ; Princeton University Press, 1985.

[27] My intention is to complete a second volume dealing with 1950 to the present which will explore these comments further and link the early institutional developments to the various problems facing modern welfare states.

social policies while the British rather ingenuously set out to simplify social politics and policymaking. A democratic Germany adopted a corporatist structure for most social benefits which the Federal Republic has gone to great lengths to coordinate with other German policies. During and after the war the Swedes continued to work on the complicated economic and social issues of making wage solidarity a reality.[28] In the initial postwar years, the American welfare state changed little. As a consequence of pluralist politics many of the basic social issues of American politics shifted to voting rights, equal opportunity and more elaborate local social services for the handicapped, disabled and aged. Momentus as these changes were, they did not alter the underlying pluralist structure of American policymaking.

Institutional regularities help reveal patterns of action within democratic governance. Indeed, as argued in Chapter 1, from a structural perspective on democratic governance one would not expect to find similar patterns of response, formulation and implementation across many policy areas. Social policy, then, is only one area of change within democracies that reveal institutional constraints at work, but it involved decisions for which the liberal states were the least well prepared. Neither the left nor the right were certain about policy options. The private sector was largely caught off-guard, and indeed never resisted welfare state policies very forcefully or very effectively. In this sense, developing welfare states was a highly political act even though many of the political consequences were unforeseen and many of the decisions were taken within the short-term perspectives of normal democratic politics. Welfare states varied because democracies do not have fixed goals and objectives.

In this respect, in a democratic context policymaking for social questions is no different from policymaking for any other objective. If free political institutions and the open competition of ideas is curtailed, welfare states can easily take on authoritarian forms. The most obvious case between the wars was of course Nazi Germany where social and economic relationships were totally subordinated to the state. Less obvious, but yet worrying from a democratic perspective on the state, were the attempts to revive

[28] See, in particular, the chapter on the Wage Fund controversy in Sweden in Hugh Heclo and Henrik Madsen, *Politics and Policy in Sweden*, Philadelphia, PA; Temple University Press, 1986.

state socialism under the guise of social and economic necessity, most clear perhaps in Mosley's proposals and his subsequent fascist movement in Britain. As we have seen, after both World War I and World War II there were a number of leading social reformers who admired wartime solidarity and pondered whether the wartime sense of sacrifice might not be preserved to invigorate welfare states. Titmuss is perhaps the most striking example in the 1950s. In varying degrees all these ideas contained threats to democratic politics because they assumed that a small elite in a totally mobilized society could determine social and economic policies without the distractions, setbacks and inefficiences of democratic governance.

For this reason how diverse political ideas affected welfare states, so easily put aside in socio-eonomic explanations of welfare states, received extensive treatment in this study. Each democracy devised its own concepts of how to reconcile the abstract goals of social justice and social equality with democratic governance. The process was not as conflictual as many contemporary theories of class politics and 'capitalist' states suggest. To understand why, it is important to grasp not only the uncertainties confronting the main political actors, but the flexibility of democratic decisionmaking. It is precisely those qualities of the democratic policy process that make it unacceptable to the extreme right and to the extreme left that enabled democracies to treat social policies in an innovative, dynamic way. The institutional regularities represent the underlying and persistent political values of the system as it historically and politically developed. The policy process enables us to see how within these constraints political and administrative forces shifted their goals, their priorities and their resources. In a political and policy sense there never were fixed objectives. Had there been such rigidities neither the institutional nor decisional capabilities displayed in the emergency of welfare states would have been possible.[29]

As this study has shown, the policy process varies not only in relation to the institutional constraints and governmental capacities, but was part of a prolonged decisional history balancing social needs and resources against a host of other policy questions.

[29] This is essentially the reason why a structural or multi-level explanation is needed. For an explanation of this view, see Douglas E. Ashford, 'Structural Analysis and Institutional Change: The Case of the Welfare State', *Polity*, March 1986.

Broadly speaking, social policies evolved from early nineteenth century forms of charity to concern with unemployment and eventually to the interdependence of social assistance and wages. Within the rubric of the liberal state charity was, and remains, the primary vehicle for social assistance and social protection. But even in this instance, there were important differences among countries in the initiatives taken by employers, the organization of charity in predominantly Protestant or Catholic societies, and of course the links between the religious and business elites and government itself. From at least the mid-nineteenth century the liberal formula for social assistance was no longer adequate, and, as time passed, it was no longer politically acceptable.

In Germany, the conservative *Verein für Sozialpolitik* attempted to redesign German social and economic policies even before unification, but like the Social Democrats, the Liberals and the Catholics were manipulated by Bismarck in order to advance his concept of state socialism.[30] In France many of the most progressive employers were Catholics, but even after the Encyclical *Rerum Novarum* the social ideas varied greatly among conservative and progressive Catholic groups. The anti-republican scheming of conservative Catholics diminished the chances of reviving effective charities.[31] In many respects the most politically effective private resistance to early social policy development was in Britain where the Charity Organization Society had ready access to elite circles and strong views about the moral purposes of assistance to the poor. For present purposes, these various efforts to rally traditional values failed because their advocates could not formulate workable policies. With this failure, the possibility of developing effective social policies outside government using voluntary methods and private resources died quite independently of the growing social and economic pressures on the democracies.

Responsibility for the aged and the poor was of course always an implicit burden of the liberal state. Not until the second evolution

---

[30] The best account of this process in English is still William Harbutt Dawson's *Bismarck and State Socialism*, London; Sonnenschein, 1891, although Hockert, Mommsen and Tempke have now revised the historical study of German social policy.

[31] Typical of the cross-cutting political loyalties in French politics, the early assistance from benevolent *patrons* was broken along religious lines. See Hatzfeld *Du paupérisme. . .*, pp. 206–8. Also Emile Laurent, *Le paupérisme et les associations de prévoyance*, Paris; Guillaumin, 1865. The Société de Prévoyance was formed in 1821.

of social policy were there acute political dilemmas. The concept of unemployment did not even exist as the early industrial recessions took place in the 1880s and the early 1900s. Although primarily an economic problem, the early responses of the democracies were conditioned by their internal trade interests, their own industrial structure and their labour movements. Though not directed primarily toward social problems, the late nineteenth-century imperialist ambitions were perhaps the closest thing to a liberal solution for industrial and employment problems that the liberal states could devise. Both French and British policymakers saw imperial strength, its trade opportunities, its stimulation of military industries, and even its nationalist appeal as ways of absorbing social discontent and providing resources to alleviate internal social and economic pressures.[32] In so far as it was a coherent strategy, these ideas were perhaps most fully developed in the British Efficiency Movement. With the possible exception of Germany, where social legislation preceded the Kaiser's Imperial designs,[33] and therefore were in reverse relationship to social and economic pressures, this conservative strategy was of course self-defeating. Not only did the workers of all the democracies demonstrate their nationalist loyalties by pouring out their blood in World War I, but the socialist movements throughout Europe rallied to the defence of their countries.

As more sensible domestic solutions arose, each government was influenced by the perceptions of policymakers, both in defining the problem and in devising workable policies. As in the case of more traditional social policies, British policymakers, Beveridge among them, concentrated on making the labour market itself work smoothly. Unemployment insurance in the 1911 Act focused on the most unstable and uncertain areas of employment. In the British tradition, the labour exchanges were a wholly nationalized scheme to link workers to jobs[34] and after the war, wage councils

---

[32] Miles Kahler, *Decolonization in Britain and France: The Domestic Consequences of International Relations*, Princeton, NJ; Princeton University Press, 1984.

[33] Bismarck took a sceptical view of imperialism which contributed to his dismissal by the Kaiser. Against the wishes of German General Staff he also felt that Germany should not impose excessively harsh conditions on France in 1871.

[34] See Jose Harris, *William Beveridge. . .*, pp. 145–67. Initially designed when Beveridge chaired a Sub-Committee of the Charity Organization Society, he saw the exchanges as the keystone for a universal plan to test unemployment insurance claims, to subsidize union insurance, and to extend unemployment protection to the non-unionized workers. The irascible Burns at the Local Government Board

were devised to protect wages in low-paid industries. In an approach that affected many aspects of British policymaking, and with the support of the TUC itself, labour problems were divorced from social policy. Few new ideas appeared between the wars because the magnitude of unemployment, even if misperceived, discouraged more ambitious thinking. As a result many decisions made little economic sense because they protected declining and inefficient industries. Whitehall's preoccupation with unemployment provided ample reasons to avoid more ambitious reconsideration of how Britain's elaborate social benefits related to wages and incomes. While Britain made full employment a pillar of the Beveridge Plan, it too reflects the failure to develop a coordinated, comprehensive policy toward the interdependence of social need and wages. Quite possibly, the last opportunity to redefine the British welfare state was lost in the 1930s.

As we have seen, the compartmentalization of labour and social policies was never this easily accomplished on the continent. Though much weaker than the TUC, French unions considered the early labour exchanges their own facility, and in their areas of strength simply took them over. Both the socialists and the unions felt that the nascent social programmes should be managed by workers. From the 1880s the government itself viewed labour organization as an issue of major political importance to the state, not just to the economy or to social tranquility. The unemployment problem was not as severe as in Britain, but the idea of a *salaire normale* was continually expanded and discussions of labour problems were linked to the more sophisticated notion of maintaining the purchasing power of all citizens.[35] Sweden actually reversed the usual historical sequence of unemployment and other social policies to wages by first constructing a concept of wage solidarity which could use wages to redistribute incomes before major social programmes were launched. For reasons that we have seen, the German ADBG and SDP were left in the backwash of autocratic

was vehemently opposed to the exchanges as a threat to union power. The law was passed in 1909 with very little debate and no division of the House.

[35] The breadth of French concern is perhaps most visible in the various reforms of the Blum government, including worker delegates in factories with over ten employees, paid vacations, the forty-hour week and revision of the 1919 collective convention law. Though in economic trouble, Blum insisted that worker purchasing power must be protected. See P. Renouvin and R. Rémond, *Léon Blum: Chef du Gouvernement*, Paris; Fondation Nationale des Sciences Politiques, 1981, pp. 246–89.

social reform and, as in other major sectoral policies in Germany, turned to building an entirely new, corporatist organization to deal with the economy. The liberal character of the American welfare state was of course preserved by avoiding any suggestion that social security was in fact related to wage and labour problems.[36]

Contrary to both utopian Marxist ideas on the left and neo-classical economic principles on the right, all the democracies sought solutions within the institutional and historical context of their own political system. The early policy responses to unemployment directly affected what may be the third phase on building welfare states, the emergency of a social democratic formula. The entrenchment of the TUC within both the Labour Party and Westminster meant that over the 1950s and 1960s the British left offered few new ideas, and those that were proposed were easily quashed.[37] The French left was split between the Communist and socialist unions, which offered two dramatically different views of how workers related to political institutions as well as to society, while political interests soon overtook the new social security system.[38] After a false start in the Federal Republic, the German left revived its ideas about corporatist management of the economy buttressed by extremely generous unemployment and social benefits. Only in the United States was there no official postwar discussion of how wages and social benefits interlock.[39] The outcomes of these trends goes beyond the scope of this study, but

[36] Edward T. Harpham, 'Federalism, Keynesianism and the Transformation of Unemployment Insurance,' in D. Ashford and E. W. Kelley, eds, *Nationalizing Social Security*, Greenwich, CN; Jai Press, 1986.

[37] In the prewar period, the New Fabian economic planners of the Labour Party were almost totally absorbed in conventional financial and banking problems. See Elizabeth Durbin, *New Jerusalems. . .*, pp. 117–85. In the postwar period, the Labour Party right wing pressed social democratic views over the 1950s, but were outweighed by the unions and Labour's left wing. See Philip M. Williams, *Hugh Gaitskell. . .*, especially p. 537–621. The classic statement was C. A. R. Crosland, *The Future of Socialism*, London; Jonathan Cape, 1956; and his later Fabian pamphlet, *A Social Democratic Future for Britain*, London; Fabian Society, 1971.

[38] The CFDT view of labour relations and labour participation can of course be directly traced to early twentieth-century socialist ideas. On the more recent divisions, see the account of Antoinette Catrice-Lorey, *Dynamique Interne de la Sécurité Sociale*, Paris; Economica, 1982, pp. 29–48, of Communist control of the major social security employees' union, the Federation Nationale des Organismes Sociales (FNOSS).

clearly the social democratic state, if it ever does emerge, will be as diversified as was the conventional welfare state of the prewar period.

The political significance of the democratic welfare state, then, can only be understood by accepting its structural complexity. At least two structural changes were occuring simultaneously. The entire fabric of early democratic governance and its institutions were undergoing a severe test, and of course all the developing democracies did not succeed in making a successful transition. The fact that enlarging the social and economic role of the state did not guarantee the survival of democratic values is grounds for caution in accepting socio-economic explanations of the welfare state. Political traditions and institutional constraints did not disappear simply because governments found their activities vastly expanded, nor is there any reason to assume that they should. The liberal democratic assumption was that each people could fashion its own government, accept its own errors and shape its own future. The second change is less widely recognized and is the basic point of this study. The policy process itself gained influence, partly by the simple expansion of bureaucracies and public finance needed for social programmes, but more important as an independent political force within democratic systems. There were no totally accurate road maps for the early social policy-makers, and there are probably none today. But there was an accumulation of programmes, budgetary commitments, technical and professional skills that gave increasing autonomy to the policy process itself.

The challenge of the welfare state concept to democratic governance was twofold. Could expanded social programmes fit within the framework of party politics, parliamentary rule and electoral competition that each democracy had in place? Could these institutional arrangements, in turn, accommodate and guide the intricate policy processes and governmental machinery that the social programmes required? As we have seen, the institutional and policy adjustments were not defined as much by social and economic principles, radical or conservative, as they were by how leaders saw possibilities of successfully integrating these new requirements with old democratic structures. Moreover, neither

[39] The major related departure was President Truman's concern for fair employment practices. Already the American welfare state was being shaped to America's major social problem, racial discrimination, and this concern permeated the more substantial efforts made under President Johnson.

institutional relationships nor policymaking were static, but inter-
acting as other institutional threats arose and as the focus of
social policies shifted over time. If there is any singular 'test' of
democracy, it was, and no doubt remains, an intricate historical
process rooted in both institutional assumptions and political
imagination.

Failure in this complex process, then, is to lose democratic
viability in the name of social and economic progress. The alternatives of the extreme left and the extreme right are in this
respect alike: both have a singular, rigid view of the institutional
foundations of democracy, the first by asserting the necessity to
reorder democracy in order to resolve underlying socio-economic
'contradictions' and the second by asserting that certain institutional relationships are inviolable. Neither accept the risks or
deal with the dynamics of existing welfare states. There were
many temptations to pursue such a destructive course during the
emergence of welfare states, on the one hand from the initial
revolutionary urges of the early Marxist movements and on the
other hand from intransigent resistance from the right. At times
the temptations of state socialism, as in Germany, or of 'war
socialism' gained popularity. The failure was to think that total
solutions to either social or economic questions are possible within
the framework of democratic governance.

In both an analytical and practical sense, the essential democratic problem is unchanged by the emergence of welfare states.
The acceptance of mass suffrage, competitive politics and elected
legislatures meant that social adjustments and social needs must
enter the political arena. As this happened, the nineteenth-century
notion of liberal state was fatally eroded, in part because it never
had a clear notion of how to deal with social and economic
problems. Neither did those who participated in the construction
of welfare states from 1900 to 1950, but they were prepared to
take political risks and to engage in free political competition.
Despite the failures and unsteady progress, the democratic policy
process demonstrated that it could respond and that it could make
major structural changes in government. The aims were never
fixed nor were the methods ever coercive. Had they been, the
emergence of welfare states would have terminated democratic
political life. In this respect, the welfare state in all its complexity and diversity is a tribute to the capacities of democratic
governance.

Bibliography

OFFICIAL DOCUMENTS

Great Britain

Parliamentary Papers (PP) 1893–1940.

Public Records Office. CAB. 27/263, 1925; 27/755, 1934 and 1935; 87/1, 1941; 87/2, 1942; 87/3, 87/7, 87/13, 1943; 87/4–5–6–7–8, 1944; 124/204, 1944; 134/697, 1945; 134/518, 1950.

Department of Health and Social Security, *Low Incomes: Evidence to the Royal Commission on Distribution of Income and Wealth*, Supplementary Benefits Commission Paper No. 6, London, HMSO, 1977.

Local Government Board, *Annual Reports*, 1900–17.

Ministry of Health, *A National Health Service*, London, HMSO, 1944, cmd. 6502.

Ministry of Health, *Annual Reports*, 1918–40.

Ministry of Reconstruction, Machinery of Government Committee (Haldane Report), London, PP, 1918, cd. 9230.

Royal Commission on the Civil Service, *First Report*, London, PP, 1912, cd. 6209; and *Second Report*, London, PP. 1912, cd. 6535.

Treasury, Committee on National Debt and Taxation, *Report* (Colwyn Report), London, PP, 1927, cmd. 2800.

Treasury, Committee on National Expenditure, *First Interim Report* (Geddes Committee), London, PP, 1922, cmd. 1581.

Treasury, *Statement of Government Policy for the Creation and Maintenance of Full Employment*, London, HMSO, 1944, cmd. 6527.

France

Journal Officiel, Débats Parlémentaires, Chambre des Députés, 1898–1910.

Journal Officiel, Débats, Assemblée Consultatif, 1945.

Journal Officiel, Débats, Assemblée Nationale Constituante, 1945–46.

Journal Officiel, Débats, Assemblée Nationale, 1946–50.

Rapport Anotelli, *Journal Officiel*, Débats de l'Assemblée Nationale, Annexes, No. 3187, avril 1930, pp. 500–643.

Rapport Buisson, *Journal Officiel*, Documents de l'Assemblée Consultatif, Annexes, No. 554, 24 juillet 1945, pp. 725–734.

Conseil d'Etat, *La Réforme des éstablissements publics*, Paris, Documentation Française, 1971.

BOOKS

Abrams, Philip. *Origins of British Sociology, 1834–1914*, Chicago, University of Chicago Press, 1968.

Abramovitz, Moses and Eliasberg, Vera F. *The Growth of Public Employment in Great Britain*, Princeton, Princeton University Press (for the National Bureau of Economic Research), 1975.

Addison, Christopher, ed. *Problems of a Socialist Government*, London, Gollancz, 1933.

Addison, Paul. *The Road to 1945*, London, Jonathan Cape, 1975.

Allen, Bernard M. *Sir Robert Morant: A Great Public Servant*, London, Macmillan, 1934.

Altmeyer, Arthur J. *The Formative Years of Social Security*, Madison, University of Wisconsin Press, 1966.

Anderson, Perry. *Lineages of the Absolutist State*, London, New Left Books, 1974.

Andler, Charles. *Vie de Lucien Herr 1864–1928*, Paris, Rieder, 1931.

Andrews, W. and Hoffman, S., eds. *The Fifth Republic at Twenty*, Albany, N.Y., State University of New York Press, 1981.

Annan, Noel. *Leslie Stephens: His Thought and Character in Relation to His Time*, London, McGibbon and Key, 1951.

Annan, Noel. *The Curious Strength of Positivism in English Political Thought*, London, Oxford University Press, 1959.

Ashford, Douglas E. *British Dogmatism and French Pragmatism: Center–Local Relations in the Welfare State*, London and Boston, Allen and Unwin, 1982.

Ashford, Douglas E., ed. *Comparing Public Policies: New Concepts and Methods*, Beverly Hills, Calif., Sage Publications, 1978.

Ashford, Douglas E., ed. *Financing Urban Government in the Welfare State*, London, Croom Helm, 1980.

Ashford, Douglas E. *Policy and Politics in France: Living with Uncertainty*, Philadelphia, Pa., Temple University Press, 1982.

Ashford, D.E. and Kelley, E.W., eds. *Nationalizing Social Security in Europe and America*, Greenwich, Conn., JAI Press, 1986.

Auspitz, Katherine. *The Radical Bourgeoisie: The Ligue de l'Enseignement and the Origins of the Third Republic, 1866–1885*, Cambridge, Cambridge University Press, 1982.

Bakke, E. Wright. *Insurance or the Dole? The Adjustment of Unemployment Insurance to Economic and Social Facts in Britain*, New Haven, Conn., Yale University Press, 1935.

Banks, Olive. *Parity and Prestige in English Secondary Education*, London, Routledge and Kegan Paul, 1965.

Barnett, Henrietta O. *Cannon Barnett, His Life, Work and Friends*, London, 1921, 2 vols, 3rd edn.

Bateman, J. *The Great Landlords of Great Britain and Ireland*, London, 1883, 4th edn.

Beer, Samuel H. *British Politics in the Collectivist Age*, New York, Knopf, 1965.

Bellom, Maurice. *Les Résultats de l'assurance ouvrière à la fin du xixè siècle*, Nancy, Berger Levrault, 1901.

Bendix, Reinhard. *Nation-Building and Citizenship*, New York, Wiley, 1964.

Berglund, Sten and Lindstrom, Ulf. *Scandinavian Party Systems*, Lund, Student Literature, 1978.

Beveridge, William H. *Power and Influence*, New York, Beechurst, 1945.

Beveridge, William H. *Unemployment: A Problem of Industry*, London, Longman's and Green, 1910 (expanded in 1930).

Bloch, Camille. *L'Assistance et l'état en France à la veille de la Révolution*, Paris, Picard, 1908.

Blum, Léon. *Le Problème de l'unité*, Paris, Libraire Populaire, 1945.

Bouglé, C., ed. *L'Ecole Normale Supérieure: D'où elle veint – où elle va*, Paris, Libraire Hachette, 1934.

Bourgin, Hubert. *De Jaurès à Léon Blum: l'Ecole Normale et la politique*, Paris, Fayard, 1938 (reprinted Paris and New York by Gordon and Breach, 1970).

Boutmy, Emile. *The English People: A Study of their Political Psychology* (trans. J.E. Courtenay), London, T.F. Unwin, 1904.

Braithwaite, W.J. *Lloyd George's Ambulance Wagon*, ed. Sir Henry N. Bunbury, London, Methuen, 1957.

Briggs, Asa and Macartney, Anne. *Toynbee Hall: The First Hundred Years*, London, Routledge and Kegan Paul, 1984.

Brown, Ernest Phelps. *The Growth of British Industrial Relations*, London, Macmillan, 1959.

Brown, Fred K. *Fathers of the Victorians*, Cambridge, Cambridge University Press, 1961.

Brown, Kenneth D. *John Burns*, London, Royal Historical Society, 1977.

Brown, Kenneth D. *Labour and Unemployment, 1900–1914*, London, Rowman and Littlefield, 1971.

Brown, Kenneth D., ed. *The First Labour Party, 1906–1914*, London, Croom Helm, 1985.

Bruce, Maurice. *The Coming of the Welfare State*, London, Batsford, 1968, 4th edn.

Brumter, Christian. *La planification sanitaire*, Doctoral thesis, Faculté de Droit et des Sciences Politiques, University of Strasbourg, 1979.

Brunot, Charles. *La Solidarité sociale comme principe des lois*, Paris, Picard, 1903.

Buchanan, James M. *Theory of Public Choice: Political Applications of Economics*, Ann Arbor, University of Michigan Press, 1972.

Bullock, Alan. *The Life and Times of Ernest Bevin, 1881–1960*, London, Heinemann, 1960, vol. 1.

Burk, Kathleen, ed. *War and the State: The Transformation of British Government, 1914–1919*, London and Boston, Allen and Unwin, 1982.

Burns, Eveline M. *The British Unemployment Program, 1920–1938*, Washington, D.C., Social Science Research Council, 1941.

Butler, David and Sloman, Anne. *British Political Facts, 1900–1975*, London, Macmillan, 1975.

Camplin, James. *The Rise of the Rich*, New York; St Martin's, 1979.

Carnoy, Martin. *The State and Political Theory*, Princeton, Princeton University Press, 1984.

Catrice-Lorey, Antoinette. *Dynamique interne de la securité sociale*, Paris, Economica, 1982.

Ceccaldi, Dominique. *Histoire des Prestations Familiales en France*, Paris, Association Nationale des Allocations Familiales, 1951.

Chadwick, Sir Edwin. *General Report on the Sanitary Condition of the Labouring Population of Great Britain*, London, Parliamentary Papers, 1842.

Chaveau, C. *Les Assurances sociales*, Paris, Payot, 1926.

Chaveau, C. *Loi sur les assurances sociales*, Paris, Libraire générale de droit et de jurisprudence, 1928.

Checkland, Sydney. *British Public Policy, 1776–1939: An Economic, Social and Political Perspective*, Cambridge, Cambridge University Press, 1983.

Chevalier, Louis. *Les Classes laborieuses et classes dangereuses à Paris pendant le première moitié du XIXe siécle*. Paris, Plon, 1958.

Cheysson, Emile. *L'Assistance des ouvrièrs contre les accidents*, Paris, Guillamin, 1888.

Cheysson, Emile. *L'Assurance rurale et le regroupement des communes*, Paris, Guillamin, 1886.

Cheysson, Emile. *L'Evolution des idées et des systèmes de retraite*, Paris, Society of Political Economy, 1902.

Clarke, Peter. *Liberals and Social Democrats*, Cambridge, Cambridge University Press, 1978.

Clark, Terry Nichols. *Prophets and Patrons: The French University and the Emergence of the Social Sciences*, Cambridge, Mass., Harvard University Press, 1973.

Clegg, Hugh, Fox, Alan and Thompson, Arthur. *History of British Trade Unionism since 1889*, Oxford, Oxford University Press, 1964.

Collini, Stephan. *Liberalism and Socialism: L.T. Hobhouse and Political Argument in England, 1880–1914*, Cambridge, Cambridge University Press, 1979.

Commons, John R. *Industrial Goodwill*, New York, McGraw-Hill, 1919.

Commons, John R. *Principles of Labor Legislation*, New York, McGraw-Hill, 1927.

Cooke, A. and Vincent, John. *The Governing Passion: Cabinet Government and Party Politics in Britain, 1885–1886*, Brighton, Harvester Press, and New York, Random House, 1974.

Cowherd, Raymond G. *Political Economists and the English Poor Laws: A Historical Study of the Influence of Classical Economics on the Formation of Social Welfare Policy*, Athens, Ohio, Ohio University, 1977.

Cowling, Maurice. *The Impact of Hitler: British Politics and British Policy, 1933–1940*, Cambridge, Cambridge University Press, 1975.

Cox, Andrew. *Adversary Politics and Land: The Conflict over Land and Property Policy in Post-War Britain*, Cambridge, Cambridge University Press, 1984.

Crosland, C.A.R. *A Social Democratic Future for Britain*, London, Fabian Society, 1971.

Crosland, C.A.R. *The Future of Socialism*, London, Jonathan Cape, 1956.

Dangerfield, George. *The Strange Death of Liberal England, 1910–1914*, New York, Putnam (Capricorn Books), 1965.

Dansette, Adrien. *Histoire religieuse de la France contemporaine*, Paris, Flammarion, 1951.

Davis, Allan. *Spearheads for Reform: The Social Settlements and the Progressive Movement, 1890–1914*, New York, Oxford University Press, 1967.

Davison, Ronald C. *British Unemployment Policy: The Modern Phase since 1930*, London, Longman's Green, 1938.

Davison, Ronald C. *What's Wrong with Unemployment Insurance?*, London, Longman's, 1930.

Dawson, William Harbutt. *Bismarck and State Socialism*, London, Sonnenschein, 1890.

Debré, Michel. *La République et son pouvoir*, Paris, Nagel, 1950.

de Courcy, Alfred. *De l'Assurance par l'Etat*, Paris, Warnier, 1894.

d'Eichtal, Eugène. *La Solidarité nationale: Ses nouvelles formules*, Paris, Picard, 1903.

Delorme, Robert and André, Christine. *L'Etat et l'économie: Un Essais d'explication de l'évolution des dépenses publiques en France, 1870–1980*, Paris, Editions Seuil, 1983.

de Moly, Henry. *L'Assurance obligatoire et le Socialisme d'état*, Paris, Guillaume, 1888.

Derfler, Martin. *Alexandre Millerand: The Socialist Years*, The Hague, Mouton, 1977.

Dérouin, H., Gory, A. and Worms, F. *Traité et practique d'assistance publique*, Paris, Sirey, 1914, 2 vols, 3rd edn.

Dommanget, Maurice. *Vaillant: Un grand socialiste, 1840–1915*, Paris, Table Ronde, 1956.

Donoughue, Bernard and Jones, G.W. *Herbert Morrison: Portrait of a Politician*, London, Weidenfeld and Nicolson, 1973.

Douglas, Roy. *Land, People and Politics: A History of the Land Question in the United Kingdom, 1878–1952*, London, St Martin's Press, 1976.

Drescher, Seymour. *Tocqueville and Beaumont on Social Reform*, New York, Harper, 1968.

Drummond, Gordon D. *The German Social Democrats in Opposition*, Norman, Okla., University of Oklahoma Press, 1982.

Dupuy, Paul. *Lucien Herr, 1863–1926*, Paris, 1927.

Durbin, Elizabeth. *New Jerusalems*, London, Routledge and Kegan Paul, 1985.

Duroselle, Jean-Baptiste. *Les Débats du Catholicisme social en France jusque 1870*, Paris, Presses Universitaires de France, 1951.

Dworkin, Ronald. *Taking Rights Seriously*, London, Duckworth, 1977.

Dyson, Kenneth H.F. *The State Tradition in Western Europe*, New York, Oxford University Press, 1980.

Easton, David. *The Political System: An Inquiry into the State of Political Science*, New York, Knopf, 1953.

Eckstein, Harry. *The National Health Service*, Cambridge, Mass., Harvard University Press, 1958.

Eckstein, Otto, ed. *Studies in the Economics of Income Maintenance*, Washington, D.C., The Brookings Institution, 1967.

Ehrmann, Henry. *French Labour from the Popular Front to Liberation*, New York, Oxford University Press, 1947.

Ellis, Adrian and Kumar, Krishan, eds. *Dilemmas of Liberal Democracies: Studies in Fred Hirsch's 'Social Limits to Growth'*, London, Tavistock Press, 1983.

Elwitt, Sanford. *The Making of the Third Republic: Class and Politics in France, 1868–1884*, Baton Rouge, La., Louisiana State University Press, 1975.

Emy, H.V. *Liberals, Radicals and Social Politics, 1892–1914*, London, Routledge and Kegan Paul, 1973.

Epstein, Abraham. *Insecurity: A Challenge to America: A Study of Social Insurance in the United States and Abroad*, New York, H.S. Smith and R. Haas, 1933.

Esping-Anderson, Gösta. *Politics against Markets: The Social Democratic Road to Power*, Princeton, Princeton University Press, 1985.

Feldman, Gerald D. *Army, Industry and Labor, 1914–1918*, Princeton, Princeton University Press, 1966.

Fenton, Steve. *Durkheim and Modern Sociology*, Cambridge, Cambridge University Press, 1984.

Fiechter, Jean-Jacques. *Le socialisme français: De l'affaire Dreyfus à la Grande Guerre*, Geneva, Libraire Droz, 1965.

Finer, Samuel. *The Life and Times of Sir Edwin Chadwick*, London, Methuen, 1952.

Flora, P. and Heidenheimer, A., eds. *The Development of Welfare States in Europe and America*, London and New Brunswick, Transaction Books, 1981.

Florinsky, Michael T. *Fascism and National Socialism: A Study of Economic and Social Policies of the Totalitarian State*, New York, Macmillan, 1936.

Ford, P. *Social Theory and Social Practice*, Shannon, Ireland, Irish University Press, 1968.

Foot, M.R.D., ed. *War and Society: Historical Essays in Honour and Memory of J.R. Western, 1928–1971*, London, Paul Elek, 1973.

Fraser, Derek. *The Evolution of the Welfare State*, London, Macmillan, 1973.

Frazer, W.M. *A History of English Public Health, 1834–1939*, London, Baillere, Tundall and Cox, 1950.

Freeden, Michael. *The New Liberalism: An Ideology of Social Reform*, Oxford, Clarendon Press, 1978.

French, David. *British Economic and Strategic Planning, 1905–1915*, London, Allen and Unwin, 1982.

Friedlander, Walter S. *Child Welfare in Germany before and after Naziism*, Chicago, University of Chicago Press, 1940.

Friedlander, Walter S. *Individualism and Social Welfare: An Analysis of the System of Social Security and Social Welfare in France*, New York, Free Press, 1962.

Galant, Henri C. *Histoire politique de la securité sociale en France, 1945–1952*, Paris, Colin, 1955.

Gallo, Max. *Le Grand Jaurès*, Paris, Laffout, 1985.

Gaudibert, Jean Claude. *Le Dernier empire français: le Crédit Agricole*, Paris, Segher, 1977.

Georges, Bernard and Tintaut, Denise. *Léon Jouhaux: Cinquantes années de syndicalism*, Paris, Presses Universitaires de France, 1962, 2 vols.

Gilbert, Bentley C. *The Evolution of National Insurance in Great Britain: The Origins of the Welfare State*, London, Michael Joseph, 1966.

Gilbert, B. *British Social Policy, 1914–1939*, Ithaca, N.Y., Cornell University Press, 1970.

Gillespie, Judith A. and Zinnes, Dina, eds. *Missing Elements in Political Inquiry: Logic and Levels of Analysis*, Beverly Hills, Calif., Sage Publications, 1982.

Godsen, P.H.J.H. *The Friendly Societies in England*, Manchester, Manchester University Press, 1961.

Goldberg, Harvey. *The Life of Jean Jaurès*, Madison, University of Wisconsin Press, 1962.

Goldthorpe, J., ed. *Order and Conflict in Contemporary Capitalism: Studies in the Political Economy of Western European Nations*, Oxford, Clarendon Press, 1984.

Gordon, Peter and White, John. *Philosophers as Educational Reformers: The Influence of Idealism in British Educational Thought and Practice*, London, Routledge and Kegan Paul, 1979.

Goschen, Sir George. *Reports and Speeches on Local Taxation*, London, Macmillan, 1872.

Goustine, Christian de. *Pouget: Les Matins noirs du syndicalisme*, Paris, Editions de la Tete de Feuilles, 1972.

Greenleaf, W.H. *The British Political Tradition: The Rise of Collectivism*, London and New York, Methuen, 1983.

Greenleaf, W.H. *The British Political Tradition: The Ideological Heritage*, London and New York, Methuen, 1983.

Grigg, P.J. *Prejudice and Judgment*, London, Jonathan Cape, 1948.

Grunow, D. and Hegner, F. *Welfare or Bureaucracy?*, Cambridge, Mass., Oelgeschlager, Gunn and Hain, 1980.

Gruson, C. *Les Origines et les espoirs de la planification française*, Paris, Dunod, 1968.

Guillot, Paul. *Les Assurances ouvrières: accidents, maladies, veillesse, chômage*, Paris, Imprimeries Centrales, 1897.

Halévy, Elie. *The Growth of Philosophic Radicalism*, London, Faber and Faber, 1928.

Hamon, Georges. *Histoire générale de l'assurance en France et à l'étranger*, Paris, Journal de l'Assurance Moderne, 1896.

Hammond, J.L. *Gladstone and the Irish Nation*, London, Longmans Green, 1938 (reprinted Hamden, Conn., Archon Books, 1964).

Harris, Jose. *Unemployment and Politics: A Study in British Social Policy 1886–1914*, Oxford, Clarendon Press.

Harris, Jose. *William Beveridge: A Biography*, Oxford, Oxford University Press, 1977.

Hatzfeld, Henri. *Du Paupérisme à la securité sociale, 1850–1940*, Paris, Colin, 1971.

Hay, J.R. *The Origins of the Liberal Welfare Reforms, 1906–1914*, London, Macmillan, 1975.

Headings, Mildred J. *French Freemasonry under the Third Republic*, Baltimore, Johns Hopkins University Studies in Historical and Political Science, 1948, vol. 56.

Heclo, Hugh. *Modern Social Politics in Britain and Sweden*, New Haven, Conn., Yale University Press, 1974.

Heclo, Hugh and Madsen, Henrik. *Politics and Policy in Sweden*, Philadelphia, Pa., Temple University Press, 1986.

Heidenheimer, Arnold J. *Adenauer and the CDU*, The Hague, Martinus Nijhoff, 1960.

Herr, Daniel and Meyer, Pierre-André. *Lucien Herr: Le Socialisme et son déstin*, Paris, Calmann-Lévy, 1977.

Hicks, Ursula. *The Finance of British Government, 1920–1936*, London, Oxford University Press, 1938.

Higgins, Joan. *States of Welfare: Comparative Analysis in Social Policy*, Oxford, Basil Blackwell and Martin Robertson, 1981.

Higham, John. *Strangers in the Land: Patterns of American Nativism, 1860–1925*, New Brunswick, N. J. Rutgers University Press, 1955.

Hill, Christopher. *The Intellectual Origins of the English Revolution*, Oxford, Clarendon Press, 1965.

Hill, Sir Norman, ed. *War and Insurance*, London, Oxford University Press, 1927.

Himmelfarb, Gertrude. *The Idea of Poverty: England in the Early Industrial Age*, New York, Random House, 1985.

Himmelfarb, Gertrude. *On Liberals and Liberalism: The Case of John Stuart Mill*, New York, Knopf, 1974.

Hirsch, Fred. *Social Limits to Growth*, Cambridge, Mass., Harvard University Press and London, Routledge and Kegan Paul, 1977.

Hirschman, A. *The Passions and the Interests*, Princeton, Princeton University Press, 1977.

Hobson, John A. *Problems of a New World*, London, Allen and Unwin, 1921.

Honigsbaum, Frank. *The Struggle for the Ministry of Health, 1914–1919*, London, Bell and Sons, Occasional Papers on Social Administration, No. 37, 1970.

Howorth, Jolyon. *Edouard Vaillant: La Création de l'unité socialiste en France*, Paris, Syros, 1982.

Howorth, J. and Cerny, P., eds. *Elites in France: Origins, Reproduction and Power*, London, Pinter, 1981.

Hunt, Lynn. *Politics, Culture and Class in the French Revolution*, Berkeley, Calif., University of California Press, 1984.

Hunt, Richard N. *The Social Democracy, 1918–1935*, New Haven, Conn., Yale University Press, 1964.

Huntingdon, Samuel P. *Political Order in Changing Societies*, New Haven, Conn., Yale University Press, 1968.

Hynes, Samuel. *The Edwardian Turn of Mind*, Princeton, Princeton University Press, 1968.

Jeanneney, J.N. *Léçons d'histoire pour une gauche au pouvoir. La faillité du Cartel (1924–1926)*, Paris, Editions du Seuil, 1977.

Johnston, T.L. *Collective Bargaining in Sweden: A Study of the Labour Market and Its Qualifier*, London, Allen and Unwin, 1962.

Jones, Greta. *Social Darwinism and English Thought*, Atlas Highlands, N.J., Humanities Press, 1980.

Jourdain, Maurice. *De l'Intervention des pouvoirs publiques en matière d'assistance par le travail*, Paris, Rousseau, 1901.

Jupp, James. *The Radical Left in Britain, 1931–1941*, London, Cass, 1982.

Kahler, Miles. *Decolonization in Britain and France: The Domestic Consequences of International Relations*, Princeton, Princeton University Press, 1984.

Keith-Lucas, Brian and Richards, Peter. *A History of Local Government in the Twentieth Century*, London, Allen & Unwin, 1978.

Kent, Christopher. *Brains and Numbers: Elitism, Comtism, and Democracy in Mid-Victorian Britain*, Toronto, University of Toronto Press, 1978.

Keynes, John Maynard. *Activities, 1940–1946. Shaping the Post-War World: Employment and Commodities. The Collected Writings of John Maynard Keynes*, ed. Donald Moggridge, vol. 27. 1980.

Klein, Rudolf. *The Politics of the National Health Service*, London, Longman, 1983.

Koblik, Steven, ed. *Sweden's Development from Poverty to Affluence, 1750–1970*, Minneapolis, University of Minnesota Press, 1975.

Kohler, P. and Zacher, H., eds. *A Century of Social Security, 1881–1981: The Evolution in Germany, France, Great Britain, Austria, and Switzerland*, Munich, Max Planck Institute, 1982.

Korpi, Walter. *The Democratic Class Struggle*, London, Routledge and Kegan Paul, 1983.

Kuhn, Thomas. *The Structure of Scientific Revolutions*, Chicago, University of Chicago, 1962.

Kuisel, Richard F. *Capitalism and the State in Modern France*, London and New York, Cambridge University Press, 1981.

Laboulaye, Eduard. *Paris en Amerique*, Paris, Charpentier, 1863.

LaCapra, Dominick. *Emile Durkheim: Sociologist and Philosopher*, Ithaca, N.Y., Cornell University Press, 1972.

Lambert, Royston. *Sir John Simon, 1816–1904, and English Social Administration*, London, MacGibbon and Kee, 1963.

Lambert, William. *Le Monopole des assurances*, Paris, Berger Levrault, 1910.

Landsberger, Henry A. *The Control of Cost in the Federal Republic of Germany: Lessons for America?*, Washington, D.C., Department of Health and Human Services, Public Health Service (DHHS Publication No. (HRA) 81-14003), 1981.

Laroque, Pierre, ed. *Succés et faiblesses*, Paris, Colin, 1961.

Laubier, Patrick de. *L'Age de la politique sociale*, Paris, Editions Techniques et Economiques, Paris, 1978.

Laurent, Emile. *Le Paupérisme et les associations de prévoyance*, Paris, Guillaumin, 1865.

Lefranc, Georges. *Essais sur les problèmes socialistes et syndicaux*, Paris, Payot, 1960.

Lefranc, Georges. *Histoire du Front Populaire, 1934–1938*, Paris, Payot, 1965.

Lefranc, Georges. *Histoire du travail et des travailleurs*, Paris, Flammarion, 1957.

Lefranc, Georges. *Jaurès et la socialisme des intellectuels*, Paris, Aubier-Montaigne, 1968.

Lefranc, Georges. *Le Mouvement Socialiste sous la Troisième République*, Paris, Payot, 1977.

Lefranc, Georges. *Le Socialisme réformiste*, Paris, Presses Universitaires de France, 1971.

Lefranc, Georges. *Les Expériences syndicales en France de 1939 à 1950*, Paris, Editions Montaigne, 1950.

Legendre, Pierre. *Histoire de l'Administration: De 1750 à nos jours*, Paris, Presses Universitaires de France, 1968.

Leiby, James. *A History of Social Welfare and Social Work in the United States*, New York, Columbia University Press, 1978.

Le Play, M.F. *La Réforme sociale en France*, Paris, Plon, 1864, vols 1 and 2.

Leroy-Beaulieu, Paul. *Essai sur la répartition des richesses et sur la tendance à une moindre inégalité des conditions*, Paris, Guillaumin, 1881.

Leroy-Beaulieu, Paul. *The Modern State in Relation to Society and the Individual*,

London, Swan Sonnenschein, 1891.

Letwin, Shirley. *The Pursuit of Certainty*, Cambridge, Cambridge University Press, 1965.

Levasseur, E. *Histoire des classes ouvrières et de l'industrie en France, 1789–1870*, Paris, Rousseau, 1903.

Levasseur, E. *Questions ouvrières et industrielles en France sous la Troisième République*, Paris, Rousseau, 1907.

Levassort, Charles. *Le Monopole des assurances*, Paris, Marchal and Billard, 1910.

Lichtheim, George. *Marxism in Modern France*, New York, Columbia University Press, 1966.

Lindenberg, Daniel. *Le Marxisme introuvable*, Paris, Calmann-Lévy, 1975.

Lindenberg, Daniel and Meyer, Pierre-André. *Lucien Herr: Le Socialisme et son déstin*, Paris, Calmann-Lévy, 1977.

Litchfield, E., ed. *Governing Postwar Germany*, Ithaca, N.Y., Cornell University Press, 1953.

Logue, William. *From Philosophy to Sociology: The Evolution of French Liberalism, 1871–1914*, Dekalb, Ill., Northern Illinois University Press, 1983.

Long, M. and Blanc, L. *L'Economie de la fonction publique*, Paris, Presses Universitaires de France, 1969.

Lovell, John. *Stevedores and Dockers: A Study of Trade Unionism in the Port of London, 1870–1914*, New York, A.M. Kelley, 1969.

Lowi, Theodore. *The End of Liberalism*, New York, Norton, 1968.

Lubenow, William C. *The Politics of Government Growth: Early Victorian Attitudes toward State Intervention 1833–1848*, Hamden, Conn., Archon Books, 1971.

Lubove, Roy. *The Struggle for Social Security, 1900–1935*, Cambridge, Mass., Harvard University Press, 1968.

Lukes, Steven. *Emile Durkheim: His Life and Times: An Historical and Critical Study*, London, Allen Lane, 1973.

Lynes, Tony. *The Unemployment Assistance Board*, London, Croom Helm, 1985.

McBriar, A.M. *Fabian Socialism and English Politics,. 1884–1918*, Cambridge, Cambridge University Press, 1962.

McClymer, John F. *War and Welfare: Social Engineering in America, 1890–1925*, Westport, Conn., Greenwood Press, 1980.

McConnel, Grant. *Private. Power and American Democracy*, New York, Random House, 1966.

MacDonagh, Oliver. *A Pattern of Government Growth, 1800–1860*, London, MacGibbon and Kee, 1961.

Macfarlane, A. *The Origins of English Individualism*, Oxford, Blackwell, 1978.

Macinol, John. *The Movement for Family Allowances, 1918–1945: A Study in Social Policy Development*, London, Heinemann, 1980.

McKechnie, W.S. *The State and the Individual: An Introduction to Political Science with Special Reference to Socialistic and Individual Theories*, Glasgow,

J. MacLehose, 1896.

MacKenzie, Norman and MacKenzie, Jean. *The First Fabians*, New York, Simon and Shuster, 1977.

MacLeod, Roy M. *Treasury Control and Social Administration*, London, Bell (Occasional Papers on Social Administration), 1968.

Macpherson, C.B. *Democratic Theory: Essays in Retrieval*, Oxford, Oxford University Press, 1973.

Madsen, Henrik Jess. *Social Democracy in Post-War Scandinavia: Macroeconomic Management, Electoral Support and the Fading Legacy of Prosperity*, Doctoral dissertation, Cambridge, Mass., Harvard University, 1984.

Maier, Charles S. *Recasting Bourgeois Europe: Stabilization in France, Germany and Italy in the Decade after World War I*, Princeton, Princeton University Press, 1975.

Marquand, David. *Ramsey MacDonald*, London, Jonathan Cape, 1977.

Marshall, T.H. *Class, Citizenship and Social Development*, London, Heinemann, 1963.

Martin, Benjamin F. *Count Albert de Mun: Paladin of the Third Republic*, Chapel Hill, University of North Carolina Press, 1978.

Martin, E.W., ed. *Comparative Development in Social Welfare*, London, Allen and Unwin, 1972.

Marwick, Arthur. *The Deluge: British Society and the First War*, Boston, Mass., Little Brown, 1965.

Mayer, Arno. *The Persistence of the Old Regime*, New York, Pantheon, 1981.

Michel, H. and Mirkine-Guetizevich, B. *Les Idées politiques et sociales de la Résistance*, Paris, Presses Universitaires de France, 1954.

Middlemas, Keith. *Politics in Industrial Society*, London, André Deutsch, 1979.

Mill, John Stuart. *Essays on England, Ireland and the Empire. Collected Works* (ed. John M. Robson), London, Routledge and Kegan Paul, 1983.

Millerand, Alexandre. *Travail et travailleurs*, Paris, Charpentier, 1908.

Minnich, Lawrence A., Jr. *Social Problems and Political Alignments in France 1893–1899: Leon Bourgeois and Solidarity*, Doctoral dissertation, Ithaca, N.Y., Cornell University, 1948.

Mommsen, W.J., ed. *The Emergence of the Welfare State in Britain and Germany*, London, Croom Helm, 1981.

Monod, Henri. *L'Assistance publique en France en 1889 et an 1900*, Paris, Imprimérie Nationale, 1900.

Montgomery, B. Gabriel de. *British and Continental Labour Policy*, London, Kegan Paul, 1922.

Moore, Barrington, Jr. *The Social Origins of Dictatorship and Democracy: Lord and Peasant in the Making of the Modern World*, Boston, Mass., Beacon Press, 1966.

Moore, David. *The Politics of Deference: A Study of the Mid-Nineteenth Century English Political System*, New York, Barnes and Noble, 1976.

Morgan, Kenneth. *Labour in Power, 1945–1951*, Oxford, Clarendon Press, 1984.

Morgan, Kenneth and Morgan, Jane. *Portrait of a Progressive: The Political*

Career of Christopher Viscount Addison, Oxford, Clarendon Press, 1980.

Moses, John A. *Trade Unionism in Germany from Bismarck to Hitler*, Totowa, N.J., Barnes and Noble, 1982, 2 vols.

Mowat, Charles. *The Charitable Organization Society*, London, Methuen, 1961.

Murray, Bruce K. *The People's Budget 1909–1910: Lloyd George and Liberal Politics*, Oxford, Clarendon Press, 1980.

Musgrave, Richard A. and Peacock, Alan, eds. *Classics in the Theory of Public Finance*, New York, Macmillan, 1958.

Newsholme, Sir Arthur. *The Ministry of Health*, London, Putnam, 1925.

O'Connor, James. *The Fiscal Crisis of the State*, New York, St Martin's Press, 1973.

Offer, Avner. *Property and Politics 1870–1914*, Cambridge, Cambridge University Press, 1981.

Olson, Mancur. *The Logic of Collective Action: Public Goods and the Theory of Groups*, Cambridge, Mass., Harvard University Press, 1965.

Olson, Mancur. *The Rise and Decline of Nations: Economic Growth, Stagflation, and Social Rigidities*, New Haven, Conn., Yale University Press, 1982.

Oualid, William, and Picquenard, Charles. *Salaires et tarifs, conventions et grèves: la politique du Ministère de l'Armement et du Ministère du Travail*, Paris, Presses Universitaires de France and New Haven, Conn., Yale University Press (for the Carnegie Peace Foundation), 1928.

Owen, David. *English Philanthropy, 1660–1960*, Cambridge, Mass., Harvard University Press, 1964.

Paxton, Robert O. *Vichy France: Old Guard and New Order, 1940–1944*, New York, Norton, 1972.

Peacock, Alan T. and Wiseman, Jack. *The Growth of Government Expenditure in the United Kingdom*, London and New York, Allen and Unwin, 1967, rev. edn.

Peel, J.D.Y. *Herbert Spencer: The Evaluation of a Sociologist*, Chicago, University of Chicago Press, 1971.

Pelling, Henry. *The Labour Governments*, London, Macmillan, 1984.

Perkin, Harold. *The Origins of Modern English Society, 1780–1880*, Toronto, University of Toronto Press, 1969.

Perkins, Frances. *The Roosevelt I Knew*, New York, Viking Press, 1946.

Persil, Raoul. *Alexandre Millerand, 1859–1943*, Paris, Société d'Editions Françaises, 1949.

Pigou, Arthur, *Economics of Welfare*, London, Macmillan, 1932, 4th edn.

Pimlott, Ben. *Hugh Dalton*, London, Jonathan Cape, 1985.

Pimlott, Ben. *Labour and the Left in the 1930s*, Cambridge, Cambridge University Press, 1977.

Pinot, R. *Les Ouvres sociales des industries métallurgiques*, Paris, Colin, 1924.

Pirouret, Roger. *La Caisse des Depots*, Paris, Presses Universitaires de France, 1966.

Plumb, J.H. *The Growth of Political Stability in England, 1675–1725*, London, Penguin Books, 1969.

Pocock, J.G.A. *Politics, Language and Time: Essays on Political Thought and*

History, New York, Atheneum, 1971.

Pryor, Frederic L. *Public Expenditures in Communist and Capitalist Nations*, New Haven, Conn., Yale University Press (The Economic Growth Center), 1968.

Rain, Pierre. *L'Ecole Libre des Sciences Politiques, 1871–1945*, Paris, Fondation Nationale des Sciences Politiques, 1963.

Ranney, Austin, ed. *Political Science and Public Policy*, Chicago, Markham, 1978.

Ratcliffe, John. *Land Policy: An Exploration of the Nature of Land in Society*, London, Hutchinson, 1976.

Rathbone, Eleanor. *The Disinherited Family*, London, Allen and Unwin, 1924.

Rawls, John. *A Theory of Justice*, Oxford, Clarendon Press, 1972, 2nd edn.

Read, Donald. *Edwardian England, 1901–1915*, New Brunswick, N.J., Rutgers University Press, 1982.

Renouvin, P. and Rémond, R. *Léon Blum: Chef du Gouvernement*, Paris, Fondation National des Sciences Politiques, 1981.

Richter, Melvin. *The Politics of the Consensus: T.H. Green and His Age*, London, Weidenfeld and Nicolson, 1964.

Rimlinger, Gustav V. *Welfare Policy and Industrialization in Europe, America and Russia*, New York, Wiley, 1971.

Roberts, B.C. *The Trades Union Congress, 1868–1921*, Cambridge, Mass., Harvard University Press, 1958.

Roberts, David. *Paternalism in Early Victorian England*, London, Croom Helm, and New Brunswick, N.J., Rutgers University Press, 1979.

Roberts, David. *Victorian Origins of the Welfare State*, New Haven, Conn., Yale University Press, 1960.

Rochetin, Eugène. *Les Assurances ouvrières: mutualités contre la maladie, l'incendie et le chômage*, Paris, Guillaumin, 1896.

Rose, Richard. *Understanding Big Government: The Programme Approach*, London, Sage Publications, 1984.

Roth, Guenther. *The Social Democrats in Imperial Germany: A Study in Working Class Isolation and National Integration*, Totowa, N.J., Bedminster Press, 1963.

Rubinow, I.M. *The Quest for Social Security*, New York, Holt, 1934.

Rueff, Jacques. *Combats pour l'ordre financier*, Paris, Plon, 1972.

Saposs, David J. *The Labor Movement in Post-War France*, New York, Columbia University Press, 1931.

Scaly, Robert J. *The Origins of the Lloyd George Coalition: The Politics of Social Imperialism, 1900–1918*, Princeton, Princeton University Press, 1975.

Schmitter, Philippe C. and Lehmbruch, Gerhard, eds. *Trends toward Corporatist Intermediation*, Beverly Hills, Calif., Sage Publications, 1979.

Schoenbaum, David. *Hitler's Social Revolution: Class and Status in Nazi Germany, 1933–1939*, New York, Doubleday, 1966.

Schonfield, Andrew. *Modern Capitalism: The Changing Balance of Public and*

Private Power, London, Oxford University Press, 1965.

Schorske, Karl. *German Social Democracy, 1905–1917: The Development of the Great Schism*, Cambridge, Mass., Harvard University Press, 1955.

Scott, John A. *Republican Ideas and the Liberal Tradition in France, 1870–1914*, New York, Columbia University Press, 1951.

Searle, G.R. *The Quest for National Efficiency: A Study in British Politics and Political Thought, 1899–1914*, Berkeley and Los Angeles, University of California Press, 1971.

Seigfried, André. *England's Crisis* (trans. H.H. Hemming), New York, Harcourt Brace, 1931.

Semmel, Bernard. *Imperialism and Social Reform: English Social Thought, 1899–1914*, Cambridge, Mass., Harvard University Press, 1960.

Sharp, Walter Rice. *The French Civil Service: Bureaucracy in Transition*, London, Macmillan, 1931.

Shinn, Terry. *Savior Scientifique et Pouvoir Social: L'Ecole Polytechnique, 1794–1914*, Paris, Presses de la Fondation Nationale des Sciences Politiques, 1980.

Sidgwick, Henry. *The Elements of Politics*, London and New York, Macmillan, 1891.

Simon, Brian. *Education and the Labour Movement, 1870–1920*, London, Lawrence and Wischart, 1965.

Skidelsky, Robert. *Politicians and the Slump: The Labour Government of 1929–32*, London, Macmillan, 1967.

Skocpol, Theda. *States and Social Revolutions*, Cambridge, Cambridge University Press, 1979.

Smith, Gordon. *Democracy in Western Germany: Parties and Politics in the Federal Republic*, New York, Holmes and Meier, 1979.

Smith, Robert J. *The Ecole Normale Supérieure and the Third Republic*, Albany, State University of New York Press, 1982.

Soltau, Roger. *French Political Thought in the Nineteenth Century*, New Haven, Conn., Yale University Press, 1931.

Somers, George C., ed. *Labor, Management and Social Policy: Essays in the J.R. Commons Tradition*, Madison, University of Wisconsin Press, 1963.

Sorlin, Pierre. *Waldeck-Rousseau*, Paris, Colin, 1966.

Spencer, Herbert. *Man vs. State*, London, Williams and Norgate, 1884.

Stearns, Peter N. *Old Age in European Society*, New York, Holmes and Meier, 1976.

Steffen, Monica. *Regulation politique et stratigies professionelles: 'Medicine liberale et émergence des Centres de Santé'*, Doctoral thesis, University of Grenoble II, Institute d'Etudes Politiques, 1983.

Stone, Deborah. *The Limits of Professional Power: National Health Care in the Federal Republic of Germany*, Chicago, University of Chicago Press, 1980.

Stone, Judith. *The Search for Social Peace: Reform Legislation in France, 1890–1914*, Albany, State University of New York Press, 1985.

Sutherland, G. *Policymaking in Elementary Education, 1870–1895*, Oxford, Oxford University Press, 1973.

Sutherland, G., ed. *Studies in the Growth of Nineteenth Century Government*, London, Routledge and Kegan Paul, 1972.

Thane, P., ed. *The Origins of British Social Policy*, London, Croom Helm, 1978.

Thirwall, A.P., ed. *Keynes as a Policy Adviser*, London, Macmillan, 1982.

Thompson, F.M.L. *English Landed Society in the Nineteenth Century*, London, Routledge and Kegan Paul, 1963.

Thompson, James M. *Louis Napoleon and the Second Empire*, New York, Columbia University Press, 1983.

Thornton, A.P. *The Habit of Authority: Paternalism in British History*, London and Boston, Allen and Unwin, 1966.

Titmuss, Richard. *Problems of Social Policy*, London, HMSO, 1950.

Tomasson, R.F., ed. *Comparative Social Research: The Welfare State, 1883-1983*, Westport, Conn., JAI Press, 1983.

Trattner, Walter I. *From Poor Law to Welfare State*, New York, Free Press, 1959, 2nd edn.

Treblicock, Clive. *The Industrialization of Continental Powers*, New York, Longman, 1982.

Vaillant, Edouard. *Assurance sociale*, Paris, Imprimérie Centrale de la Bourse, 1901.

Villey, Edmond. *Le Progrés sociale*, Paris, Presses Universitaires de France, 1923.

Villey, Edmond. *Les Périls de la démocracie française*, Paris, Plon, 1910.

Vorin, Michael. *Les Origines des caisses de securité sociale et leurs pouvoirs*, Paris, Libraire Générale de Droit et de Jurisprudence, 1961.

Walzer, Michael. *The Revolution of the Saints: A Study in the Origins of Radical Politics*, Cambridge, Mass., Harvard University Press, 1965.

Weber, Eugen. *Peasants into Frenchmen: The Modernization of Rural France, 1870-1914*, Stanford, Calif., Stanford University Press, 1976.

Welter, Rush. *Popular Education and Democratic Thought in America*, New York, Columbia University Press, 1962.

Wicksel, Knut. *Lectures in Political Economy*, New York, Macmillan, 1935.

Wicksel, Knut. *Value, Capital and Rent*, New York, Rinehart, 1954.

Wiener, Martin J. *Between Two Worlds: The Political Thought of Graham Wallas*, Oxford, Oxford University Press, 1971.

Wiener, Martin J. *English Culture and the Decline of the Industrial Spirit, 1850-1980*, Cambridge, Cambridge University Press, 1981.

Wigham, Eric. *Strikes and Government 1893-1974*, London, Macmillan, 1974.

Wilensky, Harold L. *The Welfare State and Equality: Structural and Ideological Roots of Public Expenditures*, Berkeley, University of California Press, 1975.

Williams, Philip. *Hugh Gaitskell: A Political Biography*, London, Jonathan Cape, 1979.

Winter, J.M., ed. *History and Society: Essays by R.H. Tawney*, London, Routledge and Kegan Paul, 1978.

Wolfe, Alan. *The Limits of Legitimacy: Political Contradictions of Contemporary Capitalism*, New York, Free Press and London, Macmillan, 1977.

Wrigley, C.J., ed. *A History of British Industrial Relations, 1875–1914*, Amherst, University of Massachusetts Press, 1982.

Young, Ken. *Local Politics and the Rise of Party: The London Municipal Society and the Conservative Intervention in Local Elections, 1894–1963*, Leicester, Leicester University Press, 1975.

Zeldin, Theodore. *France, 1848–1945*, Oxford, Clarendon Press, 1973, vol. 1.

Zimmern, Alfred. *Quo Vadimus*, London, Oxford University Press, 1934.

ARTICLES

Aaron, Henry. 'Social Security: International Comparisons', in Otto Eckstein, ed., *Studies in the Economics of Income Maintenance*, Washington, D.C., The Brookings Institution, 1967.

Abrams, Philip. 'The Failure of Social Reform: 1918–1920', *Past and Present*, 24 (1963): pp. 43–64.

Anderson, Charles W. 'The Logic of Public Problems: Evaluation in Comparative Policy Research', in D. Ashford, ed., *Comparing Public Policies*, Beverly Hills, Calif., Sage Publications, 1978, pp. 19–42.

Anderson, Charles W. 'The Place of Principles in Policy Analysis', *American Political Science Review*, 73 (1979): 711–23.

Ashford, Douglas E. 'A Victorian Drama: The Fiscal Subordination of British Local Government', in D. Ashford, ed., *Financing Urban Government in the Welfare State*, London, Croom Helm, 1980, pp. 71–96.

Ashford, Douglas E. 'Structural Analysis and Institutional Change: The Case of the Welfare State', *Polity*, Fall, 1986.

Ashford, Douglas E. 'The Structural Analysis of Policy of Institutions Really Do Matter', in D.E. Ashford, ed., *Comparing Public Policies: New Concepts and Methods*, Beverly Hills, Calif., Sage Publications, 1978, pp. 81–98.

Baker, John. 'Social Conscience and Social Policy', *Journal of Social Policy*, 8 (no. 2) (1979): 177–206.

Bargeton, Maurice. 'La Formation des ministères', *Revue Française des Affairs Sociales*, January–March 1971, pp. 56–86.

Beveridge, Sir William. 'Unemployment Insurance in the War and After', in Sir Norman Hill, ed., *War and Insurance*, London, Oxford University Press, 1927, pp. 229–57.

Blondel, Georges. 'Les influences de l'enseignement secondaire et l'essor économique du pays', *Réforme Sociale*, 39: January–July, pp. 193–208, and August–December 1900, pp. 439–460.

Bonnet, Charles. 'Cents ans d'histoire', *Informations Sociales*, nos 6–7, 1978, pp. 13–31.

Booth, Alan. 'An Administrative Experiment in Unemployment Policy in the Thirties', *Public Administration* (UK), 56 (Summer 1978): 139–55.

Booth, Alan. 'The Keynesian Revolution in Economic Policy-making', *Economic History Review*, Second Series, 36 (February 1983): 103–23.

Brebner, J.B. 'Laissez-Faire and State Intervention in Nineteenth-Century Britain', *Journal of Economic History*, 8 (1948): pp. 59–73.

Briggs, Asa. 'The Welfare State in Historical Perspective', *Archives Européene Sociologie*, 2 (1961): 221–58.

Briggs, Eric and Deacon, Alan. 'The Creation of the Unemployment Assistance Board', *Policy and Politics*, 2 (1973): 43–62.

Bristow, Edward. 'The Liberty and Property Defense League and Individualism', *Historical Journal*, 18 (1975): 761–89.

Brown, John. ' "Social Control" and the Modernisation of Social Policy', in P. Thane, ed., *The Origins of British Social Policy*, London, Croom Helm, 1978, pp. 126–46.

Brown, Kenneth D. 'Conflict in Early British Welfare Policy: The Case of the Unemployed Workmen's Bill of 1905', *Journal of Modern History*, 43 (Winter 1971): 615–29.

Brown, Kenneth D. 'John Burns at the Local Government Board', *Journal of Social Policy*, 6 (1977): 159–70.

Brown, Michael Barratt. 'The Welfare State in Britain', *The Socialist Register*, London, Merlin Press, pp. 185–223.

Burk, Kathleen. 'The Treasury: From Impotence to Power', in Kathleen Burk, ed., *War and the State: The Transformation of British Government, 1914–1919*, London and Boston, Allen and Unwin, 1982, pp. 84–107.

Cahnman, Werner J. and Schmitt, Carl M. 'The Concept of Social Policy (Sozialpolitik)', *Journal of Social Policy*, 8 (1979): 47–59.

Caldwell, J.A. 'The Genesis of the Ministry of Labour', *Public Administration* (UK), 37 (Winter 1959): 367–91.

Castles, F.G. and McKinlay, R.D. 'Public Welfare Provision, Scandinavia, and the Sheer Futility of the Sociological Approach to Politics', *British Journal of Political Science*, 9 (1979): 157–71.

Cheysson, Emile. 'L'Imprévoyance dans les institutions de prévoyance', *Réforme Sociale*, 6, no. 2 (July–September 1888): 273–80.

Cole, Taylor. 'Labor Relations', in E. Litchfield, ed., *Governing Postwar Germany*, Ithaca, N.Y., Cornell University Press, 1953, pp. 361–80.

Coll, Blanche D. 'Public Assistance in the United States: Colonial Times to 1860', in E.W. Martin, ed., *Comparative Development in Social Welfare*, London, Allen and Unwin, 1972, pp. 128–58.

Collier, David and Messick, Richard. 'Prerequisites versus Diffusion: Testing Alternative Explanations of Social Security Adoption', *American Political Science Review*, 69 (1975): 1296–1315.

Colson, Clément. 'L'Assurance contre le chômage', *Revue Politique et Parlementaire*, 127 (1926): 5–18.

Cripps, Sir Stafford. 'Can Socialism Come by Constitutional Methods?', in C. Addison, ed., *Problems of a Socialist Government*, London, Gollancz, 1933, pp. 35–66.

Cromwell, Valerie. 'Interpretations of Nineteenth-Century Administration: An Analysis', *Victorian Studies*, 9 (March 1966): 245–55.

Crouch, R.L. 'Laissez-Faire in Nineteenth Century Britain: Myth or Reality?', *The Manchester School*, 35 (1967): pp. 199–215.

Davidson, Roger. 'Llewellyn Smith, the Labour Department and Government Growth, 1886–1909', in G. Sutherland, ed., *Studies in the Growth of Nineteenth Century Government*, London, Routledge and Kegan Paul, 1972, pp. 227–62.

Davidson, Roger and Lowe, Rodney. 'Bureaucracy and Innovation in British Welfare Policy, 1870–1945', in W.J. Mommsen, ed., *The Emergence of the Welfare State in Britain and Germany*, London, Croom Helm, 1981, pp. 263–95.

Deacon, Alan. 'An End to the Means Test? Social Security and the Attlee Government', *Journal of Social Policy*, 11, no. 3 (1982): 289–306.

Dunn, John. 'The Identity of the History of Ideas', *Philosophy*, 43, no. 164 (April 1968): 85–104.

Eckstein, Harry. 'Authority Patterns: A Structural Basis for Inquiry', *American Political Science Review*, 67 (December 1973): 1142–61.

Elwitt, Sanford. 'Social Reform and Social Order in Late-19th-Century France', *French Historical Studies*, 11 (Spring 1980): 431–51.

Esping-Andersen, Gösta. 'Fifty Years of Social Democratic Rule: Single Party Dominance in Sweden', mimeographed 1984.

Esping-Andersen, Gösta. 'Politics against Markets: Demodification in Social Policy', paper presented to Arne Ryde Symposium on the Economics of Social Policy, Lund, Sweden, 1981.

Esping-Andersen, Gösta and Korpi, Walter. 'Social Policy as Class Politics in Post-War Capitalism: Scandinavia, Austria, and Germany', in J. Goldthorpe, ed., *Order and Conflict in Contemporary Capitalism: Studies in the Political Economy of Western European Nations*, Oxford, Clarendon Press, 1984, pp. 179–208.

Fesmire, J.M. and Beauvais, G.C. 'Budget Size in Democracy Revisited: The Public Supply of Private, Public and Semi-Public Goods', *Southern Economic Journal*, 45 (1979): 277–93.

Flora, Peter and Alber, Jens. 'Modernization, Democratization, and the Development of Welfare States in Western Europe', in P. Flora and A. Heidenheimer, eds. *The Development of Welfare States in Europe and America*, London and New Brunswick, N.J., Transaction Books, 1981, pp. 37–80.

Fowler, W.S. 'The Influence of Idealism upon State Provision of Education', *Victorian Studies*, 4 (June 1961): 337–44.

Fraser, Peter. 'The Impact of the War of 1914–1918 on the British Political System', in M.R.D. Foot, ed., *War and Society: Historical Essays in Honour and Memory of J.R. Western, 1928–1971*, London, Paul Elek, 1973, pp. 123–39.

Fry, Geoffrey K. 'Bentham and Public Administration', *Public Administration Bulletin*, 24 (August 1977): 32–40.

Gilbert, Bentley B. 'David Lloyd George: The Reform of British Land-Holding and the Budget of 1914', *Historical Journal*, 21, no. 1 (1978): 117–41.

Goldthorpe, John H. 'The End of Convergence: Corporatist and Dualist Tendencies in Modern Western Societies', in J. Goldthorpe, ed., *Order and Conflict in Contemporary Capitalism: Studies in the Political Economy of Western European Nations*, Oxford, Clarendon Press, 1984, p. 321.

Greenleaf, W.H. 'Toulmin Smith and the British Political Tradition', *Public Administration Review* (UK), 53 (1975): 25–44.

Guillaume, Gilbert. 'Agriculture', in P. Laroque, ed., *Succés et faiblesses*, Paris, Colin, 1961, pp. 179–218.

Hall, John. 'The Conscious Relegitimation of Liberal Capitalism: Problems of Transition', in A. Ellis and K. Kumar, eds, *Dilemmas of Liberal Democracies: Studies in Fred Hirsch's Social Limits to Growth*, London, Tavistock Publications, 1984, pp. 65–79.

Harpham, Edward T. 'Federalism, Keynesianism and the Transformation of Unemployment Insurance', in D. Ashford and E.W. Kelley, eds, *Nationalizing Social Security*, Greenwich, Conn., JAI Press, 1985, pp. 155–197.

Hart, Jennifer. 'Nineteenth Century Social Reform: A Tory Interpretation on History', *Past and Present*, 31 (July 1965): 39–61.

Hayward, J.E.S. 'Solidarist Syndicalism: Durkheim and Duguit', *Sociological Review*, Part I, 8 (July 1960): 17–36; and Part II, 8 (December 1960): 185–202.

Heidenheimer, Arnold. 'Education and Social Entitlements in Europe and America', in P. Flora and A. Heidenheimer, eds, *The Development of Welfare States in Europe and America*, New Brunswick, N.J., and London, Transaction Books, 1981, pp. 269–304.

Heidenheimer, Arnold J. 'Secularization Patterns and the Westward Spread of the Welfare State, 1893–1973', in R.F. Tomasson, ed., *The Welfare State, 1883–1983*, vol. 6, Comparative Social Research Annual, Greenwich, Conn., JAI Press, 1983, pp. 3–37.

Hennock, E.P. 'Poverty and Social Theory in England', *Social History*, 1 (1976–1977): 67–91.

Hinton, James. 'The Rise of a Mass Labour Movement: Growth and Limits', in C.J. Wrigley, ed., *A History of British Industrial Relations, 1905–1914*, Amherst, University of Massachusetts Press, 1982, p. 20–46.

Hume, L.J. 'Jeremy Bentham and the Nineteenth-Century Revolution in Government', *Historical Journal*, 10, no. 4 (1967): 361–75.

Keeler, John T.S. 'The Corporate Dynamics of Agricultural Modernization in the Fifth Republic', in W. Andrews and S. Hoffman, eds, *The Fifth Republic at Twenty*, Albany, N.Y., State University of New York Press, 1981, pp. 271–91.

Kristenen, Ole P. 'On the Futility of the "Demand Approach" to Public Sector Growth', *European Journal of Political Research*, 12 (September 1984): 309–24.

Kristenen, Ole P. 'The Logic of Political–Bureaucratic Decisionmaking as a Cause for Government Growth', *European Journal of Political Research*, 8 (1980): 249–64.

Kumar, Krishan. 'Pre-Capitalist and Non-Capitalist Factors in the Development of Capitalism: Fred Hirsch and Joseph Schumpeter', in A. Ellis and K. Kumar, eds, *The Dilemmas of Liberal Democracies: Studies in Fred Hirsch's 'Social Limits to Growth'*, London, Tavistock Press, 1983, pp. 148–172.

Lambert, Royston. 'Central and Local Relations in Mid-Victorian England: The Local Government Act Office, 1858–1871', *Victorian Studies*, 6 (1962): 122–39.

Landauer, Carl. 'The Origin of Social Reformism in France', *International Review of Social History*, v. 12, 1961, pp. 81–107.

Laroque, Pierre. 'Problèmes posés par les élections sociales', *Revue Française de Science Politique*, 3, no. 2 (April–June 1953): 22–30.

Levine, Daniel. 'Social Democracy, Socialism and Social Insurance, Germany and Denmark, 1918–1933', in R.F. Tomasson, ed., *Comparative Social Research: The Welfare State, 1883–1983*, Westport, Conn., JAI Press, 1983, pp. 67–86.

Lewin, Leif. 'The Debate on Economic Planning', in Steven Koblik, ed., *Sweden's Political Development from Poverty to Affluence, 1750–1970*, Minneapolis, University of Minnesota Press, 1975, pp. 282–302.

Lowe, Rodney. 'The Erosion of State Intervention in Britain, 1917–24', *Economic History Review*, 31 (May 1978): 270–86.

Lowe, Rodney. 'The Ministry of Labour, 1916–1924; A Graveyard of Social Reform?',, *Public Administration* (UK), 54 (1974): 415–38.

Lowe, Rodney. 'Welfare Legislation and the Unions during and after the First World War', *The Historical Journal*, 25 (1982): 437–41.

Mason, T.W. 'Labour and the Third Reich, 1933–1939', *Past and Present*, 33 (April 1966): 112–41.

McDougall, Mary Lynn. 'Protecting Infants: The French Campaign for Maternity Leaves, 1890s–1913', *French Historical Studies*, 13 (Spring 1983): 79–105.

Mellor, William. 'The Claim of the Unemployed', in C. Addison, ed., *Problems of a Socialist Government*, London, Gollancz, 1933, pp. 113–49.

Miller, Frederic M. 'National Assistance or Unemployment Assistance? The British Cabinet and Relief Policy, 1932–1933', *Journal of Contemporary History* 9 (April 1974): 163–83.

Mitchell, Austin. 'Clay Cross', *Political Quarterly*, 45 (1974): 165–77.

Moller, Gustave. 'The Unemployment Policy', *Annals of the American Academy*, 197 (1938): 47–71.

Moly, Henri de. 'L'Assurance obligatoire et le socialisme d'Etat,' *Réforme Sociale*, 6, no. 55 (April 1888): 706–19.

Netter, Francis. 'Annexe', Comité d'Histoire de la 2è. Guerre Mondial, Colloque sur l'Histoire de la Securité Sociale, Caen, 8–9 April 1980, p. 236.

Nettl, Peter. 'The German Social Democratic Party, 1890–1914, as a

Political Model', *Past and Present*, no. 30 (April 1965): 65–95.

Neuman, Mark. 'Speenhamland in Berkshire', in E.W. Martin, ed., *Comparative Developments in Social Welfare*, London, Allen and Unwin, 1972, pp. 85–127.

Nicholls, David. 'Positive Liberty, 1880–1914', *American Political Science Review*, 56 (1962): 114–28.

Peden, G.C. 'Keynes, the Treasury and Unemployment in the Later Nineteen-thirties', *Oxford Economic Papers* (New Series), 32 (1980): 1–18.

Richter, Melvin. 'Intellectual and Class Alienation: Oxford Idealist Diagnoses and Prescriptions', *Archives Européenes de Sociologie*, 7 (1966): 1–26.

Rollings, N. 'The Keynesian Revolution' and 'Economic Policymaking: A Comment', *Economic History Review*, Second Series, 38 (February 1985): 95–100.

Roson, Henry. 'Santé', in P. Laroque, ed., *Succés et faiblesses*, Paris, Colin, 1961, pp. 71–101.

Rueff, Jacques. 'Les Conditions du salut financier', *Revue Politique et Parlementaire*, 123 (1925): 5–11.

Salisbury, Robert H. 'The Analysis of Public Policy: A Search for Theories and Roles', in Austin Ranney, ed., *Political Science and Public Policy*, Chicago, Markham, 1978, pp. 151–78.

Schnapper, B. 'Les Sociétés de production pendant le Seconde République: l'exemple girondin', *Revue d'Histoire Economique et Sociale*, 43 (1965): 162–91.

Schnoll, Louis. 'Le Monopole des assurances', *Revue de la Prévoyance et de la Mutualité* (November 1911).

Sheridan, George J. 'Aux origines de la mutualité en France: le développement et l'influence des sociétés de sécours mutuels, 1800–1848', *La Revue de l'Economie Sociale* (July–September 1984): 17–25.

Sirinelli, Jean-Françoise. 'The Ecole Normale Superieure and Elite Formation and Selection during the Third Republic', in J. Howorth and P.G. Cerny, eds, *Elites in France*, New York, St Martin's, 1981, pp. 66–77.

Skinner, Quentin. 'Meaning and Understanding in the History of Ideas', *History and Theory*, 8 (1969): 3–53.

Soderpalm, Sven Anders. 'The Crisis Agreement and the Social Democratic Road to Power', in S. Koblik, ed., *Sweden's Development from Poverty to Affluence, 1750–1970*, Minneapolis, University of Minnesota Press, 1975, pp. 258–78.

Stein, Bruno. 'Funding Social Security on a Current Basis', in D. Ashford and E.W. Kelley, eds, *Nationalizing Social Security*, Greenwich, Conn., JAI Press, 1986.

Strawson, P.F. 'Social Morality and Individual Ideal', *Philosophy*, 36, no. 136 (January 1961): 1–17.

Tawney, R.H. 'The Abolition of Economic Controls, 1918–1921', in

J.M. Winter, ed., *History and Society: Essays by R.H. Tawney*, London, Routledge and Kegan Paul, 1978, pp. 129–86 (published in shorter form in *Economic History Review*, 13 (1943).

Thane, Pat. 'The Labour Party and State "Welfare"', in K.D. Brown, ed., *The First Labour Party, 1906–1914*, London, Croom Helm, 1985, pp. 183–216.

Thoenig, J.C. 'Local Subsidies in the Third Republic: The Political Marketplace and Bureaucratic Allocation', in D. Ashford, ed., *Financing Urban Government in the Welfare State*, London, Croom Helm, 1980, pp. 119–41.

Tilton, Timothy A. 'A Swedish Road to Socialism: Ernest Wigforss and the Ideological Foundations of Swedish Social Democracy', *American Political Science Revew*, 73 (July 1977): 505–20.

Titmuss, Richard. 'Welfare "Rights", Law and Discretion', *Political Quarterly*, 42 no. 2 (April–June 1971): 113–32.

Tocqueville, Alexis de. 'Memoir on Pauperism', *Public Interest*, 19: 110 and 118–19.

Treble, James H. 'The Attitudes of the Friendly Societies towards the Movement in Great Britain for State Pensions, 1878–1908', *International Review of Social History*, 15, no. 2 (1970): 266–99.

Tribe, Lawrence H. 'Policy Science: Analysis or Ideology?', *Philosophy and Public Affairs*, 2 (1972): 66–110.

Ullmann, H.P. 'German Industry and Bismarck's Social Security', in W.J. Mommsen, ed., *The Emergence of the Welfare State in Britain and Germany*, London, Croom Helm, 1981, pp. 133–49.

Verney, Douglas. 'The Foundations of Modern Sweden: The Swift Rise and Fall of Swedish Liberalism', *Political Studies*, 20 (March 1972): 42–59.

Wedderburn, Dorothy. 'Facts and Theories of the Welfare State', *Socialist Register*, London, Merlin Press, 1965, pp. 127–46.

Weiss, John. 'Origins of the Welfare State: Poor Relief in the Third Republic', *French Historical Studies*, 13 (Spring 1983): 47–78.

Weinsten, W.L. 'The Concept of Liberty in Mid-Century English Political Thought', *Political Studies*, 13 (1965): 145–62.

Whiteside, Noel. 'Private Agencies for Public Purposes: Some New Perspectives on Policy Making in Health Insurance between the Wars', *Journal of Social Policy*, 12, no. 2 (1983): 165–94.

Whiteside, Noel. 'Welfare Legislation and the Unions during the First World War', *Historical Journal*, 23 (1980): 857–74.

Wigforss, Ernest. 'The Financial Policy during Depression and Doom', *Annals of the American Academy of Political and Social Science*, 197 (1938): 25–39.

Wilensky, Harold L. 'Leftism, Catholicism, and Democratic Corporatism: The Role of Political Parties in Recent Welfare State Development', in P. Flora and A.J. Heidenheimer, eds, *The Development of Welfare States in Europe*, New Brunswick, N.J. and London, Transaction Books, 1981, pp. 345–82.

Zollner, Detlev. 'The Federal Republic of Germany', in P. Kohler and H. Zacher, eds, *A Century of Social Security, 1881–1981: The Evolution in Germany, France, Great Britain, Austria and Switzerland*, Munich, Max Planck Institute, 1982, pp. 15–37.

Index